DRIVING SHAREHOLDER VALUE

Value-Building Techniques for Creating Shareholder Wealth

Roger A. Morin

Sherry L. Jarrell

McGraw-Hill

New York   San Francisco   Washington, D.C.   Auckland   Bogotá
Caracas   Lisbon   London   Madrid   Mexico City   Milan
Montreal   New Delhi   San Juan   Singapore
Sydney   Tokyo   Toronto

Library of Congress Cataloging-in-Publication Data
Morin, Roger A.
    Driving shareholder value : value-building techniques for creating shareholder value /
 by Roger A. Morin and Sherry L. Jarrell
    p. cm.
    ISBN 0-07-135958-3
        1. Corporations—Valuation. 2. Industrial management. 3. Economic value added. 4.
    Corporate profits. 5. Corporations—Growth. 6. Stocks—Prices. 7. Stockholders. I. Jarrell,
    Sherry L. II. Title.

HG4028.V3 M665 2000
658.15—dc21   00–056631

McGraw-Hill
A Division of The McGraw-Hill Companies

1 2 3 4 5 6 7 8 9 0   DOC/DOC   0 9 8 7 6 5 4 3 2 1 0

ISBN 0-07-135958-3

Printed and bound by R. R. Donnelley & Sons Company.

McGraw-Hill books are available at special quantity discounts to use as premiums and
sales promotions, or for use in corporate training programs. For more information,
please write to the Director of Special Sales, Professional Publishing, McGraw-Hill,
Two Penn Plaza, New York, NY 10121-2298. Or contact your local bookstore.

 This book is printed on recycled, acid-free paper containing a minimum
of 50% recycled de-inked symbol > fiber.

*For Anna, Audrey, Marc, Melanie,
and especially Susan*

Contents

Preface

THANKS TO AN UNPRECEDENTED WAVE OF TAKEOVERS, shareholder activism, and global competition, corporate America has become acutely aware of the importance of creating economic value for shareholders. Many companies now extol the virtues of maximizing shareholder value in their mission statements, annual reports, and investor communications but fail to fully exploit the potential wealth creation from a value-based perspective. Many fail to see any direct connection between their business strategies and the market value of their business, yet company value is the direct result of such strategic decisions as which product markets to enter, how to compete, and which financial policies to embrace. Understanding the relationship between strategy, finance, and company value is the key to making consistent value-enhancing decisions.

We have written this book to help managers make the connections between strategy, financing, corporate governance, and the creation of shareholder wealth. We hope that the insights provided in this book will enable managers to uncover these key relationships in their company or business, and to manage them in ways that drive consistently superior shareholder value. *Driving Shareholder Value* lays out an approach to valuation that is anchored in a coherent set of economic principles that guide the company's strategic planning, investment policies, financing choices, and compensation plans toward increasing shareholder value. We translate the proven theories about creating corporate value into practical tools and approaches; describe how to create the best measures of business performance and how they relate directly to shareholder value; discuss how to implement a shareholder value orientation, or a "value culture," throughout the organization; and show that the key to aligning processes and decision tools with value creation is the development of appropriate internal metrics that quantify, track, and reward value-creating performance. We also show how to measure the impact of alternative business strategies on economic value, and conceptualize the value impact of competing long-term corporate strategies.

Driving Shareholder Value offers a thought-provoking yet accessible view of the step-by-step process of creating sustainable economic profits. Actual case studies demonstrate the successful implementation of value-based approaches, and empirical data document its effects on the bottom line. For the first time, a unified framework for defining and successfully implementing a value-based approach in any company is brought together in one book. The framework, called *value-based management,* or *VBM,* allows managers from all levels of the company to understand how their activities are directly linked to economic cash flows and how these economic cash flows, in turn, determine the long-term value of the company. VBM artfully combines financial and strategic management techniques to create sustainable competitive advantage at all levels of the company. By aligning internal business processes, strategies, and corporate governance and investor communications, VBM provides a common discipline, a consistent culture, and a singular focus on value for all business activities.

WHY THIS BOOK?

It might be easy to agree that the manager's goal should be to maximize corporate value, but the "how to" has been illusive. There have been many fragmented attempts over the years to develop methods that link strategy and value, including product portfolio management, competitive strategy, operational excellence, business process reengineering, benchmarking, core competence, total quality management, market positioning, employee empowerment, and so on. But these approaches fail to answer the fundamental questions: What is corporate value? How is it measured and tracked? Will the corporate plan create value? Which strategic business units are creating value? How does an organization value alternative strategies?

We owe an intellectual debt to works that explored various parts of this topic before us: Indisputably, the intellectual origins of company valuation are found in the writings of Nobel laureates Merton Miller and Franco Modigliani. Their approach was popularized and extended by several others whose work both inspired and informed our book, especially Al Rappaport's *Creating Shareholder Value,* William Fruhan's *Financial Strategy: Studies in the Creation, Transfer, and Destruction of Shareholder Value,* and Jim Copeland and Fred Weston's *Managerial Finance.* Our work has benefitted from work on valuation put forth by Joel Stern and Bennett Stewart and on real options pricing by Lenos Trigeorgis and Timothy Luehrman. The works of several important authors have benefitted our efforts in linking strategy and value throughout our book, including *Competitive Strategy* by Michael Porter, *Managing for Value: A Guide to Value-Based Strategic Management* by Bernard Reimann, and *The Value Imperative: Managing for Superior Shareholder Returns* by James McTaggart, Peter Kontes, and Michael Mankins.

Even these influential works, when taken together, seem to leave business managers with more questions than answers. For example, why are different metrics used in different parts of the organization: NPV (net present value) in capital budgeting, EPS (earnings per share) in investor communications, and ROE (return on equity) in performance evaluation? Why do institutional investors value dividend yield and growth, while companies target quarterly EPS? Why do managers ignore NPV when making strategic decisions, and what do they use instead? There seems to be no coherent framework, no synthesis, no integrated approach, no single book that puts it all together. That is why we wrote *Driving Shareholder Value.*

CHIEF FEATURES OF THE BOOK

A chief feature of this book is its integrative framework, bringing together the best of the finance-valuation-strategy trilogy into one place for the manager to refer to in the quest for consistent value-maximizing business decisions at all levels of the organization. This book is a straightforward, accessible blend of theory and practice. And the topic we address is not a fad: It is firmly anchored in rigorous economic foundations that have withstood the test of time, and its precepts are widely used in capital allocation and security valuation around the globe.

Perhaps its most exciting feature, however, is its relevance to the challenges in making business decisions in today's dynamic environment. We are the first to integrate the cutting-edge knowledge on strategic valuation to business decision making. All other approaches, including NPV, EVA (economic value added), ROIC (return on invested capital), and CFROI (cash flow return on investment), apply to the static world. Yet the business environment in which we find ourselves today is anything but static and passive; to compete successfully, we must be able to assess the impact of strategy on value. We do that through real options valuation (ROV). ROV is a rapidly evolving evaluation technique that is helpful to the manager in several ways: as a valuation framework, a decision-making process, and a way of thinking about business problems. ROV has already begun to augment or displace traditional investment valuation techniques used by corporations operating in various industries around the globe.

ROV is concerned with valuing management's flexibility to take different courses of action in response to different future scenarios. This flexibility comes in the form of real options that management may or may not exercise depending on the way relevant uncertainties are resolved. Given that a considerable fraction of shareholder value rests on the outcome of key corporate strategic decisions, it is important to bridge strategic decision making and value-based management. This linkage is magnified by the importance of large investments being made in the New Economy targeted at growth, innovation, and agility. Traditional value metrics are inadequate in capturing the true value of strategic investments.

WHO SHOULD READ THIS BOOK?

This book is directed at anyone involved in managing, or interested in the management, of a business: senior managers, middle managers, line managers, corporate finance practitioners, investors, portfolio managers, security analysts, academics, CFOs, analysts in finance departments, loan and credit officers in financial institutions, accountants, strategists, and marketers. After all, the book addresses the most fundamental questions in business:

How much is your company worth?

How much would its value be affected by each of several operating, investment, and financial policies?

Will the corporate plan create value? Which SBUs are creating value? How would alternative strategies affect shareholder value?

Which compensation plan and other corporate governance initiatives motivate the greatest corporate value? Which metrics should be used in performance targets and evaluation?

How should the business communicate with the investment community and other key stakeholders?

This book can be used for broad-based instructional purposes in executive training programs. For practitioners, the book explains how decisions in one area affect performance and opportunities in other areas and thus provides a comprehensive view of managing the entire company. It can also be used in intermediate to advanced courses in business finance and strategy.

No special knowledge or educational level is assumed. The occasionally formidable mathematics found in some other books are replaced by clear and intuitive explanations and easy-to-understand diagrams and practical applications. Technical definitions and equations are kept to a minimum. Derivations and equations are relegated to appendixes and footnotes whenever possible. A rudimentary knowledge of basic accounting, algebra, and time value of money concepts are helpful but not necessary.

Acknowledgments

MANY PEOPLE HAVE PROVIDED US WITH ASSISTANCE in preparing this book, and we would like to acknowledge their help. Our special thanks to McGraw-Hill editor Kelli Christiansen for her leadership, persistence, insight, and patience in making this book become reality. Our sincere thanks to Scott Amerman for his indefatigable editorial scrutiny and gracious support of this effort.

We extend special gratitude to Bineetha Ramachandran who was responsible for much of the content of two major chapters on corporate governance.

Where views and opinions are expressed in the book, they are our own and do not necessarily reflect the views of Georgia State University or Wake Forest University. We assume responsibility for any errors.

Readers wishing to share comments, inquiries, and suggestions beneficial in future editions are encouraged to contact us at:

Professor Sherry L. Jarrell
Babcock Graduate School
  of Management
Wake Forest University
7659 Reynolda Station
Winston-Salem, NC 27109
sherry.jarrell@mba.wfu.edu

Professor Roger A. Morin
Robinson College of Business
Georgia State University
University Plaza
Atlanta, GA 30303
profmorin@msn.com

P A R T

I

VALUATION

1

THE VALUE-BASED MANAGEMENT FRAMEWORK: AN OVERVIEW

> "We now have a solid financial blueprint for the corporation. We know which divisions are worth the most to us and how much value each will create; we know which strategies will create the most value at each division; we know the value of our stock.... In sum, we have the tools to manage our company better from a strategic and financial standpoint."
>
> —*PepsiCo executive*

VALUE-BASED MANAGEMENT, OR **VBM** FOR SHORT, is not a single idea. As anyone who has ever been involved in managing a company knows, there is no magic bullet for corporate success. No, VBM is more a single *framework* for targeting those business decisions that consistently add economic value—both immediate and long-term—to your company. The VBM framework distills the facts from the fiction in the dozens of approaches and management fads that claim to make managing easy.

In this chapter, we present an overview of the value creation process made possible by the VBM framework. The individual components of the framework are presented in modules. Subsequent chapters provide clear and complete information on how to successfully implement VBM using the ideas in each module. Throughout, actual company experiences with VBM are brought together with the abundant and fascinating empirical evidence on the impact of VBM to draw an unmistakable conclusion: VBM really does work!

Figure 1-1 displays the VBM framework and its four fundamental modules: Valuation, Strategy, Finance, and Corporate Governance. The Valuation module defines corporate value and explains the key drivers of value. The Strategy module establishes a clear link between corporate value and specific business strategies. The Finance module describes value-enhancing financial policies available to the company. The Corporate Governance module explains the actions and policies of senior management, such as performance measurement, compensation systems, and investor communications, that foster value creation.

We start with the notion that all companies, particularly public ones, should be managed to create as much wealth as possible for their owners, the shareholders. To maximize shareholder wealth, management must generate, evaluate, and select business strategies that will increase the value the company. Corporate value cannot be increased, however, unless we know what it is and how to measure it. Hence, we begin with the Valuation module of the VBM framework, the subject of Part I. There we see that the basic concepts of valuation can be universally applied to such diverse management decisions as new product development, financing, operational management, expanding abroad, corporate restructuring, managerial compensation, and mergers and acquisitions.

There are a number of valid approaches for quantifying corporate value, the best of which are covered in Chapters 5 through 8. All are deeply

FIGURE 1-1   The value-based management framework.

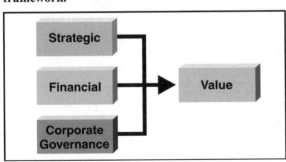

rooted in the discounted cash flow model, because this is the way that investors and capital markets actually value companies and securities. As we shall see, the value of any company is a function of the future cash flows it is expected to generate for its owners, discounted for the risk associated with those cash flows.

The emphasis on discounted long-term cash flows is not new. Capital expenditures in companies and investments in stocks, bonds, and real estate have been evaluated using discounted cash flow methods for decades. VBM simply extends that notion to the business as a whole, adds the impact of strategic decisions on value, and establishes value enhancement as the basis of corporate responsibility.

Subsequent chapters establish that value is created only when the return on capital exceeds the cost of capital. We refer to the difference between return and cost of capital as the *spread*. A straightforward example of the spread is found in banking. When you open a savings account at a friendly neighborhood bank paying 4% interest, the bank is essentially borrowing money from you at 4%. If the bank turns around and lends those funds to a business at 10%, it has created a spread of 6%, the difference between the lending rate (the *return on capital)* of 10% and the borrowing rate (the *cost of capital*) of 4%.

In this example, the spread of 6% is the value created per dollar. The greater the spread, the greater the economic profit and, therefore, the greater the market value of the bank, or any company. We show later that, *regardless of the rate of growth,* value is created only when the spread is positive. When the spread is negative, growth actually destroys corporate value!

Spread is one of three primary factors management can use to develop strategies that will increase corporate value. Factors that link management action to strategies that create value are called *drivers*. The other two drivers are scale and sustainability.

Scale refers to the dollar magnitude of the potential increase in a business opportunity—a growth business earning a positive spread on a large capital base is adding value. The larger the number of dollars put to work, the greater the potential for increasing value. Continuing with our banking analogy, the greater the amount of the loan with a spread of 6%, the greater the dollar amount of corporate value created by the bank. In other words, the bank wants to earn a spread of 6% on as large a loan as possible.

Sustainability refers to the interval of competitive advantage—that is, the time period over which the returns and growth can add to the value of the business. The longer a company can enjoy a positive spread on its investments, the greater is the amount of value created. In our bank example, the longer the loan, or the greater the number of years over which the bank can earn this spread of 6%, the more sustainable it is and the greater the value created.

Various combinations of these three key ingredients create corporate value in any setting: service or manufacturing, large or small, conglomerates or single product, domestic or international, high tech or commodity. Value creation is virtually guaranteed when a company's profitability exceeds its cost of capital. In sharp contrast, accounting profitability does *not* necessarily lead to value creation. In fact, in many cases, profitable projects actually destroy the value of the company.

Figure 1-2 summarizes the principal drivers of a company's value: the size of the spread (that is, the company's ability to earn a *return* in excess of its cost of capital); *growth* (which reflects both the amount of *capital* dollars put to work and the sustainability of the positive spread); and the *cost of capital* (which, in turn, reflects the company's risk). These factors and their interaction have enormous implications for successful business strategy, executive compensation, and performance evaluation. Target levels for each lever can be used as a basis for performance assessment and compensation. Finally, these simple levers can help managers with one of the most difficult aspects of business: the discovery of untapped opportunities for additional value creation.

Before we turn to the how-to of value creation, let's examine why companies should maximize corporate value. The business environment is

FIGURE 1-2   Determinants of value.

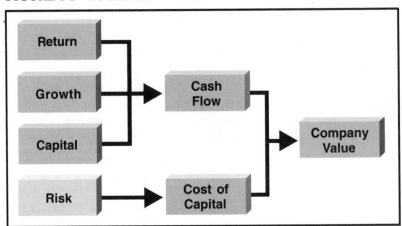

evolving dramatically. Managers are faced with unprecedented pressure to perform in all the markets where their companies compete—namely, the product market, the market for corporate control, the market for financial capital, and the managerial labor market, as shown in Figure 1-3. Moreover, the institutional forces pushing management toward a value creation focus in each of these markets are unstoppable. There is simply no dispute that managers opting for VBM will

- Make better decisions
- Earn higher salaries and bigger bonuses
- Deliver better performance to shareholders and other stakeholders

In the product market, the competitive landscape has changed dramatically, with the promise of unimaginable changes to come. New products and services are introduced daily by a variety of new and powerful competitors hailing from all over the globe. Newly deregulated companies have joined the fray. New developments in information technology have created an entire class of informed customers who know how and where to get products cheaper and faster. In some cases, the "Internet half-life" of products is measured in months, not years, with computer software a prime example.

The level and intensity of competition in the market for corporate control rival, and some say surpass, that in the product market. One inescapable lesson from the unprecedented wave of recent mergers, divestitures, and other corporate restructurings is that managers who fail to continually seek maximum shareholder value risk being replaced by those who put share-

FIGURE 1-3 **Market forces and VBM.**

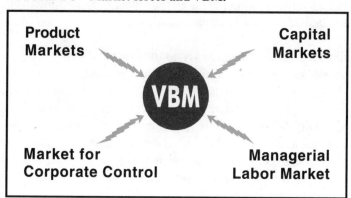

holder wealth maximization at the top of their list. Prominent investors such as Warren Buffett and activist investor groups including LENS Inc., CalPERS, and Relational Investing Inc., in their search for companies with unrealized value, have fueled the focus on shareholder value creation. The relentless search by corporate raiders and financial entrepreneurs for "value gaps," so newsworthy in the 1980s, is now so pervasive that it is considered commonplace. The bottom line? *Managers should look at their companies the same way a potential raider does—from a corporate value perspective.*

In the third of four markets in which firms compete, financial capital markets, increasingly sophisticated investors choose from a global array of available investments. As a result, players in capital markets are becoming more vocal and less patient in their expectations of value creation. Large investors intervene directly in company affairs, ousting underperforming managers and replacing board members. Institutional shareholders—the larger pension funds and mutual funds—will only intensify their intervention in corporate affairs as capital markets offer more and more investment opportunities, accelerating the inevitable adoption and institutionalization of the value perspective.

For whom would you rather work, a value-creating business or a value-destroying one? In the last of the four markets in which firms compete, the managerial labor market, we learn that the success of a company depends largely on the quality of management it attracts, and many of the best managers choose to work for a company that provides superior future opportunities for advancement and compensation. In an increasingly mobile and competitive market for skilled managerial resources, a value-creating company, particularly one in which executive compensation is value-based, will have an easier time attracting top-quality management, increasing its value creation potential, thus increasing its attractiveness for managers, and so on in a virtuous cycle.

Accounting Model of the Company Versus the Economic Model
Fundamental business value, as measured by free cash flows discounted for time and risk, has gained popularity as a superior measure of value creation. Traditional accounting-oriented metrics, like earnings per share (EPS) and return on equity (ROE), focus on past performance rather than on future cash flows and, as a result, fail to reflect the valuation factors taken into account by investors. They are not correlated with actual value creation.

The current reality in most companies is akin to a Tower of Babel. Various departments and functions speak different languages: marketing speaks about market share and growth; finance talks about earnings growth and net present value (NPV); engineering and production speak payback period and downtime; accounting and treasury talk ROE and net income; and senior management promotes EPS growth. As shown in Figure 1-4, VBM provides all managers with a common frame of reference and the same scorecard—namely, corporate value. If the value-based scorecard is also used to determine performance and compensation, VBM provides managers with the link between their actions and the strategies that are in the best interest of the company's owners. Under VBM, the universal language of value creation enables the very difficult task of aligning strategies across functions and between layers of the company.

Because of this compendium of competitive and institutional forces, the creation of corporate value will gain even more importance as the ultimate management system and measure of corporate performance in the new millennium.

VBM's Track Record
The effectiveness of VBM has been demonstrated by its successful application in a variety of corporations, including Coca-Cola, General Electric, Abbott Labs, Merck, Emerson Electric, and Equifax. The companies have exhibited stellar performance, both absolutely and relative to their peers. Their shareholders have been rewarded with substantial increases in the value of their equity holdings.

We would argue that society is better off with a VBM perpsective as well. The adoption of VBM optimizes the use of capital resources, which

FIGURE 1-4   **VBM links all management decisions to the maximization of corporate value.**

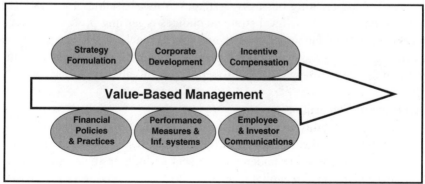

makes all stakeholders better off. For example, to maximize economic value, a company must develop, manufacture, market, and distribute the products that customers want or need and are willing to pay for. Therefore, managers seeking to maximize economic value must develop new technologies, build new plants, test new products, and create new jobs. The pursuit of value maximization requires efficient customer service, customer satisfaction, adequate supplies of goods and services, and convenience. Therefore, all the actions that help a company increase its value also benefit society at large.

SOURCES OF VALUE CREATION

As seen in the VBM framework in Figure 1-1, this book is all about value and how to achieve consistently stellar levels of corporate value. The "what," or valuation, is thoroughly discussed in module 1, Chapters 1 through 8. Modules 2, 3, and 4 present the "how," the three broad types of managerial actions—strategy, finance, and governance—that enable the company to achieve its value objectives. Strategic actions are the most important; they will have a substantial continuing effect and enhance the long-term value of the business. Financial actions involve the adoption of financing and capital structure policies that reduce the cost of capital to the company—that is, they increase the value spread. Dividend policy and financial engineering also play a role. Corporate governance actions involve creating the optimal mix of inside and outside directors on the board, adopting performance measures that are consistent with value creation, and creating compensation policies that align the interests of managers and shareholders around the goal of value creation.

VALUE CREATION: STRATEGIC DETERMINANTS

The second module of the VBM framework involves the selection and delivery of value-creating business strategies. Value-based approaches must help shape the business-level strategic choices regarding product markets, market segments, customer groups, and global reach. VBM provides both the discipline and the economic framework for linking the forces of competition and a company's competitive position to value creation.

The Curse of Competition

Sustained profitability in any industry is determined by the degree of competition in that industry. Strategically minded managers focused on increasing corporate value undertake projects as long as their expected returns exceed the cost of capital. However, the task of creating value is easier said than done. The difficulty stems from the curse of competitive markets. In perfectly competitive markets—that is, those with no entry or exit barriers and no product differentiation or cost advantages—the forces of competition ensure that all businesses eventually earn a return just equal to the cost of capital—that is, a spread of zero. This striking fact is captured in Figure 1-5. There we see the value created over the last decade by companies in the Standard & Poor's (S&P) 500 Index. Although we find substantial variability in returns, with some companies earning very high returns and others earning very low returns, companies on average earn their cost capital.

How does this happen? Consider, for example, an industry that is generating large returns. New entrants will be attracted. The additional competition and added capacity will push down prices and drive profits down to zero. In reverse, if an industry is generating returns below the cost of capital, some competitors will drop out, capacity is reduced, and prices are driven back up, producing higher returns.

As shown in Figure 1-6, there are primarily two ways of defying the curse of competition: (1) the company may enter or create economically attractive markets where favorable industry conditions generate rates of return above the competitive level, or (2) the company can build and maintain a position of relative advantage over its competitors through cost lead-

FIGURE 1-5 Ten-year average spread (ROI-WACC), 1989–1998.

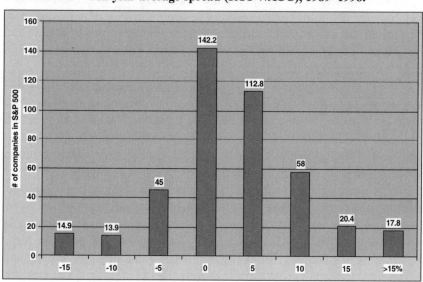

FIGURE 1-6   Strategic determinants of value creation.

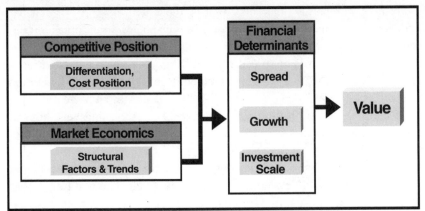

ership or product differentiation, allowing it to earn a return in excess of the industry average. We refer to the first as *market* (or *industry*) *attractiveness* and the latter as *competitive advantage*. The wide variations in both industry and company performance noted in Figure 1-5 are caused by differences in market attractiveness and competitive position, driven largely by the interaction of constantly changing economic forces and competitive strategies.

The value challenge is to break the equilibrium law of economics. The key to achieving a long-term sustainable competitive advantage is to participate in attractive markets (that is, those with a positive spread) and achieve a competitive advantage in that market (that is, a larger spread than your competitors).

The specific objective of the strategic analysis module of the VBM framework is to formulate an appropriate value-creating strategy for each business unit. The Strategy module of the VBM framework is summarized in Figure 1-7. This first task in the Strategy module is to position each business unit of the company in a market attractiveness—competitive position (MA/CP) matrix, such as the one depicted in the top center box of Figure 1-7. The horizontal axis of the matrix represents the competitive advantage, and the vertical axis represents the attractiveness of the market.

The unit's location in this matrix indicates its prospects for sustainable growth and profitability, and therefore value creation. For example, business unit A has a strong competitive position in an attractive market and is expected to sustain growth and relatively high cash flows. Therefore, the

FIGURE 1-7 Strategy module of VBM framework.

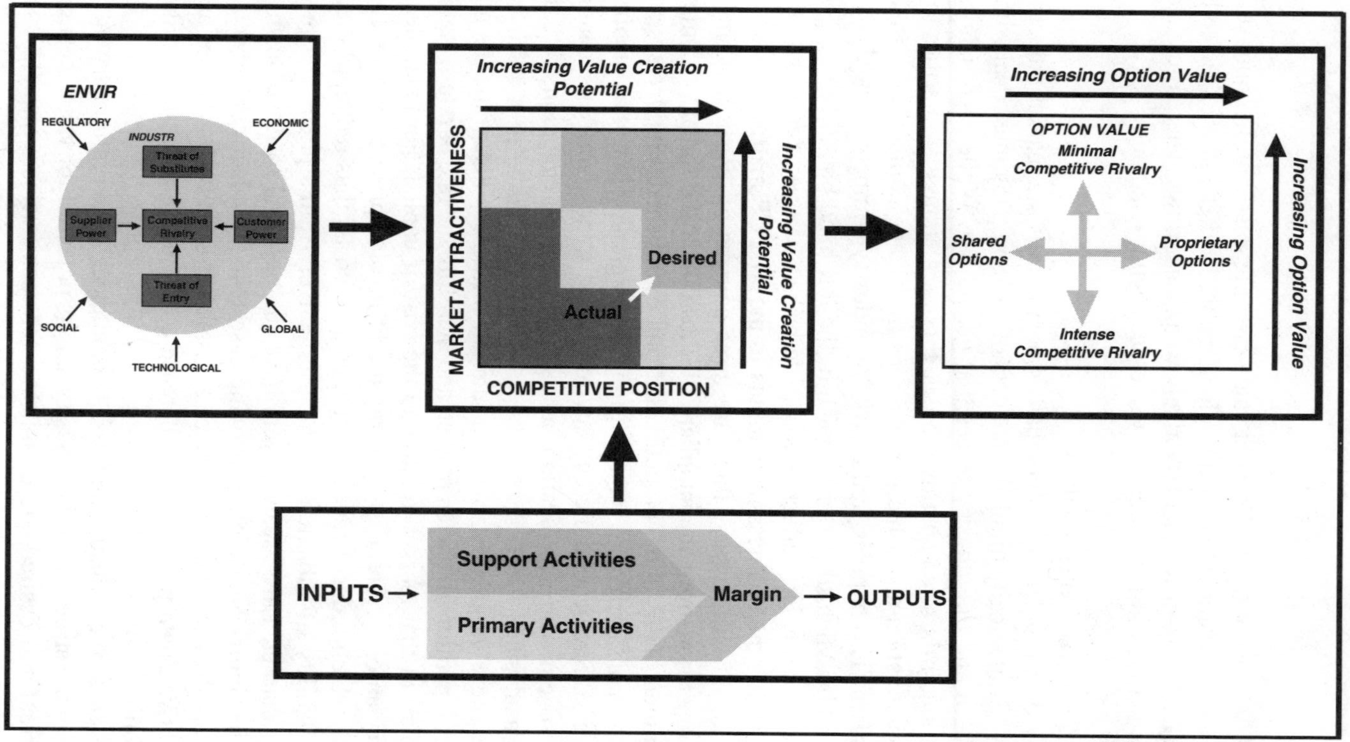

unit belongs in the upper right value-creating quadrant. In contrast, unit F has a weak competitive position in a mature market and is expected to sustain declining growth and relatively weak cash flows. Therefore, that business belongs in the lower left value-destroying quadrant.

Market Attractiveness Analysis

How do we determine a company's position on the market attractiveness axis? Strategically minded managers of any company must deal with competition and the industry forces that generate it. While each industry has a unique mix of competitive forces, there are enough similarities to allow generalization about the major forces that shape competition in most industries. The popular framework for industry/competitive analysis introduced by Michael Porter,* shown in the left-hand box in Figure 1-7, provides a particularly effective way to describe these major competitive forces and guide the business-level inputs to the MA/CP matrix.

In this framework, there are three sources of "vertical" competition (competition from the suppliers of substitutes, the threat of competition from entrants, and competition from established producers) and two sources of "horizontal" competition (the bargaining power of suppliers and buyers). Socioeconomic and environmental trends, such as technological improvements, globalization, and government deregulation, complement the analysis.

These various external and internal influences determine the intensity of competition in a given market, and therefore the rate of return on invested capital in that market, relative to the cost of capital. For example, the rivalry among current competitors might involve price or service competition, which reduces revenues or increases costs, thus reducing value. The availability of substitute products effectively limits prices and profits in any market. Large-scale buyers have the potential to drive down prices, while significant suppliers may increase costs or reduce quality of required inputs. New competitors reduce the sales of existing companies and tend to drive down prices and/or increase costs, all of which reduce the profitability in the industry.

Once the industry analysis is completed, some preliminary judgments about the structure of the industry and its potential for value creation, both current and desired, are established for each business unit. This analysis enables each business unit to be located on the vertical axis of the MA/CP matrix. Nevertheless, the analysis is still too general to allow the company

---

*Michael Porter, *Competitive Strategy* (New York, 1980), Chapter 1.

to define a particular competitive strategy. For a more refined analysis, we turn to an examination of the company's competitive position.

Competitive Position Analysis

Competitive position has a major effect on a company's profitability and continued cash flows—and, hence, on its market value. How do we establish a favorable competitive position? The key to enhancing value is creating a position in the industry that is less susceptible to direct competition and less vulnerable to erosion from the influence of customers, suppliers, and substitute goods. At the business unit level, there are two ways of gaining and maintaining such a competitive position—that is, of making markets less competitive:

1.   Differentiate the product in some key way.
2.   Achieve a cost advantage over competitors.

Product differentiation effectively limits the number of products that directly compete with your product. In the extreme, perfectly differentiated products create monopolies for that product. And, if the product is differentiated in ways that customers value, a monopoly price premium can be commanded, generating higher returns and greater corporate value.

Achieving a lower total economic cost per unit than the industry average for that product, including a charge for financial capital required to achieve the advantage, may result in value creation. Sources of economic cost advantage include economies of scale; innovative process technology; access to low-cost raw materials (particularly those in low supply); low-cost distribution channels; superior operating management; proprietary knowledge, expertise, or technology; or a low cost of financial capital. Developing a true cost advantage over your competitors will also deter new entrants into the market and reduce competition, creating monopoly pricing and another source of value creation.

Neither product differentiation nor lowest-cost production, however, guarantees value creation. Only if the cost required to differentiate the product or gain the cost advantage is smaller than the benefits produced is value created.

Value Chain Analysis

Competitive business system analysis is a fundamental tool allowing the manager to identify a company's competitive advantage or to find ways of acquiring one and keeping it. One particularly useful variation of business system analysis is provided by value chain analysis. *Value chain analysis* helps identify the company's present competitive advantages, and that of its main rivals, and those that must be developed in order to reach the desired competitive position.

Most goods and services are produced by a vertical chain of firms. Each of the activities in the value chain is a potential source of competitive advantage. The supply of bread, for example, involves a chain comprising the farmer, the miller, the baker, and the retailer. The value created in a loaf of bread may be allocated between the companies involved. In a similar way, the individual firm can be viewed as a chain of related activities. The resources and capabilities required at each stage depend upon the nature of the activity being undertaken.

Value chain analysis consists of disaggregating the company and its main rivals into a set of distinct strategic activities to better understand their respective impact on product cost and product differentiation. Only after completing such an analysis can one select a generic strategy and the appropriate competitive positioning for each product. A generic value chain is shown in the bottom box of the Strategy module in Figure 1-7. There we see that a business's value chain can be segmented into primary and support activities. Primary activities involve a product's physical creation, its sale and distribution to customers, and its service after the sale, including inbound and outbound logistics, operations, marketing and sales, and service. Support activities are those necessary for the primary activities to take place, such as human resource management, technology development, and procurement.

The value-creating potential of each primary and support activity should be examined and ranked relative to competitors' abilities, with the intent to determine areas where the company can create superior value. To illustrate, each activity involved in the inbound logistics category—such as materials handling, warehousing, and inventory control used to receive, store, and disseminate inputs to a product—is examined for its value-creating potential.

Value chain analysis provides a useful representation of the company that suggests new ways of competing. New strategies can take the form of new configurations of the chain of activities. The end result of value chain analysis is often a reconfiguration or recombination of value chain activities that creates entry barriers or superior value for customers and earns a sustainable competitive advantage. For example, FedEx altered the nature of the delivery business by reconfiguring both the primary and the support activities to create the overnight delivery business.

Another good example is provided by the airline industry. Several companies have competed successfully through redefining and reconfiguring the activities they perform. Southwest Airlines achieved remarkable success in air travel by radically pruning the number of activities they perform and substantially lowering operating costs. In contrast, American Airlines established a substantial differentiation advantage over other airlines by extending the range of its activities into a national sales and distribution network through its Sabre ticketing system.

It is possible for both the company and its suppliers to benefit from a competitive advantage by optimizing the joint use of these activities or by improving the coordination between the two chains. This is the idea, for example, behind many of the supplier initiatives undertaken within total quality management (TQM) systems. Such linkages can reduce costs and increase differentiation.

Customers also have a value chain, and the company's product is one of the inputs to its value chain. The particular degree of differentiation of a company arises from the way in which its own value chain is related to that of the customer. A company can actually develop a competitive advantage for its customers by influencing their value chain, by reducing cost or improving performance.

Strategy and Value

A cost advantage and/or the ability to differentiate a product and command a premium price affect corporate value directly. As we saw in the Valuation module, corporate value is driven by free cash flows which are, in turn, determined by sales growth, operating margin, tax rate, the amount of working capital and fixed asset investment, and the interval of competitive advantage. The various valuation frameworks covered in later chapters all contain these same critical valuation parameters.

With the framework provided by value driver analysis, we can link the qualitative aspects of strategy to the quantitative financial results with a view toward enhancing corporate value. This requires using the material on strategy and the business economics framework set forth earlier, integrating and reorienting them to a valuation framework.

Corporate Strategy

From the industry and value chain analyses, the company identifies the competitive advantages it has, or should have, for each business unit. The company's products and those of its main rivals are also compared in terms of their relative position on the MA/CP value creation matrix.

Once each business unit is located on the value creation matrix, the strategic implications for the company's management are clear. There are numerous strategic thrusts that can underlie a sustainable competitive advantage and value creation, as discussed in detail in Chapters 9 and 10.

Two of the most important strategic thrusts are differentiation and low cost, but there are others. For example, focus strategies target a market segment or part of a product line. Preemptive strategies employ first-mover advantages to inhibit or prevent competitors from duplicating or countering. Synergistic strategies rely on the specific synergies between a business and other businesses in the same company.

Several other value-creating strategic thrusts can lead to market leadership. For example, operational excellence, illustrated by Dell Computer, leads to customer convenience and cost efficiencies. Dell created a radically different and efficient delivery system for personal computers based on build-to-order manufacturing and mail-order marketing. Another example is customer intimacy in which companies such as Home Depot and Nordstrom excel at individual personalized service. Yet another example is product leadership, where companies such as Johnson & Johnson and 3M strive to produce a continuous stream of state-of-the-art products and services.

The location of each business unit on the value creation matrix will also reveal some obvious restructuring implications for the company's management. It should invest and grow the businesses in the value-creating quadrant and divest or downsize those in the value-destroying quadrant. Marginal business in the middle should be followed closely. Corporate restructuring that divests value-destroying units and increases investment in profitable ones will result in dramatic immediate creation of corporate value and improvements in stock price. Management can also create value through a regime of strategic alliances, joint ventures, acquisitions, retrenchment, and diversification activities.

Strategy and Real Options

The end result of the strategic analysis is a set of growth strategies and investment opportunities available to the company. But how do we value these strategies and opportunities? And does their value depend on when and how they are implemented?

The answer to the latter question is a resounding yes. It has been found that merely changing the timing of an investment can increase its value by 30% to 300%! And most strategies and projects involve many additional sources of managerial flexibility, each of which can add substantially to the actual value of the investment or company.

Passive management invests in a project and lets it ride. Active management keeps an eye on the project, reassessing as new opportunities evolve, as uncertainties resolve, as any new developments unfold. Test marketing is a natural example of active management: implement a smaller version of the product or idea to a limited customer base over a predetermined amount of time. Analyze the purchasing patterns and marketing successes of the product and decide whether to move into a full or modified product launch or abandon the project in favor of more promising investments.

There are many other examples of the kinds of decisions active managers face very day: the decision to expand or contract production and capacity, to defer investment while other companies incur higher startup costs, to modify features or speed up delivery, to continue with follow-on investment dollars, or to abandon the project altogether. All these decisions come under the heading of "managerial flexibility." Most strategies and projects will experience nearly every source of flexibility over time.

The methods currently in use for assigning dollar values to investments fail to recognize the value of managerial flexibility. Even discounted cash flow techniques assume passive management. This may explain managers' rather infamous and near-universal dissatisfaction with existing capital budgeting techniques and their reliance instead on their business experience and intuition.

There is a fairly new but proven technique available for assigning a dollar value to strategies that involve managerial flexibility. Merck has been using it with great success to guide its massive research and development investment strategies. It is called *real options pricing,* and it represents the final screen through which strategies are viewed in order to obtain an estimate of their true value—namely, the estimation of their *option value.*

What Are Real Options?
Option valuation is used routinely to value financial derivatives, such as call options and put options on common stocks. More recently, option valuation techniques have been applied to decisions involving capital projects and have been proposed as a method to link traditional decision rules with strategic planning. *Real options* refer to management's ability to adopt and later revise corporate investment decisions in response to unexpected or risky market developments. Real options analysis applied to corporate investments and strategies gives managers a method of identifying and valuing critical strategic decisions. Since flexibility, which is synonymous with options, can greatly change the value of a corporate investment or strategy, it should be a vital part of strategic analysis.

Until recently it was far easier to talk about options than to calculate their value. Recent seminal developments in financial theory, such as the

Black-Scholes option pricing model, and updates in computer software, now enable everyday users of spreadsheet programs and financial calculators to find the dollar value of most options embedded in a strategic decision.

Traditional valuation methods such as discounted cash flow (DCF) fail to account for management's ability to react to new information and actively affect the outcome of a strategy. This is particularly important for companies whose market value is determined by intangible assets, such as growth opportunities. An example is companies with high expenditures in research and development, such as pharmaceuticals. Another example is Internet companies whose value stems from future growth options. Most of the value of these companies is derived from their ability to exercise the option to invest in profitable discoveries and walk away from research failures.

Most critical business strategies—such as entry into new markets, new product development, the choice of operating technology, the scale and scope of investment projects, and the completion of multiphase projects—contain embedded real options, such as the ability to make follow-on investments, to abandon a project, or to wait and learn before investing. The existence of embedded real options make strategic investments quite different from scale expansion or simple replacement investment decisions. The appropriate valuation techniques for strategic investments are also necessarily different from those used to evaluate simple scale expansions. It is quite possible, for example, that a strategic growth investment appears value destroying when viewed through the lens of DCF techniques.

The interdependence between current and future strategic investments creates not only value but also the operating flexibilities that are available to the company for implementing these growth strategies. For example, must a strategic investment be implemented now, or can it be delayed in order to acquire more information on the evolution of the market? The value of these operating options will be that much greater depending on the conditions shown in the Option Value box on the right-hand side of Figure 1-7.

The value of a strategy depends on the degree of competitive rivalry and degree of exclusivity to exercise the option. As shown in Figure 1-7, the company with an exclusive option—for example, a patent—in a minimal competitive setting can fully capitalize on the value the option. Shared options, on the other hand, are less valuable. If, for example, a company has a possibility of building a plant in a new geographic market, but others may do the same, then the new plant will not create as many future opportunities. If that option is also shared by a competitor, the value of that option is not the same as for a company that faces a minimal degree of competitive rivalry.

In short, the strategic or "option" value of the investment is quite important and must be included in the valuation process. Real options analysis provides an objective measurement of the strategic value of corporate investment decisions.

Strategy and the VBM Framework: Putting It All Together

At center stage in the Strategy module is the MA/CP value creation matrix. Industry attractiveness and competitive position analysis determine each business unit's actual and desired competitive positions on the vertical and horizontal axes, respectively. Once each business unit is located on the value creation matrix, the strategic implications for the company's management are clear, and a set of growth strategies and investment opportunities available to the company are defined. The competitive strategies identified by the MA/CP analysis must be subjected to a final "option value" screen to obtain their true value.

FINANCIAL DETERMINANTS

While the Strategy module of the VBM framework focuses on product market strategies that increase the return component of the spread, the Finance module focuses on strategies that reduce the cost of capital and thus increase the spread and corporate value. These strategies are primarily financial in nature and are concerned with the right-hand side of the balance sheet.

Financial policies influence value through several channels involving capital structure and dividend policy issues. For example, value can be created for equity holders by increasing financial leverage (debt) up to a point. This, of course, is one of the sources of value that corporate leveraged buyouts (LBOs) utilize to recapture purchase price premiums. Moderate substitutions of debt for equity capital lowers the cost of capital and enhances value because of the tax savings from the deductibility of interest. As a rough approximation, each dollar of new debt should increase the company's equity value by 20 to 40 cents until the company's financial risk becomes excessive. This trade-off between risk and return and its effect on value is shown in Figure 1-8. For every business, there exists an optimal cost-minimizing, or value-optimizing, capital structure.

Dividend policy produces a similar trade-off. In the absence of worthwhile investment projects—that is, projects that generate a positive spread—a company should return excess funds to its shareholders, the legitimate owners of the company, either through dividend policy or share repurchases.

FIGURE 1-8   Financial determinants of value.

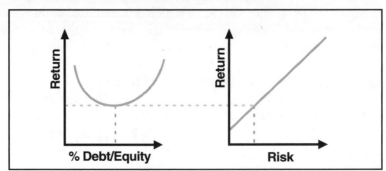

The use of risk-hedging techniques can also reduce the company's risk exposure and thus lower the cost of capital and enhance corporate value. For example, appropriate hedging transactions in the forward and futures markets for currencies and commodities can reduce foreign exchange risk and commodity price risk.

Financial engineering can enhance value by reducing risk. New financial products and security innovations designed to attract a new clientele of investors can lower the company's cost of capital.

CORPORATE GOVERNANCE

The fourth module of the VBM framework comes under the broad heading of Corporate Governance. This critical aspect of VBM involves the interactions between senior management, the board of directors, and investors, and the relationship between senior management and the operating units.

Performance Measurement

An effective management framework must incorporate a measurement system that ensures that all business activities are aligned with the overall goal of value creation and that all individuals in the organization can see and influence the direct link between their activities and the impact on corporate value. An appropriate measurement system also enhances the quality of decision making and execution within each activity.

VBM provides the appropriate focus on the only reliable measure of business unit performance—namely, value—and enables users to explicitly measure and monitor the underlying drivers of value, such as profit margins, growth, and asset management. Both the focus on value and the explicit link to the drivers of performance are particularly important in developing a truly effective managerial incentive plan, discussed in the next section. It also provides a solution for a particularly vexing problem in management; it allows business unit managers and operators to see a direct link between their activities and the resulting contribution to company-level performance.

Compensation

A major part of the incentive to take the actions required for long-term value creation must come in the form of an appropriate executive compensation plan. One of the real strengths of VBM is that it provides a means to design incentives focused on corporate value creation at all levels of the organization. Linking compensation to value-creating performance is critically important for the successful implementation of VBM—without it, VBM is likely to fail.

One way to align employee motivation with shareholder interests is to transform employees into owners/shareholders through stock options, employee stock option plans (ESOPs), or even LBOs. For operating divisions and private companies, VBM provides business-level performance measures that simulate market value creation. This enables the design of incentives that are based either directly on value measures or indirectly on the target levels of the drivers. Examples of such performance measures include economic value added (EVA)™, cash value added (CVA), shareholder value added, (SVA) and cash flow return on investment (CFROI).

Value-based incentive plans represent a major improvement over traditional incentive systems based on short-term accounting numbers such as earnings per share or sales goals. The ultimate indicator of shareholder value for publicly traded companies is the stock price, and this is why it is appropriate for companies to use stock option plans to reward their executives. For private or closely held companies, management can create "virtual" stock option plans based on the changes in stock prices of comparables, such as pure groups of companies in the same industry as the company.

It is important to point out that incentives will not work unless business-level executives see a clear connection between their activities and their rewards. VBM makes this connection transparent because it translates corporate value creation targets into business-level value drivers such as profit margins, turnover, and growth. These drivers can then become the targets on which executive incentives are based.

Investor Communications

This aspect of corporate governance deals with the company's relationships with its shareholders and the investment community. Publicly held companies are engaged in a constant tug of war with the capital markets in monitoring and mutual signaling. The company provides a steady stream of information to the markets through its annual reports, filings with the Securities and Exchange Commission (SEC), regular meetings with the investment community, and press releases. The market assimilates this and other information and incorporates its own perceptions of the company's prospects into the stock price.

The process works in the reverse as well. A company needs to understand the expectations of value creation embedded in the stock price. The stock price serves as a signal to management about the level of expected profitability required if investors are to earn a competitive rate of return. Only by exceeding the investor expectations embedded in the stock price can the company achieve superior economic returns.

Any difference between the value of the company as assessed by the stock market and management's estimate of the value of the company is called a *perceptions gap*. Perceptions gaps offer a wonderful opportunity for increasing the value of the company through more effective communication with the market. The company should be specific about its strategies: how much capital it plans to invest in various businesses, how the company is to be financed, and perhaps most important, what performance objectives are motivating management to perform. Texas Instruments forever lost a valuable opportunity to increase its market capitalization when, in 1996, it failed to adequately explain to the investing public how it planned to alter its strategy after the $3 billion sale of its highly successful defense systems unit to Raytheon. The investment community, particularly the most influential analysts and stock investors, need to know how management evaluates its own operating profitability and on what basis it rewards its people. Clear, concise, regular, and reliable communications with respect to the company's goals and strategic direction build a climate of confidence and solidify your reputation as stellar managers.

Company undervaluation represents a special case of investor miscommunication and warrants special attention: When a company's stock price is *less* than management's estimate of the value of the company, the company is much more likely to be identified by the market as a takeover target. To diminish the takeover threat, management must immediately take action to communicate how they intend to increase the true value of the company. The action might be as simple as making public statements about strategies and initiatives that have heretofore been private (that is, "inside" information). Or it could involve a repurchase of the company's shares on the open market, a more tangible signal of management's belief that the market is undervaluing its shares.

FIGURE 1-9 VBM framework: Putting it all together.

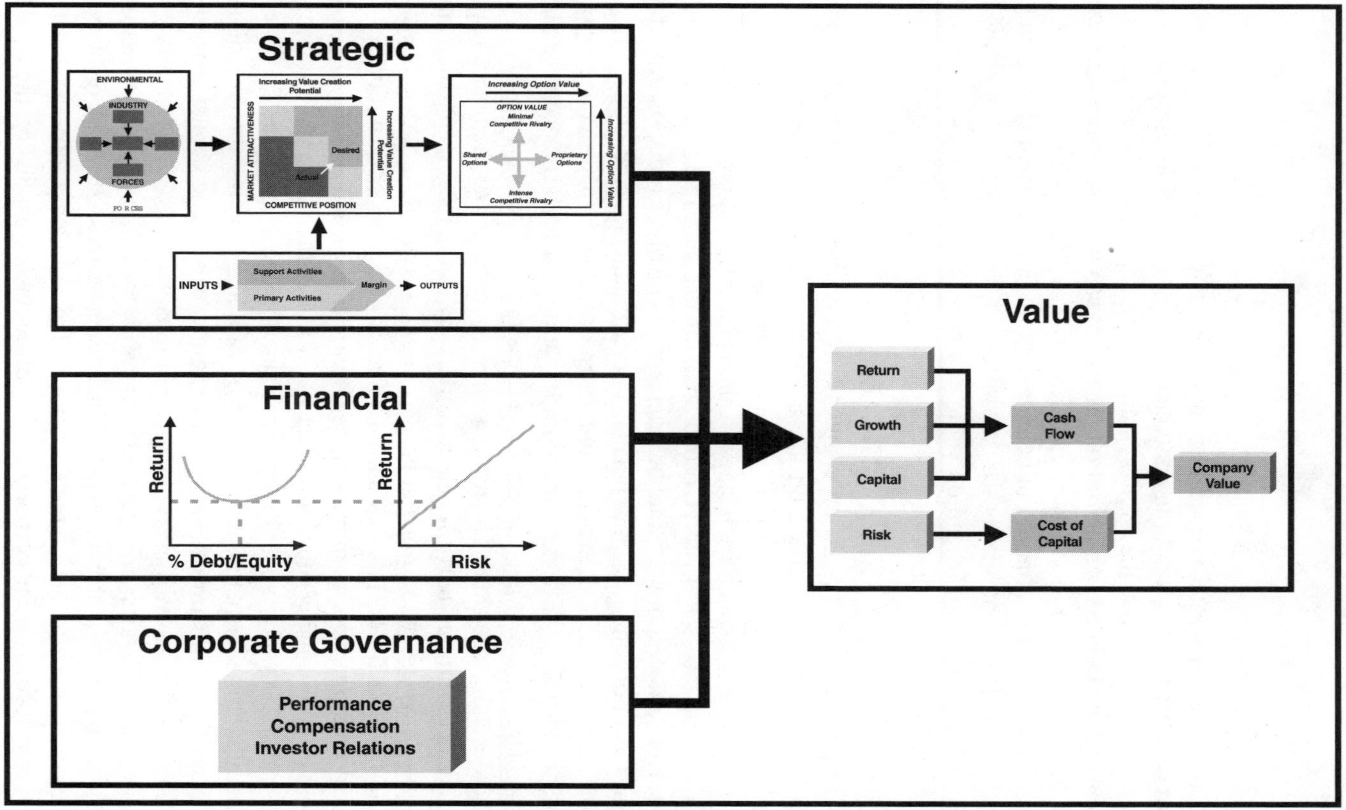

Corporate Overhead

Excessive corporate overhead consumes corporate value. The duplication of support functions at both headquarters and business levels, excess staff and personnel, and the gradual building of departmental empires (often through misguided compensation practices) can destroy shareholder value. Corporate obesity is often swept under the rug through some vague accounting allocation instead of being a distinct line item that should include all the costs of centralizing the various business units of the company. The impact of excess overhead on value can be staggering.

CONCLUSION: IT'S ALL ABOUT VALUE

The purpose of this overview chapter is to describe our integrated economic framework for managing a business. The complete VBM framework is displayed in Figure 1-9. You are urged to return to this figure frequently as you progress through each stage of the value creation process in the book.

Value stems from three broad areas of decision making: strategic, financial, and corporate. Strategic determinants involve product market strategies and portfolio planning. Financial determinants involve capital structure optimization and risk management. Corporate determinants concern governance issues, mainly executive compensation and performance evaluation.

The links between management decisions in all these areas and shareholder value are clear. The product market strategies of the business units and the corporate portfolio choices made by top management determine a set of investment and operating decisions, which, in turn, generate a series of cash flows. The real option value of managerial flexibility is a critical component of corporate value. In addition, product life cycles, competition, and many other influences will affect the size and variability of the cash flows from operations. The financing decisions influence the company's capital structure and its cost of capital. Applying the cost of capital to the cash flows determines corporate value. The capital market influences the investor's return expectation as well.

VBM provides an integrated framework for making key business decisions in all areas of management, including business strategy, resource allocation, performance targets, management compensation, and financial policy. It focuses the corporation and all its business units on the common goal of creating value for the shareholders. The remainder of the book uses a rich array of examples, illustrations, and actual case studies to provide an in-depth look at how to implement a comprehensive and successful VBM approach in which every major decision improves the value of the company.

2

WHY VALUE VALUE?

W HY SHOULD YOU VALUE VALUE? Quite simply, because everyone is better off under a value-based management (VBM) approach. With VBM, managers know how to make better decisions and can earn superior compensation, companies will perform better, investors will reap superior returns, labor will earn higher wages, and customers will enjoy better products and services.

This chapter demonstrates why the pursuit of value is easily justified on conceptual, empirical, and behavioral foundations and should be the governing objective for businesses. Moreover, the case for value maximization as the premier goal of business management is stronger today than ever, given the dramatic forces of change in all four markets where businesses compete: the markets for goods and services, corporate control, financial capital, and skilled managers.

VBM: THE NEW THINKING

So, what exactly is VBM? VBM is fundamentally a framework, or principle, that guides managers in making consistently better business decisions. VBM holds that overall business strategies should be guided by the pursuit and selection of alternatives that make the greatest contribution to the wealth of the company's owners. It provides an unambiguous mission and clear focus for management: value maximization—or else!

VBM is firmly grounded on the long-standing classical "economic view" of a business, which holds that the market value of common stock (like the value of a bond or any other investment) is the present value of a company's future expected free cash flows, discounted at a rate that reflects investors' required return for bearing risk. It is the investors' and the capital market's assessment of the relative prospects of a company—specifically its long-term cash flows and risks—that establish the market value of a company's securities.

WHAT IS VALUE-BASED MANAGEMENT?

From Coca-Cola's "A Guide to Implementing Value-Based Management, 1997," VBM is defined as the following:

> **A WAY OF THINKING.**   VBM is a set of principles that allows us to manage value at all levels of our business. Value creation becomes not just our Company's mission. It becomes the philosophy we work with daily. It becomes the framework for everything we do.
>
> **A PROCESS FOR PLANNING AND EXECUTION.**   VBM is a method of developing strategies and evaluating decisions by using value-creation principles. The method works on broad business strategies and on each associate's daily work processes.
>
> **A SET OF TOOLS.**   VBM is a set of tools for understanding what creates value—and what destroys it.

Because value is in the eye of the investor, the only correct way to measure value is from the investor's perspective. VBM explicitly introduces the perspective of current and prospective shareholders into all aspects of the management process, including strategy formulation, capital allocation, financial policy, performance measurement, investor-employee communication, and incentive compensation. Thus, business decisions are analyzed for their effects on the company's "economic value." VBM emphasizes long-term cash flow analysis and risk analysis in all aspects of managerial decision making, such as evaluating individual projects and determining the economic value of the overall strategy of the business.

The VBM approach is ultimately aimed at the goal of structuring and managing a company in a way that will create more value for its owners. Many specific valuation methodologies with this common end are discussed in subsequent chapters, including discounted cash flow, economic profit, valuation multiples, and real option valuation.

VBM is both a philosophy and a methodology for managing companies. As a philosophy, it focuses on the overriding objective of creating as much value as possible for the shareholders. The value mind-set is clearly focused on long-term cash flow and risk considerations, consistent with investor thinking and the empirical evidence from capital markets discussed in the next chapter. As a methodology, VBM provides an integrated framework for making strategic and operating decisions.

In sharp contrast to the economic view of the business, most corporate managers, directors, and company executives continue to espouse the "accounting view" of the company. This view holds that stock prices are determined primarily by reported earnings per share (EPS). In its most simplistic form, it maintains that investors respond uncritically to financial statements, mechanically capitalizing published EPS figures at standard, industrywide multiples. In such a world, the goal of corporate executives is to maximize reported earnings per share. VBM managers, on the other hand, are convinced that economic value is a more important determinant of a public company's stock price or a private company's worth than EPS, growth in sales or profits, or other traditional accounting measures. This is not to say that earnings are irrelevant. Accounting earnings may offer a reasonably good measure of corporate performance, but only insofar as they reflect real cash profitability. When earnings seriously misrepresent future operating cash flows, accounting statements distort performance and provide an unreliable guide to value.

While many corporate executives pay lip service to shareholder value in their annual reports and speeches, most have not made it part of everyday decision making. This is curious, for they already use value-based technologies in some areas of decision making, such as to evaluate capital investments and acquisitions or to calculate breakup values. Yet they fail to exploit the full potential of VBM in other areas of management.

THE EVOLUTION OF VBM

The value movement is not new and has traversed three distinct phases or generations: the number-crunching, strategizing, and integrating phases. In its original number-crunching phase in the middle 1980s, VBM focused almost exclusively on financial considerations. It started with corporate raiders who sought undervalued companies. Corporate raiders computed the value of a business based on mechanical spreadsheet valuation models, and stock price was a function of cash flows and return on equity, adjusted for risk. Businesses became tradable commodities. The emphasis was on buying and selling companies. Business units with a poor fit were divested or even liquidated, and profitable businesses with growth prospects were acquired.

While this type of corporate restructuring can certainly have a substantial immediate impact on shareholder value, the benefits are likely to be short-lived. A company can keep buying and divesting businesses for only so long; at some point it must begin to manage the remaining businesses in a way that creates economic value.

In the strategizing phase, attention shifted to operations—that is, from the right-hand side to the left-hand side of the balance sheet. The principles of VBM were extended to the management of internal operations and business strategy evaluation. VBM evolved into a technique for diagnosing business strategies. An alliance between finance and strategic planning began to emerge. Unfortunately, the approach often remained distant from actual operating decisions. It was unclear how the approach helped operating managers do a better job.

In the current integrating phase, the shareholder value movement is being absorbed into a broader and more holistic approach. It continues to best represent the owner's point of view, at a time when some boards of directors seem more intent on actively fulfilling their fiduciary role and provides a common language and shared culture across all levels of management.

VBM is becoming a more integrated approach to all aspects of decision making, including strategic planning, capital allocation, corporate restructuring, performance measurement, and incentive compensation. Thus far, however, few companies have explicitly extended VBM to their compensation systems, and even fewer to their strategic planning.

BENEFITS OF VBM

The list of companies benefiting from VBM includes a number of innovative companies that have adopted shareholder value philosophies and are publicly endorsing the approach. Examples include Coca-Cola, Berkshire Hathaway, Quaker Oats, General Electric, Wells Fargo, AT&T, Emerson Electric, Walt Disney, United Parcel Service, Lloyds Bank, BellSouth, Equifax, PepsiCo, Merck, Borg-Warner, Hillenbrand, and Marriott, to name a few. Some companies have made VBM an integral part of the management process, such as Coca-Cola, while dozens of others use various elements of the approach in pockets of excellence in their companies.

Annual reports increasingly reflect the confidence these companies have in VBM. BellSouth's annual reports state unequivocally that its primary responsibility is to its shareholders and that the company has a continuing requirement to increase the value of its shareholders' investment in BellSouth. This is not just a contemporary business phrase, but the basis for a long-term company strategy. Other examples of annual reports containing an announced value culture can be found in PepsiCo, Coca-Cola, Equifax, and UPS.

Notwithstanding the fact that the mere announcement of a move to VBM is strongly rewarded by the stock market, the empirical track record of "value" companies is impressive. Value-managed companies perform better than their peers. Figure 2-1 displays the shareholder returns for those Fortune 100 companies that espouse a shareholder value approach in their annual reports and/or in the public press relative to their peers. "Shareholder value" companies outperform their peers by 5%. An investment of $1.00 in value-oriented companies more than doubled in the five-year period covered in the study, while the same investment in the other companies was worth some $1.50. Thus, the outcome of adopting VBM is higher-value strategies and decisions which lead to improved shareholder returns and value creation.

Figure 2-2 shows the results of a study which ranked the one-year shareholder returns of the largest 1000 U.S. companies by sensitivity of CEO compensation to shareholder value. The difference in shareholder returns between the companies in the top and bottom 20% was 23%! The results are the same for the 5-year and 10-year returns. It is clear that companies with a shareholder value culture produce higher investment performance for their owners.

VBM also has a demonstrated ability to improve pay and performance. Managers do well when their companies do well. They earn raises, pro-

FIGURE 2-1   The outcome of adopting value-based management: Higher value strategies/decisions, which lead to improved shareholder returns.

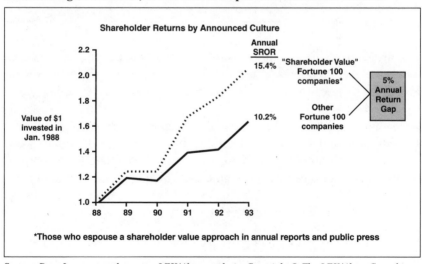

Source: Dow Jones, annual reports, LEK/Alcar analysis. Copyright © The LEK/Alcar Consulting Group, Inc.

WHAT'S IN IT FOR ME?
According to Coca-Cola:
The reason to use VBM processes is simple: Doing it creates value. We are asking you to improve your way of working—from idea through execution. You're probably thinking "I deserve a reward for all that." Well, you get several.

- **YOUR STAKE IN THE COCA-COLA COMPANY BE-COMES MORE VALUABLE**   Many managers and employees of the Coca-Cola Company own in one way or another shares of stocks in the Company. Creating value in our daily work increases the value of those shares. In short, managing for value means putting more money in your own pocket.
- **VBM OFFERS THE OPPORTUNITY TO LEARN NEW SKILLS—MARKET PLACE ANALYSIS, ECONOMIC MODELING, PROCESS IMPROVEMENT**   Using these skills will show you precisely what creates and destroys value in your area of responsibility.
- **JOB CREATION**   VBM can help secure existing jobs and create new employment opportunities.

From Coca-Cola Company's "A Guide to Implementing Value-Based Management," 1997.

motions, and valuable stock options when their companies excel. Companies that do poorly punish managers in many ways. Unhappy owners sell their shares to another company or management team that promises to do better.

In short, VBM offers the potential for superior performance, superior compensation, and superior decision making. Ultimately, improved value results in a self-reinforcing virtuous cycle that drives long-term competitive advantage, as illustrated in Figure 2-3. Greater value creation results in more resources to invest in activities that build competitive advantage, which, in turn, drives additional value creation.

THE CHALLENGE TO CREATE VALUE
Value creation is a daunting task. In a competitive economy with no barriers to entry, profits attract new companies which increase production and

FIGURE 2-2   Results of quantitative studies that rank companies by shareholder value orientations, which show that more than 5% of annual return is at stake.

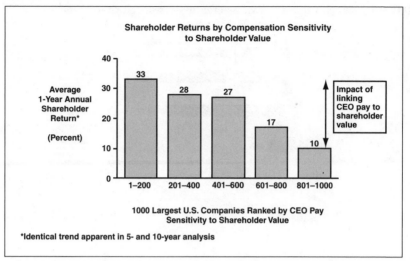

FIGURE 2-3   Shareholder value approach creating a virtuous circle that will sustain competitive advantage.

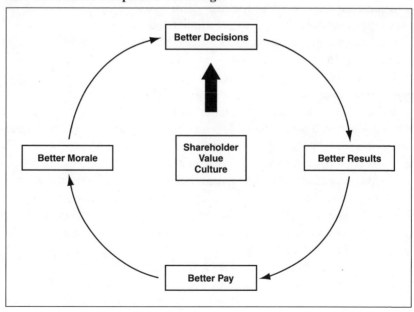

FIGURE 2-4   How have top value creators rewarded shareholders?

Industry		1999 Wall Street Journal Shareholder Scoreboard Total Shareholder Returns Value of $100 Invested on January 1, 1989	Winning Strategy

Computers	Dell Computers	54,320	• Gained "first mover advantage"
			  — Direct Internet sales
			  — "Build to order" sales

	Peer Average	1,369	

Securities Brokerage	Charles Schwab Inc.	10,548	• Leveraged brand name by selling
			  third party mutual funds
			• Achieved technology edge in
			  Internet Trading

	Peer Average	1,392	

Specialty Retailing	Home Depot	3,479	• Revolutionized home
			  improvement market with
			  — Strong customer service
			  — Big cost advantage

	Peer Average	647	

Airlines	Southwest Airlines	1,212	• Changed the rules of competition
			  by aligning entire organization
			  around low cost, efficient service
			• Avoided head-to-head competition
			  with majors

	Peer Average	466	

Conglomerates	Berkshire Hathaway	1,439	• Concentrated on businesses with
			  proven earnings performance and
			  strong management
			• Favored businesses and industries
			  unlikely to experience major change

	Peer Average	743	

Source: Copyright © The LEK/Alcar Consulting Group, Inc.

lower prices until excess economic profits are reduced to zero. Achieving and maintaining above-average economic performance is difficult. Industry factors and competitive pressures often limit management's ability to increase value even in the near term. Even companies with strong positions in attractive industries are challenged.

Creating value for investors is a demanding task for another reason. Since a company's share price already reflects current market expectations for future performance, companies can continue to outperform the market only if they continue to perform unexpectedly well.

Even so, the potential rewards to this difficult task are staggering. Figure 2-4 shows how top value creators beat the odds and exceeded their peer group's total shareholder returns over the past 10 years. While the strategies and operating styles of these companies differ widely, each company is passionate about creating shareholder value.

Management's contribution to value creation can be measured in terms of total shareholder returns (TSR) from dividends and capital gains. In Figure 2-5, for example, we see that over the 1990 to 1999 period, Dell Computer's owners realized an annual return of 140%. This compares very favorably to the average return of 48% for the computer industry and 18% for the overall stock market. In dollar terms, this means that a $1000 investment in Dell in 1995 would have grown to about $80,000 by the end of 1999. That same investment in a portfolio of other computer retailers

FIGURE 2-5 Measuring Dell Computer's performance. Annual total shareholder returns, 1995–1999.

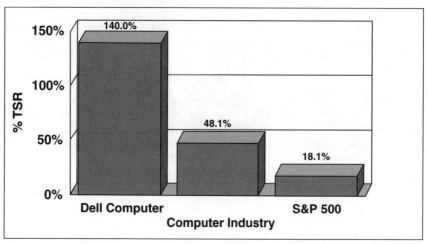

would have appreciated in value to $7000, and to only $2300 if invested in the S&P 500 Index.

There is wide variation in the TSR performance across companies over time. Figure 2-6 displays the TSR of companies in the Standard & Poor's 500 Index over the last 10 years, which ranged from −10% to nearly 50%, with an average of 14.4%.

The wide variation in value creation performance among companies underscores the remarkable opportunity for the vast majority of companies to create economic value. Even in the center region of the TSR distribution of Figure 2-6, the difference in shareholder return between second and third quartile companies is some 6% per year. For a company with a $1 billion market value currently, this represents a staggering $2 billion difference in value creation over the next decade.

The huge potential and rewards from value creation can also be seen in Figure 2-7, which shows how $1000 invested in each of the 30 Dow Jones Industrials Index companies fared over the last decade. On average, $1000 invested in the Dow grew to about $5000 in the last decade, but ranged from almost $20,000 for Citigroup to only $1600 for Goodyear Tire.

Large differences in TSR performance can be observed even for companies in the same industry with similar value creation opportunities. Table 2-1 displays the differences in annual shareholder returns between the top and bottom performers in each industry in the S&P 500 Index over the

FIGURE 2-6   Total shareholder return (S&P 500), 1990–1999.

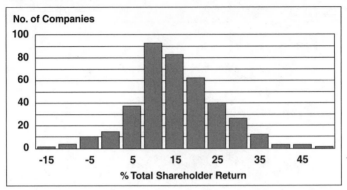

last decade. The differences are significant in many cases, and even dramatic in several instances. On average, the top performer outdistanced the bottom performer by 20%, which translates into a difference in terminal wealth of $6200 on a $1000 investment.

The vast differences in shareholder return even in the same industry strongly suggest that the potential for improving performance is enormous

FIGURE 2-7   Stock performance, Dow Jones Industrial Average Growth of $1000 invested over 1990–1999.

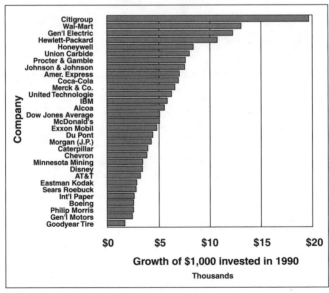

Source: Value Line Survey for Windows 01/2000.

TABLE 2-1   TSR performance within selected industries, 1990–1999.

Industry	Top Performer Company	% TSR	Bottom Performer Company	% TSR
Advertising	Omnicom Group	34.7	Interpublic Group	28.6
Air transport	Southwest Airlines	26.4	US Airways Group	−0.4
Alco-Bev	Anheuser-Busch	16.9	Seagram Co.	9.0
Aluminum	Alcoa Inc.	18.6	Reynolds Metals	6.4
Apparel	V.F. Corp.	9.4	Russell Corp.	−2.7
Appliance	Maytag Corp.	12.8	Whirlpool Corp.	9.9
Auto	Ford Motor	14.3	Navistar Int'l	2.0
Bank	Bank of New York	27.9	Bank of America	11.7
Bankmid	Northern Trust Corp.	28.7	Bank One Corp.	10.8
Beverage	Coca-Cola	21.3	PepsiCo Inc.	15.4
Brokers	Schwab (Charles)	56.8	Merrill Lynch & Co.	31.7
Building	Masco Corp.	10.1	Owens Corning	−2.3
Buildsupply	Home Depot	44.3	Lowe's Cos.	33.3
Chemdiversif	PPG Inds.	15.4	Goodrich (B.F.)	7.2
Chemical	Union Carbide	23.1	Dow Chemical	11.0
Chemspecialty	Ecolab Inc.	20.8	G't Lakes Chemical	5.7
Computer	Dell Computer	97.2	Silicon Graphics	2.9
Cosmetic	Gillette	22.6	Alberto Culver 'B'	9.8
Defense	Gen'l Dynamics	25.6	Lockheed Martin	8.6
Diversif	Honeywell Int'l	23.6	NACCO Inds. 'A'	1.3
Drug	Amgen	50.3	ALZA Corp.	4.9
Drugstor	Walgreen Co.	27.6	Longs Drug Stores	4.2
Elecequipment	Gen'l Electric	28.5	Cooper Inds.	3.1
Entrtain	Clear Channel	64.4	CBS Corp.	8.0
Finsvcs	Citigroup Inc.	34.7	Loews Corp.	0.8
Foodproc	Wrigley (Wm.) Jr.	18.9	Archer Daniels Midl'd	3.2·
Gasdistribut	ONEOK Inc.	10.0	NICOR Inc.	8.5
Gasdivrs	Enron Corp.	23.2	Consol. Natural Gas	6.9
Goldsilv	Barrick Gold	9.4	Battle Mtn. Gold Co.	−19.3
Grocery	Kroger Co.	17.7	G't Atlantic & Pacific	−5.5

(continued)

TABLE 2-1   TSR performance within selected industries, 1990–1999.
(Continued)

| | Top Performer | | Bottom Performer | |
Industry	Company	% TSR	Company	% TSR
Homebild	Pulte Corp.	16.0	Kaufman & Broad Home	8.0
Hotelgam	Mirage Resorts	10.7	Hilton Hotels	−5.7
Houseprd	Colgate-Palmolive	26.1	Ralston Purina Group	10.9
Indusrv	Equifax Inc.	14.9	Laidlaw Inc.	−11.8
Inslife	Conseco Inc.	27.7	Torchmark Corp.	7.0
Insprpty	Progressive (Ohio)	19.7	SAFECO Corp.	5.9
Instrmnt	KLA-Tencor	38.2	Polaroid Corp.	−6.8
Machine	Dover Corp.	19.9	Foster Wheeler	−5.8
Medserv	UnitedHealth Group	33.3	Humana Inc.	−2.0
Medsuppl	Medtronic Inc.	34.2	St. Jude Medical	7.0
Nwspaper	Tribune Co.	18.6	Knight Ridder	9.8
Office	Pitney Bowes	17.8	Moore Corp.	−10.6
Oilfield	Schlumberger Ltd.	10.6	McDermott Int'l	−6.0
Oilinteg	Exxon Mobil Corp.	16.9	Sunoco Inc.	−0.8
Oilprod	Apache Corp.	8.5	Burlington Resources	−1.0
Package	Sealed Air	26.1	Crown Cork	3.4
Paper	Willamette Ind.	16.5	Willamette Ind.	16.5
Paper	Weyerhaeuser Co.	14.1	Boise Cascade	1.8
Publish	McGraw-Hill	19.5	Donnelley (R.R) & Sons	1.8
Railroad	Burlington Northern	11.2	Union Pacific	4.0
Recreate	Hasbro Inc.	14.1	Brunswick Corp.	7.4
Restrnt	Wendy's Int'l	18.3	McDonald's Corp.	17.6
Retail	Wal-Mart Stores	29.3	Penney (J.C.)	−1.8
Retailsp	Gap (The) Inc.	38.8	Venator Group	−12.3
Semicond	Micron Technology	44.9	Advanced Micro Dev.	13.9
Shoe	NIKE Inc. `B'	23.6	Reebok Int'l	−5.3
Software	Microsoft Corp.	58.0	Autodesk Inc.	6.5

TABLE 2-1   TSR performance within selected industries, 1990–1999.
(*Continued*)

Industry	Top Performer		Bottom Performer	
	Company	% TSR	Company	% TSR
Steel	Nucor Corp.	14.5	Ryerson Tull	−4.4
Telequip	Tellabs Inc.	66.6	Scientific Atlanta	22.2
Teleserv	MCI WorldCom	52.8	AT&T Corp.	12.3
Thrift	Freddie Mac	25.8	Golden West Fin'l	14.8
Tire	Cooper Tire & Rubber	8.2	Goodyear Tire	5.1
Utilcent	Reliant Energy	10.1	Unicom Corp.	5.4
Utileast	Southern Co.	11.6	Niagara Mohawk	2.3
Utilwest	Edison Int'l	8.8	PG&E Corp.	4.9
Average	**Top Performers**	**25.6**	**Bottom Performers**	**5.1**

and is not likely attributable to chance. There is a strong linkage between management actions and shareholder returns which must be understood and utilized to make sound business decisions. Companies that have succeeded in linking their decisions to the objective of maximizing value have experienced spectacular value creation performance

Achieving the 1990s' 14.4% TSR in the next millennium will be difficult for all but the top-quartile performers. To be a top-quartile TSR performer during 1990 to 1999 required a minimum TSR performance of 30%, more than double the market average of 14.4%. Dell's 140% TSR, for example, puts it in the top 1% of S&P 500 companies, along with only a handful of other value exemplars such as Microsoft, Charles Schwab, Sun Microsystems, MCI Worldcom, Intel, Oracle, and Home Depot.

MAXIMIZE VALUE—OR ELSE!

Think of your business as operating and competing in four distinct markets: (1) the market for goods and services, (2) the market for corporate control, (3) the capital markets, and (4) the market for skilled managers. Forces of change and the pressures to maximize business value are intensifying in all four markets. VBM requires overcoming the external forces of competition in all four markets at once. As if this task were not challenging enough, VBM must also overcome the internal inertia of the corporate institution, or the so-called "agency issues," discussed in the following sections.

Product Market Pressures in the New Economy

The motivating forces behind the VBM movement in the product market include more intense competition, globalization, technology, deregulation, and increased volatility. Traditional barriers to entry are being eroded and aggressive competition promoted by the free movement of capital, ease of travel, spread of democracy, speed of communication, and availability of information. The breaking down of barriers is redefining the way businesses work, how products are manufactured, how goods and services are delivered, and how employees and employers think. As a result, economic profits are less sustainable.

To create shareholder value by earning excess returns, managers must find business opportunities where product prices exceed costs. The search for excess returns places tremendous pressure on managers to innovate with new product designs and applications of new technologies. They must identify products valuable enough to create customer demand and profits high enough to produce attractive returns. Excess returns evaporate quickly in an environment of continuous new product innovation, shorter and shorter product life cycles, additional capacity, and lower-cost production. A noteworthy example is the proliferation of digital commerce, which is rapidly commoditizing goods and services and threatening established participants.

Today's global, fast-changing environment puts a premium on rapid response to change—that is, the capacity to adapt quickly to new technologies in production or distribution, unanticipated shifts in consumer tastes, or major economic dislocations. That requires a coherent and integrated framework—namely, VBM. To meet such challenges, managers must understand how value is produced and maintained in any economic environment. That is the principal objective of this book.

The advantage of company size is shrinking in the new digital economy, and size alone can no longer be counted on to conceal the lack of competitive advantage. VBM frequently shows that just the opposite—namely, focus and downsizing (or "rightsizing")—actually creates more value. This view is unpopular with managers whose compensation is tied to conventional performance measures such as sales or earnings.

The advantages of integration (both horizontal and vertical) are eroding as well. The lure of vertical integration is weaker. Unbundled and disintegrated competitors can do as well, if not better. The scale economies once associated with horizontal integration are increasingly difficult to find or maintain, as evidenced by the demise of multibusiness conglomerates.

Globalization is a large part of the reason that the rules of the game are changing. For example, high-tech start-up companies saw the need for a global presence early and, carrying none of the baggage of more established companies, they were able to react more quickly and gain an early international competitive advantage.

Globalization is accelerating, and companies without a global reach will soon be at a disadvantage. In industries where profitability was once protected by substantial barriers to entry, new entry has been encouraged by deregulation, diversification by domestic companies, and multinational expansion by overseas companies. Five years ago, 2 out of 10 U.S. companies' competitors were foreign. Now it is closer to 6! The impact of globalization is pervasive, affecting the flows of goods and services, financial capital (e.g., the power of Japan and Europe), and information and knowledge in all industries. The result is a virtual real-time world marketplace.

Managers must reassess their business positions continuously in an unstable and risky environment. Witness the volatility of interest rates and foreign exchange rates and the pace of technological change. Decisions with profound effects on value must be made swiftly in areas as diverse as joint ventures, divestiture of product lines, changes in distribution channels, international expansion, corporate restructurings, and financial policies.

Pressures from the Market for Corporate Control
The second source of discipline fueling the concern for value is the market for corporate control. A business competes in the market for corporate control, as well as in the market for goods and services.

Large-scale corporate restructurings, leveraged buyouts (LBOs), raiders, and the takeover defenses were virtually unknown prior to the mid-1980s. Today, they are commonplace, and both the players in the market for corporate control and the appropriate defensive strategies have to be taken into account in making most major corporate decisions.

The restructuring movement has certainly not been inhibited by a lack of capital. Companies of all sizes have access to capital on a global scale at reasonable cost and conditions. Creative financial engineering, specialized venture capital funds, and an active high-yield debt market fuel the heated market for corporate control. Players in the market for corporate control are constantly searching for undermanaged companies, where aggressive changes in strategic directions could dramatically improve the value of the stock. In some cases, the gap between actual and potential market values, the "value gap," is so large that substantial profits can be made even after raiders pay premiums of 30% to 50% to acquire control. The presence of value gaps, combined with the availability of financial capital, has created the takeover entrepreneurs, who have been able to threaten vitually any company with a takeover, even the corporate giants. As a result, many executives recognize a new and compelling reason to be concerned with the performance of their company's stock. Successful implementation of VBM is by far the best defense against the market for corporate control.

Corporate managers must learn to look at their companies in the same way a potential raider would, constantly searching for value gaps and taking actions to correct them. To do this, management needs to become familiar with the techniques and concepts of VBM.

Indeed, it is the failure of corporate management to effectively utilize the tools of value management which makes so many companies attractive targets for acquisition and restructuring.

Pressures from the Capital Markets

The third source of discipline fueling the concern for value is the market for capital. Not only does a business compete in the product market and in the market for corporate control, it also must attract capital in financial markets in competition with all other companies. The modern executive also must focus on winning the competition for capital.

All corporate managers are basically in the same business: competing for investors' savings. While companies enjoy varying degrees of monopoly in the sale of products and services, they must compete with everyone else in the free, open market for the input factors of production, whether labor, materials, machines, or capital. The prices of these inputs are set in the competitive marketplace by supply and demand. Since investor-owned businesses must go to the open capital market and sell their securities in competition with every other issuer, they must pay the market price for the capital they require, for example, the interest on debt capital or the expected return on common equity. If competing investments offer a 10% return and your company only offers a return of 6%, not only will shareholders suffer a capital loss as the stock dives, but the company will be unable to attract capital and remain in business. Financial capital flows to the higher risk-adjusted return.

The keen interest in VBM is fueled further by the proliferation of value-oriented scorecards in the financial press and in the investment community. These scorecards report returns to shareholders, along with other measures of performance. Executives, shareholders, and the business press increasingly scrutinize business performance in terms of *shareholder value creation*. Three examples—*Business Week's* executive compensation scoreboard, Stern and Stewart's "1000 EVA–MVA" winners, and the *Wall Street Journal's* annual Shareholder Scoreboard—are noteworthy.

The broad range in executive compensation, both across and within industries, has further fueled an interest in achieving shareholder value. Considerable attention has focused recently on the problems associated with rewarding executives on the basis of short-term accounting-based indicators. As a reflection of the increasing scrutiny under which executive compensation has come, the popular business press, including *Fortune* and *Business Week,* has begun to publish data on the correlation between executives' pay and company performance measured by, among other variables, returns to shareholders. From this and other data, there is a growing recognition that executives' long-term compensation needs to be more closely tied to shareholder value creation.

Major reforms in corporate governance have occurred in the last decade. It is becoming more commonplace for large financial and other institutional investors to vote their shares against underperforming management and unreasonable anti-takeover charter provisions. There are more cases where directors challenged or even forced the ouster of senior management. The landmark ousting of General Motors' CEO in 1992 set the pace with similar fates meeting the CEOs of American Express, IBM, Apple Computer, Rubbermaid, Digital Equipment, Compaq, Delta Airline, and Eastman Kodak soon thereafter. The pay-for-performance debate continues unabated. In a world dominated by large investors whose large stakes in companies make it difficult to divest underperforming companies, large investors are devising more aggressive checks on value creation performance.

Pressures from the Market for Skilled Managers
The changing trends in business, including the information age and global competition, have resulted in increased need for senior executives who have the ability to adapt, to make decisions quickly in situations of high uncertainty, and to direct the company through transformational change. A recent survey by McKinsey shows that American companies are suffering from a shortage of executive talent.[1] An effective value-based compensation strategy is essential to attract and retain top managerial talent.

[1] Chambers, E. G., et al. 1988. "The War for Talent." *McKinsey Quarterly*. 3: 44–57.

Companies that fail to reward top value performers with excellent pay will lost their executives to those that do.

THE DEMISE OF ACCOUNTING METRICS

Performance measurement is a critical function of corporate senior management. Appropriate measures are necessary to evaluate strategies, to allocate capital among competing operating divisions of companies, to choose among investment projects, to evaluate acquisition plans, and to devise incentive-based compensation programs.

There is a growing recognition that accounting indicators can give a distorted picture of economic value for several fundamental reasons. First and foremost, economic value is determined by economic, not accounting, cash flows. Investors assess value on a cash basis rather than on an accrual basis. Second, accrual accounting numbers are strongly affected by different accounting approaches to depreciation, amortization, inventory valuation, and the like. Third, economic value is concerned with maximizing cash flows over time. Investors take into account the long-term cash-flow-generating power of a company when making investment decisions. Accounting measures are fundamentally short-term in nature.

Fourth, traditional accounting earnings and return measures fail to tell us anything about the relative riskiness of an investment. Fifth, earnings figures do not recognize the working capital and fixed asset investments required to support sales growth. Finally, earnings figures do not recognize explicitly a charge for the capital employed in the business.

In short, accounting metrics ignore the fundamental variables required for economic value: free cash flows, investment horizon, and risk. The empirical evidence discussed in Chapter 3 corroborates the economic view of a business rather than the accounting view and that investors think and act on the basis of economic value precepts.

EMPIRICAL SUPPORT FOR ECONOMIC VALUE

According to the economic value model of a business, three factors determine value: cash flows rather than earnings, long-term and short-term cash flows rather than just short-term cash flows, and risk. A substantial body of research and empirical evidence supports the economic value model. As we shall see in Chapter 3, investors care more about cash flows than net income in setting market prices for securities. A lot of executives are under the mistaken impression that capital markets are myopic and value short-term financial performance at the expense of long-term performance. In fact, most investors and institutional portfolio managers (mutual funds, bank trusts, pension funds) take a long-term view of their portfolios. Some 70% to 80% of the economic value of a business typically comes from its prospects five years or more in the future, as shown in the next chapter.

SUPERIOR DECISION MAKING

The appeal of VBM is that it provides a unified framework for making key decisions on corporate governance issues, strategy, resource allocation, performance targets, management compensation, financial policies and communications with investors and employees, and for linking all of these decisions to the maximization of shareholder value.

In practice, companies pursue a wide range of goals, akin to a corporate Tower of Babel, as shown in Figure 2-8. This diversity of goals is a reflection of the variety of different interest groups that make up the company. A company can be viewed as a coalition in which different operational goals are associated with different functional interests. For example, sales and marketing focus on revenue and market share, senior management favors earnings growth and return on equity, and production pursues output goals.

In contrast, the financial information system under the VBM approach, shown in Figure 2-9, provides companies with a consistency of analysis

FIGURE 2-8   A typical financial management system.

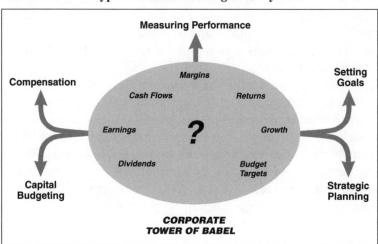

FIGURE 2-9   Simplified and focused management system.

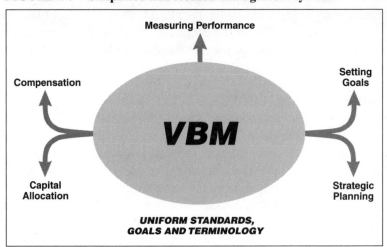

across functions, levels, and types of business decisions. In this way, those who are competing for common resources in a company will share the same framework for analyzing their businesses. In addition, the approach is not difficult to implement because it requires only a modest amount of new data (such as cash flow and the cost of capital). It also offers the benefit of overcoming the limitations of traditional accounting-based financial statements.

A properly designed and implemented VBM program energizes and empowers a company as well by creating a common language between line and staff, and between corporate and business units. VBM transcends narrow interests and provides a clear link between strategy and shareholder performance.

The VBM approach adds some important new dimensions to traditional decision making as well. For example, VBM can contribute substantially to traditional product-market portfolio methods, as can conventional techniques of competitive strategy analysis (as Chapters 9 and 10 will demonstrate). Corporate portfolio strategies can be explicitly evaluated for their potential impact on the corporation's stock market value, and so can individual business-level competitive strategies. VBM can provide the missing link between the business-level product market focus and the corporate-level concern for the stock market. Moreover, operating managers can learn to appreciate the direction and extent of their business units' impact on corporate value.

How can VBM help management identify value-creating strategies? An integral part of the VBM process is the identification of key value drivers—that is, the three to five things a business must do well to succeed, such as core skills, assets, customer needs, competitor action, and technologies. These key value drivers tend to get lost in the bureaucratic maelstrom of corporations.

VBM can add a lot to the area of compensation and investor communications as well. Value-based performance measures can be incorporated in compensation plans to encourage managers to act in the best interest of the shareholders. VBM provides a standard for investor communications that reflects how the market actually behaves.

VBM overcomes the shortcomings and distortions of accounting measures that were never designed to evaluate future strategies and future investment opportunities and reduces the corporate gamesmanship in submitting divisional plans and budgets.

VBM AND THE INSTITUTIONAL IMPERATIVE

Managers serve as agents of shareholders. Although both are stakeholders in the same company, their interests often diverge on three distinct fronts: risk position, ability to redeploy their investments, and time horizons.

As far as risk position is concerned, shareholders stand at the bottom of the totem pole of claimants to the resources of the corporation. Bankers, the government, creditors, workers—all of these "stakeholders" are first in line to be paid before shareholders can reap any gains on their investment. Executives, too, as employees of the company, have the right to payment of salaries and benefits before the claims of shareholders are met.

Executives and shareholders also differ in their flexibilities to "cash in," or liquidate, their investments. Shareholders can buy and sell freely in the securities market and at negligible transaction cost, while the executive's "stake" is far less liquid and marketable. It reaches far beyond whatever stocks are held. It extends to the human capital invested in the building of a career, including considerable industry- and company-specific knowledge. This human capital usually ties the executive to a particular industry, and the company-specific portion of that capital is largely nonmarketable.

Shareholders typically embrace longer time horizons than senior management. In the absence of special long-term compensation plans, there is little natural incentive for managers to look beyond the scope of day-to-day operations. In fact, they may not be around to witness the success or failure of projects they have approved prior to retiring.

Executives and shareholders differ fundamentally, then, in their risk positions, in their abilities to liquefy their investments, and in their time horizons. Those differences lead to differences in the ways each group measures the risks and rewards of any corporate action. In general, the differences in risk evaluation make a company's executive more averse to risk than are its shareholders.

By providing reliable and valid benchmarks for measuring performance, compensating managers, and evaluating alternative strategies, VBM helps to resolve the potential conflict of interest between shareholders and their agents, the executives entrusted with the responsibility for maintaining and increasing shareholder value. Although executive compensation plans can and should help bridge the gap between shareholders and their agents—the managers—they often compound it. A lot of executive incentive plans, for example, are based on improvements in short-term earnings and therefore actually inhibit the risky strategic decisions required to provide highly competitive returns to shareholders.

In short, value maximization requires overcoming not only the external forces of competition (competitive advantage) but also the internal forces within the corporate institution itself (agency issues).

CHALLENGES TO VBM

Some skeptics challenge value creation as the governing managerial objective. These objections are largely unfounded.

Objections to the primacy of shareholder value are mounted by capital market skeptics, who question the long-term horizon of investors. The proponents of Wall Street myopia reject the notion that capital markets impose a long-term viewpoint and argue that security investors are myopic—in other words, they are fixated on next quarter's earnings per share report. This view is inconsistent with the empirical evidence discussed earlier and reviewed in detail in the next chapter.

The stakeholder school views the corporation as a coalition of a number of interests, including shareholders, managers, and other employees. Proponents of "stakeholder capitalism" argue that the corporation is a balancer of divergent stakeholder interests. It is up to the corporation to establish a fair and equitable balance between the aspirations, rights, and concerns of employees, labor unions, customers, management, suppliers, shareholders, government, and society at large. There really is no reason to single out shareholders, according to this view.

This bureaucratic and stagnant view of a business is unappealing and leads to a dead end, for it seriously overestimates the company's market power and seriously underestimates the power of capital markets. It somehow assumes that a company is sheltered from market forces. To the contrary, customers are not captive of the company and are quick to redeploy their resources. In this new era of open, fiercely competitive global product markets, the stakeholder model becomes illusory. Similarly, investors are impersonal and fluid, quick to redeploy capital in search of a superior return.

Corporate success in creating shareholder value benefits all parties, not only shareholders. Economic surpluses make everyone better off. It is difficult to imagine a business where you can satisfy shareholders without taking care of customers and employees. Superior value performance benefits not just shareholders but also employees and customers. Employees gain security, improved opportunity, and improved compensation. Customers benefit because the company is able to attract more capital at lower cost that it can invest in activities that better meet customers' product, service, or cost needs. In the pursuit of economic value creation, management must concern itself with all aspects of company operations, including product quality, personnel training, know-how, company image, and reputation. Thus, VBM increases the value of all claims. The pursuit of economic value is consistent with the interests of all parties. Failure to consider any one party will lead to the reduction of shareholder wealth over the long term.

The case for adopting a single overriding goal for the company is supported by the fact that, in most industries, the pressure of competition, particularly of international competition and information technology, has intensified. The result has been the apparently conflicting interests of the different constituencies in the company. The underlying common interest of all stakeholders is the company's survival. Survival requires that, over the long term, the company creates economic value—that is, it earns a rate of return in excess of its cost of capital. Fewer and fewer companies in the new millennium have the luxury of being able to diverge substantially from the goal of long-run value maximization imposed by the need for survival.

In its early "number-crunching" phase, the value movement was strongly identified with the discipline of finance and its associated emphasis on theory and complex equations. This complexity stood in the way of its effective application in many companies that could have benefited from a VBM culture. Many companies simply rejected the value-based approach outright because of its complexity. Others, despite making serious efforts to implement the approach, became so involved in the method that "number blindness" set in and the financial models become the end rather than the means, thereby causing value to suffer.

Although VBM remains linked to finance, it is not about numbers. It is about a culture, a process which permeates all aspects of management. Changes in rules of the game imply changes in behavior and change in culture. Becoming a VBM company means implanting a culture of concern for value and evolving the way you think about managing your company. It is not about adopting some new sophisticated financial methodology.

In any event, the power of the personal computer has largely eliminated the fear of complex financial modeling. Recent advances in technology have put incredible analytical potential at management's disposal. Managers can now make decisions using software tools on microcomputers. New approaches thus can more readily be incorporated without displacing existing information systems. New educational programs are available from service companies and business schools to help managers understand VBM. In addition, many more consultants have taken up the shareholder value banner and are helping clients apply the concept.

Some object on the grounds that VBM is applicable principally to publicly traded companies and of limited interest to private companies. This is invalid. The tenets of VBM are equally applicable to private companies. Privately held companies are held to the same standards of value as publicly held corporations when they are bought and sold. The fundamental determinants of value that drive stock prices are the same for private and public companies; accordingly, they should provide the main criteria of any performance measurement process.

SOCIETY IS BETTER OFF

While VBM is based on a bedrock conviction that economic value creation should be the primary mission of corporate management, this is not meant to suggest that other objectives such as market position and public responsibility are unimportant. VBM is really more an acknowledgment that long-term shareholder interests—that is, value creation—should take precedence in the management decision process.

The fundamental question of why we should be concerned with shareholders extends well beyond the fact that they own the business and has to do with the fact that society's resources are limited. The way to create the greatest social wealth is to encourage every manager to maximize the economic value of the business. This decision rule leads to the greatest efficiency in allocating resources and the greatest economic good for society. The pursuit of economic value makes everyone better off.

The maximization of value is simply the maximization of what is left once you have satisfied your customers and fairly compensated your employees and all the other factors of production in your business, including capital. Residual wealth has already considered the returns to all the resources employed, to all factors of production. Focusing on what is left over after all the factors have been fairly compensated is the proper way to think about the optimal allocation of resources.

Philosophically, the emphasis on shareholder value is certainly consistent with the capitalistic social perspective of the individual as sovereign. Modern theory provides a single simple goal for company managers with well-informed investors who buy and sell stocks in efficient capital markets: maximize shareholder value. Owners can reallocate profits from their investments as they see fit, making their own consumption and investment decisions according to their preferences, risk aversion, and tax situation. The only way to simultaneously please all shareholders is to increase the value of their shares.

CONCLUSION

The primary and increasingly urgent goal for management is to create value for shareholders. More and more companies are moving VBM beyond the purely financial to all areas of management, including business strategy and compensation. They are introducing programs to educate their managers in the finer points of powerful, qualitative tools like Porter's Competitive Analysis and quantitative tools such as real options and a plethora of valuation models. They are also beginning to implement new long-term executive incentive plans pegged, in part, on the achievement of shareholder-value targets.

More and more managers and companies are adopting or considering the adoption of VBM. Executives are concerned with the performance of their company's stock but are still uncertain about how to implement the approach. The convergence of the trends and forces in product markets, capital markets, and the market for corporate control discussed earlier will compel many more corporations to examine how they can incorporate the shareholder value approach into their business planning.

There are no more excuses to postpone a serious consideration of all or part of value-based management. VBM should become the major thrust of all managerial decisions. Top management should abandon traditional

---

The Potential Contributions of VBM Are Overwhelming

- Enhance your company's competitive position in product markets, the market for corporate control, and in the capital market
- Enhance value for shareholders
- Optimize the use of resources for society broadly
- Optimize all stakeholders' interests
- Achieve better pay, better performance, better morale
- Make better decisions
- Manage assets better
- Increase your willingness to profitably redirect resources
- Bridge the gap between operations, strategy, and financial results
- Think, act, and be paid like owners
- Communicate more effectively with investors

---

accounting-based decision-making tools such as return on equity, return on assets, return on sales, and growth in earnings per share, and focus instead on value creation. VBM provides a unified approach to management decision making, whether it is to allocate capital, measure performance, restructure companies, implement value-creating business and corporate strategies, or compensate executives.

3

VALUE AND CAPITAL MARKETS

I N **CHAPTER 1,** we presented a model of value creation in which economic cash flows were determined by the (1) expected return on equity, (2) expected growth, (3) cost of equity capital, and (4) number of years over which the company can maintain the spread, defined as the difference between the actual return on equity and cost of equity capital. The cost of equity capital, in turn, is the return required by the capital market to lend equity capital to the business and is determined by an active, well-functioning capital market as the return foregone on the next best investment opportunity of similar risk.

The economic model captures the eminently sensible conclusion that a company creates true economic value when it invests in and maintains growth opportunities with a positive spread, those whose actual returns exceed their costs. A key question in assessing the viability of VBM, then, is this: Does the capital market actually subscribe to this view of economic value creation? This is the question explored in this chapter. We find strong empirical support for the economic model of a business and conclude that investors do indeed (1) think cash flow, (2) think long term, and (3) take risk into account.

CASH IS KING

A basic question in valuation is whether investors care more about cash flow or net income. The indisputable answer is cash flow. The most compelling evidence is provided by the simplest observation: When companies take actions that move earnings in one direction and economic cash flows in the other, stock prices follow the cash flows.[1] Sacrificing long-term cash flows for short-term earnings does not work: Financial markets react negatively to actions that increase earnings at the expense of cash flows and positively to those that increase cash flows at the expense of earnings. In addition, cash represents the same uniform standard worldwide and does not depend on accounting convention.

Research in capital markets behavior has also repeatedly shown, as in Figure 3-1, that there is no systematic relationship between earnings growth and stock prices. Earnings are simply not the most important measure of value. Investors do not buy and sell securities on the basis of earnings, nor do they value earnings growth for its own sake.

It is difficult to comprehend why so many managers, despite the overwhelming evidence to the contrary, continue to believe that stock prices are driven by short-term accounting numbers. One plausible explanation is the observation that stock prices do, in fact, react to unexpectedly high or low earnings reports. But a more careful analysis of this empirical regularity confirms that the stock price is reacting to the new information or *signal* contained in the earnings report about the prospects for that company's future economic cash flows.

Management should take note of the critical role of *lead steers* in the marketplace for corporate securities.[2] These dominant investors focus on economic value—the long-term cash-generating ability of the company and the risks associated with it—rather than on accounting figures that can be altered through bookkeeping and have little effect on cash.

THE LONG-TERM PERSPECTIVE OF INVESTORS

The long-term perspective of investors stands in contrast to many executives' view of the investment community, perhaps because of stock analysts' intense focus on short-term earnings per share (EPS). As a result,

---

[1] Three of many examples include (1) switching from accelerated depreciation to straight line, for which it increases reported earnings but reduces cash flows; (2) switching between first in, first out (FIFO) and last in, first out (LIFO), which decreases net income but increases cash flow; and (3) restructuring announcements disclosing management's decision to cut losses by exiting a value-decreasing line of business are greeted by significant writedowns in earnings and increases in share prices. For other examples and discussion, see Kaplan and Roll (1972).

[2] See Stuart, B. *The Quest for Value,* Harper Business, 1990.

FIGURE 3-1   P/E vs. EPS growth, S&P 400 industrial companies.

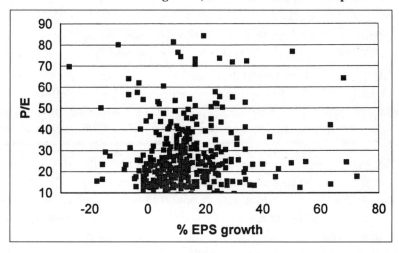

executives often imagine significant pressure to deliver and communicate short-term EPS performance, which can deflect their attention from the more important long-term value creation.

Most investors and institutional portfolio managers (mutual funds, bank trusts, pension funds) take a long-term view of their portfolios. Their holdings typically consist of companies they believe will offer superior shareholder return performance over several years. Portfolio managers may increase or decrease their holdings in a marginal stock on the basis of its short-term prospects, but they generally view the companies they hold as longer-term investments.

Contrary to commonly held beliefs, market values are not solely, or even primarily, focused on the short-term. Market myopia is a myth. In fact, the overwhelming evidence is that investors adopt a long-term perspective when assessing the value of securities.

We can think of a company's stock price as the discounted value of current earnings under a no-growth policy (referred to as the *as-is value*), plus the present value of growth opportunities (PVGO). A *growth opportunity* represents the ability of a company to invest future funds in profitable new projects. If these future investments produce a return in excess of the company's cost of capital, PVGO is positive, as shown in the following:

$$\text{Stock Price} = \text{As-Is Value} + \text{PVGO}$$
$$P = \quad E/k \quad + \text{PVGO}$$

where P = Stock price
            E = Current earnings per share
            k = Cost of equity (investor required return)
    PVGO = Present value of growth opportunities

To illustrate, consider the stock of BellSouth, which was selling near $50 in early 2000. The latest 12 months' EPS were $1.89. If BellSouth were to suddenly turn off the investment spigot and take on no new investments, the company would generate constant earnings of $1.89 in perpetuity. The discounted value of this perpetuity, assuming a return of 12%, is $1.89/0.12 = $16. In other words, only about 32% ($16/$50) of BellSouth's stock price can be attributed to its current operations. The remaining 68% ($34/$50) represents the value of future growth opportunities.

Figure 3-2 shows the results of the same analysis for other well-known companies. The darkened area of each bar shows the portion of the stock price attributable to current operations, and the remaining area shows that portion attributable to long-term growth prospects. Clearly, long-term prospects dominate stock values.

Further evidence of the market's long-term perspective is found in the proportion of stock prices attributable to long-term cash flows. To estimate this proportion, we estimate then subtract from the current stock price the present value of the expected dividends over the next five years. To illus-

FIGURE 3-2   The market believes in the long-term.

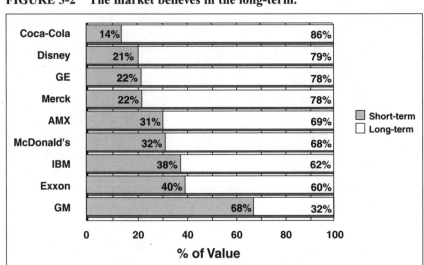

FIGURE 3-3   Long-term value index, U.S. telecommunications companies.

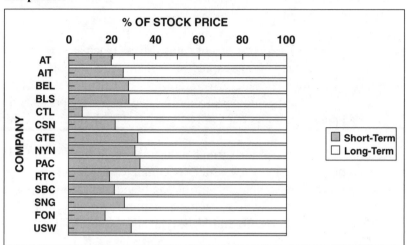

trate, consider the stock of Bell Atlantic Corporation, which was selling near the $60 range in early 2000. Its annual dividends are $1.60. Assuming a 10% dividend growth rate over the next five years and a 12.5% required return on the stock, the present value of dividends from 2001 to 2005 is $9.00, or 15% of the stock price. The remaining 85% ($51/60) of the stock price must be driven by longer-term expected cash flows.

Figure 3-3 shows the proportion of U.S. telecommunications companies' stock assignable to short-term and long-term factors. The average long-term component is 80%, and the short-term fraction is 20%. The results are much the same across most industries. Clearly, investors take a long-term view of the economic value of business.

Finally, one only need to look at Internet stocks to find near-irrefutable proof of the market's long-term thinking. The recent aggregate market value of the 40 largest Internet stocks, despite combined losses of $3 million, was $15 billion! Investors are clearly able to look far into the future and pay significant prices for shares in companies with potentially large payoffs down the road.

Value Growth Duration

Another way to capture the long-term orientation of the stock market is to estimate a company's *value growth duration,* or VGD. In pricing the shares of a company, the market implicitly assigns a finite time period over which the company is expected to create value—that is, to generate a positive spread. This period is the VGD period. After that, the company is expected to earn its cost of capital.

Estimating a company's VGD involves three steps. One, generate estimates of the market's expectations of value drivers (such as sales growth, profit margin, tax rate, working capital investment requirements, and cost of capital). Two, use the value driver forecasts to calculate annual cash flows. Three, solve for the number of years it takes before the present value of the cash flows equals the current stock price. The number of years is the VGD period.

Recent VGD estimates for various industries range from 0 to 2 years for highly competitive industries such as computer hardware to 10-plus years for food products companies with strong brand recognition (Kellogg, Coca-Cola). Companies with exceptional competitive advantage, like Home Depot, Intel, Microsoft, and Dell, typically exhibit VGDs from 15 to 25 years.

Further evidence of investors' long-term perspective can be found in the positive capital market reaction to announcements of R&D and similar investments which depress short-term earnings and have uncertain longer-term payoffs. As seen in Figure 3-4, the market value of companies increases when they announce such long-term strategic investments as joint ventures, R&D projects, capital spending programs, and product diversi-

FIGURE 3-4   Strategic announcements, abnormal stock returns.

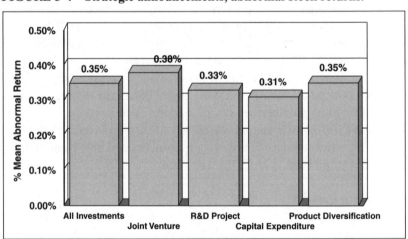

fication.[3] The average increase in stock returns with news of long-term investments is 0.35% for a two-day period, or some 60% on an annualized basis.

The association between economic value and stock price is dramatically influenced by whether or not the company is a value creator or a value destroyer,[4] as indicated by a variant of the market-to-book ratio known as *Tobin's Q*. Value-creating firms have a Q-ratio greater than one, while value-destroying ones have a Q-ratio less than one. Studies show that the stock prices of value-creating companies increase when they invest in new projects but fall when they curtail capital spending. The reverse is true for value-destroying companies.

The idea of a myopic capital market that is hypersensitive to next quarter's earnings does not square with the evidence. Even if strategic investments depress short-term financial results, they are well received by investors, who will maintain and even increase the market value of the business, particularly when management has demonstrated its capability to create value in the past.

The lesson from the empirical evidence here is simple and absolutely crucial for value-creating managers. Investors reveal their preferences in the marketplace, and these preferences materialize in stock market prices that are driven primarily by a company's long-term prospects.

RISK MATTERS

Investors do indeed take risk into account, as predicted by the economic model of a company. Figure 3-5 shows the risk and average realized returns from holding risk-free Treasury bills, intermediate and long-term government bonds, corporate bonds, large-cap common stocks and small-cap common stocks for the period 1926 to 1999. Risk is measured by the standard deviation of returns. The relationship is clear: As risk rises, so does the return.

In short, the empirical evidence strongly suggests that the market adheres to the economic model of a business. Long-term expected cash flows, adjusted for risk, are indeed the primary determinants of value.

---

[3] Evidence of the market's positive response to value-creating capital investments is provided by Woolridge, J. R., "Competitive Decline: Is a Myopic Stock Market to Blame?" *Journal of Applied Corporate Finance,* Spring 1988, pp. 26–36.

[4] See Mitra, D., Bistras, A., Owers, J., "A Direct Test of the Free Cash Flow Hypothesis," *Financial Management,* Letters, Spring 1991.

FIGURE 3-5   Long-term relationship: Risk vs. return, 1926–1999.

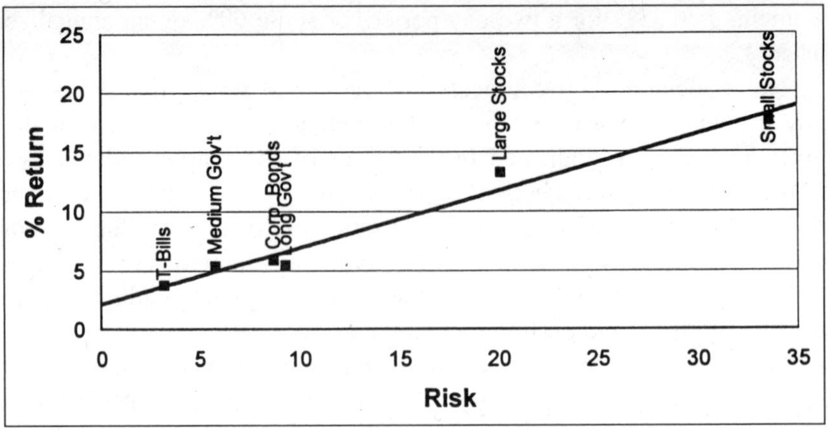

Source: Ibbotson Associates 2000 Yearbook

VALUE CREATION AND STOCK PRICES

A company's spread (again, the return relative to the cost of its funds) over time not only determines its value but also whether the company is worth more or less than its book value. One can think of book value as the cumulated capital put up by owners, and one can think of the stock price as the value placed by the owners on these investments. The ratio of the two, known as the *market-to-book ratio,* or M/B for short, is therefore the value of the dollars received for each dollar invested in the business. If a company's M/B is 2, then every dollar invested in the business by the owners has produced two dollars of economic value.

Denoting the company's return by R, its cost of capital by k, and its growth rate by g, we develop the following short-hand expression for the M/B ratio:[5]

$$\frac{M}{B} - 1 = \frac{R - k}{k - g} \tag{1}$$

This equation demonstrates that the extent to which a company's M/B ratio will depart from 1.0 depends on its ability to invest funds that earn a rate of return that exceeds their cost. The greater the spread between the company's return and its cost of capital, the more M/B will rise above 1.0,

---

[5] The derivation of this formula is shown in the appendix of Chapter 7.

FIGURE 3-6   The amount of value destroyed when a company invests in assets that produce a return less than the cost of capital. The amount is proportional to the difference between the required return and the actual return.

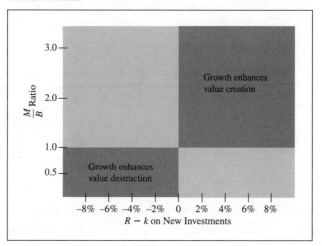

and the greater the value the business will be generating for its owners. If the company's spread is consistently positive, the business is economically profitable and its market value will exceed its book value. The reverse is also true, of course: Value is destroyed when a company invests in assets that produce a return less than the cost of capital. The amount of value destroyed is proportional to the difference between the required return and the actual return. This is shown in Figure 3-6.

To illustrate the value creation process, consider a company with an initial equity investment of $1000 and a 10% cost of equity. The company must earn enough to cover the 10% cost of equity, or $100 annually, to leave shareholders no better or worse off. (The $100, by the way, is the actual cost of the funds retained by the company. Retained earnings do not constitute a free source of capital despite the fact that such costs are ignored in the income statement by traditional accounting.) If the company earns 15% ($150 in profits), the company's investments create $50 of value annually for its owners. If the company earns 5% ($50 in profits), the company's investments will destroy $50 of value, despite the fact that this company exhibits positive growth.

TABLE 3-1   Growth, profitability, and market value.

Scenario	R	K	G	M/B
1. Medium Growth—No value creation	10%	10%	4%	1.00
2. Slow growth—Profitable	12%	10%	2%	1.25
3. Slow growth—Unprofitable	8%	10%	2%	0.75
2. High growth—Profitable	12%	10%	6%	1.50
5. High growth—Unprofitable	8%	10%	6%	0.50

Table 3-1 illustrates how various growth (g) and profitability ($R - k$) scenarios affect the M/B ratio, using Equation 1 to compute company value under each.

In the first scenario, return is equal to the cost of equity, there is no growth (and, therefore, growth has no impact on M/B), and the M/B ratio is 1.0. In scenarios 2 and 4, since return exceeds the cost of capital, we have a profitable business, and growth of a profitable business increases the M/B ratio. The greater the growth rate, the greater the amount of value created. The reverse is also true. In scenarios 3 and 5, where return is less than cost and the business is unprofitable, growth actually drives the M/B ratio lower (unless growth causes the return to rise). The greater the growth rate, the greater the amount of value destruction.

A powerful message emerges from these data: Not all growth is created equal. There is good growth and bad growth. Growth magnifies value only if it is profitable growth—that is, if $R > K$ on new investments. Growth magnifies value *destruction* if new investments yield a return less than their cost of capital.

The value created (M/B) is also a function of the volume (scale) of new investment opportunities yielding a positive spread. The investment volume is measured by the fraction of earnings retained in the business. The greater the fraction of earnings plowed back into businesses earning a positive spread, the more value is created for the owners of the business. In the above formula, the greater the reinvestment rate, the greater will be the company's growth rate, g, and the greater the M/B ratio. Again, growth acts as a magnifier for the amount of value actually created.

Value, Profitability, and Growth: Numerical Illustration
The value of investing in growth under different conditions of profitability is illustrated with the following examples. In the first illustration, en-

titled "My Cup Runneth Over,"[6] a company earns a return of 15% compared to its cost of capital of 10%. Table 3-2 shows what happens to a hypothetical original investment in this company of $100 over a 10-year period. In the first year, profit is $15, a return of 15% on a capital base of $100. Assuming a dividend payout of 50% (and thus a retention rate of 50%), half of the $15 profit is reinvested in the company, and the rest is paid out as dividends. The second year begins with a capital base of $107.50 (the original $100 plus the retained earnings of $7.50). The company continues to earn 15%, which produces earnings of $16.13 (0.15 × $107.50), of which it retains 50% and disburses 50%, and so on in successive years. The last column shows the discounted value of the cash flows generated by the company on behalf of its owners over the 10-year period, assuming a cost of capital rate of 10%. The economic value of the company is $141, compared to an initial investment of $100, for a M/B ratio of 1.41.

In the second illustration, entitled "Much Ado About Nothing," the company earns a return of 10%, which is exactly equal to its cost of capital of 10%. Table 3-3 shows what happens to the same $100 investment in this situation. In the first year, the profit is $10 (a 10% return on the capital base of $100). Assuming the 50% dividend payout and retention ratio, $5 of earnings are reinvested in the company, and the remaining earnings of $5 are remitted to the shareholders. The second year begins with a capital base of $105, which produces $10.50 in earnings, and so on in successive years. The last column shows the discounted value of the cash flows generated by the company on behalf of its owners over the 10-year period, assuming a cost of capital rate of 10%. The economic value of the company is $100, the same as the original investment of $100, for a M/B ratio of 1.00.

In the final illustration, entitled "Exit, Pursued by a Bear," the company earns a return of only 5%, which is less than its cost of capital of 10%. Table 3-4 shows what happens to the $100 investment over the 10-year period. In the first year, the profit achieved is $5, of which $2.50 is reinvested and $2.50 is remitted to the shareholders. The second year begins with a capital base of $102.50, which produces earnings of $5.125 and so on. The economic value of the company is only $66 relative to an initial investment of $100, for a M/B ratio of 0.66.

We see clearly from these examples that growing a profitable com-

---

[6] These illustrations are adapted from the pioneering work on value creation in Fruhan, *Financial Strategy: Studies in the Creation, Transfer and Destruction of Shareholder Value* (1979), Irwin Publishers, Homewood, IL.

TABLE 3-2 Value, profitability, and growth—different conditions of profitability.

My Cup Runneth Over

RETURN (R)	15%
COST OF CAPITAL (K)	10%
RETENTION RATIO	50%
M/B	1.41

RETURN = 15%

Year	Book Value of Owners' Investment	R Achieved	Profit	Retention Rate	Earnings Reinvested	Cash Flows to Owners	PV Cash Factor	PV Cash Flows
1	$100	15%	$15.00	50%	$7.50	$7.50	0.91	$6.82
2	$108	15%	$16.13	50%	$8.06	$8.06	0.83	$6.66
3	$116	15%	$17.33	50%	$8.67	$8.67	0.75	$6.51
4	$124	15%	$18.63	50%	$9.32	$9.32	0.68	$6.36
5	$134	15%	$20.03	50%	$10.02	$10.02	0.62	$6.22
6	$144	15%	$21.53	50%	$10.77	$10.77	0.56	$6.08
7	$154	15%	$23.15	50%	$11.57	$11.57	0.51	$5.94
8	$166	15%	$24.89	50%	$12.44	$12.44	0.47	$5.80
9	$178	15%	$26.75	50%	$13.38	$13.38	0.42	$5.67
10	$192	15%	$28.76	50%	$14.38	$14.38	0.39	$5.54
11	$206					$206.10	0.39	$79.46

ECONOMIC VALUE	=	$141.08
INITIAL INVESTMENT	=	$100.00
M/B RATIO	**=**	**1.41**

Source: Fruhan (1979).

TABLE 3-3 Value, profitability, and growth—different conditions of profitability.

Much Ado About Nothing

RETURN (R)	10%
COST OF CAPITAL (K)	10%
RETENTION RATIO	50%
M/B	1.00

RETURN = 10%

Year	Book Value of Owners' Investment	R Achieved	Profit	Retention Rate	Earnings Reinvested	Cash Flows to Owners	PV Cash Factor	PV Cash Flows
1	$100	10%	$10.00	50%	$5.00	$5.00	0.91	$4.55
2	$105	10%	$10.50	50%	$5.25	$5.25	0.83	$4.34
3	$110	10%	$11.03	50%	$5.51	$5.51	0.75	$4.14
4	$116	10%	$11.58	50%	$5.79	$5.79	0.68	$3.95
5	$122	10%	$12.16	50%	$6.08	$6.08	0.62	$3.77
6	$128	10%	$12.76	50%	$6.38	$6.38	0.56	$3.60
7	$134	10%	$13.40	50%	$6.70	$6.70	0.51	$3.44
8	$141	10%	$14.07	50%	$7.04	$7.40	0.47	$3.28
9	$148	10%	$14.77	50%	$7.39	$7.39	0.42	$3.13
10	$155	10%	$15.51	50%	$7.76	$7.76	0.39	$2.99
11	$163					$162.89	0.39	$62.80

ECONOMIC VALUE	= $100.00
INITIAL INVESTMENT	= $100.00
M/B RATIO	= **1.00**

Source: Fruhan (1979).

TABLE 3-4 Different conditions of profitability.

Exit, Pursued by a Bear

RETURN (R)	5%
COST OF CAPITAL (K)	10%
RETENTION RATIO	50%
M/B	0.66

RETURN = 5%

Calculation of M/B Ratio: Return = 10%, Cost of Money = 10%

Year	Book Value of Owners' Investment	R Achieved	Profit	Retention Rate	Earnings Reinvested	Cash Flows to Owners	PV Factor	PV Cash Flows
1	$100.00	5%	$5.00	50%	$2.50	$2.50	0.91	$2.27
2	$102.50	5%	$5.13	50%	$2.56	$2.56	0.83	$2.12
3	$105.06	5%	$5.25	50%	$2.63	$2.63	0.75	$1.97
4	$107.69	5%	$5.38	50%	$2.69	$2.69	0.68	$1.84
5	$110.38	5%	$5.52	50%	$2.76	$2.76	0.62	$1.71
6	$113.14	5%	$5.66	50%	$2.83	$2.83	0.56	$1.60
7	$115.97	5%	$5.80	50%	$2.90	$2.90	0.51	$1.49
8	$118.87	5%	$5.94	50%	$2.97	$2.97	0.47	$1.39
9	$121.84	5%	$6.09	50%	$3.05	$3.05	0.42	$1.29
10	$124.89	5%	$6.24	50%	$3.12	$3.12	0.39	$1.20
11	$128.01					$128.008	0.39	$49.353

ECONOMIC VALUE = $66.24

INITIAL INVESTMENT = $100.00

M/B RATIO = 0.66

Source: Fruhan (1979).

pany creates value. But a company will be unlikely to earn a return in excess of its cost of capital forever. Competitive pressures will eventually drive returns to the cost of capital after a certain number of years. The above model can easily be adjusted to allow for the projected number of years during which the company will continue to earn the positive spread. The greater the duration of a competitive advantage, the greater the M/B ratio.

The top panel of Table 3-5 shows what happens to a company's M/B ratio as the number of years that the company returns continue to exceed its cost of capital increases from 5 years to 10 years, 15 years, and 30 years, successively, for a given rate of reinvestment of 30%. When the company earns its cost of capital, the M/B ratio remains at 1.0 regardless of the length of the period. When a company earns a return in excess of the cost of funds, the M/B ratio increases exponentially from 1.0 with the length of the period of competitive advantage, and conversely.

The graph in Figure 3-7 shows how the M/B ratio increases with the spread between the return and the cost of capital for 5-year and 10-year intervals of competitive advantage, respectively.

Successive panels of Table 3-5 show what happens to the value creation as the reinvestment rate is steadily increased from 60% to 80%, 100%, and finally 150%. It is clear from these results that as the returns climb above costs and retention ratios increase, company value increases exponentially.

The observed market valuation of companies is quite consistent with the economic view of a company. Figure 3-8 displays the M/B ratios for the 30 companies in the Dow Jones Industrial Index relative to their excess returns. It is transparent that companies like Merck, Procter & Gamble, and General Electric with high returns on equity (ROE) relative to their cost of equity capital (k) are creating enormous value for their shareholders and command very high M/B ratios.

The primary reason for the scattering of observations in Figure 3-8 is differential growth rates. The higher the growth rate (investment scale) at a given positive spread, the higher the market valuation. This is demonstrated more formally in Figure 3-9, which shows the M/B ratios of the companies that make up the Standard & Poors 400 Index segregated by economic profitability (spread) and growth. The companies are ranked in descending order of spread. The first group achieved spreads in excess of 5%, the second group somewhat less, and so on. The fifth group achieved a negative spread greater than 5%. For each of the five groups, the figure shows how market value varied with sales growth. For the group of value

TABLE 3-5   M/B ratios for common stock.

Based on Cost of Equity of 10%
Future Return on Equity

Number of Years that Returns Will Continue	0%	5%	10%	15%	20%	
5 Years	0.6	0.8	1.0	1.2	1.4	30%
10 Years	0.4	0.7	1.0	1.4	1.8	of Earnings
15 Years	0.2	0.6	1.0	1.5	2.1	Are Reinvested
30 Years	0.0	0.5	1.0	1.7	2.7	

Future Return on Equity

Number of Years that Returns Will Continue	0%	5%	10%	15%	20%	
5 Years	0.6	0.8	1.0	1.2	1.5	60%
10 Years	0.4	0.7	1.0	1.4	2.0	of Earnings
15 Years	0.2	0.6	1.0	1.6	2.6	Are Reinvested
30 Years	0.0	0.4	1.0	2.2	4.6	

Future Return on Equity

Number of Years that Returns Will Continue	0%	5%	10%	15%	20%	
5 Years	0.6	0.8	1.0	1.2	1.5	80%
10 Years	0.4	0.6	1.0	1.5	2.2	of Earnings
15 Years	0.2	0.5	1.0	1.8	3.0	Are Reinvested
30 Years	0.0	0.3	1.0	2.8	7.5	

Future Return on Equity

Number of Years that Returns Will Continue	0%	5%	10%	15%	20%	
5 Years	0.6	0.8	1.0	1.2	1.5	100%
10 Years	0.4	0.6	1.0	1.6	2.4	of Earnings
15 Years	0.2	0.5	1.0	1.9	3.7	Are Reinvested
30 Years	0.0	0.2	1.0	3.8	13.6	

TABLE 3-5   M/B ratios for common stock.
(*Continued*)

Number of Years that Returns Will Continue	Future Return on Equity					
	0%	5%	10%	15%	20%	
5 Years	0.6	0.8	1.0	1.3	1.7	150%
10 Years	0.4	0.6	1.0	1.8	3.2	of Earnings
15 Years	0.2	0.4	1.0	2.6	6.6	Are Reinvested
30 Years	0.0	0.0	1.0	10.7	75.6	

creators, market value rises steeply with growth. For the low performers, the reverse is true. Once again, we see that not all growth is created equal.

Market value added (MVA), popularized by Stern Stewart & Co., has been proposed as a way to assess the wealth created by managers and bears a strong resemblance to the M/B ratio. MVA is simply the difference between the market value of a company's securities and the capital supplied by investors, and thus measures the cumulative effect of the company's economic profitability since its inception.

In their annual survey of value creation, Stern Stewart & Co. rank companies on the basis of MVA. An excerpt is shown in Table 3-6, where

FIGURE 3-7   Profitability, value creation, and the length of competitive advantage.

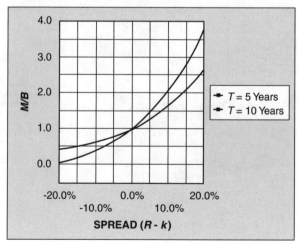

FIGURE 3-8   M/B ratio vs. spread, Dow Jones Industrials.

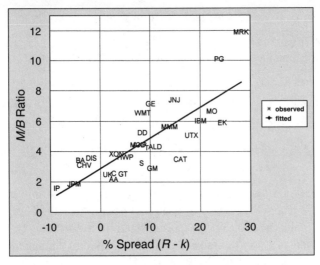

the MVAs of the top and bottom 25 companies out of a total of 1000 companies are shown for the year ending in 1998. The second column of the table displays the Long-term Value Index (LVI), which is the company's return on investment (R) divided by the cost of capital (k), as calculated by Stern Stewart & Co. If this ratio exceeds 1.0, the company's profitability

FIGURE 3-9   Value vs. spreads and growth, M/B ratios.

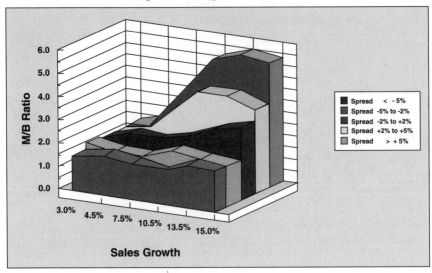

TABLE 3-6A Value creation performance.

Rank 1998	Company	MVA 1998	LVI
1	General Electric	195,830	1.3
2	Coca-Cola	158,247	3.0
3	Microsoft	143,740	3.7
4	Merck	107,418	1.6
5	Intel	90,010	2.8
6	Procter & Gamble	88,706	1.2
7	Exxon	85,557	0.9
8	Pfizer	83,835	1.7
9	Philip Morris	82,412	1.7
10	Bristol-Myers Squibb	81,312	2.0
11	Johnson & Johnson	71,433	1.6
12	Wal-Mart Stores	69,678	1.3
13	Eli Lilly	67,024	1.1
14	Cisco Systems	50,422	3.6
15	Gillette	50,209	1.6
16	IBM	49,101	0.8
17	Bell Atlantic	48,414	1.4
18	Walt Disney	46,869	0.8
19	SBC Communications	45,136	1.7
20	Dupont	42,631	1.3
21	Hewlett-Packard	42,615	1.0
22	Abbott Labs	42,443	2.1
23	Schering-Plough	41,143	2.6
24	PepsiCo	40,743	0.9
25	Lucent Technologies	39,767	1.1
976	Advanced Micro Devices	(500)	0.3
977	Boston Chicken	(549)	−0.2
978	Reliance Group Holding	(665)	0.4
979	Seagate Technology	(681)	1.8
980	Champion International	(789)	−0.3

(*continued*)

TABLE 3-6A   Value creation performance.
(*Continued*)

Rank 1998	Company	MVA 1998	LVI
981	TIG Holdings	(838)	−0.0
982	Fleming Companies	(854)	0.7
983	John Mansville	(867)	0.6
984	Asarco	(952)	0.6
985	Everest Reinsurance	(1,141)	0.8
986	Union Pacific	(1,186)	0.5
987	Provident Companies	(1,202)	1.0
988	Bethlehem Steel	(1,336)	0.4
989	Hartford Financial Services	(1,524)	0.7
990	Apple Computer	(1,594)	−1.7
991	Inland Steel	(1,669)	0.6
992	USF&G Corp	(1,961)	0.2
993	USX—US Steel	(2,090)	0.9
994	Cyprus AMAX Minerals	(2,157)	0.3
995	Kmart Corp	(2,257)	0.9
996	St. Paul Companies	(2,614)	0.7
997	Digital Equipment	(3,926)	0.0
998	RJR Nabisco	(9,530)	0.6
999	Loews Corp	(10,081)	0.4
1000	General Motors	(13,876)	0.5

Source: Stern & Stewart, Journal of Applied Corporate Finance, Summer 1999.

TABLE 3-6B   Market value added versus spread.

	Average LVI	Average MVA
Value creators	1.70	$74,588
Value destroyers	0.42	($2,594)

exceeds its cost of capital. For example, if a company's return on investment is 15% and its cost of capital is 10%, the LVI Index equals 15%/10% = 1.5. As shown in Table 3-6, it is clear that companies that rank high on the basis of MVA typically possess an LVI well in excess of 1.0 and that companies that have destroyed value (negative MVAs) have an LVI well below 1.0. On average, the top value creators have an index of 1.7, while the value destroyers have an index of 0.4.

Table 3-7 displays the value creation champions, defined as those companies who have achieved the highest average spread over the past decade and who have consistently earned a return in excess of their cost of capital year in and year out for the whole period.

Not surprisingly, these "built-to-last" companies outperformed their peers in terms of shareholder performance, with an average relative total shareholder return (TSR) of 1.20 over the past decade. Interestingly, these companies share other common traits. They focus on a core business, are global, (as measured by the high percentage of revenues from outside the United States), innovate (as measured by the rate of new product introduction), have strong leadership, espouse continuous improvement, and empowerment, and have decentralized organizational structures. At the same time, they maintain some significant control and coordination in support functions.

CONCLUSION

Success today has to be defined as the increase of the value of the business. This is not synonymous with boosting sales, assets, shareholder's equity, book value, or even ROI or EPS. None of these measures necessarily correlate with shareholder value. Traditional accounting measures such as EPS and ROI are unreliable predictors of a company's future returns to shareholders. Accounting-oriented metrics do not measure the economic value that determines stock price and are not highly correlated with superior value creation. Numerous companies have sustained double-digit EPS growth while providing minimal or even negative returns to shareholders. This is because growing companies destroy value when returns are below costs.

Some companies consistently enjoy superior shareholder returns and superior market valuations, including well-known corporate giants like Dell Computer, Intel, General Electric, and Merck, and lesser-known small- and medium-sized companies like Emerson Electric and Rubbermaid. Others consistently trade below book value and generate inferior shareholder returns regardless of stock market conditions.

TABLE 3-7   Consistent performers: 1989–1998.

Company Name	Average 10-Year Spread	Relative 10 yr TSR_S&P
	(%)	(%)
1. General Mills Inc.	105.1	82.5
2. Avon Products	80.6	151.0
3. UST Inc.	76.4	91.3
4. Gillette Co.	59.7	153.4
5. Ralston Purina Co.	36.4	73.8
6. Schering-Plough	33.4	180.1
7. Coca-Cola Co.	33.0	156.4
8. SLM HLDG Corp.	32.5	102.3
9. Unilever N V—NY Shares	25.9	115.7
10. Kellogg Co.	25.0	54.1
11. Abbott Laboratories	23.8	134.6
12. King World Productions Inc.	22.8	64.6
13. Merck & Co.	22.4	132.3
14. American Home Products Corp.	22.3	118.0
15. Philip Morris Cos., Inc.	21.4	130.2
16. Cisco Systems Inc.	20.5	
17. Bestfoods	18.1	98.0
18. Microsoft Corp.	16.0	268.9
19. Gap Inc.	15.9	226.0
20. Wrigley (WM) Jr. Co.	15.7	129.0
21. BMC Software Inc.	13.9	204.2
22. Johnson & Johnson	12.7	131.2
23. Paychex Inc.	11.1	205.1
24. Mattel Inc.	11.0	132.8
25. Franklin Resources Inc.	10.3	171.3
26. Intel Corp.	10.2	233.0
27. Anheuser-Busch Cos. Inc.	10.0	95.4
28. Fannie Mae	9.6	187.5
29. Albertsons Inc.	9.5	111.7

TABLE 3-7   Consistent performers: 1989–1998.
(*Continued*)

Company Name	Average 10-Year Spread	Relative 10 yr TSR_S&P
30. Ameritech Corp.	8.9	122.0
31. PepsiCo Inc.	8.8	119.2
32. Minnesota Mining & Mfg Co.	8.6	65.0
33. Wal-Mart Stores	7.9	154.2
34. Omnicom Group	7.8	163.9
35. Pfizer Inc.	7.7	186.7
36. Gannett Co.	7.7	85.7
37. General Electric Co.	6.8	145.5
38. Dover Corp.	6.6	104.1
39. Intl Flavors & Fragrances	6.4	71.3
40. Interpublic Group of Cos.	6.2	143.7
41. Biomet Inc.	6.1	117.1
42. Automatic Data Processing	5.8	124.1
43. Carnival Corp.	5.8	147.8
44. Genuine Parts Co.	5.7	58.4
45. May Department Stores Co.	5.7	89.4
46. Winn-Dixie Stores Inc.	5.6	113.4
47. Emerson Electric Co.	5.2	106.3
48. Alltel Corp.	4.7	111.0
49. Newell Rubbermaid Inc.	4.6	111.4
50. Sysco Corp.	4.4	121.4
Average	**18.9**	**130.5**

The observed differences in stock market valuation stem from fundamental differences in competitive performance and are not the result of a whimsical and capricious equity market. The stock market clearly subscribes to the tenets of the economic model of a company by recognizing value-creating strategies and responding rationally to the adoption of business strategies that enhance long-term expected cash flows.

C H A P T E R

THE VALUE MANAGER

> "... management realizes its boss is the shareholder ... Yes, we know we have to take care of employees and consumers, or we won't have them. It's all done with a focus on improving shareholder value."
>
> —*S. C. Weaver, Director of Corporate Planning, Hershey Foods Corp.*

WHAT DOES A VALUE MANAGER DO? How is VBM actually used to manage companies better? This chapter outlines the process of becoming a value manager. The discussion is followed by a case study adapted from an actual example. At the end of this chapter, managers should be ready to use this book to apply the principles of VBM to their own company.

VALUE-BASED MANAGEMENT: THE PROCESS

The VBM approach is useful for a variety of purposes: to provide quick diagnostics, optimally restructure the company, improve strategic planning, and devise the right executive compensation plan. VBM goes beyond these individual uses, however. Ultimately, VBM is a culture, a mind-set, a way of thinking that permeates the entire company, from top management to frontline employees. Performance metrics such as single-period accounting returns and financial ratios are set aside, and every corporate decision is made based on whether shareholder value is created.

Table 4-1 displays the timeline that successful companies employ when shifting to VBM and the key activities involved in each step. Each stage is discussed in some detail below.

TABLE 4-1 Activities at each stage of the VBM process.

Situation Assessment	Restructuring	Value-Based Planning	Value-Based Compensation
Quick and dirty analysis of the company's current position.	Value the company and each business unit.	Adopt appropriate value-based performance metrics at the corporate and business unit levels.	Tie compensation to value creation using appropriate criteria.
Surface major problems and opportunities.	Surface all strategic and operating improvements.	Understand financial and operational value drivers within each business unit.	Separate factors under management control from external factors.
Decide on a plan of action.	Evaluate all acquisition and divestiture opportunities.	Understand the hierarchy of value from the aggregate corporate level to the business unit and operational level.	Base the compensation of frontline employees on the operational value drivers.
	Evaluate financial engineering opportunities. Monitor headquarters cost.	Allocate capital based on value-creation potential.	

Adapted from Weston & Copeland, Managerial Finance, Dryden Press, 1992.

Situation Assessment

The first stage, the situation assessment, is often undertaken in response to a crisis in stock price performance. It is typically initiated by top management, often by a new CEO brought in to remedy the lackluster performance. This stage of the VBM process requires management to understand the differences between traditional accounting metrics and value-based metrics. It is during this phase that the major value creation challenges and opportunities surface and a plan of action to resolve the problems and take advantage of the opportunities takes shape.

Often an event such as a hostile takeover bid provides the catalyst for VBM. An example is Walt Disney. In 1984, Walt Disney faced takeover threats from several companies. Although the company generated positive accounting earnings, Disney was investing in projects with returns below the cost of capital. The resulting value gap was tempting to potential acquirers. In response to these threats, the board brought in Michael Eisner as the new CEO. After assessing the situation, Eisner moved to the second step of the VBM process and undertook a major restructuring effort that redeployed Disney's existing assets more efficiently, including its phenomenal brand name, and watched its stock price rise in response.

Restructuring

The restructuring phase involves taking specific actions designed to close the value gap and enhance the value-creating potential of the company. Value-based restructuring is different from much-publicized restructuring efforts such as business process reengineering, in that the primary focus is on value creation rather than individual processes, although reengineering may be a necessary component of value-based restructuring.

Value-based restructuring is best done using a framework such as the McKinsey & Co. Restructuring Pentagon. This framework, shown in Figure 4-1, proposes five stages of assessing the opportunities for unleashing value through restructuring:

1. The current market value of the company
2. The value of the company as is
3. The potential value of the company with internal improvements
4. The potential value of the company with external improvements
5. The optimal restructured value of the company

The first step in the restructuring process is to record the current market value of the company's equity and debt in Node 1. The second is to

FIGURE 4-1   Restructuring pentagon.

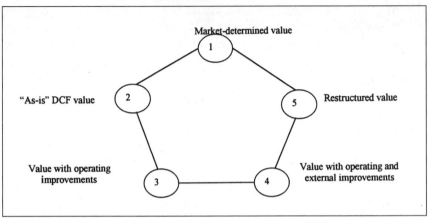

compute the value of the company under management's existing plans, the as-is value in Node 2, and compare that to the value in Node 1.

The as-is value is a reflection of the value according to management's own plans. This may differ from market value, owing to the perception gap between management and the market. When market value exceeds management's assessment of value, the market is saying that the company is worth more under different management. It becomes a takeover target. The higher market value is an indication of the potential restructured value of the company.

If the market value is less than the as-is value, two possibilities exist: Either management is too optimistic about the company's prospects or there is insufficient communication between management and the market. In either case, it signals a need for management action.

An important component of as-is valuation is to determine the discounted cash flows (DCF) value of each business unit. This allows management to distinguish value-creating from value-destroying units. Management is often surprised when fast-growing, so-called star units turn out to be value destroyers, which happens whenever growth occurs in units with a return on investment less than the cost of capital.

The next step in the restructuring pentagon is to quantify the value of potential internal strategic and operational improvements (Node 3). To undertake strategic or operating improvements, it is critical to identify the critical value drivers at both the corporate and business unit levels. Management can waste valuable time by focusing on value drivers that have little correspondence to value. Important value drivers can be determined through a DCF sensitivity analysis, where each value driver (such as growth, operating margin, working capital, and so on) is varied and its impact on DCF examined. The goal is to choose the strategy with the most value impact.

A competitive analysis of each business unit is also very useful, discussed in more detail in Chapter 9. Comparisons against competitors determine if the business unit is a first quartile performer, and if not, why it isn't. The competitive analysis of each business unit stresses the relationships among market economics, competitive position, and profitability. Business-unit managers cannot be expected to develop value-creating strategies if they do not know how much their units are worth, which drivers are responsible for the unit's value, and the degree and nature of any current and anticipated competitive advantage over industry rivals.

The fourth step in the pentagon is to consider the impact on value of external acquisition and divestiture opportunities (Node 4). Coca-Cola and Pepsi are examples of companies creating wealth by divesting underperforming businesses and focusing on the core business. Coke divested its assets in the entertainment, pasta, and wine businesses to fund the global expansion of its core beverage unit. Pepsi divested its restaurant business to focus on its core beverage business. Both have experienced superior shareholder returns, with Coke earning 130% relative to the market from 1989 to 1998, and Pepsi close behind.

It may be more difficult to create value through acquisitions, as illustrated by the case of Quaker Oats with the Snapple and Gatorade lines and Eastman Kodak with the Sterling Drugs line, although most of the acquisitions we see do create value.[1] But for every merger that goes through, 5 to 10 others were considered by the bidder and rejected as likely value destroyers. Even when the acquisition seems justified in terms of operational synergies, the difficulty of actually capturing these synergies combined with the premium paid for acquisition sometimes results in value destruction.

Once the external restructuring opportunities have been exhausted, the management should proceed to the next and final step in the restructuring pentagon, financial engineering opportunities (Node 5). The company may have excess debt capacity in the form of unused interest tax shields (see Chapter 5). Financial innovations such as derivatives enable companies to reduce the risk of their cash flows through hedging, which decreases the cost of capital and increases value.

The as-is value combined with the value of the operating, external, and financial engineering restructuring efforts provides the final optimal

---

[1] S. Jarrell, "The Long-Term Postmerger Performance of Corporate Takeovers," 2000, working paper.

restructured value of the company. The difference between the optimal re-structured value in Node 5 and the market value in Node 1 represents the maximum opportunity for the company to create shareholder wealth.

Value-Based Planning

Strategic value-based planning is essential to maintain the value momentum initiated by the restructuring process. The main objective of value-based planning is to keep the focus on value creation opportunities and to help business-unit- and corporate-level managers understand specifically how their actions affect the value of the company. To that end, the identification of appropriate performance metrics at both the corporate and business unit levels is an important part of value-based planning. For example, Ford has adopted shareholder value added (SVA) as the primary performance metric, while Coca-Cola, Quaker Oats, and AT&T have adopted economic value added (trademarked by Stern Stewart as EVA™, hereinafter referred to as EVA). Performance metrics are illustrated and compared in Chapter 11.

An essential step in value-based planning is the identification of the financial and operational value drivers of each business unit. It is critical for business unit managers to understand which of the value drivers under their control have the greatest potential impact on value. The Dupont ROE decomposition can help provide this understanding. To illustrate, in Figure 4-2 we decompose the pretax return on invested capital (ROIC) of a pub-

FIGURE 4-2   Return on capital decomposition.

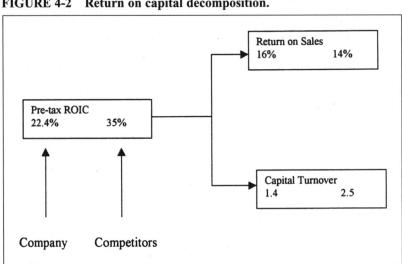

lishing company and its competitors. If the company focused on return on sales, it would seem to be doing fine, since its ROS is 16% compared to 14% for its competitors. But its ROIC of 22.4% is well below the competition at 35%. Why? The problem was poor management of working capital and plant capacity utilization. Their capital turnover was 1.4 versus an industry average of 2.5. This may not seem significant, but a value-based analysis shows that it translates into a $150 million opportunity for capital improvement. The opportunity was missed because (1) the company had been focusing on ROS instead of value creation and (2) it had never performed a thorough competitive analysis.

Once the metrics have been identified and adopted and financial and operational value drivers identified, the planning process next requires that business unit managers establish specific value objectives for each unit through dialog with the top management. Capital is then allocated to each unit based on its value creation potential.

Value-Based Compensation

The final step in the VBM journey is compensation. Value-based compensation is the lynchpin in motivating managers to make decisions and take actions that maximize value. It is a fairly complex, still-evolving process that involves tying managerial compensation to shareholder value creation. Equity ownership, stock options, SVA, and EVA targets are all different elements in a value-based compensation system.

Most companies incorporate more than one performance metric into their compensation plans, typically using different metrics at different corporate and business unit levels. For example, at Briggs & Stratton, corporate executives are compensated through a combination of options indexed to the company's cost of capital and long-term EVA targets.

In setting value-based compensation, it is essential to strike the right balance between accuracy and controllability. Accuracy ensures that only those actions that improve value will be considered. Controllability ensures that managers will not become demotivated by having their pay tied to things beyond their control. These issues are discussed in detail in Chapter 13, but we summarize the basic results here. At the corporate level, total shareholder returns (TSR) remains the most accurate measure of shareholder value creation, but because it is also influenced by external market factors beyond management's control, compensation is typically tied to TSR relative to the market or industry peer groups. Business unit compensation is often based on a combination of business-unit- and corporate-level performance, with more weight on the former because of controllability issues. By basing a portion of their compensation on corporate performance, business unit managers have the incentives to try to capture the synergies across business units. At the operational level, a substantial portion of the compensation should be tied to the achievement of specific objectives in the operational value drivers.

CASE STUDY IN VBM: BIOTECH

The case that follows chronicles the experience of a multidivisional company well on its way toward a successful implementation of VBM.[2]

Introduction

BioTech is a large, diverse medical products manufacturer. In the two decades leading up to 1990, its EPS growth had been fairly strong and its stock prices had risen steadily to a high of $39 a share in 1990. Recently, however, BioTech was not performing well. Its shareholder returns, measured by TSR, had been below both the market's and its peer groups'. Its market-to-book ratio has been falling steadily and precipitously, and the stock price had fallen to $25 per share. There was tremendous pressure on the new CEO from shareholders to reverse the company's decline in performance. It was time to do something about it.

BioTech began as a specialized manufacturer of medical surgical equipment in the early 1980s. Business was profitable, and over the next decade, the company diversified into medical and laboratory supplies through a series of acquisitions and in-house R&D. The company was divided into four major strategic business units and three smaller units, defined in terms of markets served and distribution channels employed. The four major business units were the Medical Products Group (MPG), Laboratory Products Group (LPG), Consumer Products Group (CPG), and the Electronic Instrumentation Group (EIG). The three smaller units comprised the Real Estate Development Group (REG), the Equipment Financing Group (EFG), and the Corporate Services Group (CSG). The company's business unit structure is displayed in Figure 4-3.

The company's consolidated sales were approximately $500 million. The market value of its equity prior to restructuring was $1.25 billion, some 2.7 times book value. BioTech had $375 million in debt, bringing the company's total market value to $1.625 billion.

---

[2] The case is an extension and adaptation of the BioTech case study that first appeared in Butters, et al., *Case Problems in Finance,* Irwin, 1987.

FIGURE 4-3   BioTech's organization structure.

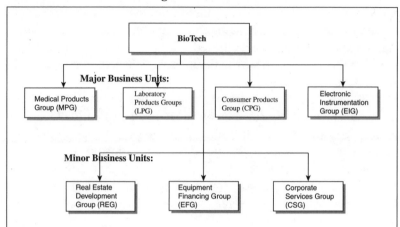

BioTech Businesses

MPG was the company's largest division. It marketed low-cost, reusable, and disposable plastic medical supplies targeted to the institutional market. The division benefited from a strong R&D team and produced a steady stream of new products with a short product life cycle, continuously upgrading and replacing its product line. The company had developed a strong reputation as an efficient manufacturer and skilled marketer.

The division operated in a rapidly growing and profitable market, as evidenced by its 17% gross margin and 17% growth rate. The unit projected that it would maintain the margin, but that the growth rate would fall slightly to a still-impressive 15%. MPG generated substantial free cash flows because of its low capital expenditures-to-sales and low net working capital-to-sales ratios. The division had experienced strong market share gains despite aggressive competition from larger and financially stronger competitors, several of which were foreign, a trend that was expected to continue.

LPG was the company's second-largest division. It produced and marketed specialized medical laboratory equipment. The laboratory products industry was capital-intensive, and LPG had high capital expenditure-to-sales and net working capital-to-sales ratios as a result. Substantial negative free cash flows were projected over the next five years. Rapid growth had exhausted plant capacity, and there was a need to expand production facilities. LPG was viewed as a major growth vehicle for BioTech, and the company consequently entertained aggressive expansion plans and capital spending for this unit in the near future. Like MPG, the division had experienced market share gains despite intense, well-financed domestic and foreign competition. LPG had enjoyed a 22% growth rate and 12% gross margin. For the future, a 16% growth rate was projected, along with a slight higher 13% gross margin.

CPG, the third-largest division, manufactured and sold staple medical supplies, destined mostly for the consumer retail market. CPG consisted of several separate smaller companies acquired over the last decade, serving complementary medical product lines. CPG's historical financial results were uneven, and it lagged behind its competitors and BioTech's other divisions. CPG had much lower growth and profit potential and much lower business risks than the two larger units. Its growth rate had declined to 10% and was expected to be remain at this level. Gross margins had declined 10% but were expected to improve slightly to 12% because of plans already underway to consolidate the various companies in the CPG group into one unit and establish a common brand name. Despite the lackluster historical performance of CPG, the consolidation of the units and the new centralized marketing thrust were expected to lead to increases in volume, margins, and returns comparable to CPG's competitors.

Jack, the new CEO, had mixed feelings about the future of CPG. The division did not fit squarely with the overall corporate strategy, which was to capitalize on a steady stream of new quality products for the institutional market. Yet its low capital expenditures and net working capital-to-sales ratios freed up modest amounts of cash flows that benefited the cash-consuming divisions and added overall stability to the corporate financial results.

The fourth major business unit, EIG, manufactured and distributed sophisticated computerized medical laboratory equipment. This market had experienced rapid growth in the last few years. The EIG business unit had high R&D costs, but it benefited from BioTech's established laboratory distribution channels. EIG had current growth rate of 20%, which was forecasted to level off at 18%. The gross margin, currently 14%, was expected to decline to 12%. Table 4-2 summarizes some important accounting data for BioTech's major business units.

Other smaller businesses were added to the corporate portfolio in the last decade. Most of these businesses were profitable, although it was unclear as to why these businesses were acquired. REG was in the property development business and managed an industrial park complex where BioTech's headquarter was located. EFG acted as the financing company

TABLE 4-2   BioTech: Growth and margin rates for the major business units.

Business Units	Current Growth Rate	Current Margin	Long-Term Forecasted Growth Rate	Long-Term Forecasted Margins
MPG	17%	17%	15%	17%
LPG	22%	12%	16%	13%
CPG	10%	10%	8%	12%
EIG	20%	14%	18%	12%

for the equipment purchased from the other divisions. CSG provided generic corporate services to all the divisions, including accounting, cash management, purchasing, personnel, credit management, and other ancillary functions.

In light of recent takeover activity, the relentless pressure from institutional investors, and the increased attention in the business press to TSR, Jack was convinced of the need to maximize economic value. It was clear to him that economic value was a far more important determinant of stock price than EPS, earnings growth, sales growth, or other traditional accounting measures.

Jack embraced VBM as a management philosophy in part to ensure that Wall Street gained the confidence he had in the company. He also realized that the ultimate boss is the owner—the shareholders. He embarked on a three-year journey to integrate the VBM approach in the company.

To anticipate the ending of the story, the results were stellar. The stock price surged 2% on the day of the announcement in the business press and more than doubled during the first three years following the adoption of VBM. This exceeded the market's rise by more than three times and outperformed its peers by a similar amount. What follows is the story of how BioTech pulled it off.

Jack implemented VBM with a five-step process spread over a three-year period:

Step 1: Situation Assessment
Step 2: Corporate Restructuring
Step 3: Value-Based Strategic Planning
Step 4: Value-Based Performance Metrics
Step 5: Value-Based Compensation

SITUATION ASSESSMENT

As seen in Figure 4-4, the company's stock price performance had been lackluster relative to the competitors' and to the stock market's performance as a whole, in part because the company had made several acquisitions that had not paid off as expected and in part because of deteriorating margins in some divisions.

Return on equity had fallen from the 17% level to the 12% level in the last few years, as shown in Figure 4-5. Institutional investors were openly malcontent and pressured management to produce better shareholder returns. Management's attempt to placate investors and to convince the market that BioTech warranted a much higher valuation were met with cynicism.

The stock underperformed its peers, suggesting that investors apparently had spotted something management had not. With its focus on earnings growth, BioTech management had failed to realize that many of its units were investing in value-destroying businesses. Many of these units were facing rising competitive pressures in maturing markets, as evidenced by their deteriorating profit margins.

Jack became convinced that earnings growth was an unsatisfactory indicator of performance. For one thing, earnings did not indicate whether the company and its various divisions were recovering their cost of capital, a requirement for value creation. Earnings also failed to reflect the amount of investment in fixed assets and working capital necessary to achieve a given growth in earnings. Finally, earnings is a single-period measure while value is driven by cash flows over the life of the asset.

Jack and his top management team also concluded that the company's "growth at any price" policy was inappropriate. The increasing competi-

---

Poor stock market performance despite high growth rates is often a signal to the management that a reevaluation of the company's value drivers is required. For example, CSX Transportation was faced with a lagging stock price, while management was spending capital to support the company's aggressive growth targets. The market was essentially saying "you are not a growth business; you are a mature business and you should be throwing off cash." Understanding the company's valuation from the market's perspective is a key component of VBM. The first step toward this is a DCF valuation.

FIGURE 4-4   Five-Year TSR: BioTech vs. market and industry group.

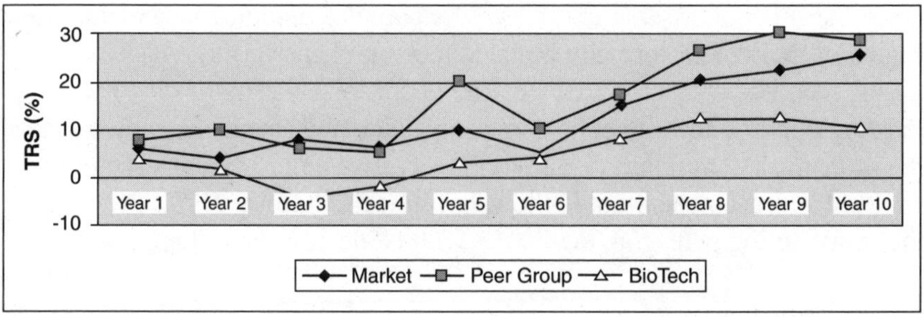

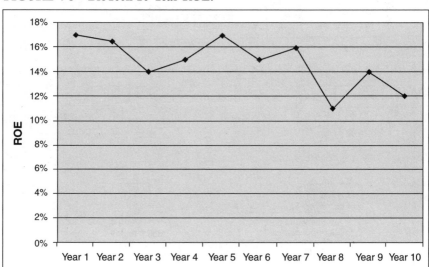

tion in the product markets was seemingly tipping the balance in favor of profitability at the expense of growth in some of BioTech's divisions, and more attention had to be devoted to the trade-offs between growth and profitability. In fact, subsequent analysis revealed that a 1% increase in corporate profit would add far more value than a 1% increase in growth. This is a fairly typical discovery for most companies as they begin their VBM process.

BioTech settled on the DCF approach to evaluating business units and business strategies.

FIGURE 4-5   BioTech 10-Year ROE.

RESTRUCTURING

Once the situation assessment phase was completed, top management, at the urging of their CEO, formally initiated a comprehensive value-based restructuring exercise, with an initial goal of uncovering the more obvious value-creating opportunities quickly to make a quick and favorable impression on the investment community. Later, more pervasive and enduring structural and strategic improvements would follow. To frame the exercise, BioTech employed the restructuring pentagon, beginning with Node 1, current market value.

Current Valuation

BioTech stock was trading at $25 per share and had 50 million shares outstanding, for a total market equity of $1.250 billion. With $375 million in total debt, the total market value of the company was $1.625 billion. This is the value at Node 1 in Figure 4-6.

Jack noted that BioTech's stock had underperformed the market and its peers, particularly around the time of acquisition activity. For example, BioTech paid $125 million for Surgitech in the mid-1980s when its market value was about $90 million, a $35 million or 39% premium. Figure 4-7 shows that on the day of the takeover announcement, BioTech stock fell by $3 per share, or $33 million in total market value, almost the full $35 million premium BioTech paid to acquire Surgitech. Apparently, Wall

FIGURE 4-6   BioTech restructuring pentagon.

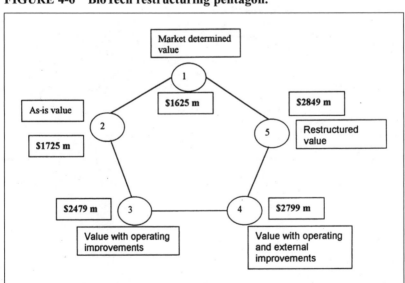

FIGURE 4-7   BioTech: SurgiTech's Impact on Stock Price.

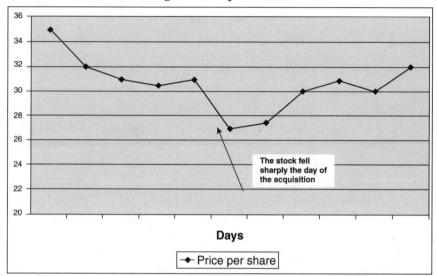

Street was skeptical about the deal and, in fact, BioTech had not implemented any changes since the acquisition, so there was little reason for Surgitech to be worth any more after the merger than before.

Jack discovered similar transfers of value in other past acquisitions. The cumulative impact of BioTech's acquisition program was startling: shareholder value had been *reduced* by $125 million over the past several years. This happened despite accounting-based analyses that showed the acquisitions to be profitable. Growth had been achieved, but at considerable cost. The shareholders would have been better off if BioTech had either made better investments or simply distributed the cash to the shareholders through dividends or stock repurchases.

The current analysis continued at the divisional level. Table 4-3 summarizes the financial results of each of BioTech's main businesses for the past five years. MPG generated both high ROI and earnings growth. LPG experienced strong earnings growth but low returns on capital because of heavy capital expenditures. Its cost of capital was high due to the unit's above-average risk. The high cost of capital and low ROI combined to produce a negative spread. CPG had low earnings growth and ROI. The cost of capital for this division was lower than average, reflecting its lower business risk and resulting in a positive spread. EIG displayed strong earnings growth but low returns on capital because of large capital expenditures.

TABLE 4-3   BioTech divisions: Performance summary.

| | 5-Year Average | | | |
Division	Earnings Growth	ROI	Cost of Capital	Spread
MPG	17%	22%	11%	11%
LPG	22%	9%	15%	−6%
CPG	10%	9%	7%	2%
BioTech	**15.55%**	**16.35%**	**10.30%**	**6.05%**

The net result across BioTech's four major units was an earnings growth of 15.5%, an ROI of 16.35%, and a spread of 6%.

Figure 4-8 displays a cash flow analysis of BioTech and its various divisions over the last five years, showing that the company had generated substantial free cash flow in MPG, most of which had been recycled into LPG and EIG. So little cash remained for shareholders that BioTech had to borrow just to maintain dividends. Jack suspected that the cash generated by MPG was reinvested in businesses that did not create an adequate return to shareholders.

Finally, various security analyst reports on the company revealed that the investment community doubted BioTech's commitment to shareholder value. The analysts were very negative about BioTech's lack of a coherent corporate strategy and its overinvestment in unprofitable businesses.

BioTech's As-Is Value

To determine the as-is value of the company, the benchmark for the impact on value of various restructuring strategies, Jack and his senior management task force conducted a rigorous strategic and financial DCF analysis of the constituent parts of the company in much the same way a raider would. They sought answers to the questions a raider would ask:

- Has each business unit achieved a position of competitive advantage? Is the advantage sustainable?
- Do competitively disadvantaged businesses have realistic opportunities to improve?
- Are the economic returns in each business improving or declining?
- How do returns compare with relevant industry benchmarks?
- Should the business units where returns exceed the cost of capital increase assets?

FIGURE 4-8   BioTech cumulative 5-year cash flow map.

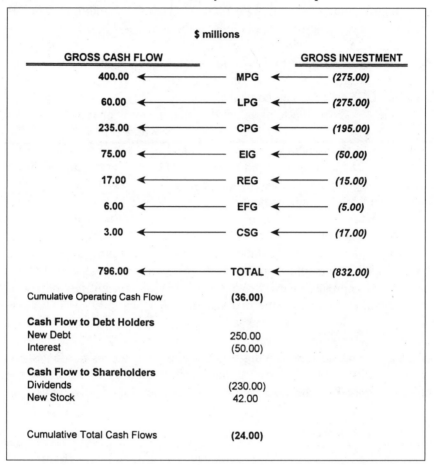

	\$ millions	
GROSS CASH FLOW		GROSS INVESTMENT
400.00 ←	MPG ←	(275.00)
60.00 ←	LPG ←	(275.00)
235.00 ←	CPG ←	(195.00)
75.00 ←	EIG ←	(50.00)
17.00 ←	REG ←	(15.00)
6.00 ←	EFG ←	(5.00)
3.00 ←	CSG ←	(17.00)
796.00 ←	TOTAL ←	(832.00)

Cumulative Operating Cash Flow	(36.00)
Cash Flow to Debt Holders	
New Debt	250.00
Interest	(50.00)
Cash Flow to Shareholders	
Dividends	(230.00)
New Stock	42.00
Cumulative Total Cash Flows	(24.00)

- Should the business units where returns are below the cost of capital curtail investment?
- Can the businesses free up cash to return to shareholders and still maintain their competitiveness?
- Will the business's projected financial performance result in superior shareholder return performance?

BioTech's DCF approach followed a self-acquisition model. The as-is value of each division is computed on the basis of projected future cash flows. Cash flow is calculated by adding depreciation back to net income and subtracting capital expenditures and changes in working capital. The cash flow projections for each division were based on projected sales growth, profit margins, working capital, and capital expenditures requirements based on simple extrapolations of the last few years' operating results. The final year residual value is calculated in the same way it would be in an acquisition. The free cash flows are discounted at the cost of capital estimate developed by the finance department for each business to yield the DCF value of the company.

Table 4-4 shows the total value of the company relative to its market value and broken down by division. The most obvious finding was that the as-is value of the company (shown on Node 2 in Figure 4-6) was approximately $1725 million compared to the capital market's estimate of $1625 million. The company's actual market value was only 94% of the economic value calculated by management.

This meant one of two things. One possibility is that management is right, and either the market did not buy management's forecasts for the company or it did not understand them. Management must seek to close this perceptions gap either through more effective communication with the market and improved investor relations or through outright repurchase of its undervalued shares on the market. The other possibility is that management may, in fact, be wrong and its forecasts too optimistic. In both cases, the perceptions gap warrants further analysis.

The second obvious finding was that three businesses accounted for more than 80% of the company's total market value, as shown in the pie chart in Figure 4-9. The other four businesses contributed only 16% of the

TABLE 4-4   BioTech's market value by division.

	As-Is Equity Value ($ million)	Book Value ($ million)
MPG	863	300
CPG	345	150
EIG	259	83.8
LPG	129	242
RPG	86	28
EFG	35	18
CSG	9	16.3
BioTech	1725	838.1
Total Market Value	**1625**	

FIGURE 4-9   BioTech "as is" value by division.

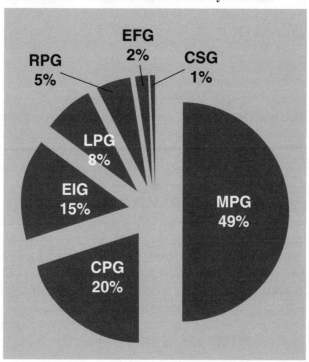

value and consumed nearly 36% of total assets and a good part of management's attention. This is a remarkably consistent discovery early in the VBM process: most of the value of a company comes from a handful of business unit activities.

BioTech's clear value star was MPG, where a book value investment of $300 million had yielded $863 in value. On the other hand, the DCF analysis showed that both LPG and CSG had values of about 50% of their investment cost to the company. So even if the managers of LPG and CSG achieved their business plans perfectly, they would destroy corporate value.

The business portfolio of BioTech illustrates the magnitude of the value gap that can be produced by pursuing inappropriate business strategies. BioTech had invested $242 million, or nearly 30% of its book value, in LPG. LPG's cash flows when discounted back amounted only to $129, a value gap of $113. This value deficit was produced by an operating strategy designed to foster growth. The key element of the plan was a massive capital-spending program designed to bolster the LPG distribution network's capacity and eliminate a competitive cost disadvantage. BioTech management was enamored by the high growth of LPG, without realizing that the negative spread of the division was destroying value. The same was true of the CSG division.

Potential Value of Internal Improvements

Once it understood its as-is value, the company took a careful look at the operations of each business unit to discover what, if any, internal strategic improvements could improve the company's value—for example, cost-cutting initiatives, efficiency drives, discontinuation of unprofitable product lines, consolidation of operations, reduction in headquarters costs, improvement in the management of working capital, increased focus on research and development efforts, and improvement in marketing, sales, and distribution.

The first step in developing internal improvements plans was to identify the value drivers for each division. Jack and his team isolated those drivers with the most impact on value for each division by means of a systematic sensitivity analysis conducted with a spreadsheet model of each division. The value driver analysis is shown in Figure 4-10. Typically, different divisions have different key value drivers. For example, earnings growth was the primary value driver for MPG, while operating margin was the primary value driver for LPG.

FIGURE 4-10   Value drivers for MPG, LPG, CPG, and EIG.

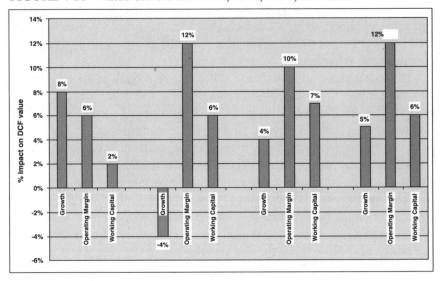

Jack and his team studied the specific plans of each division. Jack had isolated LPG as the division most in need of operating improvements. LPG was a good fit with BioTech's core competency of producing innovative, high-technology products for the institutional market, but the company's focus on growth was misplaced as long as it ignored profitability. Jack and his team devised a series of operating improvements designed to increase the profitability of LPG, described in Table 4-5.

When added together from the various divisions, these strategic and operating improvements were worth an additional $754 million, as shown in Table 4-6. If all the potential value from these improvements is realized, the company's value would rise to $2479 million, which is Node 3 on the restructuring pentagon in Figure 4-6.

BioTech's management treated VBM not merely as a financial exercise, but as a basis for business strategy formulation. The VBM analysis was the starting point for reevaluating and reformulating corporate and business strategies. Value spreadsheet models were created for each division in order to estimate the value impact of each strategy, leading to the identification and adoption of the "shareholder value" maximizing strategy.

Potential Value of External Improvements

One of Jack's major concerns was the company's diversification strategy. Although the diversification program was considered a success by many in the company, Jack's instincts told him that the program had distracted

TABLE 4-5   Potential LPG value improvements.

	$ millions
As-Is Value	129
Internal Improvements:	Potential Value Impact
Increase AR collections by 30%	150
Reduce inventory by 10%	50
Raise prices by 10%	85
Reduce operating costs by 5%	95
Reduce sales force by 10%	50
Increase returns on R&D by 20%	65
	495
Final value with internal improvements	**624**

TABLE 4-6   BioTech: Potential value with internal improvements.

$ millions

Division	As-Is Value	Value with Internal Improvements	% Difference
MPG	863	950	10.14%
LPG	345	624	80.87%
CPG	259	400	54.59%
EIG	129	350	170.53%
REG	86	90	4.35%
EFG	35	50	44.93%
CSG	9	15	73.91%
Value	**1725**	**2479**	**43.71%**
Market Value	1625	1625	
Value Gap	**100**	**854**	
% of market value	6.15%	52.55%	

management from its core business, and corporate value had suffered as a result.

Jack knew that BioTech's core competence was to develop innovative, high-technology product for the professional life science market and that the company's expansion into the consumer market through CPG was meant to leverage its R&D efforts. However, the VBM analysis confirmed that BioTech lacked the distribution channels to be successful in this highly competitive market.

The company's diversification into equipment financing, real estate, and corporate services was a result of chance rather than a part of a well-thought-out plan, a typical side effect of many diversification strategies that ignore value creation, and a decline in corporate value followed. Meanwhile, BioTech's competitive advantage in the medical and laboratory products markets was rapidly eroding, and these unrelated businesses took up a lot of the company's resources, including management time.

The VBM analysis confirmed that many of BioTech's operating units were destroying corporate value, and Jack's instincts about the diversification strategy were born out. Jack concluded that a more streamlined strategy in which the company would shed its unrelated businesses and refocus its resources on its core businesses was essential for BioTech to regain a strong competitive position in its core markets and to maximize shareholder wealth.

Jack realized that BioTech could significantly increase its value through abandoning its diversification strategy and changing its business portfolio. Table 4-7 summarizes the external restructuring VBM analysis. CPG was a good divestment candidate. It targeted the consumer market and, as such, was a poor fit with BioTech's competency in the institutional market. CPG was worth more to a company with an established distribution channel in the consumer market. REG and EFG also commanded higher selling prices than their value as part of the BioTech portfolio, although EFG's liquidating value was higher than its sales price.

Jack decided to sell the CPG and REG units and to liquidate the EFG group, unlocking $320 million in value. CSG was cut down by half by outsourcing a number of its corporate support services. BioTech would refocus on its core competency of developing products for the institutional market. The final value with operating and external improvements was estimated to be $2799 million, shown as Node 4 on the restructuring pentagon in Figure 4-6.

Potential Value of Financial Engineering

Financial engineering focuses on the capital structure of the company: the mix of debt and equity capital and its impact on the cost of capital. The

TABLE 4-7   BioTech Divisions: Comparison of external value estimates and internal improvements value.

| | $ millions | | | |
Division	Value with Internal Improvements	Strategic Buyer	LBO	Liquidation
MPG	950	900	850	700
LPG	624	600	620	500
CPG	400	700	550	375
EIG	350	325	300	270
REG	90	95	90	85
EFG	50	55	45	65
CSG	15	NA	NA	NA

VBM task force conducted a thorough analysis of BioTech's cost of capital with the aim of reducing it through one of several possible courses of action, including increased use of debt financing, stock repurchases, modified dividend policy, stock splits, and improved investor relations.

A key finding was that the company was underutilizing its debt capacity. The analysis showed that BioTech had a higher weighted average cost of capital than its industry peers and its 0.45 debt-to-equity ratio was among the lowest in the industry. The company could increase its leverage to 0.50 without affecting its debt rating. The present value of the tax shield from this increase in debt was estimated to be $50 million—a significant financial engineering opportunity. The final node was in place; the restructured value of the company was estimated at $2849 million, shown as Node 5 on the restructuring pentagon of Figure 4-6.

BioTech's Final Restructuring Plan
The potential for value-enhancing internal (operating and financial) and business portfolio adjustments determine the company's maximum possi-

TABLE 4-8   BioTech: Summary of restructuring actions.

Division	Action
MPG	Increase advertising, R&D Build marketing Cut operating costs Improve working capital
LPG	Cut operating costs Raise prices Reduce sales force Increase R&D returns Improve working capital
CPG	Sell
EIG	Increase prices Cut operating costs Improve working capital
REG	Sell
EFG	Liquidate
CSG	Cut, outsource
Financing	Increase debt ratio to capture tax shields

ble present value. The elements of BioTech's final restructuring plan are summarized in Table 4-8.

The difference between this optimal restructured value and the current market value—the value gap—shows the potential profit available to a raider from acquiring and restructuring the company. The value gap in the case of BioTech is an astounding $1224 million. The impact of the various elements of the restructuring plan on value is shown in Table 4-9. The proportion of value creation in each phase is representative. According to data provided by the McKinsey Group, on average, about 64% of the value creation opportunities come from strategic and operating opportunities directly under management's control, 22% come from acquisitions or divestitures, and the balance, about 14%, come from financial engineering opportunities.

The plans were implemented over a three-year period. BioTech's stock price increased 72% relative to its peers, capturing nearly all of the value from restructuring.

TABLE 4-9   BioTech: Total value created through restructuring.

		$ millions		
Division	As-Is Value	Restructuring Action	Restructured Value	% Difference
MPG	863	Operating Improvements	950	10.14%
LPG	345	Operating Improvements	624	80.87%
CPG	259	Sell	700	170.53%
EIG	129	Operating Improvements	350	170.53%
REG	86	Sell	95	10.14%
EFG	35	Liquidate	65	88.41%
CSG	9	Cuts, Outsource	15	73.91%
Debt Tax Shields	NA	Increase debt ratio to 0.6	50	NA
Final Value	**1725**		**2849**	65.16%
Market Value	1625		1625	
Value Gap	**100**		**1224**	
% of market value	6.15%		75.32%	

VALUE-BASED STRATEGIC PLANNING

Following the success of the restructuring campaign, Jack and his team decided that VBM should not be a one-shot deal but should be implemented as an ongoing "living" strategic plan. By institutionalizing the approach, management would continuously monitor and reexamine the policies and strategies followed by each business unit for their impact on shareholder value. Regular planning sessions focused on identifying the value drivers that the business unit managers have under their control and establishing specific value objectives in conjunction with top management. Capital would be allocated on the basis of the value creation potential of each business unit.

A competitive analysis of each business unit was undertaken on an ongoing basis. The analysis for LPG revealed that although it outperformed the competition based on margin, it was outclassed on ROI. The reason for the poor performance was the poor management of working capital and plant capacity utilization. LPG's inventory turnover lagged behind that of its competitors. The opportunity of improving capital management turned out to be worth $50 million. The opportunity had been obscured by the company's focus on profit margin instead of value creation and by the simple fact that a comprehensive competitive analysis had never been undertaken.

A comprehensive value driver analysis was performed for each business unit. Both macro- and operational-level micro drivers were identified. An example is provided in Table 4-10 for the LPG division. The primary value drivers at the macro level for LPG were identified as operating margin and working capital improvements. For this division, spending more

TABLE 4-10   Macro and micro drivers for LPG.

Macro Drivers	Micro Drivers
Operating Margin	
	Increase prices
	Reduce operating costs
	Reduce sales force
Working Capital	
	Reduce inventory
	Improve AR collection

capital to grow the business actually destroyed value because the spread was negative. LPG's micro-level drivers were price increases, operating cost reduction, increasing accounts receivable turnover, and reducing inventory. Concentrating on these micro drivers will improve operating margin and working capital and thereby improve value.

The largest unit, MPG, could benefit almost equally from market share growth and margin improvements. An implication was that price increases that raise operating margins are useless if sales growth erodes as a result. Operating margin and working capital were the primary value sources for EIG.

VALUE-BASED PERFORMANCE MEASURES

The next step in the VBM process was to adopt a set of performance measures. Jack and his top management team considered a number of candidates, among them EVA, SVA, TSR, TBR, and CFROI (these measures are discussed in detail in Chapter 12). The key concerns for the management were the accuracy, simplicity, and relevance of the candidate performance measure(s). The measure had to accurately reflect value created. The outcome of the measure had to lie reasonably within the employee's control for it to be of relevance. It also had to be simple enough to be understood by employees at all organizational levels. These criteria were especially important since Jack planned to tie a considerable portion of the employee's compensation to the measure of choice.

After evaluating each metric on these three criteria, Jack and his management team decided that no one metric satisfied all the needs of the company. They decided to adopt the hierarchy of measures displayed in Figure 4-11. TSR relative to a peer group was used as the criteria at the

FIGURE 4-11   BioTech: The metric pyramid.

corporate management level. Top management was rewarded when BioTech's performance exceeded that of the peer group—that is, when its shareholders enjoyed superior returns. At the divisional management level, SVA was adopted. The operational value drivers for each division were identified and a portion of the front-line employees' compensation was tied to the achievement of value driver targets. A portion of the divisional managers' compensation was also tied to corporate TSR to incent them to be concerned about corporatewide synergies. Finally, all capital allocation decisions were made based on DCF valuation.

VALUE-BASED COMPENSATION

Jack wanted to ensure that the newly found value culture would become firmly implanted at BioTech. He knew that the long-term success of the VBM program would depend on the sustained commitment of key executives. With strong top management involvement and support, a three-pronged attack was launched. It consisted of (1) a focused training program, (2) a modified strategy review process, and (3) a value-based incentive system.

The training program centered on the restructuring pentagon and valuation methodologies, and the modified strategy review process focused on a quarterly review of micro and macro value drivers and a progress report on value created, with areas of weakness defined and approaches refined.

Once top-level and business unit managers reached a comfort level with the VBM process and made it a part of their culture, the third step consisted of tying a portion of executive compensation, either directly or indirectly, to shareholder value. Curiously, despite the fact that they were now expected to make decisions on the basis of future cash flows and value creation, BioTech's managers were still being rewarded on the basis of accounting performance measures.

Implementation of VBM control and reward systems occurred late in BioTech's VBM adoption process. First, a reliable value metric had to be identified, and then this metric had to be clearly linked to an equitable incentive system. This proved challenging. Nonetheless, with this final step, BioTech finally had succesfully integrated its strategic and financial plans, management targets, and reward system.

The final solution was a complex system of bonuses. At the operational level, bonuses were tied to current performance on the operational metrics. Divisional-level bonuses were three-tiered. The first bonus tier was tied to the unit's current ROI. The second tier was tied to the unit's long-term SVA, and the third to the relative corporate TSR. Top management compensation was based on long-term TSR relative to a peer group. Jack considered TSR relative to the market but decided that a peer group was more relevant, since the management will not be penalized if the entire industry falls out of favor with the investors.

CONCLUSIONS

As the experiences of BioTech and a growing number of Fortune 1000 companies have demonstrated, a well-orchestrated VBM program consisting of planning, education, and incentives can prove very profitable to shareholders.

The BioTech example is fairly typical of what companies can expect on their journey in adopting VBM. Many have already initiated the VBM situation assessment and have taken the first steps into the restructuring phase. Although many companies have confronted the external improvement stage, few use VBM for internal improvement purposes. Even fewer have incorporated planning, performance metrics, and compensation in their VBM systems.

A handful of large companies stand out for adopting the complete VBM system. They include Briggs & Stratton, CSX, Harnischfeger Industries, and National Semiconductor. The shareholders of these companies have been rewarded with superior gains. Briggs & Stratton's stock price lingered between $15 and $30 before VBM. Following a successful VBM implementation, the stock price rose to $45. CSX, Harnischfeger, and National Semiconductor shareholders experienced similar success stories. According to a CSX representative, "The greatest single benefit of VBM is that CSX is now viewed very favorably by the investment community, as evidenced by the fact that our stock has outperformed both the S&P 500 and our peer group over the long term."

5

CHAPTER

DCF VALUATION: SPREADSHEET APPROACHES

VALUATION, OR THE ESTIMATION OF THE CURRENT MARKET DOLLAR VALUE OF AN ASSET, is ubiquitous in business. Nearly every business decision involves valuation. In capital markets, security analysts use valuation to find mispriced stocks, brokers use valuation in buy/sell decisions, investment bankers use it to identify takeover target companies and set offer prices in initial public offerings, and institutional lenders evaluate collateral by valuing the company's equity cushion. Inside the company, valuation drives capital budgeting, capital restructuring, and strategic planning decisions.

A wide variety of valuation approaches are in use, from simple to complex, which managers in all functional areas find indispensable. In general terms, these can be reduced to three: discounted cash flow (DCF) value, comparables, and option value. Over time, the financial community has come to rely most heavily on DCF methods, particularly in capital budgeting and merger and acquisition activities, with traditional net present value (NPV) heading the list, although adjusted present value (APV) and economic profit have recently gained popularity. The option value approach is also gaining favor because of its unique ability to overcome some limitations of the other approaches and because the power of personal computers has greatly simplified its implementation.

In this and the following chapter, we discuss DCF techniques. Comparables valuation approaches are covered in Chapter 7, and real options valuation in Chapter 8. This chapter is divided into three sections. The first lays the basic foundations of valuation theory. The second describes spreadsheet approaches to valuation, including the free cash flow, flows to equity, and adjusted present value methods, with more space devoted to the increasingly popular free cash flow and adjusted present value approaches. The third section elaborates on the actual estimation of cash flows.

THE BASICS OF VALUATION

Classical valuation theory holds that the true, or intrinsic, value of an asset is determined by its ability to generate future cash flows. The fundamental value of the asset is the discounted sum of all future cash flows that will be received by the owner of the asset, referred to as the *present value.* The concept of present value is designed to estimate how much an investment is worth today—that is, to determine a fair price for an asset given its expected future cash flows. Note that asset owners and investors care only about cash, as discussed in Chapter 3. Cash is king in asset valuation.

Present Value

In essence, the application of classical valuation theory involves estimating and adding up the present values of the future cash flows expected by the owner of that asset. Consider an investment that is expected to pay $100 one year from now. Its value today depends on the cash flow and on its *discount rate,* or *opportunity cost*—that is, the return one could expect to make on other investments of comparable risk. If competing investments offer a 10% return, then an investment of $90.91 today will compound to $90.01 × 1.10, or $100, one year from now. So, $90.91 is the present value of an investment that promises $100 a year from now with a 10% discount rate.

The process of computing present values of future sums is known as *discounting,* or *capitalizing.* To determine the present value of a future sum, the future amount is multiplied by a discount factor available from standardized financial tables for various combinations of discount rates and the number of time periods. Easier still, there are numerous specialized financial calculators and spreadsheet software programs available on the market today to perform these calculations.

The present value of any future stream of cash flows can be determined by this approach, as shown schematically in Figure 1-2 in Chapter 1. The

FIGURE 5-1   Logic of DCF valuation.

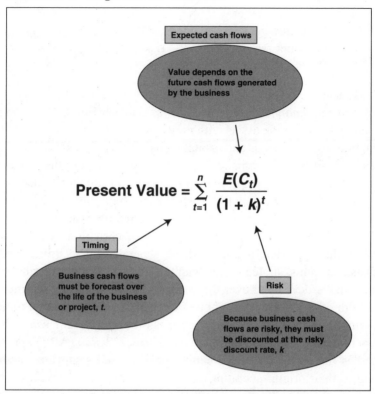

formula for the present value of an amount, F, due in n years, given k as the discount rate, is given by:

$$PV = \frac{\text{Future Value}}{1 + \text{Discount Rate}} = \frac{F}{(1 + k)^n} \tag{1}$$

Equation 1 is the fundamental formula that underlies the determination of economic value, shown schematically in Figure 5-1.

Thus, the fundamental determinants of value are the expected long-term cash flows from the asset, discounted for time value and for the risk inherent in the cash flow stream. Formally, this is given by:

$$V = \sum_{t=1}^{n} \frac{\text{Free Cash Flows}_t}{(1 + k)^t}$$

$$V = \frac{C_1}{(1 + k)^1} + \frac{C_2}{(1 + k)^2} + \frac{C_3}{(1 + k)^3} + \cdots + \frac{C_n}{(1 + k)^n}$$

where V = Value
      n = Life of the asset
      C_t = Cash flow in period t
      k = Discount rate reflecting the riskiness of the estimated cash
          flows

It is clear from the above discussion that the value of any asset is a function of the *amount, timing,* and *risk* of its cash flows. The economic rationale behind valuing assets with their cash flows is that shareholder returns come from dividends and capital gains (future dividends) which must be paid in cash by the company. Moreover, the claims of other stakeholders, including creditors, employees, managers, and suppliers, must also be paid in cash from the company's cash flows. The ability of the company to service all its claims lies in its ability to generate cash.

The present value of any future stream of cash flows can be determined by this approach, including those generated by securities, companies, business units, strategies, and capital projects. Several variants of the approach have developed over the years to handle a variety of situations in a wealth of contexts. When applied to cash flows from capital projects, for example, the approach is referred to as the *net present value* (NPV) approach. Another variation, the *adjusted present value* (APV) approach, unbundles the cash flows from capital projects and segregates them according to their origin: operating cash flows, financing flows, tax-related flows, and so on. The *flows-to-equity* (FTE) approach values the cash flows accruing to shareholders. A recent addition to the DCF family is the *economic profit* approach. This model expresses the value of the company as the sum of the original capital investment and the discounted forecasts of economic profits.

Examples: How Investors Evaluate Bonds and Stocks

When applied to securities such as bonds or common stocks, the value of the security equals the present value of the future cash inflows discounted at the investor's required return (the cost of equity). With bonds, the future cash flows are the coupons, if any, plus the principal or face value. For example, what is the value of a bond with a $150 coupon per year for three years and a principal of $1000 three years from now if the opportunity cost of money for investments of comparable risk is 15%? Timelines of cash flows are exceptionally useful in valuing assets. The timeline of this bond's cash flows are shown in Figure 5-2.

FIGURE 5-2   Time line of bond's cash flows.

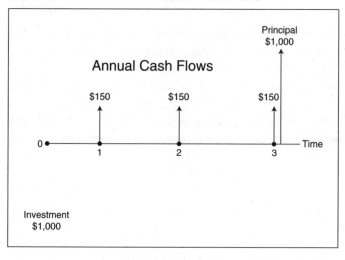

Applying Equation 1 or using present value tables or spreadsheet software to calculate the present value of each future cash flow and then their sum, we find that the present value of this bond investment is as follows:

$$PV = \$150/(1 + 0.15) + \$150/(1 + 0.15)^2 + (\$150 + \$1000)/(1 + 0.15)^3$$
$$= \$130.43 + \$113.42 + \$756.14$$
$$= \$1000$$

With common stocks, the expected future cash flows are the dividends and future changes in the resale value of the stock. Consider an investor with a one-year holding period. If a dividend of $5 and resale price of $26 are expected at the end of the year, and the stock is fairly risky and requires a 24% return (Chapter 11 is devoted to estimating discount rates), then the present value of the cash flows from the investment in this stock is

$$P_0 = \frac{\$5}{1 + 0.24} + \frac{\$26}{1 + 0.24} = \$25$$

More generally, if we represent the expected dividend by D_1, the expected stock price by P_1, and the discount rate by k, we have:

$$P_0 = \frac{D_1}{1 + k} + \frac{P_1}{1 + k}$$

If the investor plans to hold this stock for two years, and a dividend of $5.25 and a resale price of $27.30 are expected at the end of the second year, we have

$$P_0 = \frac{\$5.00}{1 + 0.24} + \frac{\$5.25}{(1 + 0.24)^2} + \frac{\$27.30}{(1 + 0.24)^2}$$

The analysis can be extended to any number of holding periods. We can always replace the expected future stock price with its future expected dividend and the next period's expected share price. Regardless of the investor's holding period, the next purchaser of the stock will pay a price that reflects the present value of dividends beyond that period, so that the price of a share of common stock is simply the present value of the infinite stream of future cash flows or expected dividends:

$$P = \sum_{t=1}^{\infty} \frac{D_t}{(1 + k)^t}$$

This and other stock valuation equations are derived in the appendix to Chapter 7.

Example: How Managers Evaluate Capital Projects

The decision to invest in inventory, receivables, or plant and equipment is remarkably analogous to the investor's decision to purchase bonds and stocks: There is an initial cash outlay in exchange for expected future cash flows over the life of the asset. As above, the present value of a capital project is the discounted value of its expected future cash flows. The *net* present value (NPV) of the project is its present value less the (present value of its) required investment. The venerable NPV rule has been around for decades and is widely used by companies in analyzing the economic viability of capital projects.

$$NPV = \sum_{t=1}^{n} \frac{\text{Cash Flows}_t}{(1 + k)^t} - \text{Investment}$$

where n = number of periods of cash flow
k = opportunity cost of capital, or discount rate

To illustrate, a company invests $100,000 in a capital project that is expected to generate revenues of $20,000 per year for 10 years. The discount rate for this project is 12%. The NPV is simply the present value of a 10-year $20,000 annuity less the initial investment of $100,000:[1]

$$NPV = \sum_{t=1}^{10} \frac{\$20,000}{(1 + 0.12)^t} - \$100,000 = \$13,000$$

---

[1] The present value of a 10-year $20,000 annuity is obtained from a financial calculator or by multiplying the amount by the appropriate present value factor for annuities obtained from a specialized financial table. The factor here is 5.650. The present value of the annuity is thus $20,000 × 5.650 = $113,000. The NPV is $113,000 − $100,000 = $13,000.

FIGURE 5-3   Capital project valuation.

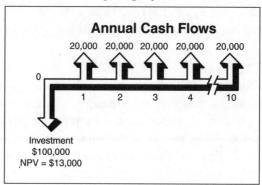

As summarized in Figure 5-3, since the NPV is positive, the project creates economic value and should be accepted by the company.

Example: How Companies Should Evaluate Alternative Strategies

The classical valuation approach is applicable to the evaluation of some alternative strategies as well. Strategies are, at their most basic level, just sets of investments over time. An illustration will help here. Figure 5-4 shows how a company can use NPV analysis to evaluate a business unit's strategy. (NPV typically captures a strategy's minimum value. For strategies with growth options and other opportunities for active management, we need the real options valuation approach to valuation, discussed in Chapter 8.) Suppose a business unit of a company plans to add a new color scanner to its product line. To evaluate the strategy, the company must project five-year financial statements and the incremental cash flows generated by the scanner. The estimated cash flows are discounted by an appropriate cost of capital, say 12%, to arrive at an estimate of the present value of the strategy, shown in Figure 5-4 to be $6519. If this present value is greater than the

FIGURE 5-4   Corporate business unit PV of business strategy.

	2001	2002	2003	2004	2005	beyond 2005
Planned cash flows	$570	$630	$700	$800	$850	$850
Discount factor (12%)	0.893	0.797	0.712	0.636	0.567	4.729
2000 Present Value	$509	$502	$498	$508	$482	$4,019
TOTAL PV	**$6,519**					

required investment costs, this strategy will add value to the company. This analysis helps managers to estimate the value creation of this and alternative strategies, and to select those that add the most value to the company.

SPREADSHEET APPROACHES TO VALUATION

If we think of a company or business unit as a bundle of projects or a pool of assets, then valuing a company or business unit is fundamentally no different than valuing bonds, stocks, capital projects, or passive strategies. The economic value of the bundle is the sum of the present value of the future expected cash flows of each of the assets in the bundle.

The spreadsheet approach generates estimates of an asset's future cash flows by first examining the level and drivers of the cash flows in its historical financial statements and then projecting those cash flows into the future after adjusting them for anticipated changes in the economic conditions of the industry, the company's competitive position in that industry, and its peers' strategies, actions, and financial parameters.

The spreadsheet approach can be implemented in several ways depending on data availability and the particular circumstances. The principal variations are the free cash flow (FCF), flows-to-equity (FTE), and adjusted present value (APV) approaches.

Free Cash Flow and Flows-to-Equity Approaches

The DCF valuation of a company can be structured with either the FCF, also known as the all-entity approach, or the FTE approach. Figure 5-5 depicts the equivalence of these two approaches with the use of a simple balance sheet. In economic valuation, as in accounting, the two sides of the balance sheet must be equal. Therefore, we should be able to value an asset by evaluating its cash flows from either an operating or financing perspective and obtain the same result.

The FCF approach focuses on the asset, or operations, side of the business. Since a business has an infinite life, it is convenient to break down the economic value of a business into two components, as in Figure 5-6.

The first component is the present value of all forecasted cash flows from operations during some predetermined forecast period. The second component represents the value of the company beyond the forecast period and is referred to as the *continuing, residual,* or *terminal value.* The terminal value is the value of the business as a going concern at the end of the forecast period and is estimated from the cash flows forecast to come after the explicit forecasting period.

FIGURE 5-5   DCF valuation.

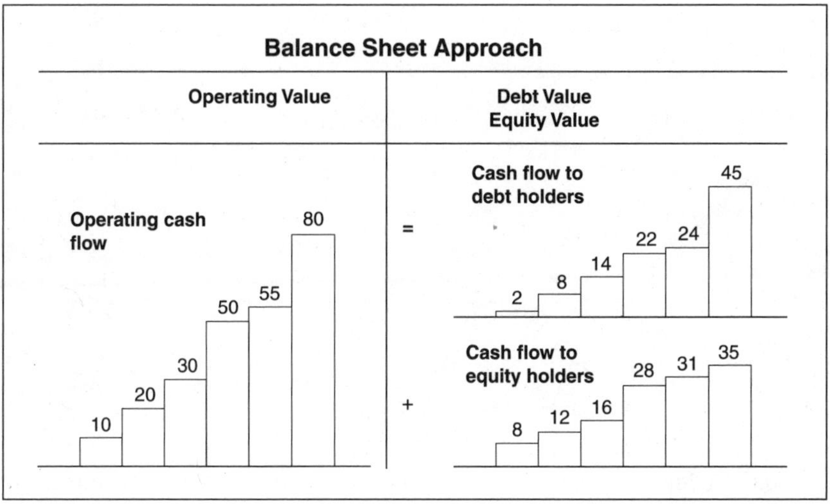

The free cash flows from assets or operations are discounted by the company cost of capital. The company cost of capital is the weighted average of the returns required by the company's bondholders and shareholders and is called the *weighted average cost of capital,* or WACC. The WACC is discussed in detail in Chapter 11.

There are four distinct steps to the FCF approach to company valuation:

Step 1: Forecast the free cash flows available to all investors over a finite horizon (usually 5 to 10 years). The final year of the horizon is called the *terminal year.*

Step 2: Forecast the free cash flows beyond the terminal year.

Step 3: Discount the free cash flows by the WACC. The present value represents the value of the free cash flows available to debt and equity holders as a group.

Step 4: Subtract the current market value of debt from the present value of the free cash flows, and add the value of any nonoperating assets excluded from the original free cash flow forecasts (e.g., marketable securities or real estate held for sale) to arrive at the estimated value of equity.

The FCF approach is illustrated with the following example. XYZ.com is considering acquiring Portal.com and is trying to assess its fair market

FIGURE 5-6 Approach to valuation.

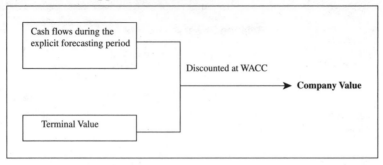

value. Portal.com's abridged financial statements are shown in Table 5-1. The $60,000 of free cash flows generated by Portal.com in 2001 is the difference between the cash revenues and cash outlays derived from its income statement and balance sheet, as shown at the bottom of Table 5-1.

Figure 5-7 shows Portal.com's cash flows sorted into two sets of components: one from operations and the other from investments (working capital and fixed assets). Cash *in*flows are produced by revenues. Cash *out*flows include operating expenses, taxes, and additions to working capital and fixed assets. The difference between cash inflows and outflows is the free cash flow produced by the company.

The spreadsheet cash flow projections over the next five years for Portal.com are exhibited in Table 5-2. The projections start with the first year's free cash flow of $60. Free cash flow is the portion of operating income not reinvested by the company and is defined as after-tax operating profits less the change in total capital accounts. Equivalently, free cash flow is the net cash flow available for distribution to investors—that is, the company's after-tax operating earnings before interest, less any additional investment in working capital and fixed assets:

$$\text{Free Cash Flow} = \text{EBIT}(1 - T) + D - \Delta\text{Working Capital} - \Delta\text{Fixed Assets}$$
$$= \$5{,}250(1 - 0.40) + \$250 - \$1{,}340 - \$2{,}000$$
$$= \$60$$

where EBIT = Earnings before interest and taxes
$\quad\quad\quad T$ = Marginal tax rate
$\quad\quad\quad D$ = Depreciation

The first row of Table 5-2 is Portal.com's projected revenues, starting at $12,000 and growing at 25%. Operating costs are subtracted from rev-

TABLE 5-1 Portal.com financial statement.

Balance Sheet

	2001	2000	Change
Cash	$250	$100	$150
Receivables	$2,600	$1,500	$1,100
Inventory	$2,600	$1,500	$1,100
Property, plant, & eqpt	$6,000	$4,000	$2,000
Accum deprec	$750	$500	$250
Net property, plant, & eqpt	$5,250	$3,500	$1,750
Total Assets	$10,700	$6,600	$4,100
Accounts Payables	$3,570	$2,560	$1,010
Long-Term Debt	$2,000	$2,000	$0
Common Equity	$5,130	$2,040	$3,090
Total Liabilities & Owners Equity	$10,700	$6,600	$4,100

Income Statement

	2001
Sales	$12,000
Cost of Sales	$3,500
Selling, general, admin	$3,000
Depreciation	$250
Total expense	$6,750
Interest	$100
Income before tax	$5,150
Taxes (40%)	$2,060
Net income	$3,090

(*continued*)

enues to arrive at earnings before depreciation, interest, and taxes (EBDIT), which also grow at 25%. Depreciation is subtracted to arrive at earnings before interest and taxes (EBIT). Taxes at 40% of EBIT are subtracted, depreciation is added back, and changes in total capital requirements (net working capital plus net property, plant, and equipment) are subtracted from EBIT to arrive at the free cash flows for each year.

TABLE 5-1   Portal.com financial statement.
(Continued)

	Free Cash Flows
	2001
Cash Flows—Operations	
Revenue	$12,000
Cash Expenses	$6,500
Taxes*	$2,100
Total	$3,400
Cash Flows—Investments	
Working Capital	$1,340
Fixed Assets	$2,000
Total	$3,340
Free Cash Flows	**$60**

A tax rate of 40% is applied on taxable income, which is sales minus operating costs and depreciation of $250.

The terminal value of Portal.com is the present value of its cash flows after year 5. If we assume that cash flows remain constant at their year 5 level of $845 into infinity, and the discount rate is 12%, then the terminal value as of the end of year 5 is the present value of the perpetuity, or $845/.12 = $7044. (Terminal or continuing values are discussed in Chapter 6). Discounting the free cash flows and terminal value by Portal.com's cost of capital of 12%, we find a present value of $5245, which is the value of Portal.com to XYZ.com.

The present value of cash flows under the FCF approach is the value of the company as a whole, including both debt and equity. To compute the equity value from the value of the firm as a whole, the value of debt must be netted out. Figure 5-8 illustrates the procedure. Note that we do not subtract the value of other liabilities, such as accounts payable. Their influence on firm value has already been considered in the process of forecasting free cash flows.

Table 5-2 indicates that, based on a cost of capital of 12%, Portal.com's total value is estimated at $5245 million. From that, debt of $2000 is subtracted to arrive at an equity value of $3245. Dividing by the 100 shares outstanding, we arrive at a value for Portal.com of $32 per share. This is slightly higher than the prevailing stock price of $29, indicating potential

FIGURE 5-7 Portal.com 2001 valuation cash flows.

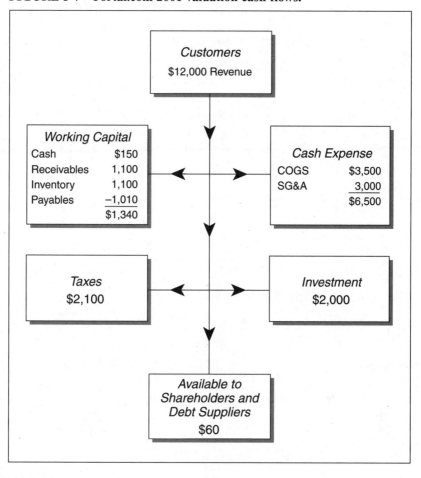

synergies from the acquisition. If XYZ.com pays more than $32 per share, it is making a value-destroying investment and its own stock price will decline. If if pays less than $32 per share and if the cash flow projections materialize, it will be enhancing value and its stock price will increase.

To the extent that a company maintains any nonoperating assets that will generate cash flows not considered in the cash flow forecasts, the value of those assets must be added at this stage. Common examples are marketable securities, land held for sale, and excess pension fund assets. Adjustments should also be made for the expected cost of any obligations not recorded on the balance sheet and not already considered in earnings projections. An example would be the anticipated costs to repair environmental damage. On

TABLE 5-2 Portal.com free cash flows projections and valuation.

Free Cash Flows		2001	2002	2003	2004	2005
1. Sales		$12,000	$15,000	$18,750	$23,438	$29,297
2. Oper costs excluding dep.		$6,500	$8,125	$10,156	$12,695	$15,869
3. Earnings bef. dep., interest, tax (EBDIT)		$5,500	$6,875	$8,594	$10,742	$13,428
4. Depreciation (Dep)		$250	$300	$360	$432	$518
5. Earnings bef interest & tax (EBIT)		$5,250	$6,575	$8,234	$10,310	$12,909
6. Less 40% Taxes on EBIT		$2,100	$2,630	$3,294	$4,124	$5,164
7. Plus Depreciation		$250	$300	$360	$432	$518
8. Less Capital Expenditures		$2,000	$2,400	$2,880	$3,456	$4,147
9. Less Additions to Working Capital		$1,340	$1,675	$2,094	$2,617	$3,271
10. *Free Cash Flow*		$60	$170	$327	$545	$845
11. Terminal Value (See Note)						$7,044
12. Total Free Cash Flow		$60	$170	$327	$545	$7,890
NPV at 12%	$5,245					
Less Debt	$2,000					
Equity Value	$3,245					
Shares outstanding	100					
Intrinsic Value per share	$32					
Recent Share Price	$29					
Discount of Price from Value	11%					

Note: The terminal value is estimated using the perpetuity valuation model: TV = FCF (year 5)/WACC. This estimate assumes a WACC of 12%

FIGURE 5-8   Free cash flow valuation.

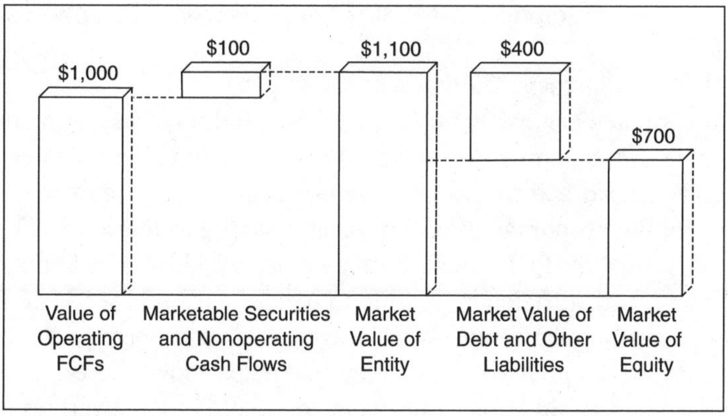

Source: Weston and Copeland, op. cit.

the other hand, if the effects of unrecorded liabilities have already been included in the cash flow projections, they must be ignored. A good example is found in operating leases. If the earnings projections already reflect expected rent payments on these leases, they need not be considered.

There are often questions regarding adjustments to cash flow estimates for the effects of cash balances. In Portal.com's case, the adjustment is unnecessary because the cash flow forecast in Table 5-2 already includes interest income from cash equivalents. In addition, the value of cash is already embedded in the present value estimate because the cash needed to keep operations running smoothly was captured in the cash flow from operations. To adjust cash flow estimates for this cash would constitute double-counting.

An alternative approach is to treat cash and cash equivalents as a nonoperating asset, exclude the interest income on that asset from the cash flow projections, and add its current value to the present value of the projected cash flows. However, since some cash is necessary just to maintain operations, only the "excess" cash should be a candidate for such treatment.

A final adjustment would be required in cases where the company has potentially dilutive securities outstanding. The market value of options and warrants, as well as the market value of the conversion feature of convertible securities, should be deducted from firm value. Estimation of such amounts can be quite complex and lies outside the scope of this chapter. However, for many if not most firms, the amounts involved are relatively small. Portal.com, like most high-technology entrepreneurial companies, has employee stock options outstanding, but they represent claims to shares constituting a very small portion of the outstanding stock. Their value would be an even smaller fraction of the value of outstanding shares, because there is a cost (the exercise price) associated with exercising the options.

Free Cash Flow Approach: Multidivisional Company

The FCF approach can easily be extended to a multibusiness company. The equity value of the company is the sum of its individual units' values, less corporate overhead and the value of senior claims (debt, preferred stock). Cash-generating corporate assets are usually added to the resulting value.

In conclusion, the FCF spreadsheet approach to valuation is familiar, easy to implement, and sufficiently flexible to handle most real-world complexities—hence, its popularity and wide usage. Managers relate to the method because they are familiar with its capital budgeting roots. More importantly, the approach is a useful initial framework for identifying the various sources of value in a company and searching for value-creating opportunities.

Flows-To-Equity Approach

As illustrated in Figure 5-5, there are two equivalent ways to value a company. One is the FCF approach, where the company's free cash flows are discounted at the WACC. The other is the flows-to-equity (FTE) approach, where the residual cash flows to equity holders are discounted at the equity cost of capital:

$$\text{Value of Equity} = \sum_{t=1}^{n} \frac{\text{Flows-to-Equity}_t}{(1 + k_e)^t}$$

where k_e = Cost of equity

Residual cash flows are the cash flows available to equity holders after all expenses, tax obligations, and interest and principal repayments have been taken out. The easiest way to calculate FTE is to subtract the flows to debt holders from the company's free cash flows. Another way is to add dividends paid to the value of common shares repurchased less the value of new shares issued:

$$\text{FTE} = \text{Dividends} + \text{Share Repurchases} - \text{Shares Issued}$$

In the absence of shares issued or repurchased, FTE reduces to dividends paid to shareholders. Viewed this way, FTE is simply the portion of earnings not reinvested by the company and thus can also be defined as earnings less changes in equity capital:[2]

$$\text{FTE} = \text{Earnings} - \Delta\text{Common Equity Capital}$$

[2] This is true as long as the company follows "flow-through" accounting.

Table 5-3 illustrates the various methods of computing FTE using the Portal.com example.

How do the FCF and FTE approaches compare? The FCF method is generally considered to be simpler and more convenient to use, and can be applied to either the business unit or company level. It does not require information on debt repayment or interest payments, as does FTE, information which is generally not even available at the business unit level.

Finally, the discount rate must be estimated with extreme care when capital structure or dividend policy changes are contemplated. Fairly complicated modeling circularities are required to yield capital costs that are

TABLE 5-3   Portal.com flows-to-equity estimation—Direct, long, short-cut methods.

Defining Flows to Equity: Direct Method	
Dividends	0
+ Share repurchases	0
− Share issuances	0
Total flows-to-equity	**0**
Defining Flows to Equity: Long Method	
Earnings after taxes	3,090
+ Depreciation	250
+ Increases in interest-bearing debt	0
+ Increases in non-interest-bearing debt	1,010
= Sources of cash	4,350
Fixed capital investment	**2,000**
+ Increase in current assets	2,350
= Uses of cash	4,350
Equity cash flow =	**0**
Defining Flows to Equity: Short Cut	
Earnings after taxes	3,090
− Equity Invested	3,090
Equity cash flow =	**0**

consistent with market value capital structures under either approach. For that reason, the adjusted present value, discussed next, is often preferable. The APV approach has the added bonus of providing the manager with better information on sources of value, as we demonstrate shortly.

Adjusted Present Value Approach

Whereas the NPV approach bundles all financing side effects into the discount rate, the adjusted present value (APV) approach unbundles NPV into its separate components to allow the manager to isolate the side effects of financing on value. APV helps managers begin to identify an important source of value.

APV is equal to the base-case NPV plus the value of all financing side effects. *Base-case NPV* is the value of the project under all-equity financing. Financing side effects include the flotation expenses incurred in issuing new securities, the value of interest tax shields, and the impact of subsidized financing through loan guarantees, among others.

APV = Base-Case NPV + Value of Financing Side Effects

- Tax shield
- Bankruptcy
- Issue costs
- Agency costs

Typically, the APV method discounts the company's free cash flows at the unlevered (no debt) cost of capital and adds to that the present value of the tax shield, which is given by the product of the corporate tax rate, T, and the dollar amount of debt, D:[3]

$$APV = \text{Base-Case NPV} + T \times D$$

---

[3] For debt that is assumed to be outstanding in perpetuity, the tax saving is the tax rate, T, times the interest payment, rD. The present value of this perpetual savings is $TrD/r = TD$.

This calculation gives a value for the entire company, from which the value of the debt is deducted in order to arrive at an estimate of the equity value.

Sound economic valuation requires that cash flows be discounted at a rate consistent with the risk of those cash flows. Pure business cash flows should be discounted at the cost of capital for the unlevered (all-equity) company. And the debt tax shield is valued by discounting the future annual tax savings at the pretax cost of debt. Appropriate discount rates and other cost of capital issues are discussed in Chapter 11.

APV example. BioTech is evaluating a $10 million capital investment in a new generation of a self-administered computerized testing kit for diabetes recently developed in Europe. The investment is to be set up as a wholly owned European subsidiary. The project's financing calls for $5 million debt (10-year, 8% or $400,000 annual coupon with 10% cost of debt) and $5 million of cash through an injection of equity from the parent. The after-tax cash flows from the project are estimated at $2 million per year for 10 years plus $6 million in cash salvage value. BioTech's tax rate is 40%, and the required return for this risky project if all-equity financed is 15%. BioTech management wants to know the venture's APV.

The upper panel in Table 5-4 summarizes the project's data and assumptions, and the middle panel displays the resulting cash flows. The base-case NPV is $11.52 million, obtained by discounting the business cash flows at 15%, the unlevered cost of equity. The lower panel provides the amortization schedule for BioTech's debt financing. Annual tax savings are obtained by multiplying the annual interest payments by the tax rate of 40%. The present value of these tax shields, $0.86 million, is added to the base-case NPV of $11.52 million to obtain an APV of this project of $12.38 million. Subtracting the required investment of $10 million generates a net APV of $2.38 million.

APV versus NPV. In practice, the estimates provided by the various valuation methods are close but not identical. Differences can be due to using book-value versus market-value weights in computing the weighted average cost of capital, minor differences in the assumed cost of debt or equity, or to dynamic capital structure changes.

When should you use APV over the venerable NPV approach? There are three major situations when the APV approach may be preferable. First, the traditional NPV-WACC approach is perfectly appropriate only in the fairly unrealistic situation where the project, strategy, or operation under

TABLE 5-4 BioTech investment project adjusted present value method.

Investment	$10,000
Financing	
Debt	$5,000
Equity	$5,000
Life	10 years
After-tax cash flows	$2,000 per year
After-tax salvage	$6,000
Cost of debt	10%
Unlevered cost of equity	15%
Principal payments	$400 for 9 years
Last principal payment	$1,400
Tax rate	40%

	Year 0	Year 1	Year 2	Year 3	Year 4	Year 5	Year 6	Year 7	Year 8	Year 9	Year 10
After-tax cash flows		$2,000	$2,000	$2,000	$2,000	$2,000	$2,000	$2,000	$2,000	$2,000	$2,000
Salvage											$6,000

Base case NPV   **$11,521**

	Year 0	Year 1	Year 2	Year 3	Year 4	Year 5	Year 6	Year 7	Year 8	Year 9	Year 10
Loan balance BOY		$5,000	$4,600	$4,200	$3,800	$3,400	$3,000	$2,600	$2,200	$1,800	$1,400
Interest		$500	$460	$420	$380	$340	$300	$260	$220	$180	$140
Principal repayment		$400	$400	$400	$400	$400	$400	$400	$400	$400	$1,400
Loan balance EOY	$5,000	$4,600	$4,200	$3,800	$3,400	$3,000	$2,600	$2,200	$1,800	$1,400	$0
Tax shields		$200	$184	$168	$152	$136	$120	$104	$88	$72	$56

PV tax shields   **$863**

APV   **$12,383**

Net APV   **$2,383**

	Year 0	Year 1	Year 2	Year 3	Year 4	Year 5	Year 6	Year 7	Year 8	Year 9	Year 10
Debt ratio	50%	46%	42%	38%	34%	30%	26%	22%	18%	14%	0%
Cost of equity	18.0%	17.6%	17.2%	16.8%	16.5%	16.3%	16.1%	15.8%	15.7%	15.5%	15.0%
WACC	12.0%	14.1%	14.2%	14.2%	14.3%	14.4%	14.5%	14.6%	14.6%	14.7%	15.0%

consideration is an exact replica of the company in terms of both risk and capital structure.

Second, in NPV, the discount rate is adjusted to pick up any value attributable to financing. For example, the cost of debt in the WACC is converted into an after-tax rate to pick up the value of interest tax shields. But for most modern-day corporate restructurings, buyouts, joint ventures, and cross-border investments, properly adjusting the WACC would require extensive and complex adjustments for the tax shields, dynamic capital structures, subsidies, and exotic debt securities associated with these deals. The result is that NPV is both impractical and most likely wrong in these applications. APV, by separating out the value impact of financing, can be used to properly evaluate the more complex and dynamic transactions of today. The same issues lead us to prefer APV for valuing individual business unit operations.

Third, and perhaps most importantly, APV is superior in providing information to managers about the sources of value creation. The APV approach allows the manager to separate operational and financing elements and to focus on the sources of value from each. By unbundling base-case cash flows, APV leads to superior accountability at the operational level and does a better job of identifying the fundamental value drivers of a business.

Earlier in Table 5-2 we determined the value of Portal.com using the traditional NPV approach. In Tables 5-5 and 5-6, we value Portal.com again, this time using APV. The steps involved in calculating APV are similar to those involved with the FCF method:[4]

- Prepare performance forecasts and base-case incremental cash flows for the business.
- Discount base-case cash flows and terminal value to present value.
- Evaluate financing side effects.
- Add the pieces together to get an initial APV.
- Tailor the analysis to the managers' needs.

The first step consists of forecasting the incremental cash flows of the company in the same manner as in the NPV approach. The forecasts are displayed in Table 5-5. Next, the base-case cash flows and terminal value are discounted at 13.5%, the cost of equity of a comparable all-equity company. The resulting base-case NPV is $4510.

---

[4] The methodology and the example that follows are adapted from a case study presented in "Using APV: A better tool for valuing operations," by T. Luehrman, *Harvard Business Review*, May–June 1997, pp. 145–154.

The financing side effects are next. In this case, they consist primarily of the income shielded from taxes by the deductibility of interest payments. The present value of the tax shield is $662, obtained by multiplying the annual interest payments (assumed to continue indefinitely as the company refinances maturing debt) by the tax rate, then discounting by the cost of debt. The two sources of value are added together in the fourth step to obtain $5172, the APV of the project.

The crucial step for managerial purposes is the fifth and final one where the various sources of value are examined separately. In Table 5-6, base-case cash flows are unbundled into the cash flows associated with each value creation initiative undertaken by XYZ.com's management. It is likely that different initiatives are the responsibility of different managers. The top panel of Table 5-6 shows the baseline cash flows derived from current operations and management strategies. These generate Portal.com's as-is baseline business value of $1897.

Each successive panel of Table 5-6 shows the incremental cash flows associated with each of XYZ.com management's initiatives: margin improvements, net working capital improvements, asset sales, and a higher growth profile. The four categories of operating improvements collectively add $2614 in value. Figure 5-9 shows the various sources of value improvement uncovered by an APV evaluation of Portal.com. There we see that about two-thirds of the anticipated value creation stems from short-term initiatives such as divesting unproductive assets and reducing working capital needs. The balance comes from long-term strategies like improving margins and increasing growth.

WHERE DO CASH FLOWS COME FROM?

Free cash flow (FCF) is the net cash flow available to all investors, including bondholders, other creditors, preferred stockholders, and common stockholders. It is the portion of operating income not reinvested by the company and is thus defined as net operating profits after tax (or NOPAT) less the change in total capital accounts:[5]

$$FCF = NOPAT - \Delta Total\ Capital$$

NOPAT is earnings before interest and taxes (EBIT) after taxes, that is, EBIT $(1 - T)$ where T is the corporate tax rate.

---

[5] This is true as long as the company follows flow-through accounting. The approach used here, particularly in Tables 5-6 and 5-7, is adapted from J.F. Weston, J.A. Siu, and B.A. Johnson, *Takeovers, Restructuring & Corporate Governance,* 3d ed. (2001), Prentice Hall, Chapter 9.

TABLE 5-5 Portal.com APV analysis.

Step 1: Prepare Base-Case Cash Flow Forecasts

Base-Case Cash Flows

	2000	2001	2002	2003	2004	2005
Sales		$12,000	$15,000	$18,750	$23,438	$29,297
Oper costs excl. deprec.		$6,500	$8,125	$10,156	$12,695	$15,869
Earnings bef. depr., int., tax (EBDIT)		$5,500	$6,875	$8,594	$10,742	$13,428
Depreciation (Dep)		$250	$300	$360	$432	$518
EBIT		$5,250	$6,575	$8,234	$10,310	$12,909
− Taxes @ 40%		$2,100	$2,630	$3,294	$4,124	$5,164
= EBIT $(1 - T)$		$3,150	$3,945	$4,940	$6,186	$7,745
+ Depreciation		$250	$300	$360	$432	$518
= Operating cash flow		$3,400	$4,245	$5,300	$6,618	$8,263
− Change net working capital		$1,340	$1,675	$2,094	$2,617	$3,271
− Capital expenditures		$2,000	$2,400	$2,880	$3,456	$4,147
− Change other assets		$0	$0	$0	$0	$0
= Free cash flow of assets		$60	$170	$326	$545	$845

Step 2: Discount Base-Case Cash Flows

Base-Case Value

	2000	2001	2002	2003	2004	2005
Free cash flow of assets		$60	$170	$326	$545	$845

130

	2000	2001	2002	2003	2004	2005
Terminal value of assets						$6,262
Discount factor @ 13.5%		0.88	0.78	0.68	0.60	0.53
Present value, each year		$53	$132	$223	$328	$3,774
Base-case value (total)	**$4,510**					

Step 3: Evaluate Financing Side Effects

Interest Tax Shields

	2000	2001	2002	2003	2004	2005
Interest tax shield		$40	$40	$40	$40	$40
Terminal value tax shields						$800
Discount factor @ 9.5%		0.91	0.83	0.76	0.70	0.64
Present value, each year		$37	$33	$30	$28	$534
PV Tax Shields	**$662**					

Step 4: Add the Components of Value to Get APV

	2000	2001	2002	2003	2004	2005
Base-case value	$4,510					
Side effect: tax shields	$662					
APV	**$5,172**					

TABLE 5-6 Portal.com APV analysis.

Managerial Information

Step 5: Customize Analysis to Suit Managers' Needs

Baseline Performance

	2000	2001	2002	2003	2004	2005
EBIT		$5,040	$6,312	$7,905	$9,898	$12,393
− Taxes @ 40%		$2,016	$2,525	$3,162	$3,959	$4,957
= EBIT $(1 - T)$		$3,024	$3,787	$4,743	$5,939	$7,436
+ Depreciation		$250	$300	$360	$432	$518
= Operating cash flow		$3,274	$4,087	$5,103	$6,371	$7,954
− Change Net Working Capital		($1,940)	($1,725)	($2,094)	($2,617)	($3,271)
− Capital expenditures		($2,000)	($2,400)	($2,880)	($3,456)	($4,147)
= Free cash flow, baseline		($666)	($38)	$129	$298	$536
Terminal value, baseline						$3,694
Discount factor @ 13.5%		0.88	0.78	0.68	0.60	0.53
Present value each year		**($587)**	**($29)**	**$88**	**$179**	**$2,245**
Baseline business value	**$1,897**					

Increments: Value-Creation Initiatives

	2000	2001	2002	2003	2004	2005
1. Margin improvement						
Incremental EBIT		$158	$197	$247	$309	$287

132

	Year 1	Year 2	Year 3	Year 4	Year 5	Value
– Taxes @ 40%	$63	$79	$99	$124	$115	
= Cash increment	$95	$118	$148	$186	$172	
Increment to terminal value					$1,189	
Present value, each year @ 13.5%	$83	$92	$101	$112	$722	
Value of margin improvement						**$1,111**
2. Net working capital improvement						
Incremental cash flow	$700	$75				
Present value, each year @ 13.5%	$617	$58				
Value of working capital improvement						**$675**
3. Asset sales						
Incremental cash flow	$375	$300	$175			
Present value, each year @ 13.5%	$330	$233	$120			
Value of asset sales						**$683**
4. Higher steady-state growth						
Incremental terminal value					$274	
Present value, each year @ 13.5%					$145	
Value of higher growth						**$145**
Sum of baseline and increments						**$4,511**
+ Value of interest tax shields						**$662**
= Adjusted present value						**$5,172**

FIGURE 5-9   APV is rich in information.

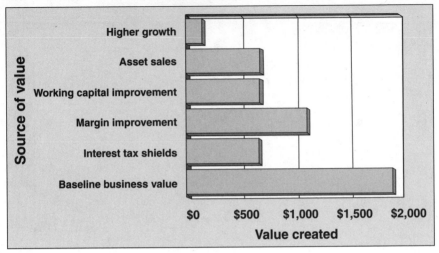

By virtue of the equality of the two sides of the balance sheet, the change in total capital equals the change in working capital plus the change in fixed assets. Thus, FCF is NOPAT less the additional investment required in working capital and fixed assets:[6]

Free Cash Flow = NOPAT − Δ Working Capital − Δ Fixed Assets

This is the classic and most widely used definition of FCF,[7] although several variations are observed in practice. Table 5-7 revisits Portal.com to illustrate the alternative methods for computing free cash flows, derived from its financial statements provided in Table 5-1. All the various methods will produce the same FCF of $60 if implemented properly.

---

[6] Total capital is simply the sum total of investor-contributed capital—that is, the sum of interest-bearing debt, preferred equity, and common equity. Since sources of funds must equal uses of funds, it is also equal to total assets less non-interest-bearing liabilities (NIBLs).

[7] Free cash flows from operations are the after-tax earnings available to service the financing claims—that is, before interest. To the extent that EBIT is calculated after depreciation, the latter must be added back. Because depreciation is a noncash charge which was subtracted from earnings to compute taxes due, it must be added back to EBIT to obtain a true cash flow figure:

Free Cash Flows = EBIT$(1 - T)$ + Depreciation
                          − Capital Expenditures − Working Capital Needs

TABLE 5-7   Cash flow computation alternative methods.

Free Cash Flow—Gross Basis	
Bottom-Up Approach:	
Net Income	3,090
+ Dep	250
= Cash flow from operations	3,340
+ After-tax interest $f(1 - T)$	60
= Cash operating income (gross)	**3,400**
− Gross investment	**3,340**
= Free cash flow	**60**
Top-down approach:	
EBDIT$(1 - T) + T$(Dep)	3,400
− Gross investment	3,340
= Free cash flow	**60**
Free Cash Flow—Net Basis	
Bottom-Up Approach:	
Net Income	3,090
+ After-tax interest	60
= Cash operating income $X(1 - T)$	3,150
− Investment	3,090
= Free cash flow	**60**
Top-Down Approach:	
EBIT$(1 - T)$	3,150
− Net investment	3,090
= Free cash flow	**60**
Free Cash Flow—Classic Method	
NOPAT	3,150
− Change in working capital	1,340
− Change in fixed asset	1,750
= Free cash flow	**60**

The gross basis and net basis FCFs differ only in their treatment of depreciation, both as an expense on the income statement and as an investment offset on the balance sheet. With the gross basis approach, fixed asset investments are subtracted from cash operating income on a gross basis—that is, before depreciation. Depreciation is added back to net income to arrive at cash operating income. Under the net basis approach, fixed asset investments are subtracted from cash operating income net of depreciation. There is no need to add depreciation back to net income under the net basis approach, since it has already been subtracted from gross investment.

FCF can be computed either from a "bottom-up" or "top-down" perspective for either approach, as illustrated in Table 5-7. Under the bottom-up approach for the gross basis, depreciation is added back to net income to arrive at cash flow from operations. After-tax interest is added back to cash flow from operations to obtain the total cash operating income available for asset investment and for distribution to all creditors and shareholders. Gross investment is subtracted from the cash operating income to arrive at free cash flow. Under the top-down approach, the after-tax earnings before depreciation and interest is simply added to the tax shield from depreciation to arrive at the cash operating income. Gross investment is then subtracted to arrive at free cash flow.

The lower panel of Table 5-7 shows the FCF calculations under the net basis approach with both the bottom-up and top-down perspectives. The calculations are identical to those under the gross basis approach except that net rather than gross investment is subtracted from cash operating income and there is no need to consider depreciation when computing cash operating income. The top-down net basis approach is labeled "Classic Method" in the lower panel, where free cash flow is defined as NOPAT less the additional investment required in working capital and fixed assets.

Table 5-8 shows other ways of computing FCF. Under the direct method, financing cash flows are added back to equity cash flows to obtain the FCFs available to all investors. Under the long method, FCFs are obtained by subtracting the various uses of cash from the various sources of cash, reminiscent of the cash flow statement found in most company annual reports.

In practice, particularly at the business unit level, the top-down net basis approach, labeled the "Classic Approach," is the most convenient and economical in terms of required information:

Free Cash Flow = EBIT$(1 - T)$ − ΔWorking Capital − Δ Fixed Assets

TABLE 5-8   Free cash flows estimation—direct, long, short-cut methods.

Estimating Free Cash Flows: Direct Method

Equity cash flows	0
Financing cash flows	
After-tax interest	60
− Debt issuance	0
Total financing	60
Free cash flows	**60**

Estimating Free Cash Flows: Long Method

NOPAT	3,150
+ Depreciation	250
+ Increases in interest-bearing debt	0
+ Increases in non-interest-bearing debt	1,010
= Sources of cash	4,410
Fixed capital investment	2,000
+ Increase in current assets	2,350
= Uses of cash	4,350
Free cash flow	**60**

Defining Free Cash Flows: Short Cut

NOPAT	3,150
− Total capital reinvestment	3,090
Free cash flow	**60**

Source: Approach adapted from J. M. McTaggart, P. W. Kontes, and M. C. Mankins, *The Value Imperative: Managing for Superior Shareholder Returns,* The Free Press, 1994.

Estimating Future Cash Flows of a Company

Estimating future cash flows is a critical step in calculating the value of a company. This is best done using a value driver approach, where cash flows are calculated from the underlying value drivers of the company. The three main drivers of cash flow are return, growth, and capital (Figure 1-2 in Chapter 1). This is simply common sense: A company that earns higher profits for each dollar invested will be worth more than one earning less. Similarly, a firm with higher growth on a larger capital base will create more value than one with lower capital growth if they both are earning the same return on their invested capital.

Tables 5-9 and 5-10 illustrate how to calculate cash flows from the underlying fundamental value drivers of a company. First, some definitions:

NOPAT	Net Operating Profits after Tax
Capital	Total capital invested in the company including operating working capital, net fixed assets, and other assets
Net investment	Incremental capital in each period that is invested in the company
Free cash flow	NOPAT − Net Investment
ROIC	Return on Invested Capital
	NOPAT/Invested Capital

In Table 5-9, Companies A and B have the same capital invested and cost of capital, but different ROIC, leading to different cash flows. Company A has the higher ROIC and thus the higher value.

TABLE 5-9   Cash flow calculation: Value driver approach.

EXAMPLE 1						
Company A		**Return on Invested Capital 22%**				
	Year 0	Year 1	Year 2	Year 3	Year 4	Year 5
NOPAT		220	231	243.1	256.3	270.6
Capital	1000	1050	1105	1165	1230	1300
Net investment		50	55	60	65	70
Free cash flow		170	176	183.1	191.3	200.6
Cost of capital	15%					
Discounted cash flow value		$610.41				
Company B		**Return on Invested Capital 17%**				
	Year 0	Year 1	Year 2	Year 3	Year 4	Year 5
NOPAT		170	178.5	187.85	198.05	209.1
Capital	1000	1050	1105	1165	1230	1300
Net investment		50	55	60	65	70
Free cash flow		120	123.5	127.85	133.05	139.1
Cost of capital	15%					
Discounted cash flow value		$427.02				

TABLE 5-10 Cash flow calculation: Value driver approach.

EXAMPLE 2

Company A		Return on Invested Capital		22%		
	Year 0	Year 1	Year 2	Year 3	Year 4	Year 5
NOPAT		220	235.4	247.5	260.7	275
Capital	1000	1070	1125	1185	1250	1320
Net investment		50	55	60	65	70
Free cash flow		170	180.4	187.5	195.7	205
Cost of capital	15%					
Discounted cash flow value		$621.33				

Company B		Return on Invested Capital		22%		
	Year 0	Year 1	Year 2	Year 3	Year 4	Year 5
NOPAT		220	231	243.1	256.3	270.6
Capital	1000	1050	1105	1165	1230	1300
Net investment		50	55	60	65	70
Free cash flow		170	176	183.1	191.3	200.6
Cost of capital	15%					
Discounted cash flow value		$610.41				

In Table 5-10, both A and B have the same ROIC, but A has more capital invested than B and thus has the higher value.

Strategic Grounding of Cash Flow Forecasts

Forecasting FCFs combines a historical analysis of the company (or business unit) financial statements and an extrapolation of the financial statements based on current strategy and value drivers. Regardless of the computational method used, long-range cash flow forecasts must be grounded in a solid economic and strategic analysis of the company. Valuation exercises are only as credible as the cash flow forecasts on which they rest. This is discussed further in Chapter 9.

We continue our discussion of DCF valuation methods in the next chapter, where we focus on DCF formula approaches and variations developed by consulting firms.

C H A P T E R

DCF VALUATION: FORMULA APPROACHES

I
N THIS CHAPTER, we examine the formula approach to valuation. The formula approach uses the same cash flow data as the spreadsheet approach, but its presentation is more compact. While the approaches yield the same valuation results, they each possess their own charms and weaknesses.

In the first section, formula approaches to valuation are presented and compared with spreadsheet approaches. Valuation approaches popularized by various consulting firms, including economic profit, are discussed in the second and third sections. The fourth section addresses the estimation of continuing value, common to all DCF valuation approaches. The fifth section points out some words of caution in applying DCF, and the last section discusses limitations of the DCF approach.

SPREADSHEET APPROACH TO VALUATION

The value of a company can be viewed as the sum of its as-is value and the value of its growth opportunities. The as-is value is the present value of the perpetual EBIT stream generated by existing assets. The value of future growth depends on the volume of the company's future investments, I, and the return on those investments, r, in excess of the cost of the capital invested, k. As shown in the appendix of this chapter, we can express the value of a company V as follows:

$$V = \frac{\text{EBIT}_1}{k} + \sum_{t=1}^{\infty} \frac{I_t(r_t - k)}{k(1 + k)^t}$$

As-Is value   Value of growth
                            opportunities

This expression is both revealing and powerful. Note that growth only contributes to value if the return earned by the company on its new investments exceeds the cost of capital—that is, if the company earns a positive
spread. Otherwise, the second term in the above equation is negative.

Although there are many valuation formulas, all are anchored on the idea
that the value of a company is the present value of free cash flows. The differences stem from assumptions on the particular pattern of free cash flows.
Table 6-1 shows four widely used valuation formulas, with Model 3,
"Temporary supernormal growth followed by no growth," the most popular.[1]

The numerical example in Table 6-2 contrasts the spreadsheet and formula approaches to valuation. The upper panel displays the spreadsheet

---

[1] This section draws heavily from J.F. Weston, J.A. Siu, B.A. Johnson, op. cit., Chapter 9.
Derivations of the formulas are available from the authors upon request.

TABLE 6-1   Company valuation—Free cash flow formulas.

Model 1, No Growth:

$$V = \frac{\text{NOPAT}_0}{k}$$

Model 2, Constant Growth:

$$V = \frac{\text{NOPAT}_0(1 - b)(1 + g)}{k - g}$$

Model 3, Temporary Supernormal Growth, Then No Growth:

$$V = \text{NOPAT}_0 (1 - b) \sum_{t=1}^{n} \frac{(1 + g_s)^t}{(1 + k)^t} + \frac{\text{NOPAT}_0(1 + g)^{n+1}}{k(1 + k)^n}$$

Model 4, Temporary Supernormal Growth, Then Constant Growth:

$$V = \text{NOPAT}_0 (1 - b) \sum_{t=1}^{n} \frac{(1 + g_s)^t}{(1 + k)^t} + \frac{\text{NOPAT}_0(1 - b)}{k - g} \times \frac{(1 + g)^{n+1}}{(1 + k)^n}$$

where NOPAT_0 = Initial after-tax earnings before interest and taxes (EBIT).

b = Rate of investment per period divided by NOPAT.

g = Growth in free cash flows. The subscript s refers to supernormal growth.

n = Number of periods of supernormal growth.

k = The company's weighted average cost of capital WACC.

TABLE 6-2   Spreadsheets vs. formula approaches: Portal.com.

	2000	2001	2002	2003	2004
Free Cash Flows					
1. Sales	$10,000	$12,500	$15,625	$19,531	$24,414
2. Total capital	$5,000	$6,250	$7,813	$9,766	$12,207
3. Operating costs	$5,500	$6,875	$8,594	$10,742	$13,428
4. Earnings before interest & tax (EBIT)	$4,500	$5,625	$7,031	$8,789	$10,986
5. Less taxes on EBIT	$1,800	$2,250	$2,813	$3,516	$4,395
6. NOPAT	$2,700	$3,375	$4,219	$5,273	$6,592
7. Less investments	$1,250	$1,563	$1,953	$2,441	
8. *Free cash flow*	$1,450	$1,813	$2,266	$2,832	$6,592
9. Terminal value*					$54,932
10. Total FCF		$1,813	$2,266	$2,832	$61,523
DCF at 12%	$44,539				

The terminal value is estimated using the perpetuity valuation model: TV = FCF(year 5)/WACC. This estimate assumes a WACC of 12%.

Formula Approach: Model 3 (Supergrowth followed by no growth)

EBIT initial	$4,500
Tax rate	40%
After-tax profits	$2,700
b	0.4630
r	54%
g	25%
n	3
k	12%
$(1 + g)/(1 + k)$	1.1161
Value first term	$5,440
Value second term	$39,099
Value	$44,539

approach and yields a value of $44,539. Inserting the data from the bottom panel of the table into Model 3 produces the same value. Each approach helps the manager focus on different elements of the valuation task: The spreadsheet method allows the manager flexibility in projecting cash flows; the formula approach helps focus attention on value drivers.

Table 6-3 shows a sensitivity analysis obtained by varying the principal drivers—namely, the return on investment, the cost of capital, the growth in free cash flows, the number of years of supernormal growth, the reinvestment rate (retention ratio), and the tax rate.

The sensitivity analysis indicates that when returns exceed the cost of funds, an increase in investment requirements or opportunities exerts a powerful influence on value. Case 1, the base case, has an initial value of $44,542. Case 2 doubles the scale of the profitable investment which causes growth to increase, and raises value by $9000. Case 3 increases profitability, which also causes growth to increase, for a combined effect on value of $6000. Subsequent cases show the impact of varying the cost of capital (k), the period of supernormal growth (n) and the tax rate (T), on

TABLE 6-3   Sensitivity analysis of varying the value drivers.

	k	b	r	g	n	T	Value
Initial case							
1	0.12	0.46	0.54	0.25	3	0.40	$44,542
Change *b, g, r*							
2	0.12	0.60	0.54	0.32	3	0.40	$53,783
3	0.12	0.60	0.60	0.36	3	0.40	$59,625
4	0.12	0.70	0.54	0.38	3	0.40	$61,476
Initial case, vary *k*							
5	0.11	0.46	0.54	0.25	3	0.40	$49,362
6	0.13	0.46	0.54	0.25	3	0.40	$40,485
Initial case, vary *n*							
7	0.12	0.46	0.54	0.25	2	0.40	$38,459
8	0.12	0.46	0.54	0.25	4	0.40	$51,331
Initial case, vary *T*							
9	0.12	0.46	0.54	0.25	3	0.35	$48,254
10	0.12	0.46	0.54	0.25	3	0.45	$40,830

value. Increases in the cost of capital and tax rate obviously reduce value. Increasing the period of supernormal growth, however, has the most dramatic impact on value, as one would expect.

SPREADSHEET VERSUS FORMULA APPROACHES

The spreadsheet and formula approaches tend to complement one another, but each has its distinct advantages. The spreadsheet approach is familiar to managers because of its similarity to financial statements. It can also serve as a powerful tool for educating managers in the concepts of value creation. Because it is easy to perform sensitivity analysis with personal computer spreadsheet software, a large number of variables that may impact the value of a company may be examined. Managers can gain a rich understanding of the dynamics of their business and the behavior of the key value drivers. As managers gain a better, more rigorous understanding of the operation of their business and its impact on value, they will also be able to better communicate the results to other managers and the investment community.

The disadvantage of spreadsheets is that they tend to lull managers into a false sense of security with their appearance of precise projections. Projections are subject to forecasting error and are not always consistent with the business framework from which they were determined. Spreadsheets can become too complex very quickly, obscuring the true underlying economic and strategic forces.

Formula approaches can also improve a manager's insight into the critical factors that affect value. Formulas can easily become cumbersome, however, particularly if a large number of variables and interactions are considered. In addition, restrictive assumptions are often necessary to keep a formula tractable.

The choice between spreadsheet valuation and formula valuation essentially involves a trade-off between insights and complexity, and as usual, some combination of the two is best. Spreadsheets are often used to analyze data patterns that facilitate the use of formulas, and formulas are often used to determine the continuing value of a company needed to complete the spreadsheet valuation. The formula and spreadsheet approaches also provide mutual checks on the reasonableness of the procedures and accuracy of the valuations. For example, to test whether the increased complexity of the spreadsheet approach has a significant impact on valuation, you could break the problem down into a small number of critical value drivers, value each with the appropriate formula, sum the values, and compare the sum with the spreadsheet valuation.

VALUATION MODELS: ENTER THE CONSULTANTS

The intellectual foundation of all DCF valuation models is the classic 1961 work of Nobel laureates Modigliani and Miller. They demonstrated that the same basic valuation model could be developed using (1) current earnings plus future investment opportunities, (2) stream of dividends, (3) stream of earnings, or (4) stream of free cash flows. Modigliani and Miller's classic valuation model is equivalent to the free cash flow model of temporary supergrowth followed by no growth in Table 6-1 (derivation available from authors upon request).

Leading consulting firms and practitioners in valuation methodology employ variations of the basic valuation expressions in Table 6-1, although they sometimes use different notation and symbols. Three noteworthy examples are discussed in the following sections.

From Theory to Practice: The McKinsey Valuation Approach

The McKinsey valuation model is a simplified version of the classic M&M equation:

$$\text{Value} = \text{As-Is Value} + \text{Present Value of Growth Opportunities}$$

$$= \frac{\text{Current After-Tax Profits}}{\text{Cost of Capital}} + \frac{(\text{Return} - \text{Cost of Capital})}{\text{Cost of Capital}}$$
$$\times \text{\$Invested} \times T$$

$$V = \frac{\text{NOPAT}}{k} + \frac{(r - k)}{k} \times I \times T$$

where the symbols are as before except that T is now the number of years the company can earn returns above the cost of capital. This approach spotlights the critical role of the spread $(r - k)$, and how it determines the degree to which value is increased beyond that of a zero-growth company. Notice that when a company earns a return equal to its cost of capital, the second term evaporates. We are left with the as-is value of a zero-growth company.

In this approach, the first source of value is current business operations. To value current business operations, the expected level of NOPAT is capitalized at a cost of capital that reflects the risk inherent in prospective operating cash flows. The value of existing assets, then, is simply a perpetuity of the anticipated free cash flows.

The second term captures the value of future investment growth opportunities. Investors will capitalize into today's stock price the ability of management to invest funds (I) over a limited period of years (T), in projects whose anticipated returns (r) exceed the rate of return available to investors from comparable risk ventures (k). The simplified M&M variation again provides rich insights into the factors that drive economic value—namely the spread, scale, and interval of competitive advantage.

From Theory to Practice: The Stern-Stewart Approach

The Stern-Stewart approach is analogous to the free cash flow valuation model for temporary supernormal growth followed by no growth. It compresses the model into two multipliers or "interest factors" as follows:

Value = Value of Supernormal Growth Period

+ Value at End of Growth Period

= FCF_1 (Interest Factor 1) + $NOPAT_1$ (Interest Factor 2)

$NOPAT_1$ is the net operating profit after tax forecast for the coming year, and FCF_1 is what is left of NOPAT after reinvestment. Interest Factors 1 and 2 are as follows:

$$\text{Interest Factor 1} = \frac{\text{FVIFA}(h\ \%,\ n\ \text{years})}{1 + k}$$

$$\text{Interest Factor 2} = \frac{\text{FVIF}(h\ \%,\ n\ \text{years})}{k}$$

where FVIFA is the future value interest factor of an annuity, and FVIF is the future value interest factor for a single cash flow.

From Theory to Practice: The Rappaport Valuation Approach

Alfred Rappaport pioneered the use of financial valuation models and strategic planning to improve shareholder returns and is largely responsible for the shareholder value movement as we know it today. In his approach, value is the present value of cash flows, but cash flows are defined as after-tax operating profit less required investment:

$$\text{Cash Flow} = S_{t-1}(1 + g)\ m\ (1 - T) - S_{t-1}\ g\ (w + f)$$

where S_{t-1} = Sales in the prior year
g = Growth rate in sales
m = Profit margin
T = Tax rate
w = Working capital requirement
f = Fixed asset investment as a percentage of sales.

This cash flow expression embodies all the key inputs required to employ the basic valuation model for temporary supernormal growth followed by no growth:[2]

Last year's sales	$100 million
Sales growth	10.5%
Operating profit margin	8.0%
Incremental fixed asset investment as a % of sales	24.0%
Incremental working capital investment as a % of sales	18.9%
Cash income tax rate	35.0%
Cost of capital	10.0%

It is relatively straightforward to insert the Rappaport numbers into Model 3 in Table 6-1. With a profit margin of 8% on sales of $100 million, net operating profit is $8, and NOPAT is $5.2 (with a tax rate of 35%). Growth g is 10.5% for $n = 5$ years and the cost of capital k is 10%. The only variable that appears to be missing, the investment rate b, can be estimated using variables from Rappaport's approach.[3] In this example, b is 0.7839 and $(1 - b)$ is 0.2161. Substituting these quantities into the classic valuation formula, we obtain a company value of $58 million, the same answer as Rappaport obtains before adding marketable securities and deducting the market value of debt.

This valuation approach has the appeal of simplicity and familiarity to managers because free cash flows are defined by familiar accounting quantities such as profit margin and working capital requirements. Profit margin, however, is not always an appropriate benchmark for comparing economic profitability among companies in different industries with different capital intensities. An aircraft manufacturer like Boeing clearly has a lower turnover and higher profit margin per unit than a supermarket company like Kroger.

---

[2] Rappaport, *Creating Shareholder Value* (1999), p. 48.

[3] $I_t = (w + f)(S_t - S_{t-1}) = (w + f)[S_{t-1}(1 + g) - S_{t-1}] = (w + f)gS_{t-1} = (w + f)gS_t/(1 + g)$; but $NOPAT_t = m(1 - T)S_t$, so that $S_t = NOPAT_t/m(1 - T)$

So, $I_t = (w + f)g\, NOPAT_t/m(1 - T)(1 + g)$

And the reinvestment rate b becomes:

$$b = I_t/NOPAT_t = (w + f)g/m(1 - T)(1 + g)$$

ECONOMIC PROFIT APPROACH TO VALUATION

Economic profit is the difference between a company's actual earnings and what it would have earned if its profitability (R) had just covered its required rate of return, or cost of capital, k or WACC:

$$\text{Economic Profit} = \text{Invested Capital} \times (R - k)$$

Consider a company with $1000 of invested capital whose investors require a 12% rate of return. This corresponds to earnings of $120. If this company actually earned 20%, or $200, its economic profits would be $80:

$$\text{Economic Profit} = \$1000 \times (20\% - 12\%) = \$200 - \$120 = \$80$$

The difference between the company's return and its cost of capital is called its *abnormal return,* in our example 8%. Economic profits of $80 are abnormal earnings.

There is another way to look at economic profit. Going back to the above definition of economic profit, the product of invested capital and return R is simply NOPAT, while the product of invested capital and the cost of capital k is simply a dollar capital charge:

$$
\begin{aligned}
\text{Economic Profit} &= \text{Invested Capital} \times (R - k) \\
&= \text{Invested Capital} \times R - \text{Invested Capital} \times k \\
&= \text{NOPAT} - \text{Capital charge}
\end{aligned}
$$

Of course, this alternative calculation yields the same value for economic profit:

$$
\begin{aligned}
\text{Economic Profit} &= \text{NOPAT} - \text{Capital charge} \\
&= \$1000 \times 20\% - \$1000 \times 12\% \\
&= \$200 - \$120 = \$80
\end{aligned}
$$

The company earns $80 per year more than investors require to part with their funds.

Economic profit, which actually goes all the way back to the nineteenth-century economist Alfred Marshall, provides a simple VBM perspective to the evaluation of business performance that takes into account profits, cost of capital, and capital employed, all at once. The concept is that every business employs capital in the form of plant, inventory, working capital, and other assets. Further, companies incur a cost to use this capital. When a company earns a return on its capital investments that is greater than its cost of capital—that is, when the company experiences a positive spread—economic profit is improved by investing more capital.

In the case of a negative spread, more capital actually decreases economic profit. This is a crucial concept in value creation and distinguishes good growth from bad.

The economic profit approach to valuation states that a company's value equals the sum of its original invested capital C_o plus the present value of its economic profits, PV(EP):

$$V = C_o + \text{PV(EP)}$$

This makes intuitive sense. Market value should be high when a company earns an abnormal profit. If a company earns only its WACC each period, then EP = 0, and its value merely equals its invested capital. A company's value can diverge from its invested capital only if its return on capital diverges from its cost—that is, if EP differs from zero.

We can think of the company as a capital budgeting project. The initial invested capital represents the initial cash investment and measures only the project's scale, without regard to profitability. The present value of economic profit represent the project's net present value (NPV), which depends on both profitability and scale. Going back to the above numerical example, the company's economic profit is $80 each year. Under the economic profit approach, the company's value is given by:

Value = Invested capital + Present Value of Projected Economic Profit
  V = $1000 + PV(EP)
    = $1000 + $80/0.12
    = $1000 + $667 = $1667

We obtain the same answer by discounting the company's free cash flow. Operating profit equals free cash flow in the absence of growth. The present value of a perpetual free cash flow of $200 is simply $200/0.12 = $1,667.

Two other versions of the economic profit valuation approach are Stern Stewart & Co.'s economic value added (EVA) and market value added (MVA) models, discussed in detail in Chapter 12.

ESTIMATING CONTINUING VALUE

Regardless of the valuation approach employed, an estimate of continuing value is required. In the Portal.com example in Table 5-2, the forecasts extend to the year 2005, the "terminal year." Since the value of the company depends on cash flows over the remainder of Portal.com's life, the analyst must adopt some simplifying assumption about the cash flows beyond the year 2005. There are three prevalent methods for estimating the continuing value of the company: perpetuity, constant growth, and multiples.

Continuing Value: Perpetuity Method

The most common method and the one that stands on firm economic grounds is the *perpetuity method*. The method assumes that the cash flow in the terminal year will continue at a constant rate forever. The continuing value is then the present value of a perpetuity beginning at the terminal year.[4]

The perpetuity method is based on the simple economic proposition that there is no free lunch, at least not for any extended period of time. Any company that is able to generate returns greater than the minimum return required by investors (cost of capital) will eventually attract competitors. When competitors move in, the returns of the company are ultimately driven down (as a result of price cutting, for example) to the cost of capital. In final equilibrium, there are no excess returns.

In the face of competition, it is increasingly difficult for a company to extend its supernormal profitability to new projects year after year. Empirical research shows that company ROEs generally revert to normal levels within 5 to 10 years in a competitive environment. Therefore, it is reasonable to treat cash flows beyond that period as if they were a perpetuity.

Returning to Portal.com (Table 5-2), if we assume that the company reaches competitive equilibrium in the year 2005, we can greatly simplify the calculations. By treating sales as if they will remain constant at the 2005 level, we arrive at an estimate for free cash flows of $845 per year.[5] Using a discount rate of 12%, the present value in 2005 of the cash flows for the years beyond 2005 is thus equal to:

Present Value of Cash Flows beyond 2005 $= \$845/0.12 = \$7044$

---

[4] The present value of a perpetuity is simply the value of the expected annual cash flow stream divided by the rate of return:

$$\text{PV of a Perpetuity} = \frac{\text{Annual Cash Flow}}{\text{Rate of Return}}$$

For example, the present value of a $100 perpetuity at 10% is $100/0.10 = $1000.

[5] Note that the perpetuity calculation is based on operating profit (profit before deducting the cost of investments required to expand capacity) rather than on free cash flow. This is because we do not need to take into account the additional investments in fixed and working capital during the post-forecast period. Although these investments may help increase the future cash inflows, as long as they are earning only the cost of capital rate of return, any increase in cash inflows will be exactly offset by the investment cash outflows required to grow the business. In the perpetuity method, it is assumed that the cost of maintaining existing capacity equals the depreciation expense, which has been deducted to arrive at operating profit before tax.

The value as of the end of 2000 would be obtained by discounting $7044 million for five years to the present:

Present Value of Continuing Value $= \$7044/(1 + 0.12)^5 = \$4000$ million

The amount $4000 million is the so-called *terminal value*, or *continuing value*, of the firm.

$$\frac{\text{Continuing}}{\text{Value}} = \frac{\text{Perpetual Operating Profit after Tax}}{K} \times \frac{\text{Discount}}{\text{Factor}}$$

Continuing Value: Constant Growth Method

This variation of the perpetuity method assumes that the cash flows will grow (or decay) at the rate g forever. The approach is more aggressive but may also be more realistic. This method, typically referred to as the "Gordon Model," estimates terminal value as:

$$\text{Terminal Value} = \frac{\text{FCF}_{2006}}{k - g}$$

The FCF for 2006 is the FCF for 2005 compounded for one period at g:

$$\text{Terminal Value} = \frac{\text{FCF}_{2005} (1 + g)}{k - g}$$

This give us the present value as of the end of 2005. If we assume a growth rate of 3.5% and discount rate of 12%, the present or continuing value in 2000 is equal to $5843, which is about $1800 million higher than our terminal value estimate based on the assumption of no growth in abnormal profitability. Higher later growth rates can be justified by assuming more aggressive marketing efforts. A growth rate less than inflation implies that the business is contracting in real terms.

There are circumstances under which a company can certainly maintain a competitive advantage that permits it to achieve returns in excess of the cost of capital for a certain period of time. When that advantage is protected with entry barriers, such as patents or a strong brand name, the company may be able to maintain it for many years. If a manager believes that supernormal profits can be extended to larger markets for many years and the competitive equilibrium postponed, then a longer time horizon should be used for forecasting growing cash flows. With hindsight, we know that companies such as Dell Computer, Microsoft, Coca-Cola, and Wal-Mart have been able not only to maintain their competitive edge but to expand it across increasing investment bases.

The DCF approaches to estimating terminal value and their rationale are summarized in Table 6-4.

There are limitations to the constant growth approach. First, it may not fully recognize the cash outflows that are likely to be required for continued growth. Second, it ignores capital structure. The growing cash flows can often lead to severe changes in capital structure (e.g., high debt/equity ratios) that are either undesirable or economically unrealistic. Third, there is no assumption about the economic return on the investment required for the growth. Thus, the net present value of the growth in perpetuity can yield a value less than, equal to, or greater than that of the perpetuity method (where the economic assumption of growth yielding NPV = 0 is invoked). Finally, as the perpetuity growth rates approach the long-term cost of capital, the residual value will explode and rise toward infinity because the denominator in the formula goes toward zero. This is unrealistic.

TABLE 6-4   DCF approaches to estimating terminal value.

$g = 0$	In a perfectly competitive market, in the long term, companies earn their cost of capital, resulting in zero economic profit and, hence, zero cash flow growth rate.
$g =$ industry average	Zero growth rates may be too conservative in the cases of some industries. In that case, it is reasonable to assume that companies' cash flow will grow at the average industry rate.
$g =$ Forecasted long-term inflation growth rate	Usually, both revenues and costs are equally affected by inflation, and hence, inflation has no or little effect on a firm's growth rate. In some cases, especially in certain consumer industries, inflation affects the revenues more than the costs. In this case, the forecasted perpetual inflation growth rate is a good proxy for the firm's revenue growth rate and consequently its cash flow growth rate.
$g =$ Forecasted long-term GDP growth rate	It is reasonable that in the long term, the growth rate of companies will fade to that of the growth rate of the overall economy. If a company grows at a sustained rate higher than that of the economy, eventually it will become larger than the economy itself, which, of course, is not possible.

Continuing Value: Multiples Method

The third method of estimating continuing value involves estimating a market value for the equity of the business using a projected multiple, such as the market-to-book (M/B) or price/earnings (P/E) ratio. Since multiples are discussed extensively in the next chapter, we provide only an overview here.

As a starting point, the analyst examines the recent M/B and P/E ratios for the company in question and companies that are comparable in terms of such variables as size, industry, and risk. Next, the future value of the equity is determined by multiplying the projected (book) common equity by the M/B ratio or the projected earnings by the P/E ratio. The value of the debt is added to the projected value of the common equity to arrive at the projected total value of the company, which must then be discounted to the present at the company's cost of capital.

The advantage of using the multiples method is that it focuses managers on the longer term prospects of the business strategy. The multiples projections must be made on the basis of a careful analysis of long-term trends in technology, competition, customer needs and other relevant factors. Chapter 7 demonstrates the linkages between the multiples and growth, profitability, and value creation.

This is particularly important for relatively new businesses that can be expected to continue to grow in periods well beyond the limited planning horizon, such as in embryonic industries like computer technology and telecommunications. A conservative perpetuity assumption would make little sense for these kinds of businesses. The perpetuity assumption would, of course, also be inappropriate for businesses heading for a decline, since their returns are almost certain to dip below the firm's cost of capital.

Selecting the Terminal Year

How long should the forecast horizon be? We used five years in the Portal.com example. Why not 7, 10, or 20 years? When the competitive equilibrium assumption is used, the proper answer is whatever time is required for the firm's returns on incremental investment projects to reach that equilibrium—an issue that turns on the sustainability of the firm's competitive advantage. The historical evidence indicates that most firms in the United States should expect ROEs to revert to average levels within 5 to 10 years. Exceptions include companies that are so well insulated from competition (perhaps because of a patent or the power of a brand name) that they can extend their investment base across new markets for many years and still expect to generate supernormal returns.[6]

PRACTICAL ISSUES IN VALUATION
Apples and Oranges
In implementing any DCF-based valuation methodology, it is important to properly match cash flows and discount rates. While the FCF and FTE approaches use different definitions of cash flow and discount rates, they yield consistent estimates as long as the same assumptions are made. The bias from discounting company cash flows at the cost of equity or equity cash flows at the WACC is demonstrated in Table 6-5. The effects of using the wrong discount rate are clearly visible in the last two calculations. When WACC is mistakenly used to discount the flows-to-equity, the positive bias in the value of equity is $1597. When free cash flows are discounted at the cost of equity, the value of the company is understated by $1743.

The Double-Counting Fallacy
Since the free cash flow valuation approach requires the cash flows available to all providers of capital, the cash flow from operations should be expressed on a pre-interest but post-tax basis. That is, interest expense on debt should not be deducted in arriving at free cash flow, and amounts deducted for taxes should reflect what tax payments would be due if the firm had no interest deduction. Intuitively, it might seem reasonable that the cash flows to the firm should reflect the tax benefits from interest expenses. However, this tax benefit is already reflected in the weighted average cost of capital through the use of after-tax cost of debt and will be double-counted if it is also in the cash flows. To net out interest expense under the FCF approach would be double-counting the effects of debt.

Inflation: Apples and Oranges Again
In the presence of inflation, the analysis must either explicitly adjust for inflation or treat all variables in real terms. The discount rate is already a nominal rate because investors consider expected inflation rates when setting required rates of return. Investors recognize that inflation erodes purchasing power, and they demand an inflation premium in addition to the

---

[6] Note that the return on incremental investment can be normal even while the return on total investment (and therefore ROE) remains abnormal.

TABLE 6-5   Valuation approaches.

Free cash flow vs. flows-to-equity

	FCF	FTE
EBIT	$2,103	$2,103
Interest		($175)
Income before tax	$2,103	$1,928
Tax (34%)	$715	$656
Net income	$1,388	$1,272
Add back depreciation	$500	$500
Less investments	($500)	($500)
Cash flow	$1,388	$1,272
Present value	$10,850	$8,350
Discount rate	12.79%	15.24%
Value of the firm (V)	$10,850	
Value of the debt (D)	$2,500	
Value of equity (E)	$8,350	$8,350
Value with wrong k	$6,607	$9,947

real return in order to be compensated for time, risk, and the erosion of purchasing power.

Inflation can be incorporated by expressing all cash flows in nominal terms and then by using the nominal cost of capital, k_n:

$$V = \sum_{t=1}^{n} \frac{\text{Nominal Cash Flows}_t}{(1 + k_n)^t}$$

The expected inflation is incorporated into cash flows and discount rates at the time of the analysis, and value is estimated on that basis. Nominal cash flows incorporate expected inflation. The process of estimating nominal cash flows requires the analyst to make estimates not only of expected inflation in the general price level but also of expected price increases in the specific goods and services that the firm either sells or uses. Thus, an analyst making nominal cash flow predictions for Delta Airlines would have to predict price increases in airline tickets to obtain revenues and the inflation rate in the price of oil to estimate costs.

We get the same valuation result if we express all cash flows in real terms and then discount by using the real cost of capital. The relationship between nominal and real cash flows is determined by expected inflation:

$$\text{Real Cash Flow}_t = \frac{\text{Nominal Cash Flow}_t}{(1 + \Pi)^t}$$

where Π = Expected inflation rate in the general price level

The effects of inflation on real cash flows will largely depend on the difference between the inflation in the prices of the goods and that in the cost of the resources that the company uses. If a company can increase prices on goods it sells at a rate faster than the rate at which its costs go up, real cash flows will increase with inflation. If not, the real cash flows will go down.

The relationship between nominal and real discount rates also depends on the expected inflation rate:

$$\text{Real Discount Rate}_t = \frac{\text{Nominal Discount Rate}_t}{(1 + \Pi)^t}$$

When the expected inflation rate is low, the difference between the nominal discount rate and expected inflation can be used as an approximation for the real discount rate.

Consistency is the important consideration. Real cash flows should be discounted at the real discount rate and nominal cash flows should be discounted at the nominal discount rate.

In practice, it is preferable to express cash flows in nominal dollars—that is, to include inflation effects in the cash flow estimates and then to discount by the nominal cost of capital. This is because it allows various cash flow components (labor costs, materials, expenses, and so on) to be adjusted at differing inflation rates.

Although no explicit inflationary component appears in the perpetuity method formula, this approach does not ignore inflation. Instead, it implicitly assumes that on a present-value basis, any inflationary increases in profits are offset by an inflationary increase in investments required to generate those profits. That is, the net present value of the inflationary effects is zero.

"Normalizing" the Operating Profit
If the operating profit in any year is abnormally high or low, it will yield misleading results when used as a basis for the perpetuity calculation. This problem occurs most frequently with companies in cyclical industries,

where the calculated residual value will be abnormally high in boom years and abnormally low in bust years. Normalizing or smoothing the operating profit can compensate for this effect.

Cross-Border Investments

When valuing cash flows originating in a foreign country and denominated in a foreign currency, the manager can pursue two different approaches: (1) discount the foreign currency cash flows at the foreign discount rate, then convert to dollars, or (2) convert the foreign currency cash flows to dollars and discount at a U.S. discount rate. In theory, the two approaches should yield the same estimate of value in the home currency.

FIGURE 6-1   Comparison of two valuation approaches for cross-broader investments.

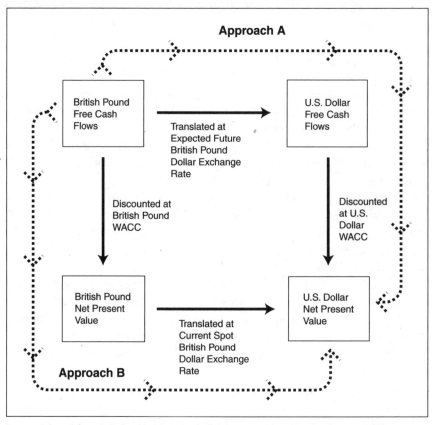

Source: Adapted from R.E. Bruner, *Case Studies in Finance: Managing for Corporate Value Creation, Instructor's Resource Manual,* 3d edition, Irwin, McGraw-Hill, 1999, pp. 736–750.

Figure 6-1 shows the steps involved in deriving the dollar NPV from British pound cash flows and the two alternative valuation approaches. In the first approach, the manager converts the British pound flows to dollars, using the forecast of the forward pound/$ exchange rate implied in currency exchange markets and/or interest rate parity conditions. The dollar cash flows are discounted using a dollar WACC. The end result is a DCF value denominated in U.S. dollars. The dollar WACC estimate must reflect both the systematic risk (beta) of the company's industry and the foreign equity market risk and political risk. A reasonable procedure is to price the business risk from the capital asset pricing model (CAPM), covered in Chapter 11, and the cost of debt for comparable U.S. companies. The political risk can be estimated from the difference between the yields of U.S. Treasury bonds and foreign currency government bonds of similar maturities.

In the second approach, the manager discounts British pound cash flows using a British pound WACC, and then converts the British pound into a dollar DCF using the spot exchange rate. This poses the challenge of adjusting for country risk. We have more to say on this in Chapter 11.

As a practical matter, most U.S. managers prefer the first method, which uses the more reliable U.S. discount rates. Local risk-free rates in emerging foreign markets are poor indicators of inflation expectations and thus are of doubtful value when managed by central banks. Second, the market risk premium required for estimating the proper discount rate is very difficult to estimate because of the generally short trading histories in these countries. Third, there are often no pure-play companies whose shares are traded and offer the basis for risk estimates.

Whichever approach is selected, you should strive for consistency between the currency of cash flows and the WACC. British pound cash flows should be discounted using a British pound WACC, and U.S. dollar cash flows should be discounted using a U.S. WACC.

APPLICABILITY OF DCF

DCF valuation is based upon expected future cash flows and discount rates. Given these informational requirements, this approach is easiest to use for assets (companies) whose cash flows are currently positive and can be estimated with some reliability for future periods, and where a proxy for risk is readily available.

The further we get from this idealized setting, the more difficult DCF becomes. For companies that are expected to fail or for distressed companies that are expected to lose money for some time in the future (e.g.,

Internet stocks), estimating future cash flows is difficult, and DCF valuation does not work very well. In the case of cyclical companies, whose cash flows rise during economic booms and fall during recessions, expected future cash flows must be smoothed out unless the analyst is able to predict the timing and duration of economic recessions and recoveries. For companies involved in mergers and acquisitions, there is the difficult task of incorporating the effects of synergy into the estimates of future cash flows and the effect of changing management on cash flows and risk.

For companies experiencing major changes in investment and financing policy, such as changes in ownership structure (leveraged buyouts, spinoffs), asset structure, capital structure, and dividend policy, future cash flow estimates must reflect the effects of these changes. The discount rate must be adjusted to reflect the new business and financial risk in the company as well. This is discussed further in Chapter 11.

To value private companies or corporate divisions, we must rely on comparable publicly traded companies for estimates of discount rates, and errors from poor or unavailable comparables bias our estimates of value.

DCF values depend heavily on several key assumptions. If the underlying assumptions are incorrect, DCF models give a distorted picture. For this reason, valuation professionals rarely work with a single estimate of company value. They typically bound the range of possible outcomes through extensive sensitivity analysis.

In most DCF valuations, it is not unusual for the terminal value to represent a large fraction of the total discounted cash flows. For example, in our valuation example of Table 6-2, the terminal value represents 75% of the total value. Since the terminal value estimate is hinged on the long-run cash flow forecasts, the latter become key to a good valuation.

The final valuation estimate is sensitive to the choice of the terminal growth rate. Because the perpetual growth model assumes constant growth forever, it is unreasonable to assume a very aggressive rate, particularly given the bounds represented by competitive forces. One could reasonably assume that a company will be able to maintain the growth in cash flows at least at the rate of inflation, the rate of population growth, or the growth in real GNP. One method of dealing with the discomfort of specifying growth rates is to determine that rate at which the NPV just equals zero or that rate at which the valuation reproduces the current stock price, then consider the reasonableness of that rate. This can easily be done using a spreadsheet "back solver" function, or by trial and error.

"It Doesn't Need Positive NPV—It's Strategic"

One fundamental problem with NPV analysis is that it assumes that managers take a passive approach to managing. NPV fails to recognize that there are many decision points in a real investment project where the option exists to go forward or abort. These "managerial flexibilities," or options, have significant value that NPV ignores. These issues are discussed in Chapter 8.

CONCLUSION

Managers face three basic types of valuation problems: operations, strategic opportunities, and ownership claims. Operations problems involve assets already in place—say, an ongoing business, a new equipment purchase, or an existing product. Such investments are best valued with APV. Opportunities are essentially possible future operations, such as R&D investments, marketing expenditures, or new technology platforms. These are best valued with real options in Chapter 8. The third category—ownership claims—involves claims that companies issue against the value of their operations and opportunities, including joint ventures, partnerships, strategic alliances, or project financing. Such interests are best valued with the flows-to-equity method.

We close this chapter by noting that the right valuation tool for each and every business circumstance is available for the manager to use to create value for his or her company.

Formula Approaches to Valuation

ONSIDER A COMPANY WITH NO DEBT that generates an annual cash flow equal to net operating income (EBIT), less any new working capital and plant & equipment expenditures (I). Assume the corporate tax rate is zero. The annual cash flow stream generated by the company is therefore given by the difference between EBIT and capital expenditures, I, as shown on Table 6-6.

The EBIT in any given year is equal to last year's EBIT plus the dollar return on new capital invested, the latter being given by the percentage return on new capital invested times the amount of new capital. (For a fuller discussion of issues raised in the appendix, see Weston and Copeland.) For example, the free cash flow in the second year, $EBIT_2$ is given by $EBIT_1 + r_1 I_1$. Table 6-7 shows the resulting cash flow pattern over time.

The free cash flow in a given year n is therefore equal to the first year's $EBIT_1$ plus the cumulative returns from all the prior years' capital investments:

$$EBIT_n = EBIT_1 + \sum_{t=1}^{n-1} r_t I_t \qquad (1)$$

The value of the company is then simply the present value of the annual free cash flows shown in Table 6-6, discounted at the cost of common equity capital k:

$$V = \sum_{t=1}^{n} \frac{\text{Free Cash Flows}_t}{(1 + k)^t}$$

$$V = \frac{\text{EBIT}_1 - I_1}{(1 + k)^1} + \frac{\text{EBIT}_1 + r_1 I_1 - I_2}{(1 + k)^2} + \frac{\text{EBIT}_1 + r_1 I_1 + r_2 I_2 - I_3}{(1 + k)^3}$$
$$+ \cdots + \frac{\text{EBIT}_1 + \Sigma\, r_t I_t - I_n}{(1 + k)^n} \tag{2}$$

After some routine, although tedious, algebraic simplifications of the above equation, we can obtain the following expression for the present value of the company V:

$$V = \frac{\text{EBIT}_1}{k} + \sum_{t=1}^{\infty} \frac{I_t(r_t - k)}{k(1 + k)^t} \tag{3}$$

or

Value = Value of Assets in Place + Value of Future Growth Opportunities

Constant Growth Valuation Formula

Although valuation formulas come in many shapes, colors, and sizes, they all emanate from the idea that the value of a company is the present value of free cash flows. The different flavors stem from the particular pattern of free cash flows assumed over time. One popular variation is to assume that the amount of net new investment, I, is a constant proportion b of free cash flows each year:

$$I_t = b\,(\text{EBIT}_t) \tag{4}$$

TABLE 6-6   Free cash flows.

Year	Cash Inflow	Cash Outflow	Free Cash Flow
1	EBIT_1	I_1	$\text{EBIT}_1 - I_1$
2	EBIT_2	I_2	$\text{EBIT}_2 - I_2$
3	EBIT_3	I_3	$\text{EBIT}_3 - I_3$
4	EBIT_4	I_4	$\text{EBIT}_4 - I_4$
5	EBIT_5	I_5	$\text{EBIT}_5 - I_5$
6	EBIT_6	I_6	$\text{EBIT}_6 - I_6$
$\vdots$	$\vdots$	$\vdots$	$\vdots$
n	EBIT_n	I_n	$\text{EBIT}_n - I_7$

TABLE 6-7   Free cash flows.

Year	Inflow	Outflow	Free Cash Flow
1	$EBIT_1$	I_1	$EBIT_1 - I_1$
2	$EBIT_1 + r_1 I_1$	I_2	$EBIT_1 + r_1 I_1 - I_2$
3	$EBIT_1 + r_1 I_1 + r_2 I_2$	I_3	$EBIT_1 + r_1 I_1 + r_2 I_2 - I_3$
$\vdots$	$\vdots$	$\vdots$	$\vdots$

It follows that the free cash flow in any given year is

$$\begin{aligned} EBIT_t &= EBIT_{t-1} + rI_{t-1} \\ &= EBIT_{t-1} + rbEBIT_{t-1} \\ &= EBIT_{t-1}(1 + rb) \end{aligned} \tag{5}$$

Financial analysts frequently refer to b as the retention rate, for it measures the proportion of cash flows retained in the company for further investments. Note also that the product of the return on these investments r and the retention rate b equals the growth rate of free cash flows, g, so that $g = rb$, and:

$$EBIT_t = EBIT_{t-1}(1 + g) \tag{6}$$

We can substitute Equation 6 into Equation 2 and obtain a simple equation for the value of a company that grows forever at a constant rate g:

$$V = \frac{EBIT_1(1 - b)}{k - g} \tag{7}$$

We can easily extend this expression to a world with taxes and to companies that use debt financing in their capital structures by using EBIT after taxes and using WACC instead of the cost of equity:

$$V = \frac{EBIT_1 (1 - T)(1 - b)}{WACC - g} = \frac{NOPAT(1 - b)}{WACC - g} \tag{8}$$

This valuation expression is widely used and is known as the *constant growth* model of a company. It is frequently used to calculate the terminal value of the company in spreadsheet models.

VALUATION MODELS: THE GENESIS

Modigliani and Miller's classic valuation model, from which all other valuation approaches derive, is equivalent to the free cash flow model of temporary supergrowth followed by no growth, and it gives the same result. By assuming that a company's special investment opportunities are available over some finite time period of n years, they arrived at the following valuation model:

$$V = \frac{\text{NOPAT}_0 \, (1 + g)}{k} \left\{ 1 + \frac{b(r - k)}{g - k} \left[\frac{(1 + g_s)^n}{(1 + k)^n} - 1 \right] \right\}$$

where NOPAT_0 = Initial after-tax earnings before interest and taxes (EBIT)

b = Rate of investment per period divided by NOPAT

g = Growth in free cash flows. The subscript s refers to supernormal growth.

n = Number of periods of supernormal growth

k = The company's weighted average cost of capital (WACC)

To illustrate numerically, we return to the same Portal.com example used to illustrate the free cash flow valuation model with temporary supernormal growth, followed by no growth. Substituting the same numbers from that example into the above equation, we obtain the same numerical result, namely $44,539.

COMPARABLES APPROACH TO VALUATION

D
CF VALUATION METHODS REQUIRE DETAILED, multiyear forecasts, and thus place heavy demands on the manager. This chapter is about a simpler valuation approach based on price multiples of "comparable" companies.

To draw on a common analogy in the real estate business, the value of a personal residence is frequently determined by examining transactions on comparable homes. Similarly, under the multiples approach, the value of an asset is derived from the pricing of "comparable" assets, standardized with variables such as earnings, book value, or revenues. For example, industry-average price/earnings (P/E) ratios are often used to value a company—the assumption being that its industry competitors are the most comparable, and the market, on average, prices these companies correctly. Other multiples in wide use are the market-to-book (M/B) and price/sales (P/S) ratios. Other price ratios that play a role in valuation analysis include price/cash flows, price/dividends, and market value/replacement value (Tobin's Q).

The comparables approach estimates price or value multiples for a company simply by using the multiples of comparable companies. The challenge is to identify truly "comparable" companies. When less than perfect comparables can be identified, which is generally the case, the next challenge is for the analyst to control for all the variables that can influence the multiple. In practice, methods for controlling for these variables range from the naive

167

(using industry averages) to the sophisticated (multivariate structural models between the company and its comparables). One distinct advantage of the comparables approach is that it relies on the market to undertake the difficult task of deciphering the effects of expected growth and profitability on value.

PRICE/EARNINGS RATIO METHOD

This method involves estimating the market value of the equity of a business from its projected earnings by using the P/E ratio of comparable companies. The P/E ratio is measured by dividing the market value of the company's equity by net income. The P/E ratio multiplied by the company's earnings gives the company's stock value. For example, if earnings are forecast to be $3 million and the appropriate comparable earnings multiple is 20, the forecast equity value is $60 million. It is common practice to perform this calculation on a per-share basis, in which case P/E is measured by dividing the stock price by earnings per share (EPS). The expected market value of equity is then computed by multiplying the projected EPS of the business by the P/E of comparable companies.

The P/E valuation procedure begs the question of what determines the P/E ratio. To answer that question, it is useful to construct multiples based on various formulas. Some simple mathematics of valuation are required before we can proceed. According to the fundamental classical valuation theory presented in Chapter 5, the value of any asset is the present value of its expected future cash flows. In the case of common stocks, the value of the share price is the present value placed on expected equity cash flows, or dividends. The fundamental valuation equation for common stocks is

$$\text{Price} = \sum_{t=1}^{\infty} \frac{\text{Dividends}_t}{(1 + \text{Discount Rate})^t} = \sum_{t=1}^{\infty} \frac{D_t}{(1 + k)^t} \qquad (1)$$

The model can be translated into the familiar terminology of P/E ratios by expressing the dividends each year as a proportion of earnings, commonly called the dividend payout ratio, or p. As shown in the appendix to this chapter, by expressing dividends as the payout ratio times earnings, and each year's earnings as an expected growth rate from the previous year's earnings, Equation 1 can be greatly simplified to produce several useful expressions for the P/E ratio. If the discount rate and the dividend payout are assumed constant and if growth rates are assigned some simple pattern, the P/E formulas become intuitive and tractable.

Table 7-1 shows four P/E ratio expressions that result from various simplifying assumptions about growth. The four growth scenarios assume increasingly aggressive growth rates generating progressively higher P/E ratios.

TABLE 7-1   P/E expressions.

$(k = 10\%,\ \text{payout} = 0.60,\ g = 9\%,\ T = 10\ \text{years})$

Scenario	Formula	P/E
1. Earnings lasting T years:	$p/k(1 - 1/(1 + k)^T)$	3.7
2. Perpetual no-growth earnings:	p/k	6.0
3. Growth in earnings for T years, no growth thereafter:	$\dfrac{p}{k - g}\left[\dfrac{1 - (1 + g)^T}{(1 + k)^T}\right] +$ $\left[\dfrac{p(1 + g)^T}{k(1 + k)^T}\right]$	10.7
4. Growth in earnings in perpetuity:	$p/(k - g)$	60.0

The first formula assumes constant (no-growth) earnings lasting T years. The second formula assumes a perpetual constant earnings stream. The third formula assumes that the company reinvests the fraction $(1 - p)$ of its earnings for the T years that the return on investment (r) is expected to exceed the cost of investment (k)—that is, for as long as growth adds value. Beyond T years, only zero net present value projects are expected. This formulation is reminiscent of the Modigliani and Miller valuation approach discussed in the previous chapter. The fourth formula assumes constant perpetual growth.

Table 7-1 provides an illustrative numerical example as well. The company is assumed to pay out 60% of its earnings as dividends and to experience a growth rate of 9%. A 10% discount rate is assumed. In the case where earnings have zero growth and cease altogether in 10 years, the P/E ratio is only 3.7. If no-growth earnings are maintained in perpetuity, the P/E ratio rises to 6. If earnings exhibit positive growth over 10 years, the P/E reaches 10.7. And in the case of constant perpetual growth, the P/E soars to 60.

The P/E formulas have shortcomings, of course. They assume that the rates of return on investment are constant, yet P/E ratios change over time as the determinants of their value—including interest rates (discount rates), growth prospects, and future dividend payouts—change. P/E ratios also vary across companies and industries at a point in time, reflecting differences in expected growth and risk.

Nevertheless, these simplified P/E formulas can provide very useful valuation benchmarks for investors and analysts. P/E ratios are essentially compact proxies for investor expectations about the timing, growth, and risk of a company's future cash flows and its dividend distribution policy. One can think of the P/E ratio as a summary statistic of the company's future prospects.

The reasonableness of a company's P/E ratio can be checked by comparing today's P/E ratio with the following:

- Its average level of the past 5 to 10 years, both on an absolute basis and relative to the P/E for a broad market index. The latter neutralizes common factors that affect the overall stock market, such as a decline in interest rates.

- The P/E of companies that are as comparable as possible in terms of fundamental valuation factors, including profitability, reinvestment opportunities, operating characteristics, and financial risk.

- A calculation of what the company must do in absolute performance terms to warrant a given P/E ratio.

MARKET-TO-BOOK RATIO METHOD

This method involves estimating the market value of the company's equity from its projected (book) common equity by applying the market-to-book ratio (M/B) of comparables. The M/B ratio is measured by dividing the market value of equity by book value.[1] It is common to use the per-share version, in which case the M/B ratio is measured by the comparable's stock price divided by its book equity per share. An example will clarify this. In early 2000, BellSouth common stock sold for $43 per share, and its book value, obtained by dividing the total book value of common equity by the number of shares outstanding, was reported at $8.20 per share. The resulting M/B ratio is $43/$8.20 = 5.2. The high premium to book value reflects the value BellSouth management has created with shareholders' historical investment dollars and is expected to create in the future. If BellSouth were deemed comparable in terms of its managerial skills, growth prospects, and risk to a small telecommunications company with a book value of $200 million, then managers would assign it a market value of 5.2 times book of $200 million, or $1041 million.

Recall from the previous chapter that the value of a company equals the sum of its initial book value B and the present value of its economic profits, PV(EP):

$$M = B + \text{PV(EP)}$$

---

[1] Book value as a measure of economic value ignores the key roles of profitability and reinvestment opportunities and is therefore of little help. Book value fails to reflect how much a company is earning on its capital. Liquidation value is appropriate, obviously, only if the management plans to dissolve the enterprise.

This can easily be translated into an expression for the M/B ratio by dividing both sides by book value B:

$$\frac{M}{B} = 1 + \frac{PV(EP)}{B}$$

This expression shows that the M/B ratio is greater than, less than, or equal to 1 as the present value of economic profits is greater than, less than, or equal to 0, respectively. Only if profitability exceeds the cost of capital will value be created. This makes economic sense: High M/B ratios should be associated with abnormally profitable opportunities, and vice versa. M/B ratios should vary across companies according to differences in their future economic profits, which in turn, depend on future ROEs, growth in book value, and risk (the driver of differences in discount rates).

A simple example illustrates this important point. Consider a company with a book value of equity per share of $10. Assume the market's required return on equity is 12% for companies in that risk class. If the $10 book value of equity earns $1.20 per share, or 12%, the market price will be set at $10, and the M/B will equal $10/$10 = 1, since the market's required return at that price will also be $1.20/$10, or 12%. If the $10 book equity per share earns less—say, 6%—the market price has to fall in order for the market's required return to be 12%. In this case, the price falls to $5, since $0.60/$5 = 12%, and the M/B ratio falls to $5/$10 = 0.50. If, on the other hand, the $10 book equity per share earns 18%, or $1.80 per share, the market price has to rise to $15 in order for the market's required return to be 12% ($1.80/$15 = 12%), and the M/B rises to $15/$10 = 1.5.

The appendix to this chapter develops the formal relationship between company profitability r the cost of capital k and the M/B ratio, and shows that the M/B equals 1.3 if $r = k$, is greater than unity if $r > k$, and less than unity if $r < k$:

$$M/B \; \substack{>\\=\\<} \; 1 \text{ as } r \; \substack{>\\=\\<} \; k$$

Q- RATIO METHOD

The market value of a company's securities clearly exerts an important influence on the company's incentive to invest in productive assets. If the market value of a company's stocks and bonds exceeds the cost of establishing productive capacity, there is an incentive to raise new capital and establish more productive capacity, since such investments increase stock price.

The relationship between the market value of a company's securities and the replacement cost of its assets in current dollars is embodied in the Q ratio, defined as follows:

$$Q = \frac{\text{Market Value of a Company's Securities}}{\text{Replacement Cost of Company's Assets}}$$

At the corporate level, the Q ratio is equivalent to the M/B ratio of net assets adjusted for inflation. If $Q > 1$, a company has an incentive to invest because the value the stock market assigns to its net assets (or equity plus long-term debt) is greater than their actual replacement cost—that is, the company's return on its investments exceeds its cost of capital. Conversely, if $Q < 1$, a company has a disincentive to invest. In the long run, the Q ratio is driven to one. This is because profits encourage entry, which, in turn, expands production and lowers prices, profits, and, finally, market values. Over time, the market value of a company's securities will fall to the replacement cost of its assets.

The Q ratio simulates the investor's perspective on value by focusing on the relationship between the amount investors initially put at risk and its current market value. As with any investment, such as common stock, what investors originally put in must be adjusted for inflation to be meaningfully compared to what they actually get back.

To apply the Q ratio, a control group of comparable companies is used to establish an appropriate Q ratio. This ratio is multiplied by the replacement cost value of equity-financed assets in a subject company to obtain a market value:

$$\text{Value} = Q \times \text{Replacement Value}$$

A simple balance sheet method for calculating a company's Q ratio uses the following formula:

$$Q = \frac{\text{MVE} + \text{FVD}}{\text{RC}}$$

where MVE (Market Value of Equity) = RC − FVD
    RC   = Replacement cost of "net assets"
    FVD = Face value of debt, straight preferred

Net assets are total assets at replacement cost less current liabilities (other than debt) and deferred credits (other than investment tax credits).

TABLE 7-2   Value of Eastern Power Co.'s equity at adjusted replacement cost.

	($000,000)
Common equity	$150
Minority interest common equity	5
Convertible preferred	2
Value of equity at historical cost	157
+	
Difference between net plant at replacement and historical cost	80
Value of common equity at adjusted replacement cost	$237
The market value of the Eastern Power Co. is calculated as follows:	
Value of equity at replacement cost	$237
	×
Comparable risk companies Q-ratio	0.80
Market value of equity	$210

For the replacement cost of assets, either trended original cost or the actual replacement cost data required by the SEC in 10K reports can be used.

The example shown in Table 7-2 will help illustrate. The Q ratio applicable to the Eastern Power Co. is estimated as follows. The average Q ratio for a sample of risk-equivalent companies is estimated at 0.85, computed from the market value of their publicly traded debt and equity securities, and the replacement costs of the companies' net plant and equipment and inventories as contained in their 10K reports. The value of Eastern Power Co.'s common equity at adjusted replacement cost is estimated from the information contained in the current annual report.

Of course, the resulting Q ratio can only be as accurate as the replacement cost data on which it is based, typically derived from 10K reports. The lack of verifiability and the subjective nature of this data are weaknesses with the method. For private companies, the problem of generating suitable replacement cost data is even more formidable; trended original cost proxies could serve instead.

OTHER MULTIPLE-BASED METHODS
Other multiple-based valuation methods include the price-to-sales, price-to-cash, and price-to-EBITDA ratios. Price-to-sales ratios (P/S) can be

viewed as the product of price/earnings ratios and earnings-to-sales (profit margin) ratios:

$$P/S = \frac{P}{E} \times \frac{E}{S} = P/E \times \text{Margin}$$

Thus, in addition to the factors that explain variation in P/E ratios, P/S ratios should vary with expected profit margins. Companies with higher expected margins should be worth more in dollar sales. This is why one would expect pharmaceutical companies to have higher P/S ratios than grocery store chains, and established brand-name companies to have higher P/S ratios than recent entrants.

Price-to-cash-flow ratios, as used in practice most notably by Value Line, actually rarely employ pure cash flow measures. This is because cash flow from operations is sensitive to fluctuations in working capital accounts, and thus provides a noisy indicator of value. Instead, EBITDA (operating earnings before interest, taxes, depreciation, and amortization) is typically used in the denominator. It is important when calculating any multiple of sales, operating earnings, or operating cash flows that the numerator includes not just the market value of equity but the value of debt as well. In other words, the ratio should be unlevered (includes the value of debt in the numerator), because the denominator reflects earnings before interest.

MULTIPLES IN PRACTICE

Application of price multiples from comparable companies appears straightforward: you simply identify similar companies, calculate the desired multiples, then apply the multiple to the data of the company being valued. Table 7-3 provides a numerical example of valuing a company with multiples. The first column displays typical multipliers and their magnitude based on the market data of comparable companies. The second column shows the company's own projected data for each multiplier. In the last column, the multiplier is applied to the company data to arrive at an estimate of continuing value for the equity component of total value. The average estimate from all the multipliers is $34 million. Adding the book value of debt of $10 million brings the total estimate of continuing value to $44. If using this technique to estimate continuing value in a DCF analysis, the latter must then be discounted back at the company's WACC.

Application of price multiples is not so simple in practice. Identification of companies that are really comparable is often quite arbitrary and difficult. There are also some choices to be made concerning

TABLE 7-3   Value estimates.

Multiplier	Company Data	Continuing Value
1.5 × book value	$23.2	$34.8
9 × cash flow	$3.6	$32.4
7 × EBIT	$4.3	$30.1
25 × 2000 earnings	$1.5	$37.5
20 × 2001 earnings	$1.7	$33.0
Average estimate		**$33.6**

how the multiples will be calculated. Finally, explaining the variation of multiples across companies, and the applicability of another company's multiple to the subject company, requires a thorough understanding of the determinants of each multiple.

You must be careful in using a P/E ratio from an industry average or a single comparable to value a subject company or business unit. The P/E ratio is not always a reliable indicator of economic value because it is based on accounting earnings, which can be greatly affected by alternative accounting conventions, and it fails to account for risk, the time value of money, or investment requirements. Moreover, if the earnings in any year are abnormally high or low (because of the write-off of nonrecurring restructuring charges, for example), the P/E method will yield misleading results. This problem is particularly acute for companies in cyclical industries. Using normalized or averaged earnings over the business cycle may help circumvent this difficulty.

The same criticisms apply to the M/B ratio, since it is based on the book value of equity, an accounting variable. For example, a company's book value increases whenever it capitalizes rather than expenses its investments, even though this has no effect on economic cash flows or value. The M/B ratio of a given company could also reflect a variety of sources of value creation or destruction, such as restructuring charges, intangibles (brand name, management skill), write-offs, potential liabilities, and so on.

The other problem with using multiples based upon comparable companies is that any valuation error incorporated in the market value is reflected in the multiple. If, for example, the market has overvalued all computer software companies, then using their average P/E ratio to value an initial public offering for a new computer software company will lead to an overvaluation of its stock. In contrast, DCF valuation is based on company-specific growth rates and cash flows and is less likely to be influenced by market errors in valuation.

No effective means exist for accurately forecasting future P/E or M/B ratios, although the P/E and M/B formulas developed above offer benchmarks for quantifying the various factors that influence these ratios. Finally, when using the P/E or M/B multiple to estimate continuing value, there is an inherent inconsistency in using accounting numbers to estimate continuing value, which, in turn, is evaluated in conjunction with the intervening free cash flows to arrive at an estimate of economic value.

Selecting Comparable Companies

Ideally, comparable price multiples should come from companies with the most similar operating and financial characteristics. Companies within the same industry are obvious candidates. Even within narrowly defined industries, however, it is often difficult to find a similar company. Frequently, a close competitor cannot be used because it exists as a division within a diversified company. For example, if a manager is looking to medical service goods companies as proxies for BioTech's Medical Product Division, the closest competitor in the consumer market is Abbott Labs, which also manufactures agricultural and chemical products. Moreover, Abbott Labs does not disclose financial data for its medical products division, and even if it did, there is no observable market price for only that part of the business. Similar issues arise with other candidate comparables such as Johnson & Johnson and C.R. Bard.

Other issues arise when tentative comparables are foreign companies. Even if the foreign companies' financials are converted to U.S. generally accepted accounting principles (GAAP), it is unlikely that their accounting policies are truly similar enough.

One way of dealing with the inevitable heterogeneity of comparable companies is to average across all companies in the industry in the hope that various sources of incomparability cancel each other out. Another approach is to focus on those companies within the industry that are most similar according to informed judgment.

Forecast Versus Historical Multiples

Price multiples can include measures of either past or future performance. *Trailing P/E multiples,* for example, use the latest 12 months of earnings in the denominator. *Leading P/E multiples* use an earnings forecast for the next year. If reliable forecasts are available, as they typically are for most larger companies, it is generally best to base the price multiple on that, because stock prices are driven by expected future performance.

One note of caution on trailing P/E ratios: They can be substantially distorted by accounting anomalies such as transitory gains and losses, non-recurring gains or losses, or other unusual recent performance. Leading multiples can also be distorted but are less likely to include nonrecurring gains and losses in the denominator.

Interpreting and Comparing Multiples

Even across truly comparable companies, price multiples may vary considerably. Analysis based on comparables requires careful consideration of the factors that might explain why some companies' multiples should be higher than others. By relating the P/E and M/B ratios to their fundamental determinants, as in Table 7-1, management can gain a better understanding of the usefulness of price multiples to valuation. Another way to improve the usefulness of a P/E or M/B ratio analysis is to use a computer spreadsheet model to quickly and accurately compute the appropriate multiple from the formulas provided in this chapter's appendix, given assumptions on such value drivers as spread, growth, and cost of capital, and thus verify how reasonable the observed ratios are. For example, P/E ratios should vary positively with expected growth and negatively with risk. In the special no-growth case, the P/E ratio should approximate the reciprocal of the cost of equity capital, thus placing it in the range of 7 to 10 for a cost of equity in the range of 10% to 15%.

When using an array of multiples across a sample of comparable companies, it is not unusual for one company to be high on one multiple and low on another. Consider, for example, the two most commonly used multiples: P/E and M/B. Both multiples vary positively with expected earnings growth. However, M/B is determined by the level of future earnings relative to book value, while P/E is determined by growth in future earnings relative to current earnings. As a result, a company can have a relatively high P/E, because depressed near-term earnings are expected to grow substantially, but because they are not expected to be high relative to book value (i.e., low ROE), its M/B ratio is lower than that of the other companies.

In general, the M/B and P/E ratios will both be high when a company is expected to grow quickly and to enjoy abnormally high ROEs during the growth period. These are the "rising stars." "Falling stars" are companies that still enjoy high ROEs on existing investments but are no longer growing very fast. Such companies have high M/Bs but relatively low P/Es. Recovering companies that are expected to rebound from depressed earnings levels but will be prevented by competition from resuming high ROEs have high P/Es and low M/Bs. Finally, companies with both unfavorable earnings growth and poor ROE prospects—the "dogs"—carry low M/Bs and P/Es.

The differences in ratios across companies, even companies that are closely related, render valuation based on multiples an inherently rudimentary technique. The impact of such differences can be mitigated by focusing on average multiples across the comparable companies, but there is still no guarantee that the average applies perfectly or even well to the company being valued.

Valuation of companies is a difficult and uncertain business, and no technique can alter that underlying reality. The manager can only apply the techniques as intelligently as possible to minimize the estimation errors from the underlying economic uncertainties.

DCF VALUATION VERSUS MULTIPLES

The chief attraction of multiples is that they are easy to grasp and simple to use. They can be used to obtain value estimates of companies and assets quickly, and are particularly useful when there are a large number of comparable companies traded on financial markets and when the market prices these companies correctly on average.

Valuation based on DCF requires detailed, multiple-year forecasts on a variety of parameters, including growth, profitability, and cost of capital. These techniques supply the proper conceptual framework for thinking about what creates value, and they offer the advantage of forcing the analyst to make both the forecasts and assumptions explicit. Doing so minimizes unrealistic or internally inconsistent assumptions, but it places high demands on the analyst. Moreover, the detailed approaches are vulnerable to estimation errors.

Valuation techniques based on price multiples of comparable companies are less demanding than DCF. They take advantage of the information embedded in the stock price of comparables by the marketplace and avoid some estimation errors by "letting the market decide" on the valuation parameters. For example, application of a P/E ratio does not require the user to explicitly specify the company's cost of capital or growth rate. It simply assumes that whatever such parameters' values may be, they are similar to those for companies deemed "comparable."

The primary difficulty with using price multiples lies in identifying companies that are truly comparable. An understanding of the determinants of various multiples can help the analyst assess the degree of comparability and explain why differences in multiples should be expected across companies.

The various alternatives to valuation each have their own advantages, and in a given setting, one may be more useful than another. In general, however, there is no universal "best" valuation method; important insights are gained from using more than one approach, which may explain why most analysts triangulate—that is, apply several methods to examine the same company.

A word of caution is in order, however. A limitation of both DCF and multiples valuation is that neither take into consideration the option value of a project or strategy. Many resource allocation and capital investment decisions involve significant option value. We discuss real options pricing in Chapter 8. Ideally, then, capital allocation decisions should be made using a combination of a DCF method such as NPV or APV, the multiples method, and the real option method.

As discussed in Part II of this book, "Strategy," option pricing is not just a valuation tool. It is also a systematic framework for creating critical strategic advantage. Successful companies have applied the concepts of real option valuation to produce superior shareholder returns by following the strategy of maximizing the value of their real option portfolio—that is, by making investments to secure the upside while insuring against the downside.[2] Real option value is synergistic with shareholder value. In fact, when DCF techniques fail to reproduce observed stock prices, the difference is typically explained by the capital market's recognition of embedded option value. Managers who follow a strategy of maximizing the option value of their portfolio will maximize shareholder value as well.

[2] K. Leslie, and M. Michaels. "The Real Power of Real Options," *Corporate Finance,* January 1998, pp. 13–20.

Common Stock Valuation and Market Multiples

CONSISTENT WITH THE BASIC TENET OF CLASSICAL VALUATION THEORY, stock value equals the present value of future cash inflows discounted at the investor's required return (the cost of equity). Consider an investor with a horizon of n years. The investor buys stock at the beginning of year 1, expects to receive dividends D_1 at the end of year 1, D_2 at the end of year 2, and so on, and expects to sell the stock at a price of P_n at the end of year n. If the investor's required return corresponding to the riskiness of those expected cash flows is k, the present value, and hence the price, of all the future expected cash flows from owning the stock is

$$P_0 = \frac{D_1}{1 + k} + \frac{D_2}{(1 + k)^2} + \frac{D_3}{(1 + k)^3} + \cdots + \frac{D_n}{(1 + k)^n} + \frac{P_n}{(1 + k)^n} \qquad (1)$$

In abbreviated form, the equation can be compressed as:

$$P = \sum_{t=1}^{n} \frac{D_t}{(1 + k)^t} + \frac{P_n}{(1 + k)^n} \qquad (2)$$

Alternately, the value of common stock can be expressed as the present value of an infinite stream of dividends, justified by assuming that either the investor has an infinite investment horizon, or the expected resale price at the end of a finite horizon P_n is in itself the present value to the new purchaser of the expected dividends following year n:

$$\text{Present Value} = \frac{D_1}{1 + k} + \frac{D_2}{(1 + k)^2} + \frac{D_3}{(1 + k)^3} \ldots \text{and so on} \quad (3)$$

In abbreviated form, the equation can be compressed as:

$$P = \sum_{t=1}^{\infty} \frac{D_t}{(1 + k)^t} \quad (4)$$

COMMON STOCK VALUATION AND THE P/E RATIO

In Equation 5, we can express expected dividends in any given year as expected earnings times the expected payout ratio p:

$$D_{t+1} = E_{t+1} \, p \quad (5)$$

The earnings in any given year can, in turn, be expressed as an expected growth rate from the previous year's earnings:

$$E_{t+1} = E_t(1 + g)^t \quad (6)$$

Substituting Equation 8 into Equation 7, we can rewrite Equation 5 as:

$$P = \frac{E_1 p}{1 + k} + \frac{E_2 p}{(1 + k)^2} + \frac{E_3 p}{(1 + k)^3} + \cdots \quad (7)$$

$$P = \frac{E_1 p}{1 + k} + \frac{E_1 (1 + g) p}{(1 + k)^2} + \frac{E_1 (1 + g)^2 p}{(1 + k)^3} + \cdots \quad (8)$$

Factoring out E_1 from both sides, we obtain an expression for the P/E ratio:

$$P = E_1 \left[\frac{p}{1 + k} + \frac{(1 + g) p}{(1 + k)^2} + \frac{(1 + g)^2 p}{(1 + k)^3} + \cdots \right] \quad (9)$$

or, in much simpler form:

$$P = E_1 \, [P/E]$$

where P/E is shorthand for all the elements in the bracketed expression in Equation 9.

Equation 9 can be reduced to much simpler expressions for the P/E ratio if the discount rate and the dividend payout are assumed constant and if growth rates are assigned some simple pattern, as illustrated in Table 7-1 earlier in the chapter.

Similar expressions can easily be developed for the M/B ratio simply by observing that the expected earnings E_1 in Equation 9 is the company's return on equity capital r times the book value of the investment B:

$$E_1 = r B$$

We can substitute rB for E_1 in Equation 9 and obtain an expression relating a company's M/B ratio and its determinants.

THE STANDARD DCF MODEL OF STOCK VALUATION

The general common stock valuation model embodied in Equation 3 is not very operational, since it requires an estimation of an infinite stream of dividends. By assigning a particular configuration to the dividend stream, a more operational formula can be derived. Assuming that dividends grow at a constant rate forever, that is

$$D_t = D_0 (1 + g)^t \qquad (10)$$

where g = expected dividend per share growth, and substituting these values of future dividends per share into Equation 3, the familiar reduced form of the general dividend valuation model is obtained:

$$P_0 = \frac{D_1}{k - g} \qquad (11)$$

This fundamental valuation equation states that the market price of a share of common stock is the value of next year's expected dividend discounted at the market's required return net of the effect of growth. Consider the following market data for Southern Company:

Current dividend per share = $1.62
Required return   = 12%
Expected dividend growth = 4%

From Equation 11, the standard DCF model produces a stock price of:

$$P_0 = \frac{D_1}{k - g} = \frac{D_0(1 + g)}{k - g} = \frac{\$1.62(1 + 0.04)}{0.12 - 0.04} = \$21$$

Note that next year's expected dividend is the current spot dividend increased by the expected growth rate in dividends. The growth rate g can be estimated using several techniques. One way is to extrapolate the historical compound growth of dividends over some recent period. Another is to use consensus analysts' long-term growth forecast reported by the Institutional Brokers' Estimate Service (IBES) or Zacks Investment Research on their respective websites.

Note also that the standard DCF model does not apply to growth stocks. In Equation 11, it is clear that as g approaches k, the denominator gets progressively smaller, and the price of the stock infinitely larger. If g exceeds k, the price becomes negative, an implausible situation. In the derivation of the standard DCF valuation model in Equation 11, it was necessary to assume that g was less than k in order for the series of terms to converge. With this assumption, the present value of steadily growing dividends becomes smaller as the discounting effect of k in the denominator dominate the effects of such growth in the numerator.

THE M/B RATIO, PROFITABILITY, AND THE COST OF CAPITAL

The relationship between company profitability r, the cost of capital k, and the M/B ratio can be demonstrated by a simple manipulation of the standard DCF equation. Starting from the seminal DCF model of Equation 11:

$$P_0 = D_1/(k - g) \tag{12}$$

and expressing next year's dividend D_1 as next year's earnings per share E_1 times the earnings payout ratio $(1 - b)$, we have:

$$D_1 = E_1 (1 - b) \tag{13}$$

Substituting into Equation 12:

$$P_0 = \frac{E_1 (1 - b)}{k - g} \tag{14}$$

But next year's earnings per share E_1 are equal to the expected rate of return on equity r times the book value of equity per share B at the end of the current year:

$$E_1 = r B \tag{15}$$

Substituting Equation 15 in Equation 14:

$$P_0 = \frac{rB(1 - b)}{k - g} \tag{16}$$

Dividing both sides of the equation by B, and noting that $g = br$:

$$P_0/B = \frac{r(1 - b)}{k - br} = \frac{r - br}{k - br} \tag{17}$$

We can also express the same relationship as a function of growth by substituting the growth rate g for br in the above expression:

$$P_0/B = \frac{r - g}{k - g} \tag{18}$$

From Equations 17 or 18, it is clear that the M/B ratio will be equal to 1 if $r = k$, greater than 1 if $r > k$, and less than 1 if $r < k$:

$$M/B \overset{>}{\underset{<}{=}} 1 \text{ as } r \overset{>}{\underset{<}{=}} k \tag{19}$$

Another interesting expression for the M/B ratio is obtained by subtracting 1 from both sides of Equation 18 and collecting terms:

$$P_0/B - 1 = \frac{r - k}{k - g} \tag{20}$$

This expression asserts that the extent to which a company's M/B ratio deviates from 1 depends on the spread between its profitability and the cost capital, $r - k$. If the spread is positive, the M/B will be above 1. The converse is also true: If the spread is negative, the M/B will be less than 1.

REAL OPTIONS VALUATION

A VARIETY OF VALUATION TOOLS HAVE BEEN DESCRIBED IN PRE-
VIOUS CHAPTERS—discounted cash flow, multiples, and others.
These tools are widely used—sometimes in isolation, but more
often in combination—to make a wide variety of business
decisions. For certain kinds of business decisions, however—
those involving high levels of uncertainty, growth, and strategy—all of
these valuation techniques are routinely rejected when they contradict the
instinct or business judgment of management. And the truth is that, in
many cases, they should be. There is a better way.

Consider a manager with an idea for a new product. Say the required
R&D investment for this product is $10 million. If the R&D results are
favorable, a pilot plant can be constructed for $25 million. Subsequent full-
scale commercialization would require an additional $100 million. The to-
tal investment of the R&D, pilot plant, and commercial plant phases is
$135 million. Traditional NPV analysis would compare the required in-
vestment of $135 million to the cash flow projections and, if NPV is pos-
itive, management would accept the project.

What is wrong with this picture? Two things. One, high-risk projects like
this one are often assigned higher discount rates, which increases the odds
that the resulting NPV will be negative and the project will never get off the
ground. Two, NPV analysis assumes that management will proceed with the
entire sequence of investments, even if it is uneconomical to do so. The truth

of the matter is that the pilot plant will not be built unless the R&D phase is favorable, and the full-scale commercial plant will not be built unless the pilot plant is profitable. That is, NPV assumes passive management and ignores the fact that as time passes managers gain important information about demand, costs, capabilities, and the reaction of competitors that can and should be used to alter the cash flows and risks of projects already underway.

Good managers use their knowledge, skill, and experience to manage the uncertainties in their business to protect the value of the company. Excellent managers *create* corporate wealth by seeking, embracing, and exploiting the opportunities that uncertainty represents. They do this by pursuing policies that maintain flexibility on as many fronts as possible. This flexibility is what provides managers with the opportunity to exploit upside outcomes and avoid downside ones.

Managerial flexibility is what transforms risk and uncertainty into opportunities to create value. In fact, as seen in Figure 8-1, the greater the uncertainty, the bigger the role for flexibility, and the more certain it is that the proactive manager will be able to create value.

It is this idea of managerial flexibility that provides for the analogy between financial options on stocks and the "real" options found in most business decisions. This analogy, in turn, allows us to value managerial flexibility in much the same way we value financial options. The two concepts together have been coined *managerial options*.

Managerial options exist whenever management has the right, but not the obligation, to take some action. Most projects possess or can be infused with some sort of managerial flexibility, and any such flexibility gives the project the characteristics of options. An investment in research and development gives the company the right, but not the obligation, to acquire the benefits of R&D for the cost of commercialization. Oil ex-

FIGURE 8-1   Expected value with and without managerial flexibility.

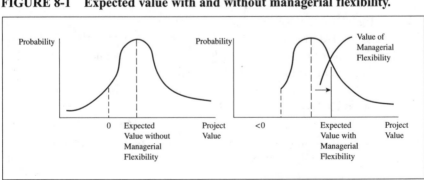

ploration rights give the company the opportunity to extract but not the obligation to do so. Test marketing gives the company the right to expand to full product introduction. Staged financing gives the lender the right but not the obligation to provide second-stage financing. Preemptive investment in emerging markets creates the opportunity to scale up to full production if conditions become favorable. The opportunity to switch between producing a component part and outsourcing is a valuable option, as is cross-training workers to perform other tasks as market demand shifts.

Consider the timeline of the stages in a typical risky business investment in Figure 8-2. At several points along the timeline, new information on such critical factors as market demand, technological and design capabilities, costs, and the likelihood of success become available. At each point, management will decide whether to continue with the investment as planned, alter it in some way, or abandon it altogether.

Options are analogous with flexibility in decision making precisely because the holder of the option can exercise the option at his or her discretion to take advantage of an opportunity. Similarly, the hallmark of flexible management is the use of discretion in light of new information to pursue value-creating opportunities and avoid value-destroying developments.

Figure 8-3 shows a simple investment decision as it appears at time zero, as management is assessing its likely cash flows, risks, scale, and duration to determine whether it will add value to the company. It includes a simple "continue or abandon" decision at each stage. As the investment unfolds and uncertainties about economic conditions are resolved, the manager has access to more information about the probabilities of success and likely cash flows—that is, about the investment's value-creating potential for the organization.

FIGURE 8-2   Typical managerial decision-making timeline.

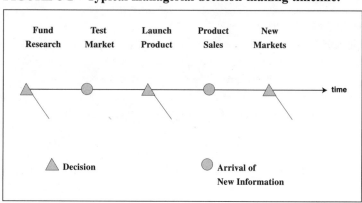

FIGURE 8-3   Decision tree with managerial flexibility.

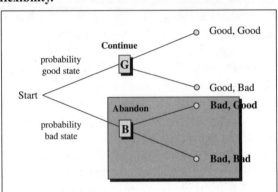

The decision tree is useful for visualizing the difference between passive and flexible management. If the investment depicted in Figure 8-3 was managed passively—that is, the manager did not exercise the right to abandon or otherwise alter the project once underway—then the correct value of this investment is the present discounted value of all expected future cash flows. If management used its discretion, however, they would abandon the project in period 2 if the bad state occurred, and the entire bottom node and its associated losses would be avoided. The value of the project is clearly higher under flexible management.

Managerial flexibility has quantifiable value because it can be used to protect the gains and limit the losses of business investments, and the dollar values of both actions are measurable. Before we show how to value real or managerial options, however, we need to review option pricing as it applies to financial assets.

FINANCIAL OPTIONS

Financial options are financial instruments that give the owner the right, but not the obligation, to buy the underlying asset for the exercise price on or before the exercise date. The option owner may also choose to let the option expire unexercised if the exercise price is greater than the asset's prevailing market price.[1] Options, because they cost a fraction of what

---

[1] These examples are for call options. Put options give the owner the right to sell the underlying asset and will be exercised if the exercise price is greater than the underlying asset price at expiration.

the underlying asset costs, are a type of leverage. European options allow exercise only on the exercise date. American options permit early exercise.

The logical breakthrough that led to the option pricing model is both simple and elegant: If one can replicate the payoffs from the option with payoffs from a combination of common stock and borrowing, then in the absence of arbitrage profits, the price of the option must equal the price of the stock-borrowing "option equivalent."

Let's illustrate by pricing a one-year call option on VBM Corporation stock. Assume the cost of borrowing r is 10 percent, the exercise price X is $160, the current stock price S is $140, and next period's stock price S_1 is either $110 or $210. As we shall see, we need not specify the probability of the stock price rising or falling next period to value the option. The payoff of the call option next period will either be $0 (if the stock price moves to $110, in which case we will let the option expire) or $50 (if the stock price moves to $210, in which case we will exercise the option and pay the exercise price of $160 for stock now valued at $210), which we denote as a payoff pattern of [$0, $50].

This is illustrated graphically in Figure 8-4 by the characteristic "hockey stick" payoff pattern created by the call option.

Outcomes	$S_1 = \$110$	$S_1 = \$210$
Option Value	$0	$S_1 - X$
		$= \$210 - \$160$
		$= \$50$
Option Equivalent Value		
One share stock	$110	$210
Loan repayment (principal + interest)	−$110	−$110
Total payoff	$0	$100

Compare this [$0, $50] payoff with the payoff from borrowing $100 (the present value of $110, the amount needed to make the total payoff equal to zero in one of the two states of the world, necessary to replicate the option payoff pattern) at 10%, and buying one share of VBM Corporation stock for $140. We see that in the down state of the world, our payoff is again $0, and in the up state of the world, our payoff is $100, the difference between the stock value of $210 and the principal and interest repayment of $110.

The total payoff from the "borrowing plus stock" investment is [$0, $100], the same as the payoff from owning two call options. Therefore,

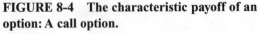

FIGURE 8-4   The characteristic payoff of an option: A call option.

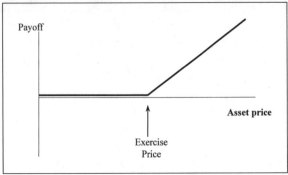

the price of two call options equals the price of the stock/borrowing option equivalent. The price (or cost or value) of the option equivalent is the cost of the stock less the present value of borrowing, or $140 − $100 = $40. Since the stock/borrowing position costs twice the equivalent call option, the call option must be worth half of that, or $20.

Notice that owners of call options can delay purchasing the underlying stock until more information becomes available. In this way, options allow a less costly, lower-risk, and more valuable way to obtain an asset. For only a fraction of the cost of buying the asset outright, option owners have the right to purchase the asset on or before some specified future date, when more and better information about the value of that asset will be available. As importantly, by purchasing the option, we have acquired the right to *not* buy the stock if doing so creates a loss. As we will see, the ability to avoid or limit losses is a significant source of the value of managerial flexibility.

In short, financial options create two distinct advantages. First, we tie up fewer funds today by purchasing the option to obtain the asset instead of the asset itself, which frees up funds to pursue other promising business opportunities. Second, we create value by purchasing the right to wait until more information becomes available before committing to the asset or not. In this example, spending $20 on the option today creates value no matter what the stock price does: If it rises to $210, the option gives us the right to purchase the stock for only $160, creating $50 in value; if it falls to $110, the option gives us the right to walk away, leaving a $30 loss on the table, the difference between the stock's current value of $110 and the $140 we would have originally paid for it.

All options give us the right to exploit upside risk and limit downside exposure. In essence, options enable investors to control risk and to shape the outcomes they face. This is the most attractive and valuable feature of options,[2] and it is the fundamental reason that managerial flexibility creates value.

Real Options

Real options are, in the simplest sense, options on real assets. Simply put, financial options give their owners the right, but not the obligation, to purchase or sell some asset; real options give the manager the right, but not the obligation, to pursue successful investments. Real options pricing attempts to value flexible management.

Following are real-world examples of real options pricing applications in industry today:

*   Shell Oil's planning group uses real options analysis extensively in analyzing capital projects and investment strategies. One is a timing option, secured through the purchase of a license to develop an oil field. The most important option is to further postpone development of the oil field, spend further sums of money, or drill some holes in order to extend the license. This is a classic real option involving sequential investments (to limit loss), a great deal of uncertainty, and a high potential reward.

*   Enron used real options thinking to discover that they could earn substantial returns by building relatively inexpensive and inefficient gas-powered electric facilities. By operating these plants only when profitable and allowing them to sit idle the rest of the time, Enron had purchased the flexibility to benefit from wildly fluctuating electricity prices.

*   Hewlett-Packard (HP) applied real options analysis to maximize the value of its printer business. The demand for printers varies across different parts of the world, both in terms of number of printers and the particular configuration of features and sales price. To maximize profits, HP needed to provide customized printers in the correct quantities for each region. Real options analysis showed that by producing a more generic product locally and having it customized at each of the regional warehouses actually saved money, despite

[2] Bernstein, *Capital Ideas: The Improbable Origins of Modern Wall Street,* NY Free Press, 1992, p. 6.

the fact that total production costs were higher. Delaying the customization until later in the production process when more and better information on demand was available created significant additional economic value.

- Cadence Design Systems developed an option valuation method to value intellectual property licenses, which it gave to Intel and Toshiba.[3] This was designed to aid collaboration between high-tech companies and streamline bringing new products to market.

- At Merck, R&D investments are analyzed in an options framework. R&D requires sequential investments with the ability to abandon the research at several points and involves high risks, an ideal set of circumstances for option valuation.

- When Intel purchased Level One Communications, it purchased access to manufacturing expertise in a complementary business. The chips made by Level One fit a specific purpose not currently served by Intel and one that is in high demand because of the growth of the Internet. This gives Intel the flexibility to shift resources into producing different types of chips as demand fluctuates.

Unlike financial options, real options are not neatly packaged or clearly defined. They vary from project to project and company to company. Some real options—investment decisions that create managerial flexibility—are easy to see. Most executives, for example, can readily understand why investing today in R&D or in a new marketing program can generate the possibility of successful new products or markets tomorrow. But the analogy is more difficult to see—and certainly to quantify—with most real-world capital projects. The journey from insight to application, from calls and puts to strategy and timing, is difficult, time-consuming at first, and somewhat frustrating. Like most worthwhile activities, however, the effort to learn to recognize embedded options—which exist in nearly every business decision—has many benefits, some obvious, others unforeseen. Perhaps the biggest downfall from learning how to recognize the many managerial options embedded in business decisions is catching the "real options disease"—once afflicted, you will see options everywhere! But this is a good thing, because the manager cannot manage what he or she cannot see.

[3] P. Coy, "Exploiting Uncertainty: The Real-Options Revolution in Decision-Making," *Business Week,* June 7, 1999, p. 122.

Before we explore the basic types of real options, it is helpful to make a couple of general observations about real options pricing. The first observation is that strategic investments have been made by corporate America for decades without benefit of a real options framework, so why is it useful now? One industry executive observed that his company had approved R&D expenditures through years of budgets cycles without ever mentioning real options benefits. Ironically, R&D is a classic example of the type of investment that would rarely be justified were it not for the options such expenditures provide management to extend successful research projects with follow-up investments.

Our point is that while executives may not have explicitly used real options analysis, *implicitly they have.* Indeed, R&D activity in corporate America has historically been justified by the "gut feeling" or "intuition" about its strategic value, in part because standard financial analysis routinely shows R&D to be negative NPV. Rather than providing an indictment of real options pricing, however, such observations should encourage a more vigorous pursuit of tractable real options pricing as the only approach capable of quantifying the value potential of business "instinct."

Competing in the new economy with inflexible management is like playing basketball with ski boots on. Real options analysis lets you kick off those clunkers and sprint down the floor.[4]

The second observation is that while many real options occur naturally, particularly in the natural resources and other extractive industries, others must be planned or built in at some extra cost (e.g., the option to expand capacity or alter input or output configurations next year, made possible by building more flexible but costly production facilities today). We return to this point when we discuss the strategic implications of real options analysis, but it is useful to keep it in mind as we move now to consider the common forms of real options.

---

[4]Coy, op. cit., p. 124.

Although specific examples of actual real options are numerous, most managerial options take a limited number of forms. By understanding and becoming more familiar with these forms, managers will become better · able to both spot the options in their own decisions and seize opportunities to create optionlike flexibility in their organizations. A numerical example of each of these real options is provided in the appendix to the chapter.

Common Types of Real Options
In this section we'll look at some common types of real options. Keep in mind that the lists may not be exclusive or exhaustive.

Timing option

- Option to learn
- Option to delay
- Option to defer
- Option to accelerate

The timing option occurs when one can put off a decision until some date in the future. This allows management to determine if more, less, or the same amount of resources should be spent (slower, faster, or at the same rate) on the project at that future date. The option to delay or defer can be created through licensing agreements, up-front fees, or exclusive contracts, and it is particularly valuable in periods of high interest rates (the option to delay is a call option, whose value rises with interest rates, explained below). It may appear that the option to delay and learn before committing to a strategy is always good, but this overlooks the very real possibility that delaying allows competitors to enter the market and establish a dominant market share. For this reason, the option to delay is usually most valuable in industries with proprietary technology, patents, licenses, or other barriers to entry.

Capital budgeting involves not only *whether* to invest but *when* to invest. Most capital budgeting decision rules, like payback, NPV, and internal rate of return, focus only on the static "go/no-go" decision. Real options pricing allows us to value the more dynamic components of capital budgeting and strategy: the *when* to invest. Do we invest now or wait? Do we invest the full amount now or in stages? How long should the stages be? Should the parties renegotiate at the end of each stage? Which scenario creates more value? A real-options framework enables us to improve the timing of strategic investments because of the natural analogy between optimal investment timing and exercising a call or a put at the best time. An example here might help.[5]

Suppose a company planned to introduce an interactive CD-TV system, and a software company had been invited to participate in the venture. You have a choice between two alternatives: (1) Immediately begin full-scale production of game software on CDs for the new interactive TV, or (2) Receive an exclusive license to manufacture and distribute the software at a future time of your choosing. The license would in all likelihood be preferable, since it would give you the option to defer investment until you had a better idea of the size of the market for interactive CDs. This kind of option to delay is also valuable during periods of volatile interest rates, since the ability to wait can allow managers to raise capital for projects when interest rates are lower.

Keep in mind, though, that the option to delay is valuable only if it more than offsets any harm that might come from delaying. For example, if you delayed implementing the interactive CD-TV project, some other company might establish a loyal customer base or determine a standard that would make it difficult for your company to later enter the market. Of course, your license might head off this possibility. Usually, the option to delay is most valuable to companies with some type of barrier to entry. We talk more about the proprietary nature of some real options when we explore strategy in the next two chapters.

Notice that the option to delay is not the same as doing nothing. A company must expend funds to obtain the right to delay, just like one must buy a call option to have the right to purchase the stock later.

The cash flows from a business capital investment play the same role as dividend payments on a stock. When a stock pays no dividends, the call option is always worth more alive than dead and should never be exercised early. But when dividends are paid, the ex-dividend price and the possible payoffs to the call option fall, and early exercise may be warranted. Think of the extreme case where a company pays out a liquidating dividend: The stock price is zero and the call is worthless. Any in-the-money call would optimally be exercised just before this liquidating dividend.

Dividends do not always prompt early exercise, but if they are sufficiently large, call option holders capture them by exercising just before the ex-dividend date. We see managers acting in the same way: When a proj-

---

[5] This example is adopted from Brigham, Gapenski, and Ehrhardt, *Financial Management: Theory and Practice* (9th Edition), Dryden Press, p. 520.

ect's forecast cash flows are sufficiently large, managers "capture" the cash flows by investing (exercising) right away. But when the forecast cash flows are small, managers are inclined to hold on to their option rather than investing, even when the project NPV is positive. This explains why some managers are reluctant to commit to positive-NPV projects. This caution is rational as long as the option to wait is sufficiently valuable and the risks of waiting are not great.

Staging option

- Time-to-build option
- Staged investments or staged financing option
- Option to default

Staging investment as a series of outlays creates the option to default or change the enterprise mid-project should conditions become unfavorable. This is the option to sell and as such is a put option.

The development of a project can almost always be considered to be a series of options, and each stage in the development is an option on the future stages. Staged investments can be valued as a compound option.

This is both an operating option—from the point of view of the borrower—and a financing option—from the point of view of the lender. Should both parties be made aware of the value added by the staging option, more efficient sharing of gains through negotiation would result in the undertaking of a greater number of profitable investments.

Operating or capacity option

- Option to alter the scale of operations, i.e., to expand or contract
- Option to temporarily shut down and restart
- Option to abandon for salvage value
- Option to exit
- Option to build versus buy; own versus outsource; buy versus lease

The operating or capacity option allows companies to manage their productive capacity in response to changing market conditions. One such option is the option to exit, or better yet, to abandon for salvage value should conditions become unfavorable. In addition, many projects can be structured so that they contain options to reduce or temporarily suspend operations rather than completely close them down. Such options are common in natural resource projects, including mining, oil, and timber.

Other facilities can be structured so that they contain the option to expand production or expand into a new geographical market. Much of today's investments in Eastern Europe, China, and Russia are justified mostly on the basis of the embedded options to expand or shut down as we gain experience with these emerging markets.

Flexibility option or option to switch

* Option to switch use of inputs
* Option to switch output mix
* Flexible production technology option

The flexibility option allows managers to switch inputs in a manufacturing process. An example would be modifying power-generating systems to permit switching between coal, oil, and gas, depending on their costs. It generally costs more to build a flexible plant up front, but input flexibility can pay for itself rapidly if input prices are volatile.

Growth options.   The option to grow is used when an initial investment is required for further development—when it is a prerequisite or link in a chain of interrelated projects that lead to future growth opportunities. The future growth opportunities might take the form of a new-generation product or process, the discovery of oil reserves, access to a new market, application, or technology, or strengthening of core capabilities. This is a very common type of real option, and real-world examples are abundant: research and development, test marketing, loss leaders, patents, joint ventures, and strategic acquisitions like bidder toeholds in targets, leases on undeveloped land, and investments in information technology, to name just a few.

New product option.   The new product or brand-name extension option is the option to add complementary products or successive generations of the original product. For example, Toshiba probably lost money on its first laptop computers, a clear loss leader, but the manufacturing skills and brand-name recognition it gained helped turn its subsequent generations of laptop computers into moneymakers. In addition, Toshiba used its experience and name recognition in laptops as an entry fee into the desktop computer market segment.

Sequential or Multiple Interacting Options

Most projects are, in fact, combinations of various real options, combining calls that enhance the upward potential and puts that protect against downward movements in project value. The sequencing of the options—whether calls are followed by puts or puts followed by calls—obviously has an impact on the overall value of the compound real option. It is likely that the combined option value will be different from the simple sum of the individual option values; some research shows that, in general, the combined value is a bit less than the sum of the individual option values but still substantially greater than the value of the investment without its embedded options.

The Drivers of Option Value: Real and Financial

Option pricing theory tells us that there are five primary drivers of value for a simple call option: the stock price, the exercise price, the risk-free rate of interest, the time to maturity, and the riskiness of the cash flows of the underlying asset. (Other factors, such as ownership rights and contract terms, are also important determinants of option value; we take these up in Chapter 10, where the strategic advantages of real options pricing are explored further.) Each of these variables in turn has a natural interpretation when viewed from within real investments with option characteristics, like real estate, new products, oil exploration, and so on. Table 8-1 lists the five drivers of option value. Let's look at each of these determinants of option value more closely.

TABLE 8-1   Drivers of option value.

	Financial Option	Real Option
Underlying asset price	Stock price	Value of developed project
Exercise price	Exercise price	Expenditures for project assets
Time to maturity	Contract's maturity	Time to expiration; license period
Interest rate	Risk-free interest rate	Time value of money
Volatility	Standard deviation of stock returns	Volatility of project cash flows

Underly asset price, S.   The higher the price of the underlying asset rises, the more likely the call will be "in the money" at expiration (i.e., the more likely the asset price will be greater than the exercise price), and the higher the call value.

Exercise price, X.   The lower the exercise price, the less one has to pay for the asset upon exercise, and the more valuable the call option.

What we are really interested in is the asset-to-exercise price ratio. As the asset/exercise price ratio increases, the spread between the market value of the asset and what one has to pay for it widens, increasing the value of any call option on that asset. We can see the analogy between real and financial options developing if we recast the characteristic hockey stick payoff patterns of financial options into its real options counterpart, as shown in Figure 8-5.

Time to maturity, horizon, or deferability, *t*.   As the time to maturity increases, the option has more value because there is more time for the asset price to rise relative to the exercise price. A capital-budgeting analogy to the financial option's time to maturity might include the period of time during which the scale-up decision may be realistically deferred. The ability to defer committing funds or capital to a project gives the manager additional time to examine the course of future events and to gain more information. The manager also has the prerogative of expanding the project as favorable events unfold, or cutting the losses as unfavorable events unfold. The longer the time frame, the greater the odds that a positive turn of events will occur (regardless of whether the company is currently in the bad state of affairs or not), thus unambiguously increasing the project's profitability. The ability to defer alone easily transforms many a negative NPV project into an attractive investment opportunity.

Level of interest rates, *r*.   This one takes some explaining. Investors who buy stock by way of a call option are really buying the stock on installment credit. They purchase the option contract today, but thus do not pay the exercise price for the stock until, and if, they exercise the option on the exercise date. The delayed payment is more valuable the higher the interest rate

FIGURE 8-5   Real option hockey stick payoff pattern.

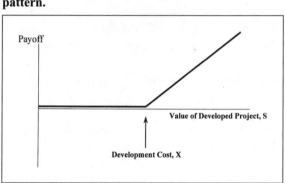

(the "value of time") and the more periods there are to maturity (see previous option). The higher the interest rate, the lower the present value of the cash outlay needed to exercise the managerial option, or the more one could earn on the funds if invested in the meanwhile. Notice, however, that a rise in the interest rate also lowers the present value of the cash flows of the base case project. Generally, but not always, the net effect is that high interest rates raise the value of projects, particularly those with expansion options.

Volatility or risk, σ.   The volatility of a financial option is measured by the standard deviation (or variance, σ^2) of the underlying stock price. Perhaps surprisingly, the higher the standard deviation of the underlying stock price, the more valuable the option on the stock. Why? Because of the asymmetry facing the owners of options—all options, both financial and real. It is this asymmetry that weakens DCF valuation techniques and requires that we use real options pricing to put a dollar value on managerial flexibility. The asymmetry calls the manager into action.

Take call options, for example: If the price goes above the exercise price, call option owners benefit from every increase in stock price. But if the stock price falls below the exercise price, the option has no value, no matter how far below the exercise price the stock price falls. There is a lower bound on the loss from holding the option, and that is the price of the option itself. There is no effective upper bound on the value of the option, which rises with volatility.

The real option interpretation of risk concerns the variability in the underlying asset's cash flows as driven, by example, by changes in demand for the product. The capital budgeting counterpart says that the greater the risk associated with the investment, the more valuable the option on it. This again arises because of the asymmetry of gains and losses. A big upside potential confers highly positive NPV. But large downside events do not necessarily flow through to the bottom line because of the option available to management to not scale up, or to even abandon. A large zero is no bigger than a small zero. This means that the riskier the project, the greater the odds of a large gain without a corresponding increase in the size of the potential loss.

THREE APPROACHES TO SOLVING FOR REAL OPTION VALUE
Following are three viable approaches used to solve for real option values:

1.   *The Decision Tree Approach.*   The appendix for this chapter works through several detailed examples using the decision tree approach. Two important observations are in order. First, notice that we do not

need the risky discount rate to value real options, which greatly simplifies the valuation task. Second, we need not abandon NPV analysis to calculate the value of investments with embedded options. Specifically, the value of the company or project including its managerial (real) options can be most easily expressed as the NPV of the company "as is" plus the value of all sources of managerial flexibility. The good news is that we can continue to use the discounted cash flow methods developed earlier in the book even for strategic investments if we correctly augment those calculations with the value of managerial flexibility.

2.   *The Option Pricing Model.*   The seminal, Nobel Prize–winning option pricing model developed by Black and Scholes[6] is a multiperiod version of the simple options pricing derivation discussed previously and encompasses the same five drivers of option value. As such, it is at once both more realistic—that is, it takes several possible price outcomes into account in each of several intervening periods—but also more dependent on the validity of the underlying assumptions.

Accepting the assumptions that underlie the Black-Scholes formula, it is actually easier to use than forecasting future cash flows and calculating the appropriate probability distribution throughout the binomial tree. All we need to do is input the five option value drivers—the value of underlying asset, exercise price, time to expiration, volatility, and the risk-free rate—into the Black-Scholes options pricing formula and solve the formula using any one of the many handheld calculators, spreadsheet programs, or website programs available today. This approach is used extensively on Wall Street and also has taken some industries, including oil and gas and pharmaceuticals, by storm.

Three of the five option input variables—namely, the exercise price, time to expiration, and risk-free rate—are readily available. The other two—the value of the underlying asset and its volatility—must be estimated. If there is a publicly traded stock whose cash flows vary with that of the project, we can appropriately use the variability of its cash flows to proxy for the volatility of the real investment project's cash flows. The value of the underlying asset—that is, the real investment or strategy under consideration—can be

---

[6] The approach is well covered in Brealey and Myers, *Principles of Corporate Finance,* 6th edition (2000), New York: McGraw Hill, or any text on options.

TABLE 8-2 Call option pricing table

Call option values, percent of share price
SHARE PRICE DIVIDED BY PV (EXERCISE PRICE)

STANDARD DEVIATION TIMES SQUARE ROOT OF TIME	.40	.45	.50	.55	.60	.65	.70	.75	.80	.82	.84	.86	.88	.90	.92	.94	.96	.98	1.00
.05	.0	.0	.0	.0	.0	.0	.0	.0	.0	.0	.0	.0	.0	.0	.1	.3	.6	1.2	2.0
.10	.0	.0	.0	.0	.0	.0	.0	.0	.0	.1	.2	.3	.5	.8	1.2	1.7	2.3	3.1	4.0
.15	.0	.0	.0	.0	.0	.0	.1	.2	.5	.7	1.0	1.3	1.7	2.2	2.8	3.5	4.2	5.1	6.0
.20	.0	.0	.0	.0	.0	.1	.4	.8	1.5	1.9	2.3	2.8	3.4	4.0	4.7	5.4	6.2	7.1	8.0
.25	.0	.0	.0	.1	.2	.5	1.0	1.8	2.8	3.3	3.9	4.5	5.2	5.9	6.6	7.4	8.2	9.1	9.9
.30	.0	.1	.1	.3	.7	1.2	2.0	3.1	4.4	5.0	5.7	6.3	7.0	7.8	8.6	9.4	10.2	11.1	11.9
.35	.1	.2	.4	.8	1.4	2.3	3.3	4.6	6.2	6.8	7.5	8.2	9.0	9.8	10.6	11.4	12.2	13.0	13.9
.40	.2	.5	.9	1.6	2.4	3.5	4.8	6.3	8.0	8.7	9.4	10.2	11.0	11.7	12.5	13.4	14.2	15.0	15.9
.45	.5	1.0	1.7	2.6	3.7	5.0	6.5	8.1	9.9	10.6	11.4	12.2	12.9	13.7	14.5	15.3	16.2	17.0	17.8
.50	1.0	1.7	2.6	3.7	5.1	6.6	8.2	10.0	11.8	12.6	13.4	14.2	14.9	15.7	16.5	17.3	18.1	18.9	19.7
.55	1.7	2.6	3.8	5.1	6.6	8.3	10.0	11.9	13.8	14.6	15.4	16.1	16.9	17.7	18.5	19.3	20.1	20.9	21.7
.60	2.5	3.7	5.1	6.6	8.3	10.1	11.9	13.8	15.8	16.6	17.4	18.1	18.9	19.7	20.5	21.3	22.0	22.8	23.6
.65	3.6	4.9	6.5	8.2	10.0	11.9	13.8	15.8	17.8	18.6	19.3	20.1	20.9	21.7	22.5	23.2	24.0	24.7	25.5
.70	4.7	6.3	8.1	9.9	11.9	13.8	15.8	17.8	19.8	20.6	21.3	22.1	22.9	23.6	24.4	25.2	25.9	26.6	27.4
.75	6.1	7.9	9.8	11.7	13.7	15.8	17.8	19.8	21.8	22.5	23.3	24.1	24.8	25.6	26.3	27.1	27.8	28.5	29.2
.80	7.5	9.5	11.5	13.6	15.7	17.7	19.8	21.8	23.7	24.5	25.3	26.0	26.8	27.5	28.3	29.0	29.7	30.4	31.1
.85	9.1	11.2	13.3	15.5	17.6	19.7	21.8	23.8	25.7	26.5	27.2	28.0	28.7	29.4	30.2	30.9	31.6	32.2	32.9
.90	10.7	13.0	15.2	17.4	19.6	21.7	23.8	25.8	27.7	28.4	29.2	29.9	30.6	31.3	32.0	32.7	33.4	34.1	34.7
.95	12.5	14.8	17.1	19.4	21.6	23.7	25.7	27.7	29.6	30.4	31.1	31.8	32.5	33.2	33.9	34.6	35.2	35.9	36.5
1.00	14.3	16.7	19.1	21.4	23.6	25.7	27.7	29.7	31.6	32.3	33.0	33.7	34.4	35.1	35.7	36.4	37.0	37.7	38.3
1.05	16.1	18.6	21.0	23.3	25.6	27.7	29.7	31.6	33.5	34.2	34.9	35.6	36.2	36.9	37.6	38.2	38.8	39.4	40.0
1.10	18.0	20.6	23.0	25.3	27.5	29.6	31.6	33.5	35.4	36.1	36.7	37.4	38.1	38.7	39.3	40.0	40.6	41.2	41.8
1.15	20.0	22.5	25.0	27.3	29.5	31.6	33.6	35.4	37.2	37.9	38.6	39.2	39.9	40.5	41.1	41.7	42.3	42.9	43.5
1.20	21.9	24.5	27.0	29.3	31.5	33.6	35.5	37.3	39.1	39.7	40.4	41.0	41.7	42.3	42.9	43.5	44.0	44.6	45.1
1.25	23.9	26.5	29.0	31.3	33.5	35.5	37.4	39.2	40.9	41.5	42.2	42.8	43.4	44.0	44.6	45.2	45.7	46.3	46.8
1.30	25.9	28.5	31.0	33.3	35.4	37.4	39.3	41.0	42.7	43.3	43.9	44.5	45.1	45.7	46.3	46.8	47.4	47.9	48.4
1.35	27.9	30.5	33.0	35.2	37.3	39.3	41.1	42.8	44.4	45.1	45.7	46.3	46.8	47.4	47.9	48.5	49.0	49.5	50.0
1.40	29.9	32.5	34.9	37.1	39.2	41.1	42.9	44.6	46.2	46.8	47.4	47.9	48.5	49.0	49.6	50.1	50.6	51.1	51.6
1.45	31.9	34.5	36.9	39.1	41.1	43.0	44.7	46.4	47.9	48.5	49.0	49.6	50.1	50.7	51.2	51.7	52.2	52.7	53.2
1.50	33.8	36.4	38.8	40.9	42.9	44.8	46.5	48.1	49.6	50.1	50.7	51.2	51.8	52.3	52.8	53.3	53.7	54.2	54.7
1.55	35.8	38.4	40.7	42.8	44.8	46.6	48.2	49.8	51.2	51.8	52.3	52.8	53.3	53.8	54.3	54.8	55.3	55.7	56.2
1.60	37.8	40.3	42.6	44.6	46.5	48.3	49.9	51.4	52.8	53.4	53.9	54.4	54.9	55.4	55.9	56.3	56.8	57.2	57.6
1.65	39.7	42.2	44.4	46.4	48.3	50.0	51.6	53.1	54.4	54.9	55.4	55.9	56.4	56.9	57.3	57.8	58.2	58.6	59.1
1.70	41.6	44.0	46.2	48.2	50.0	51.7	53.2	54.7	56.0	56.5	57.0	57.5	57.9	58.4	58.8	59.2	59.7	60.1	60.5
1.75	43.5	45.9	48.0	50.0	51.7	53.4	54.8	56.2	57.5	58.0	58.5	58.9	59.4	59.8	60.2	60.7	61.1	61.5	61.8
2.00	52.5	54.6	56.5	58.2	59.7	61.1	62.4	63.6	64.6	65.0	65.4	65.8	66.2	66.6	66.9	67.3	67.6	67.9	68.3
2.25	60.7	62.5	64.1	65.6	66.8	68.0	69.1	70.0	70.9	71.3	71.6	71.9	72.2	72.5	72.8	73.1	73.4	73.7	73.9
2.50	67.9	69.4	70.8	72.0	73.1	74.0	74.9	75.7	76.4	76.7	77.0	77.2	77.5	77.7	78.0	78.2	78.4	78.7	78.9
2.75	74.2	75.4	76.6	77.5	78.4	79.2	79.9	80.5	81.1	81.4	81.6	81.8	82.0	82.2	82.4	82.6	82.7	82.9	83.1
3.00	79.5	80.5	81.4	82.2	82.9	83.5	84.1	84.6	85.1	85.3	85.4	85.6	85.8	85.9	86.1	86.2	86.4	86.5	86.6
3.50	87.6	88.3	88.8	89.3	89.7	90.1	90.5	90.8	91.1	91.2	91.3	91.4	91.5	91.6	91.6	91.7	91.8	91.9	92.0
4.00	92.9	93.3	93.6	93.9	94.2	94.4	94.6	94.8	94.9	95.0	95.0	95.1	95.2	95.2	95.3	95.3	95.4	95.4	95.4
4.50	96.2	96.4	96.6	96.7	96.9	97.0	97.1	97.2	97.3	97.3	9.73	97.4	97.4	97.4	97.5	97.5	97.5	97.5	97.6
5.00	98.1	98.2	98.3	98.3	98.4	98.5	98.5	98.6	98.6	98.6	98.6	98.7	98.7	98.7	98.7	98.7	98.7	98.7	98.8

Note: Based on Black-Scholes model. To obtain corresponding European put values, add present value of exercise price and subtract share price.

Source: Brealey & Myers, *Principles of Corporate Finance,* McGraw Hill, 5th edition (1996) pages AP12–AP13.

TABLE 8-2   Call option pricing table (*Continued*)

SHARE PRICE DIVIDED BY PV (EXERCISE PRICE)

1.02	1.04	1.06	1.08	1.10	1.12	1.14	1.16	1.18	1.20	1.25	1.30	1.35	1.40	1.45	1.50	1.75	2.00	2.50	
3.1	4.5	6.0	7.5	9.1	10.7	12.3	13.8	15.3	16.7	20.0	23.1	25.9	28.6	31.0	33.3	42.9	50.0	60.0	.05
5.0	6.1	7.3	8.6	10.0	11.3	12.7	14.1	15.4	16.8	20.0	23.1	25.9	28.6	31.0	33.3	42.9	50.0	60.0	.10
7.0	8.0	9.1	10.2	11.4	12.6	13.8	15.0	16.2	17.4	20.4	23.3	26.0	28.6	31.1	33.3	42.9	50.0	60.0	.15
8.9	9.9	10.9	11.9	13.0	14.1	15.2	16.3	17.4	18.5	21.2	23.9	26.4	28.9	31.2	33.5	42.9	50.0	60.0	.20
10.9	11.8	12.8	13.7	14.7	15.7	16.7	17.7	18.7	19.8	22.3	24.7	27.1	29.4	31.7	33.8	42.9	50.0	60.0	.25
12.8	13.7	14.6	15.6	16.5	17.4	18.4	19.3	20.3	21.2	23.5	25.8	28.1	30.2	32.3	34.3	43.1	50.1	60.0	.30
14.8	15.6	16.5	17.4	18.3	19.2	20.1	21.0	21.9	22.7	24.9	27.1	29.2	31.2	33.2	35.1	43.5	50.2	60.0	.35
16.7	17.5	18.4	19.2	20.1	20.9	21.8	22.6	23.5	24.3	26.4	28.4	30.4	32.3	34.2	36.0	44.0	50.5	60.1	.40
18.6	19.4	20.3	21.1	21.9	22.7	23.5	24.3	25.1	25.9	27.9	29.8	31.7	33.5	35.3	37.0	44.6	50.8	60.2	.45
20.5	21.3	22.1	22.9	23.7	24.5	25.3	26.1	26.8	27.6	29.5	31.3	33.1	34.8	36.4	38.1	45.3	51.3	60.4	.50
22.4	23.2	24.0	24.8	25.5	26.3	27.0	27.8	28.5	29.2	31.0	32.8	34.5	36.1	37.7	39.2	46.1	51.9	60.7	.55
24.3	25.1	25.8	26.6	27.3	28.1	28.8	29.5	30.2	30.9	32.6	34.3	35.9	37.5	39.0	40.4	47.0	52.5	61.0	.60
26.2	27.0	27.7	28.4	29.1	29.8	30.5	31.2	31.9	32.6	34.2	35.8	37.4	38.9	40.3	41.7	48.0	53.3	61.4	.65
28.1	28.8	29.5	30.2	30.9	31.6	32.3	32.9	33.6	34.2	35.8	37.3	38.8	40.3	41.6	43.0	49.0	54.0	61.9	.70
29.9	30.6	31.3	32.0	32.7	33.3	34.0	34.6	35.3	35.9	37.4	38.9	40.3	41.7	43.0	44.3	50.0	54.9	62.4	.75
31.8	32.4	33.1	33.8	34.4	35.1	35.7	36.3	36.9	37.5	39.0	40.4	41.8	43.1	44.4	45.6	51.1	55.8	63.0	.80
33.6	34.2	34.9	35.5	36.2	36.8	37.4	38.0	38.6	39.2	40.6	41.9	43.3	44.5	45.8	46.9	52.2	56.7	63.6	.85
35.4	36.0	36.6	37.3	37.9	38.5	39.1	39.6	40.2	40.8	42.1	43.5	44.7	46.0	47.1	48.3	53.3	57.6	64.3	.90
37.2	37.8	38.4	39.0	39.6	40.1	40.7	41.3	41.8	42.4	43.7	45.0	46.2	47.4	48.5	49.6	54.5	58.6	65.0	.95
38.9	39.5	40.1	40.7	41.2	41.8	42.4	42.9	43.4	44.0	45.2	46.5	47.6	48.8	49.9	50.9	55.6	59.5	65.7	1.00
40.6	41.2	41.8	42.4	42.9	43.5	44.0	44.5	45.0	45.5	46.8	48.0	49.1	50.2	51.2	52.2	56.7	60.5	66.5	1.05
42.3	42.9	43.5	44.0	44.5	45.1	45.6	46.1	46.6	47.1	48.3	49.4	50.5	51.6	52.6	53.5	57.9	61.5	67.2	1.10
44.0	44.6	45.1	45.6	46.2	46.7	47.2	47.7	48.2	48.6	49.8	50.9	51.9	52.9	53.9	54.9	59.0	62.5	68.0	1.15
45.7	46.2	46.7	47.3	47.8	48.3	48.7	49.2	49.7	50.1	51.3	52.3	53.3	54.3	55.2	56.1	60.2	63.5	68.8	1.20
47.3	47.8	48.4	48.8	49.3	49.8	50.3	50.7	51.2	51.6	52.7	53.7	54.7	55.7	56.6	57.4	61.3	64.5	69.6	1.25
48.9	49.4	49.9	50.4	50.9	51.3	51.8	52.2	52.7	53.1	54.1	55.1	56.1	57.0	57.9	58.7	62.4	65.5	70.4	1.30
50.5	51.0	51.5	52.0	52.4	52.9	53.3	53.7	54.1	54.6	55.6	56.5	57.4	58.3	59.1	59.9	63.5	66.5	71.1	1.35
52.1	52.6	53.0	53.5	53.9	54.3	54.8	55.2	55.6	56.0	56.9	57.9	58.7	59.6	60.4	61.2	64.6	67.5	71.9	1.40
53.6	54.1	54.5	55.0	55.4	55.8	56.2	56.6	57.0	57.4	58.3	59.2	60.0	60.9	61.6	62.4	65.7	68.4	72.7	1.45
55.1	55.6	56.0	56.4	56.8	57.2	57.6	58.0	58.4	58.8	59.7	60.5	61.3	62.1	62.9	63.6	66.8	69.4	73.5	1.50
56.6	57.0	57.4	57.8	58.2	58.6	59.0	59.4	59.7	60.1	61.0	61.8	62.6	63.3	64.1	64.7	67.8	70.3	74.3	1.55
58.0	58.5	58.9	59.2	59.6	60.0	60.4	60.7	61.1	61.4	62.3	63.1	63.8	64.5	65.2	65.9	68.8	71.3	75.1	1.60
59.5	59.9	60.2	60.6	61.0	61.4	61.7	62.1	62.4	62.7	63.5	64.3	65.0	65.7	66.4	67.0	69.9	72.2	75.9	1.65
60.9	61.2	61.6	62.0	62.3	62.7	63.0	63.4	63.7	64.0	64.8	65.5	66.2	66.9	67.5	68.2	70.9	73.1	76.6	1.70
62.2	62.6	62.9	63.3	63.6	64.0	64.3	64.6	64.9	65.3	66.0	66.7	67.4	68.0	68.7	69.2	71.9	74.0	77.4	1.75
68.6	68.9	69.2	69.5	69.8	70.0	70.3	70.6	70.8	71.1	71.7	72.3	72.9	73.4	73.9	74.4	76.5	78.3	81.0	2.00
74.2	74.4	74.7	74.9	75.2	75.4	75.6	75.8	76.0	76.3	76.8	77.2	77.7	78.1	78.5	78.9	80.6	82.1	84.3	2.25
79.1	79.3	79.5	79.7	79.9	80.0	80.2	80.4	80.6	80.7	81.1	81.5	81.9	82.2	82.6	82.9	84.3	85.4	87.2	2.50
83.3	83.4	83.6	83.7	83.9	84.0	84.2	84.3	84.4	84.6	84.9	85.2	85.5	85.8	86.0	86.3	87.4	88.3	89.7	2.75
86.8	86.9	87.0	87.1	87.3	87.4	87.5	87.6	87.7	87.8	88.1	88.3	88.5	88.8	89.0	89.2	90.0	90.7	91.8	3.00
92.1	92.1	92.2	92.3	92.4	92.4	92.5	92.6	92.6	92.7	92.8	93.0	93.1	93.3	93.4	93.5	94.0	94.4	95.1	3.50
95.5	95.5	95.6	95.6	95.7	95.7	95.7	95.8	95.8	95.8	95.9	96.0	96.1	96.2	96.2	96.3	96.6	96.8	97.2	4.00
97.6	97.6	97.6	97.6	97.7	97.7	97.7	97.7	97.8	97.8	97.8	97.9	97.9	97.9	98.0	98.0	98.2	98.3	98.5	4.50
98.8	98.8	98.8	98.8	98.8	98.8	98.8	98.8	98.9	98.9	98.9	98.9	98.9	99.0	99.0	99.0	99.1	99.1	99.2	5.00

STANDARD DEVIATION TIMES SQUARE ROOT OF TIME

Note: Based on Black-Scholes model. To obtain corresponding European put values, add present value of exercise price and subtract share price.

Source: Brealey & Myers, *Principles of Corporate Finance,* McGraw Hill, 5th edition (1996) pages AP12–AP13.

estimated using the discounted cash flow methods described in Chapters 5 and 6.

3. *The Option Pricing Tables.*   These tables have been created to help the user solve for the value of the option as well. On one axis is the underlying asset's price divided by the present value of the exercise price (discounted by the continuous risk-free rate of interest); on the other is the annual standard deviation of the asset's return times the square root of the time to expiration. The values in the table are the call option value expressed as a percent of the current underlying asset value. We obtain the call option value by first locating the figure in the table corresponding to the value of each of the two dimensions on the axes, and then multiplying that figure by the stock price. A standard call option pricing table is duplicated in Table 8-2.

Notice two things about the figures in the table. One, they rise with the ratio of the asset value to the (present value of the) exercise price. That is, the value of the call option increases as the value of the underlying stock increases and/or the present value of the exercise price decreases. In addition, the figures in the table rise with the product of volatility and time remaining. As we saw earlier, as volatility or time to maturity rises, so too does the chance that the option will be in the money at expiration. We return to the option pricing table in Chapter 10, when we use its ideas to help visualize and formulate value-creating strategies.

Deriving the Value of Real Options: Operating and Financing

You may choose to skim or carefully review the following overview, depending on your technical background and interests. In either case, however, note that the mathematical setup of the problem is the same each time and is essentially just a decision tree with various possibilities depicted at each decision point. We believe this captures visually how most individuals regard investment decisions intuitively. The real challenge in applying the real options technique is to be able to recognize the particular option involved in a given strategy, and then to treat that option consistently throughout the analysis.

EXAMPLE: AN OIL EXTRACTION AND REFINERY PROJECT

Here we develop real options pricing by applying it to a series of operational, strategic, and financial options embedded in a typical capital investment.[7] A large oil company has a one-year lease to start drilling on undeveloped land with potential oil reserves. Initiating the project may re-

---

[7] This example was adapted from an article by Lenos Trigeorgis, "Real Options and Interactions with Financial Flexibility," *Financial Management,* Autumn 1993, pp. 202–224.

quire exploration costs, followed by road construction and other infrastructure outlays I_1. This would be followed by outlays for the construction of a new processing facility I_2.

Extraction can begin only after construction is completed—in other words,
cash flows are generated only during the operating stage that follows the last
outlay. During construction, if market conditions deteriorate, management can
choose to forgo any future planned outlays. Management can also choose to
reduce the scale of operation by $c\%$, saving a portion of the last outlay, I_C, if
the market is weak. The processing plant can be designed up front such that,
if oil prices turn out higher than expected, the rate of production can be enhanced by $x\%$ with a follow-up outlay of I_E. At any time, management can
salvage a portion of its investment by selling the plant and equipment for salvage value or switch them to an alternative use with value A. An associated
refinery plant (which may be designed to operate with alternative sources of
energy inputs) can convert crude oil into other refined products.

PRINCIPLES OF VALUING REAL OPTIONS

Suppose we are faced with an opportunity to invest $I_0 = \$104$ (in millions)
in an oil project whose gross value in each period will either move up by
80% or down by 40%, depending on oil price fluctuations. A year later, the
project will have an expected value from subsequent cash flows of $180
million if the oil price moves up ($C+ = 180$) or $60 if the oil price moves
down ($C- = \$60$), all in millions of dollars. There is an equal probability
($q = 0.5$) that the price of oil will move up or down in any year. Let S be
the price of oil (or of a twin security that is traded in the financial markets
and has the same risk characteristics as the real project under consideration). Both the project and its twin security have an expected rate of return
(or discount rate) of $k = 20\%$. The risk-free rate is $r = 8\%$.

We assume throughout that the value of the project V_t (i.e., the present value in each year t of its subsequent expected cash flows) and its twin
security price S_t (i.e., the oil stock price, or simply the price of oil in dollars per barrel) move through time as follows:

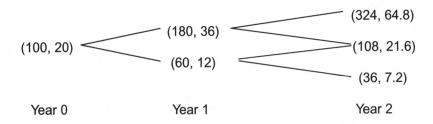

| Year 0 | Year 1 | Year 2 |

For example, the pair (V_0, S_0) represents a current gross project value of \$100 and a spot oil price of \$20 a barrel (or \$20 per share of oil stock).

Under traditional NPV capital budgeting, the current value of this investment would be obtained by discounting the project's end-of-period values by the appropriate discount rate (which, with real assets, is typically the discount rate of the traded twin security):

$$V_0 = (0.5 \times 180 + 0.5 \times 60)/1.20 = 100$$

and subtracting the investment costs, $I_0 = 104$, gives:

$$\text{NPV} = V_0 - I_0 = 100 - 104 = -4$$

Traditional discounted cash flow analysis would reject this negative NPV project. Let's compare the investment decision made using real options valuation. The basic idea is that management can replicate the payoff to equity by purchasing a specified number of shares of the twin security and financing the purchase in part by borrowing a specific amount at the riskless interest rate. The ability to construct a riskless "synthetic" portfolio out of the twin security and bonds is what enables us to price real options without regard to actual probabilities, q, or the risky discount rate, r. Essentially, the synthetic portfolio enables us to obtain the same solution from evaluating expected cash flows using risk-neutral probabilities, p, and riskless discount rates, r_f, as we do using actual probabilities and risky discount rates:

$$E = \frac{pE^+ + (1 - p)\, E^-}{(1 + r_f)}$$

where E is the expected value of the equity holder's claim across the upstate (E^+) and downstate (E^-), and p is given by

$$p = \frac{(1 + r_f)S - S^-}{(S^+ - S^-)}$$

The risk-neutral probability p can be estimated from the price dynamics of either the twin security S (which usually has better available historical data) or oil. Here:

$$p = \frac{(1.08 \times 20) - 12}{(36 - 12)} = 0.4$$

As a check, note that we do indeed arrive at the same present value using p and the risk-free rate as we did above using q and the risky discount rate:

$$V_0 = \frac{pC^+ + (1 - p)\,C^-}{(1 + r_f)} = \frac{0.4 \times 180 + 0.6 \times 60}{(1.08)} = 100$$

Assume in what follows that if any part of the required investment outlay, having a present value of $104, is not going to be spent immediately, it is placed in escrow earning the risk-free rate of interest, 8%. This assumption is not crucial, but it simplifies the analysis. Assume all-equity financing through the first several examples that follow. You may want to refer frequently to the project's cash flow tree provided earlier.

1. *Option to Defer Investment.* The option to wait is analogous to a call option on project value V with an exercise price equal to the required outlay next year $I_1 = 104 \times 1.08 = 112.32$:

$$E^+ = \max(V^+ - I_1, 0) = \max(180 - 112.32, 0) = 67.68$$

$$E^- = \max(V^- - I_1, 0) = \max(60 - 112.32, 0) = 0$$

The project's total value (i.e., the expanded NPV that includes the value of the option to defer) using the equations for E and p given above is

$$E_0 = \frac{pE^+ + (1 - p)\,E^-}{(1 + r_f)} = \frac{0.4 \times 67.68 + 0.6 \times 0}{(1.08)} = 25.07$$

Using Expanded NPV = NPV + Option Value, the value of the option to defer provided by the lease is nearly one-third the project's gross value:

Option to Defer = Expanded NPV − Passive NPV
$$= 25.07 - (-4) = 29.07$$

2. *The Option to Expand (Growth Option).* Management may have the option of expanding the scale of production by $x = 0.50$ by incurring a follow-up investment outlay of $I_E = 40$, provided oil prices and market conditions turn out better than originally expected. The original investment opportunity is seen as the initial-scale project V, plus a call option on a future opportunity, or $E = V + \max(xV - I_E, 0) = \max(V, (1 + x)V - I_E)$:

$$E^+ = \max(V^+, 1.5V^+ - I_E, 0) = \max(180, 270 - 40) = 230$$

$$E^- = \max(V^-, 1.5V^- - I_E, 0) = \max(60, 90 - 40) = 60$$

The value of the investment opportunity with the option to expand is

$$E_0 = \frac{pE^+ + (1 - p)\,E^-}{(1 + r_f)} - I_0$$

$$= \frac{0.4 \times 230 + 0.6 \times 60}{(1.08)} - 104 = 14.5$$

and the value of the option alone is $14.5 - (-4) = 18.5$, or 18.5% of the gross project value.

3. *Options to Abandon for Salvage Value or Switch Use.* As market conditions change and the relative prices of inputs, outputs, or plant resale value fluctuate, equity holders may find it preferable to abandon the current use of the asset by switching to a cheaper input or more profitable output, or by simply selling the plant's assets. Let the project's value in its best alternative use A (or the salvage value for which it can best be exchanged) fluctuate over time as:

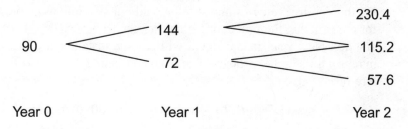

| Year 0 | Year 1 | Year 2 |

Notice that the project's current salvage value ($A_0 = 90$) is below the project's value in its present use ($V_0 = 100$); otherwise, management would have switched use immediately. Notice also that the schedule of salvage or alternative values have been designed to generate a 20% expected return, although with lower risk. In this case, if the market keeps moving up, it would not be optimal to abandon the project early for salvage value. However, if it moves down, management may find it desirable to switch use (i.e., in year 1 exchange the present use value of 60 for a higher alternative use value of 72). Thus, equity holders can choose the maximum of the project's value in its present use V or its value in the best alternative use A—that is, $E = \max(V, A)$:

$$E^+ = \max(V^+, A^+) = \max(180, 144) = 180$$

$$E^- = \max(V^-, A^-) = \max(60, 72) = 72$$

The value of the investment opportunity including the option to expand is

$$E_0 = \frac{pE^+ + (1 - p)\,E^-}{(1 + r_f)} - I_0$$

$$= \frac{0.4 \times 180 + 0.6 \times 72}{(1.08)} - 104 = 2.67.$$

The value is highly dependent on the schedule of salvage or alternative use values.

4. *The Option to Default (on Planned Staged Cost Installments) During Construction.* Management may abandon a project during construction to save any subsequent investment outlays if the upcoming required investment exceeds the value from continuing the project, including any future options. Suppose the $104 present value of the investment can be staged as a series of installments: $I_0 = \$44$ start-up costs, with the remaining $60 placed in an escrow account earning the risk-free rate of interest to be paid out as a follow-up outlay for constructing the processing plant in year 1 ($I_1 = \$60 \times 1.08 = \$64.80$). Next year, management will pay the installment cost only in return for a higher project value from continuing, for a payoff picture of $E = \max(V - I_1, 0)$:

$$E^+ = \max(V^+ - I_1, 0) = \max(180 - 64.80, 0) = 115.20$$
$$E^- = \max(V^- - I_1, 0) = \max(60 - 64.80, 0) = 0$$

The value of the investment including the option to default is

$$E_0 = \frac{pE^+ + (1 - p)\,E^-}{(1 + r_f)} - I_0$$

$$= \frac{0.4 \times 115.20 + 0.6 \times 0}{(1.08)} = -1.33$$

The value of the option to abandon alone is $-1.33 - (-4) = 2.67$. This value is, of course, dependent on the particular cost schedule.

Any of the above examples can be extended to a discrete multiperiod setting with any number of nodes or stages. As the number of steps increase, the discrete time solution approaches its continuous Black-Scholes equivalent.

We now move to examples of financial flexibility, or the ability to adjust the company's debt level over time, or "recapitalization," and explore the many real-world interactions among financing flexibility and operating options.

5.   *Equity Holder's Option to Default on Debt (Limited Liability).*   So far, we have assumed an all-equity financed company. If we allow for debt financing, then the value of the project to equity holders can potentially improve by the additional amount of financial flexibility, or the option to default on debt payments deriving from limited liability.

Let's reevaluate the original oil project investment with project financing. Assume the oil project is the entire company. Consider, for example, venture capital financing of a single-project start-up oil company. Suppose initially that venture capitalists (or "junk bond" purchasers) would be content to provide funds in exchange for contractually promised fixed-debt payments with a return of 16.7%, the rate on bonds of comparable risk. Suppose that the company borrows $I^D{}_0 = \$44$ out of the immediate required outlay of $104 against the investment's expected future cash flows, to be repaid with interest in two years. The balance, $I^E{}_0 = \$60$, is supplied by the company's equity holders.

Equity holders, of course, have an option to acquire the company value V—which, in the meantime, is "owned" by the debtholders (in this case, the venture capitalists)—by paying back the debt (with imputed interest) at the exercise price two years hence. Thus, in year 2, equity holders will pay back what they owe the debtholders ($D_2 = 44 \times 1.167^2 = 59.22$) only if the investment value exceeds the promised payment, else they will exercise their limited liability rights to default and surrender the project's assets to the debtholders and receive nothing: $E_2 = \max(V_2 - D_2, 0)$.

Thus, depending on whether oil prices move up in both years $(++)$, up in one year and down the next $(+-$ or $-+)$, or down in both years $(--)$, the equity holders' claims in year 2 will be

$$E_2{}^{++} = \max(V_2{}^{++} - D_2, 0) = \max(324 - 59.92, 0) = 264.08$$

$$E_2{}^{+-} = \max(V_2{}^{+-} - D_2, 0) = \max(108 - 59.92, 0) = 48.08$$

$$E_2{}^{++} = \max(V_2{}^{--} - D_2, 0) = \max(36 - 59.92, 0) = 0$$

The value of the equity holders' claim back in year 1, depending on whether the oil market was up or down, would be

$$E_1^+ = \frac{p\,E_2^{++} + (1-p)\,E_2^{-+}}{(1+r)} = \frac{0.4 \times 264.08 + 0.6 \times 48.08}{(1.08)}$$

$$= 124.52$$

$$E_1^- = \frac{p\,E_2^{+-} + (1-p)\,E_2^{--}}{(1+r_f)} = \frac{0.4 \times 48.08 - 0.6 \times 0}{(1.08)}$$

$$= 17.81$$

Finally, moving another step back to year 0, the present value of the oil company investment opportunity with partial debt financing is

$$E_0 = \frac{pE^+ + (1-p)\,E^-}{(1+r_f)} = \frac{0.4 \times 124.52 + 0.6 \times 17.81}{(1.08)}$$

$$= -4.0.$$

The expanded NPV value is the same as the NPV of the equity-financed project, confirming that debt financing at the 16.7% equilibrium interest rate, a rate that already reflects a premium for the equity holders' option to default, is a zero-NPV transaction. The company compensates the lenders *ex ante* through a fairly priced default option premium embedded in the equilibrium interest rate in exchange for financial flexibility.

6.   *Potential Interaction between Operating and Financial Default Flexibilities.*   Revisit the operating default scenario above, but suppose that the start-up funds $I_0^D = \$44$ were borrowed as before from venture capital sources or by issuing junk bonds. $I_1^E = \$64.80$, as before. The value of the equity holders' claims in year 2 (with debt repayment) remains unchanged, but in year 1, it now becomes the maximum of (1) its value in the previous case (in the absence of any outlay for continuing), minus the "equity cost" I_1^E now due, or (2) 0 (if the project performs poorly and equity holders default)— that is, $E_1 = \max(E_1 - I_1^E, 0)$:

$$E_1^+ = \max(V^+ - I_1, 0) = \max(124.52 - 64.80, 0) = 59.72$$

$$E_1^- = \max(V^- - I_1, 0) = \max(17.81 - 64.80, 0) = 0$$

We find that the value of the investment with both operating and financial default flexibility is $22.12, and the incremental value of the operating default option in the presence of financial flexibility is $22.12 - (-4) = \$26.12$, or about one-fourth of the gross investment value, far exceeding the value of the equivalent operating option to default under the all-equity financing case above, where the value was \$2.67. *This confirms that the incremental value of an option in the presence of other options may differ significantly from its individual value in isolation and that financial and operating flexibility options may interact.*

7. *Venture Capitalists' (Lenders') Option to Abandon via Staged Debt Financing.* Suppose the venture capitalists insisted on providing sequential financing, such that $I_0^D = \$22$ (to be repaid at 16.7% interest, or \$29.96 two years hence) and $I_1^D = \$22 \times 1.08 = \$23.76$, contingent on successful interim progress. Following a successful first stage, the second stage would be less risky so that a lower 12% rate would be agreeable (with the \$23.76 to return \$26.61 a year later). The equity holders would thus also need to contribute $I_0^E = \$22$ toward the \$44 upfront cost for infrastructure, as well as $I_1^E = \$41.04$ (=\$64.80 $-$ \$23.76) toward the potential second-stage \$64.80 processing plant cost one year later, if the venture at that time seems worth pursuing.

Suppose that the venture capitalists would choose to provide second-stage financing at the lower 12% rate only if the first stage is successful (i.e., following a "+" oil price state in period 1), but would otherwise choose to abandon the venture midstream. Equity holders' value in the intermediate states in year 2 may differ, contingent on first year apparent success:

$$E_2^{++} = \max(V_2^{++} - (I^D{}_{0-2} + I^D{}_{1-2}), 0)$$
$$= \max(324 - (29.96 + 26.61), 0) = 267.43$$
$$E_2^{+-} = \max(V_2^{+-} - (I^D{}_{0-2} + I^D{}_{1-2}), 0)$$
$$= \max(108 - 56.57, 0) = 51.43$$

following an apparently successful first year, or

$$E_2^{-+} = \max(V_2^{-+} - I^D{}_{0-2}, 0) = \max(108 - 29.96, 0) = 78.04$$
$$E_2^{--} = \max(V_2^{--} - I^D{}_{0-2}, 0) = \max(36 - 29.96, 0) = 6.04$$

following an unsuccessful first year, when only the upfront debt repayment need be made. If there were no outlays required in period 1, the value of the equity holders' claim would be, in the positive state:

$$E_1^{+} = \frac{p\,E_2^{++} + (1 - p)\,E_2^{+-}}{(1 + r_f)}$$

$$= \frac{0.4 \times 267.43 + 0.6 \times 51.43}{(1.08)} = 127.62$$

and in the negative state:

$$E_1^{-} = \frac{p\,E_2^{-+} + (1 - p)\,E_2^{--}}{(1 + r_f)}$$

$$= \frac{0.4 \times 78.04 + 0.6 \times 6.04}{(1.08)} = 32.36$$

Since equity holders actually need to contribute 41.04 in period 1 for the venture to proceed, the correct (revised) value is the maximum of the above value in the absence of any outlays minus the "equity cost" I_1^{E}, or zero (if the venture performs poorly and is abandoned in midstream)—that is, $E_1 = \max(E_1 - I_1^{E}, 0)$:

$$E_1^{+} = \max(E_1^{+} - I_1^{E}, 0) = \max(127.62 - 41.04, 0) = 86.58$$

but when E_1 in the negative state is 0, after a disappointing first stage, the venture would be abandoned. Finally, the time-0 value of equity holders' claims becomes

$$E_0 = \frac{p(E_1^{+}) + (1 - p)(E_1^{-})}{(1 + r_f)} - I_0^{E}$$

$$= \frac{0.4 \times 86.58 + 0.6 \times 0}{(1.08)} - 22 = 10.07$$

Thus, the value of equity's default options, offset by the venture capitalists' option to abandon by refusing to provide second-stage financing, is $10.07 - (-4) = 14.07$, or 14% of the gross project value. This is less than the 26% option default value found above, when venture capitalists could not abandon. The venture capitalists should thus be willing to pay a premium of up to 12% of the project value ($12 million) to preserve their option to abandon via staged debt financing, which provides the equity holders a negotiating window to obtain better financing terms, such as saving on debt interest costs.

As this last example should demonstrate, structuring the financing deal in contingent stages to more closely match the inherent resolution of uncertainty over the investment's different stages can make both parties better off. Even after a bad interim state, entrepreneurs can, for example, prevent abandonment of the venture by the lenders by renegotiating more appropriate second-stage financing terms given the revealed higher risks, thus generating mutual gains by solving the underlying agency or underinvestment problems.

PART

II

STRATEGY

9

BUSINESS STRATEGY

I N THE VALUE-BASED MANAGEMENT FRAMEWORK, there are three
broad types of managerial actions that lead to value creation: strategic, financial, and corporate governance. This chapter focuses on
the first module, strategy. Strategic actions are the most important
to value creation; they will have the most substantial and longest-
lasting effects on the value-creating potential of the company. The VBM
framework provides the explicit link between value creation and those economic forces that determine both the degree of competition in a particular market and the company's relative position within that market, a link
made stronger by the common language and discipline provided by an un-
wavering focus on economic value creation.

As our BioTech manager in Chapter 4 discovered, managers create
value when they invest in assets whose returns exceed their (economic)
costs. The ability to *systematically* create economic value remains elusive,
however, due primarily to the "curse of competition." A perfectly competitive market is one in which there are no barriers to entry or exit, no
product differentiation, and no cost or information advantages. In a competitive equilibrium, then, companies earn their cost of capital—a zero
spread—and create zero economic value. How does this come about?
Consider an industry that is generating superior profits and creating economic value. New entrants are attracted, which increases production, lowers prices, and drives profits down to zero. Likewise, exit from unprofitable industries ensures that prices rise to generate zero economic returns.
This striking truth about the forces of competition was displayed in Figure

1-5 in Chapter 1. There we saw that although there was tremendous variation in the rates of return earned by any given company in a year, companies earn their opportunity cost of capital on average.

Yet some companies *do* create value—routinely. Hewlett-Packard has enjoyed 20% annual growth for close to 20 years. How is this? Fundamentally, the same competitive forces that move the *average* company toward a zero-profit equilibrium handsomely reward the *superior* company that continues to find ways to compete, innovate, and repeatedly break the law of economic equilibrium. A company can break this law by (1) participating in less-than-competitive markets, where the rates of return are greater than costs, and (2) creating strategies that provide the business with a unique competitive advantage over its rivals. Viewed this way, a value-creating strategy is the systematic search for attractive markets in which the business can earn returns in excess of the industry average, combined with actions that then protect and sustain those conditions for as long as possible.

The specific objective of the strategic analysis module of the VBM framework is to formulate appropriate value-creating strategies across all the business units of the company. This task requires us to first perform a factual, thorough, and objective analysis of the existing market economics and competitive position of each product or business unit within the company. Second, this analysis is used to generate well-grounded and realistic forecasts of the level, risk, growth, and sustainability of the cash flows—that is, the drivers of value—associated with each product or business. In this way, managers have the data they need to determine the value-creating potential of each business. These steps are depicted in Figure 1-6 in Chapter 1.

This analysis enables us to position each strategic business unit on the value-based market attractiveness/competitive position (MA/CP) matrix in Figure 9-1. The vertical axis of the matrix represents the attractiveness of the market, and the horizontal axis captures the competitive advantage of the business unit relative to its rivals. We then take the best—and most enduring—strategic lessons from the competitive analysis approach and combine them with valuation tools that appropriately capture the effects of strategy on value.

VALUE-CREATING MARKET ATTRACTIVENESS ANALYSIS
A complex array of forces and interplay determines the attractiveness of an industry at a point in time. Porter's work on the five competitive forces provides a useful framework for summarizing the rules of competition internal to an industry. In this framework, the industry's rate of return on in-

FIGURE 9-1   Value-based market attractiveness / competitive position matrix.

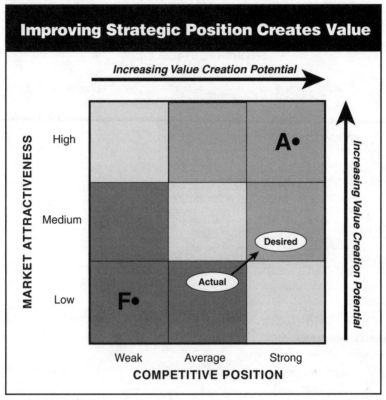

Source: B.C. Reimann, "Stock Price and Business Success: What Is the Relationship?," *Journal of Business Strategy,* Spring 1987.

vested capital (ROI) relative to its cost of capital—that is, the *spread*—is determined by five sources of competitive pressure, two from "vertical" competition (the bargaining power of suppliers and customers) and three from "horizontal" competition (competition from substitutes, entrants, and rivalry among established producers). Each plays a role in explaining why some industries are historically more profitable than others. The interplay of the five forces is depicted in Figure 9-2.

When combined with an analysis of the external factors governing an industry's potential performance, managers can develop a fairly thorough understanding of the nature of competition in an industry and better identify opportunities to avoid or forestall the zero-profit equilibrium that awaits the complacent company.

FIGURE 9-2   Porter's industry analysis framework.

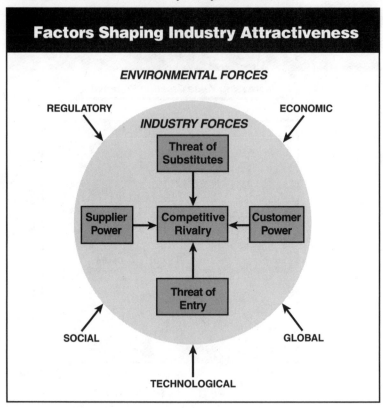

The Relative Bargaining Power of Customers

When customers have more power than sellers, they can lower industry profitability by forcing down prices or demanding costly services. The bargaining power of customers depends on their bargaining leverage and price sensitivity. Bargaining leverage, in turn, depends on the following factors:

*   Concentration and purchase volume
*   Relative switching costs
*   Quality of information
*   Availability of substitute products
*   Ability to vertically integrate (integrate backwards)

The customers' price sensitivity of demand is a function of the following factors:

- Cost or price of an item relative to total purchase costs
- Product differentiation
- Importance of brand identity
- Importance of customer quality/performance targets
- Customer profitability

Buyers' relative bargaining leverage.   Bargaining leverage ultimately rests on the ability to credibly and effectively refuse to deal with the other party. The more concentrated the buyers, the more difficult it is for a supplier to replace lost customers; and the bigger the purchases, the greater the damage from the loss. Independent retailers in Europe and North America formed buying groups to leverage their bargaining power.

The better informed buyers are, the more effectively they can bargain. Essential is the ability to compare the prices and qualities. Doctors and lawyers do not normally display the prices they charge, nor do traders in the bazaars of Tangier and Istanbul. Knowledge of price is of little value, however, if the quality and attributes of the product are unknown, as they are with baldness treatments, investment advice, management consulting, and other experience goods. In these industries, buying power is weak.

Finally, there is the ability to enter the other party's business through vertical integration. Large food processors such as Heinz and Campbell's Soup have reduced their dependence on metal can suppliers by manufacturing their own. Leading retail chains have increasingly displaced the brands of the major manufacturers with their own-label products. Backward integration need not necessarily occur; a credible threat may suffice.

Buyers' price sensitivity.   The sensitivity of buyers to price depends on many things, including the importance of the item in their budget. Also, the less differentiated the supplier's products, the more willing buyers are to switch on the basis of price unless brand identity is very important.

The more important the industry's product to the quality of the buyer's product, the less price-sensitive buyers are. As competition in the personal computer industry has become increasingly focused on the range and sophistication of available software, so has the bargaining power of the leading software houses. A central strategic weakness of IBM's position in the personal computer industry is its dependence on Microsoft's operating systems.

Finally, the greater the competition between buyers, the lower their margins, and the greater their eagerness to achieve price cuts from suppliers. One consequence of intense international competition in the auto-mobile industry has been the increased pressure on component suppliers to lower prices, improve quality, and speed up delivery.

The Relative Bargaining Power of Suppliers

Factors that influence the relative bargaining power of suppliers include the following:

- Supplier concentration relative to users
- Differentiation and switching costs
- Completeness of information
- Ability to integrate forward
- Critical nature of inputs to the user's business
- Relative importance of industry to the supplier group
- Presence of substitute inputs

Concentrated suppliers selling to diverse customers with high switch-ing costs have relative bargaining power. The highly concentrated oil in-dustry is often powerful enough to influence profits in customer industries that find it expensive to convert from oil.

Studies produced by the Profit Impact of Market Strategy (PIMS) Program show that supplier power is significantly increased by forward integration into its customer's own industry, reducing the customer's ROI by 2 percentage points, and that unionization typically reduces supplier profits.

Threat of New Entrants

If an industry is earning a return on invested capital in excess of the cost of capital, companies will want to enter. Unless entry is barred, the rate of profit must fall to the competitive level. It may not even be necessary for entry to actually take place; the threat of entry may be sufficient to con-strain prices. Consider an airline that offers the only service between two cities. It will be less willing to charge higher fares if other airlines can ex-tend their routes to cover the same two cities. Empirical studies have found that entry barriers can add 5 percentage points to return on equity. Familiar entry barriers include the following.

Capital investment requirements. The capital costs of getting estab-lished in an industry can be so large as to discourage all but the largest companies. In television broadcasting, Rupert Murdoch spent hundreds of millions of dollars in capital costs and operating losses to establish his Fox Broadcasting as the fourth U.S. network.

Economies of scale.   In some industries, particularly capital- or research-intensive ones, efficiency requires producing at a very large scale. Economies of scale in the development and manufacture of cars, for example, have squeezed out small independents such as Jaguar and Saab, and made it a very difficult industry to enter. Saturn was established only with the help of General Motors. New entrants are faced with the choice of entering either on a small scale and accepting high unit costs, or on a large scale and running the risk of costly underutilization of capacity while they build up sales volume. In the U.S. cereal market, for example, production economies of scale occur at approximately 5 percent of sales. Since a successful brand may gain only a 1 percent share, a new company would need to score five winners, a virtually impossible feat.

Absolute cost advantages.   Irrespective of scale economies, established companies may have a cost advantage over entrants across all levels of output. Such advantages are usually associated with "first-mover advantages." By being early in the industry, established companies are more likely to have been able to acquire low-cost sources of raw materials. By being in the industry longer, they benefit from economies of learning. Delaware, for example, has a virtual lock on (re)incorporating companies despite similar corporate governance environments in other states, primarily because they have been doing it for so long.

Product differentiation.   In an industry where products are differentiated, established companies possess an advantage over new entrants by virtue of brand recognition and customer loyalty. The percentage of U.S. consumers loyal to a single brand varies from under 30 percent in batteries to 71 percent in cigarettes. New entrants into highly differentiated markets must spend disproportionately on advertising and promotion. In producer goods, too, bonds between suppliers and their customers based on loyalty and understanding of reciprocal needs are often strong. In business services such as auditing and investment banking, established relationships create formidable entry barriers.

Access to channels of distribution.   For consumer goods manufacturers, the biggest barrier may be distributors' preferences for established companies' products. Limited capacity within distribution channels (e.g., shelf space), risk aversion, and the fixed costs associated with carrying an

additional product result in distributors' reluctance to carry a new manufacturer's product. Research has found that late entrants into consumer
goods markets incur additional advertising and promotional costs amount-
ing to 2.12% percent of sales revenue.

Governmental and legal barriers.   It has been claimed, notably by econ-
omists of the Chicago School, that the only really effective barriers to entry are those created by government. In industries such as taxicab services, banking, and telecommunications, entry may require a license granted
by a public authority. In knowledge-intensive industries, patents, copy-
rights, and trade secrets are frequently the most effective barriers to entry.
In industries subject to heavy government involvement through regulation,
procurement, and environmental and safety standards, new entrants may
be at a disadvantage because of the costs of becoming an "approved supplier."

Retaliation.   The effectiveness of any barrier to entry depends on the entrants' expectations as to possible retaliation by established companies.
Proposals to launch new newspapers frequently lead to threats of advertising rate cuts and increased promotion by the incumbent. In 1987, IBM
used threats of litigation over patent and copyright infringement to deter
competitors from cloning its personal computers. The effectiveness of
threats of retaliation depends on their credibility. Threats of aggressive
price competition against new entrants are only credible, for example, when
backed by excess capacity or inventories.
      The likelihood of retaliation also depends on industry conditions. If
entrants restrict themselves to market segments where they do not compete directly with established companies, a reaction is less likely. The
Japanese entry into the U.S. consumer electronics market was accomplished by circumventing the U.S. distribution barriers by initially sup-
plying the U.S. retailers' own brand products and focusing on market segments that domestic producers viewed as unattractive, such as monochrome
and portable televisions. From there they adopted a strategy of "cascading
segment expansion" to move from market niches to market dominance.

      The effectiveness of barriers to entry also depends heavily on the re-
sources of would-be entrants. Barriers which are effective in impeding new
companies may be ineffective in thwarting established companies in other
industries with the financial resources, skills, and transferable brand im-
ages to enter and compete effectively. American Express leveraged its

brand name to enter other financial services, and Procter and Gamble relied on its marketing strengths to enter health product markets.

The Threat of Competitive Substitutes

The potential for value creation in an industry is determined by the maximum price that customers are willing to pay. This depends primarily on the availability of substitutes. Where there are few substitutes for a product, as in the case of gasoline or cigarettes, consumers are willing to pay more. If there are close substitutes for a product, then any increase in price will cause some customers to switch. The extent to which the threat of substitutes constrains industry pricing depends on three factors:

- The relative price performance of substitutes
- The customer's costs of switching to substitutes
- The customer's propensity to substitute

The relative price performance of substitutes.   If two products meet the same customer needs and one performs better than the other, the price of the superior product determines the maximum price for the inferior product. For batteries of identical size and voltage, the one with the shorter life expectancy will only sell if it undercuts the price of the longer-life battery. Where products meet more complex needs and none dominate all performance dimensions, a niche position in the market may be sustainable despite premium pricing. Harley-Davidson has achieved market leadership in "super-heavyweight" motorcycles with cycles priced substantially above equivalent Japanese models, despite inferior speed, acceleration, and technical sophistication.

The customer's costs of switching to substitutes.   If the costs of switching are substantial, a substitute would have to offer significant performance and/or price advantages before the buyer will switch. Federal Express apparently met this higher performance standard for a large number of shippers that switched from the low-priced alternative offered by the U.S. Postal Service. Computer replacement part suppliers, whose end users placed a very high premium on speedy delivery, are an example of shippers that switched to FedEx.

The customer's propensity to substitute.   The critical issue in the discussion on substitutes is the willingness of the buyer to substitute. Even though substitutes may exist, customers may be unresponsive to changes in relative prices. For example, efforts by city planners to relieve traffic congestion either by charging the motorist or subsidizing public transport have been remarkably ineffective in encouraging motorists to forsake their cars.

One effective strategic response to threats from substitutes is to un-bundle the product into several distinct products or services, thereby re-defining the market and the degree of relative competition for each un-bundled product segment. The pooling and reselling of mortgages in tranches according to their maturity dates is an example.

The Rivalry Among Existing Competitors
For most industries, a major determinant of the overall state of competi-tion is the interaction among the businesses within the industry. A key question then in forming strategy is "How do the existing competitors in-teract?" In some industries, companies compete aggressively on price. In others, rivalry focuses on advertising, innovation, and other nonprice di-mensions. Among the major factors determining the nature and intensity of competition between established companies are

- Industry sales growth
- Industry concentration and competitive balance
- Diversity of competitors
- Product differentiation
- Cost conditions
- Excess capacity and exit barriers

Industry sales growth.   The impact of growth on potential value creation depends on where the product is in its growth life cycle: Early-stage growth is more likely to sustain entrants and profits and thus be value creating; Later-stage growth is more likely to accompany negative spreads and be value destroying. In short, while average profitability defines the level of market attractiveness, growth defines the *degree* of market attractiveness.

Industry concentration and competitive balance.   Seller concentration refers to the number of competitors in an industry and their relative sizes. An industry dominated by a single firm, such as Xerox's dominance of plain-paper copiers during the early 1970s, displays little competition, and the dominant firm can exercise considerable discretion over the prices it charges. Where an industry comprises a small group of leading compa-nies, price competition may also be restrained, either by outright collusion or, more commonly, through *parallelism* of pricing decisions, such as in the U.S. airline industry.

Diversity of competitors. The ability of the companies in an industry to avoid competition depends not only on the number of companies but also on their similarities in terms of origins, objectives, costs, and strategies. The U.S. steel industry, before the advent of overseas competition and the new mini mills, was composed of similar companies headed by managers with similar outlooks.

Product differentiation. The more similar are the offerings of rivals, the more willing are customers to substitute between them, and the greater is the incentive for companies to cut prices in order to expand business. Price is the sole basis of competition for undifferentiated products, or "commodities." By contrast, in industries where products are highly differentiated, such as perfumes, pharmaceuticals, and management consulting services, the effectiveness of price competition is limited, and even when these differentiated industries contain several producers, profits can be very high.

Cost conditions. The aggressiveness with which rivals compete for market share is crucially dependent on the cost conditions that they face. The higher the ratio of fixed to variable costs, the greater the willingness of companies to reduce prices in order to use spare capacity.

Excess capacity and exit barriers. The propensity of companies in an industry to resort to aggressive price competition depends critically on the balance between capacity and output. The presence of unused capacity encourages companies to compete for additional business in order to spread fixed costs over a greater sales volume. Excess capacity is most commonly the result of declining market demand, although overinvestment may play a role. The duration of excess capacity depends on the "barriers to exit," or the costs and other impediments to leaving an industry. Where resources are specialized or employees are entitled to job protection, barriers to exit may be substantial.

The importance of exit barriers also depends on the level of commitment of the competitors to spend whatever is needed to maintain their position. In general, an undiversified company that has made major investments in facilities or sources of supply will be highly committed. Gallo, for example, has nearly all its sales tied to wine and has extensive vertical integration. It thus has a high level of commitment. A commitment to a business can also be created when that business supports other parts of a company. A retailer may need to remain in several undesirable sites to maintain a critical mass regionally.

In summary, despite considerable empirical research into the relationship between industry structure and profitability, the results are far from conclusive, perhaps because the variability of firm performance within industries is so great. Most contentious is the impact of seller concentration on profitability. The impact of some of the other variables on profitability is more clear. Studies using the PIMS database show that the rate of market growth is positively associated with profitability, although cash flow declines with very high growth caused by the greater investment needs of growing businesses. Excess capacity has a depressing effect on both ROI and return on sales (ROS), particularly in capital-intensive businesses.

Industry Attractiveness: External Factors
The five forces model focuses on the internal determinants of the competitiveness of an industry, but external forces can have a significant impact on average profitability as well. One high-tech producer of specialty medical equipment learned this the hard way when, despite a thorough analysis of the factors driving industry competitiveness, its business was thrown into disarray when the federal regulator with whom its management team had worked extensively suddenly resigned. The product launch was delayed and eventually scrapped, at a significant loss of millions of dollars.

Clearly, even though managers have less direct control over external forces, their impact on the company's ability to develop strategies to create and sustain value must be factored into the analysis. The problem is that the company's external environment consists of an almost limitless array of potentially important factors. Even though your analysis will not and probably should not attempt to cover every possible external environment configuration, a sound economic analysis will consider the prevailing and projected conditions in most of the following areas, each of which can have a major impact on the potential attractiveness of the industry:

- Regulatory and legal forces
- Macroeconomic forces
- Global forces
- Social forces
- Technological forces

Regulatory and legal forces. The regulatory environment determines the set of laws governing business. Regulation (and deregulation) can affect each of the five forces of competition, but the most obvious may be the barriers to entry. Deregulation in the telecommunications and airline industries, for example, has spawned a host of new competitors. The way companies respond to these changes determines whether the new environment enhances or destroys their ability to generate and sustain profits.

Many other examples of the effects of regulation on business and its ability to develop strategies to create value exist. Some key areas to keep in mind in a thorough external economic assessment include tax reform, disclosure and reporting, licensing, international trade policy, patent and copyright protection, equal opportunity employment, occupational health and safety, product safety, fuel economy, and environmental pollution.

Macroeconomic forces. General economics conditions such as recession, inflation, interest rates, and unemployment affect the average profitability of industries. The macro level of these forces, however, obscures dramatic differences across industries. Some industries or regions can experience very tight labor markets, for example, while others have labor to spare. In addition, a given level of a macroeconomic variable can have quite a varied impact across industries. The same level of general price inflation, for example, affects highly price-sensitive industries like banks and homebuilders, while price-insensitive industries like producers of insulin remain unaffected.

Global forces. There is little question that the existence of world trade and international competition has transformed the nature of competition in a great many U.S. industries. The most prevalent impact has been to increase the speed with which profit levels in affected U.S. industries fall to the cost of capital, reducing the spread to zero and drastically limiting their value-creating potential. This need not mean, however, that some companies will not earn abnormal profits. In some cases, the existence of foreign trade has enabled domestic companies to reap substantial profits. Auto parts suppliers, for example, recognized that foreign customers reduced their dependence on domestic buyers, improving their bargaining power and profits.

Social forces. Social forces change the way people live, eat, play, work, and even die, and this changes their relative demand for new and existing goods and services. Recognizing social trends early enables a business to be first. The growth in the number of failed marriages, for example, coupled with the general increase in the number of women in the workforce, has led to an increase in the level and quality of all varieties of child care.

Often it is a business from outside the industry whose managers have the freedom and perspective to think outside of the box and innovate ways to compete that respond early and well to social trends. Rival, a relative newcomer to the appliance industry, invented the Crock-Pot. Raytheon, a defense contractor, introduced the microwave oven.

Technological forces. This is a very broad category, involving the people, processes, and products that transform inputs into outputs. Technological improvements either increase the efficiency with which products are produced or increase the menu of available goods and services. Clearly, the vast increase in the value of the U.S. stock market and the growth rate of the U.S. economy is due in large part to technological advances. The average attractiveness of any given industry depends heavily on the relative opportunities and threats posed by new technologies. Even so, technologies probably represent a much more dramatic opportunity to raise a company's *marginal* return on investment relative to its competitors.[1]

In summary, various external and internal influences jointly determine the current intensity of competition in a given market and, therefore, the upper and lower limits on the rate of return on invested capital that can be earned relative to the cost of capital. From this we can estimate the average level of profitability in a market. This combined with the projected rate of growth in that market helps determine the level and degree of attractiveness in that industry. Growth magnifies the impact of (superior and negative) spreads on value, an impact that varies depending on where the business stands in its product life cycle. The analysis of market economics helps management determine which industries to target and which product lines to retain.

WEAKNESSES WITH PORTER'S INDUSTRY ANALYSIS
Managers must be careful to recognize that not all forces are created equal. They need to focus on the factors most critical to their industry's attractiveness. In addition, Porter's analysis is static, while industry structure is

---

[1] A study by the MIT Center for Information Systems Research suggests that the impact of information technology on such variables as productivity may have been insignificant for a number of industries, but that individual companies, like Xerox, successfully exploited the new technologies and realized marked gains in productivity and profits. The typical firm in the industry apparently failed to implement the new technology and suffered losses, pulling the industry average profit down to the cost of capital.

increasingly dynamic in this high-tech, global era. The framework fails to focus on important trends in industry structure or to provide a framework for visualizing the threats and opportunities represented by future industry structures. Scenario planning may assist in filling this gap.

Porter's strategic approach tends to be adversarial, which ignores the wisdom accumulated over the last decade about the benefits of cooperation. Not all competitors are threats; some can be valuable partners in joint ventures, licensing agreements, supplier agreements, and other strategic alliances.

Finally, Porter's approach assumes that the companies in an industry are fairly homogenous. It is likely, of course, that companies in the same industry are more similar than not, but this does not mean that the focus of *strategy* should be on their similarities. Strategy should focus on how the company, its product offering, and strategic choices are unique. The emerging *strategic group analysis* begins to provide some rigor to this concept.[2]

VALUE-CREATING COMPETITIVE POSITION ANALYSIS
Competitive position has a major effect on a company's profitability and continued cash flows, and, hence, on its market value. We need only refer to the earlier observation that the spreads within an industry are much greater than those between industries to recognize that a company's relative competitive position has a far greater impact on the value-creating possibilities for a company than does average market profitability. In addition, while a business *can* take steps to alter the degree of *average* industry profitability, it is much more likely that the company has more immediate and significant control over its relative profitability.

How do we situate a business on the competitive position axis of the MA/CP matrix? How do we establish a favorable competitive position? The key to enhancing value is creating a position in the industry that is less susceptible to direct competition and less vulnerable to erosion from the influence of customers, suppliers, and substitute goods. At the business unit level, Porter has identified two generic ways of gaining and maintaining such a competitive position, that is, of making markets less competitive:

- Differentiate the product in some key way
- Achieve a cost advantage over competitors

---

[2] Hax and Majluf. *The Strategy Concept and Process: A Pragmatic Approach.* Upper Saddle River, NJ: Prentice Hall, 1991.

The combination of these two types of competitive advantage with the scope of their strategic target yields Porter's well-known generic strategies, shown in Figure 9-3.

Generic Strategy #1: Product Differentiation

Product differentiation effectively limits the number of products that directly compete with your product. In the extreme, perfectly differentiated products create monopolies for that product. If the product is differentiated in ways that customers value—the only relevant version of differentiation for our purposes—a monopoly price premium can be commanded, generating higher returns and corporate value.

In strategic terms, a business unit's product is differentiated if customers perceive it to be of sufficiently higher quality, lower risk, or better performance to pay a premium over competitors' offerings. These perceived differences on the part of customers enable the company to break the equilibrium law of economics and either charge a premium relative to their competitors and maintain market share, or gain market share by charging the same price as their competitors for a superior product.

It is important to understand that it is not enough to simply offer a *different* product. *Different* products are not necessarily *differentiated* products. It is not uncommon for managers to overestimate the uniqueness of their products, probably because they are so familiar with the product's attributes and advantages. The problem is that these optimistic forecasts lead to overpriced products and value-destroying strategies. It is very important for business managers to first determine whether their customers do, in fact, perceive their product or service as truly differentiated, and then to mea-

FIGURE 9-3   Porter's generic competitive strategies.

	Sources of Competitive Advantage:	
	Unique Value as Perceived by Customer	Lowest Cost
Broad (industry-wide)	Overall Differentiation	Overall Cost Leadership
Narrow (segment only)	Focused Differentiation	Focused Cost Leadership

Strategic Scope

Source: Porter, op. cit.

sure the price premium the customer is willing to pay for the improvement in the offering. The only meaningful differentiation in a value-based management system is one that enables companies to charge a premium for their product. Companies with differentiated products may alternatively choose to forgo the premium and grow market share. Either way, value is created. The magnitude of a differentiation advantage can be explicitly measured over time by (1) the size of the price premium, if market shares are stable; (2) the increase in market share, if pricing is kept at competitors' levels; or (3) the combination of price premiums and gains in market share. These measures, not managers' perceptions, are the true test of whether the product represents a differentiation advantage for the business.

Not all differentiation advantages create value. Only when the combined premium and market share effects are large enough to recover the costs and investments required to distinguish the product does the differentiation advantage create value for the company. A careful analysis of costs, customer perceptions, premiums, and market share over time is required to objectively determine the value-creating potential of the differentiation strategy.

Many companies that undertake such an analysis are surprised to learn that their presumably differentiated products have been priced to lose market share over time. Almost any product can become insufficiently differentiated in the eyes of customers to warrant a price premium. Customers may become more sophisticated over time as they gain experience with some products and are less willing to pay for features that engineers inside the company may add. Typically, only a careful survey of current, lost, and potential customers can reveal the offering advantage represented by a product. The judicious use of customer surveys—gathering only data directly relevant to the strategic issue at hand—is a useful way of maintaining data on the strategic actions and reactions of competitors as well.

The goal of differentiation strategies is to create value by differentiating those products or services whose price premium exceeds the total economic costs required to generate the (perceived) improvement in the offering. There are many ways to differentiate a product. The easiest to describe, but perhaps most difficult to achieve, is offering the highest-quality product or service as perceived by the customer. Mercedes-Benz and American Express Travelers Services come to mind as two products able to charge a premium based on actual quality. A company might also use superior advertising to enhance the customer's perceptions of quality, regardless of the actual differences in quality. Clorox Bleach is chemically identical to competing brands, yet advertising has enabled the business to charge a premium for perceived differentiation for many years. Another way, though harder to implement, is to differentiate by reducing the customer's perceived risks. Until the era of open systems, IBM was able to command a differentiation premium through the high vendor-switching costs produced by its proprietary software and architecture.

In general, a company can successfully differentiate its product or service offering by

- Improving the quality of the offering itself
- Improving how the offering is promoted
- Lowering the risk associated with the offering

Table 9-1 shows examples of the first two strategies to differentiate products, improved product offering and product promotion. Gillette's Sensor razor is an example of an improved product offering. By increasing the comfort feature of a razor that still gave a close shave, Gillette was able to add $500 million in revenues with a 40 percent operating margin. The company's ROI increased from 20 to 26 percent and its stock price doubled, largely because of this product offering differentiation strategy. An interesting example of a successful product promotion differentiation strategy is found in Van Heusen, the men's shirtmaker. Their customer research found that women make 70 percent of all men's clothing purchases. By targeting its ad campaign to women's magazines, the company successfully differentiated its product without changing its product.

Improving product quality in ways customers appreciate generally requires a thorough understanding of how customers use the product or service, their purchasing habits and income levels, and a painfully objective assessment of how customers *really* view the business unit's current offerings. Focus groups, observing the customer interacting with the product, test mar-

TABLE 9-1   Differentiation strategies.

Improve Product Offering	Improve Product Promotion
Add features	Increase advertising effectiveness
Improve performance	Increase sales promotion
Shorten time to market	Increase direct selling effectivenes
Improve appeal of packaging	Enhance merchandising
Enhance service/warranty	Liberalize credit
Improve convenience	

keting, and timely customer surveys are some useful techniques for gaining these insights into opportunities for profitable differentiation.

In addition, for the differentiation strategy to create and sustain economic value, it must be consistent with the strategic assessment of the business unit. For example, for business units with a competitive advantage in an attractive market, differentiation strategies should focus on enhancing growth while maintaining profits. Recall from Chapter 3 that increasing the scale (or growth or market share) of any product earning a positive spread increases corporate value. Based on extensive research of the preferences of the frequent snacker and medium-to-light snacker segments, Frito-Lay decided that it could maintain its product differentiation while growing market share. It did so by extending its product line, revitalizing its packaging, and perfecting its distribution. On the other hand, if the strategic characterization reveals that the business unit is earning below-average industry profits but is in an attractive market, then its differentiation strategy should focus on how to improve the offering's profitability.

We must be careful, however. There may be wide differences in profits across product lines and customer segments. Value will be enhanced if these differences influence the differentiation strategies pursued. This will likely result in a mix of product promotion and offering strategies. A wonderful example is found in the typical department store chain, with its many products and customer segments, the combination of which varies across geographic regions and through the ups and downs of changing customer tastes.

Constant vigilance and an objective assessment of purchasing and pricing trends in a product's market are required to guarantee that product differentiation still creates value. Only if the cost or investment required to differentiate the product is smaller than the benefits produced is value created.

Generic Strategy #2: Cost Advantage

The most reliable competitive strategy is simply to be able to charge a lower price for your good or service than your rival and still earn money. To be profitable, this requires that your total economic costs be lower than your rival's. A low-cost position tends to insulate the company against all five forces of competition. It protects the company from supplier power by giving it a cushion to absorb input cost increases. Customer power and availability of substitutes is limited, since prices can only be driven down to the cost of the most efficient producer. The same factors that lead to lowest cost and large minimum-efficient scale (high fixed capital expenditures) also represent significant barriers to entry. Finally, a company's lower costs protect it from the inroads of competitive rivalry, since the rivals will compete away their profits before the lowest cost producer will.

Achieving a lower total economic cost per unit than the industry average for that product, including a charge for the financial capital required to achieve the advantage, typically results in value creation. Lowest-cost production does not, however, guarantee value creation: Only if the economic cost and/or investment required to gain the cost advantage is smaller than the benefits produced is value created. That is, the product must be viewed as close enough to the competition that the discount pricing needed to increase market share does not wipe out the cost advantage.

The emphasis on the proper measurement of costs is crucial. Without a full recognition of the charge for capital, for example, a company that invests heavily to reduce operating costs might actually increase the true economic costs per unit if the investment capital charges exceed the reduction in operating costs. A striking example of this is seen in General Motors in the mid-1980s. The company spent billions of dollars on automation and robotics, only to burden itself with such high per-unit costs that Ford, who had been concentrating on improving efficiency and customer satisfaction, was able to price its offerings more competitively and still earn profits. Acknowledging the full economic costs of each strategy not only helps the line manager understand the true costs of operations but also makes it easier to measure the impact of cost-advantage strategies on value creation.

Just as in the case of product differentiation, a relative cost advantage enables the company to either price its product or service lower than the competitors' in order to gain market share while maintaining its profits, or match competitor's prices and increase profitability. Unlike product differentiation, however, a true economic cost advantage can be measured and thus verified in only one way: by comparing the total economic cost per unit of a business against the comparable cost of its competitors, information obtained either by direct observation or by using publicly available financial statements to infer business unit costs (sometimes referred to as benchmarking).

Sources of economic cost advantages include economies of scale, economics of scope, innovative process technology, access to low-cost raw materials (particularly those in low supply), low-cost distribution channels or access to customers, superior operating management, proprietary knowledge, expertise, or a low cost of financial capital. Developing a true cost advantage over your competitors will also deter new entrants into the market and reduce competition, creating monopoly pricing and another source of value creation.

TABLE 9-2   Cost advantage and asset strategies.

Redeploy Assets and Activities	Reduce Unit Costs in Each Activity
Outsource products	Process innovation and control
Outsource services	Reduce waste and rework
	Improve design (involve customers)
Vertically or horizontally integrate to bring outsourced activities in-house	Reduce cycle time
	Increase utilization
	Relocate facilities
	Implement supplier agreements
	Increase relative costs to competitors (e.g., through ownership of assets, access, or other barriers)

Table 9-2 shows various cost advantage and related asset strategies.

Typically, it is difficult to build a competitive cost advantage through low-cost access to raw materials, because the suppliers of these materials prefer to sell to as many buyers as possible. It is not impossible, however. Procter & Gamble was able to gain such an advantage by helping a Japanese company finance a plant for producing polyacrylate, a key ingredient in Procter & Gamble's best-selling superabsorbent Ultra Pampers. The financing agreement essentially locked up the supply of this extremely scarce raw material, effectively blocking any of P&G's rivals from producing a competing product. Unless the company owns a resource that is in limited supply, like OPEC, or enters into long-term contracts restricting access (like P&G in the example above, or as movie studios did with major stars in the 1930s and 1940s), sustaining such a cost advantage is generally quite difficult.

Superior process technology is a more reliable source of cost advantage, particularly when it can be made proprietary. A process technology is superior if it has a large impact on total economic cost. The Microsoft and Netscape search engines are examples of superior process technologies that reaped large profits for an extended period.

Low-cost access to either distribution channels or customers can be a source of significant advantage in many markets. Limited access to broadcast frequencies is an example, as is having a prime location in a retail market. Packaged-food companies use brand name and introduce self-competing products—like the ready-to-eat breakfast cereal industry—to dominate shelf space at grocery stores and thus secure low-cost access to customers.

A illustrative example of a value-creating cost advantage strategy is found in a large glass container business that discovered through an extensive market attractiveness and competitive position analysis that the average competitor earned negative economic profits, and given the fiercely competitive nature of the industry and bargaining power of customers, this company in particular would probably never produce a profit under its current strategy.[3] Since product differentiation opportunities were limited, the company undertook an extensive cost analysis. The analysis determined that the two most important strategic cost and asset drivers to this business were plant siting (because of its impact on shipping costs, which were substantial for the bulky yet fragile glass containers) and capacity utilization (since fully 75% of production costs in this capital-intensive industry were fixed).

Two alternative cost strategies were developed. One involved decreasing the number of plants from six to four. This raised capacity utilization from 60% to 85% but also increased the maximum shipping distance to 300 miles. The predicted ROE was 15%, a significant improvement over the historical ROE of 4%. The other alternative involved closing five of the six plants and building a new modern facility so that the company could operate two modern plants at 90% capacity. These plants would operate at unit costs well below any competitor in the market, but raised the minimum shipping distance to 500 miles and reduced expected volume. The ROE on this plan was higher, at 17%. After more analysis on the expected growth rates generated by each alternative, which are dependent on a thorough analysis of customer profitability data as well, the company chose the first alternative which, despite its slightly lower ROE, was expected to generate significantly more economic value over time. Management implemented the four-plant configuration and was indeed profitable and healthy within three years, as predicted.

The most important source of a competitive advantage, however, has to be superior operating management. There are innumerable examples of companies with distinctive and long-term cost advantages that can only be explained by their unique command over the purchasing, manufacturing,

---

[3] This example is drawn from McTaggart, Kontes, and Mankins, *The Value of Superior Shareholder Returns.* New York: The Free Press, 1994.

marketing, distribution, human resource, and/or business processes within the company. Typically, these companies have studied their processes extensively, frequently using the tools afforded by total quality management and just-in-time production techniques, to reduce their costs by eliminating waste, defects, and rework, minimizing cycle time, and reducing inventory storage. (All of this presumes that they are designing and producing a product or service in demand by the customer, of course.) A recent study found that companies that implemented mature and extensive total quality management systems, a goal reached by only about one in four companies that tried, improved their operating net income per employee by about $3000 per year, a result that was independent of the change in the number of employees.[4]

We need to distinguish, however, between simple operational excellence and strategic positions that create value. To the extent that best practices diffuse easily throughout an industry, efficiencies may improve but profits do not. In the extreme, after all, benchmarking simply makes firms more similar. Strategies that sustain value over the long run will include cost advantage strategies, but these will just prevent the company from falling behind, not enable the company to move ahead.

Combining Differentiation and Low-Cost Strategies
Typically, it is very difficult for a business to undertake both differentiation and low-cost strategies and do both well. Companies that try usually devote a separate organizational unit to each strategy or create autonomous units that serve distinct segments with one or both strategies, both of which require considerable resources and effort. Perhaps the research coming out of the PIMS database showing that the very highest returns are reserved for those who can somehow manage to combine the two gives companies the incentive to keep trying despite the odds.

The most likely source for low-cost differentiation strategies is a new technological innovation that generates an increase in product quality accompanied by low-cost inputs, production, and/or distribution. Inland Steel's new $20 million information system, which tracks its production schedules and inventory levels, is one such example. The system saves money internally by reducing downtime and trimming inventory storage

---

[4] G. Easton and S. Jarrell. "The Effects of Total Quality Management on Corporate Performance: An Empirical Investigation." *Journal of Business,* Volume 71, No. 2, 1998, pp. 253–307.

costs. At the same time, it creates a differentiation advantage by providing its customers (who have proprietary access to the system) a way to track the real-time progress of their orders, thus lowering their processing and inventory management costs.

Generic Strategy #3: Pricing

A complete description of a company's current competitive strategy includes details not just on how the company differentiates its product offerings or manages the business unit's costs, but also on how the company prices its products and services. As we have seen earlier, answers to the first two questions will determine the firms' sustainable competitive advantage, or its ability to earn and maintain superior economic profits. Pricing strategies, frequently overlooked by managers, help determine the impact of a company's competitive advantage on value creation. For advantaged businesses, prices can either be set equal to competitors to build market share due to superior products or increased above competitor levels to create value through increased margins and profit levels. Basic pricing strategies take the following forms:

Price to Build/Protect Market Share If:	Price to Build/Protect Margins If:
Current returns exceed capital cost	Current returns below capital cost
High current growth	Low market growth
High leverage/scale economies	Low leverage/scale economies
Low current market share	High current market share
Competitor inertia	Reactive competitors

Optimal pricing strategies are highly complex. Since the pricing decisions of companies are so visible to customers, pricing strategies need to be explored carefully before committing to one or the other. Much like optimal dividend policies, stable prices are like an implicit contract with customers. Repeated violations of this contract can permanently undermine the trust of the customer in the business and significantly damage the company's bottom line.

Value Chain: Identifying Strategies to Sustain Competitive Advantage

That Inland Steels' unique dual strategy may be hard to sustain brings us to the question of the factors determining the sustainability of a competitive advantage. No generic strategy will create value unless it yields a competitive advantage over a long enough period to recoup the required investment and capital costs and margins lost to secure market share. Sooner or later, the competition is going to replicate the source of any successful strategy. The more successful the strategy, the higher the profits and the greater the incentives for competitors to find a way to enter the industry. We need methods for finding ways to sustain competitive advantage. Porter's Value Chain is one such method.

Value chain analysis is built on the observation that a vertical chain of firms produces most goods and services. The supply of bread, for example, involves a chain comprising the farmer, the miller, the baker, and the retailer. The value created in a loaf of bread may be allocated between the companies involved. The value may be added by the efficiency of the manufacturing process, the distribution system, and so forth. Each of the activities in the value chain is a potential source of competitive advantage.

Different manufactured items have different value chains. A disposable-pen company's value may come from marketing and efficient distribution, whereas a machine tool manufacturer's advantage may come in efficient production and service. In this view, value chain analysis helps identify the company's present competitive advantages—and that of its main rivals—and those that must be developed to reach the desired competitive position.

In a similar way, the individual business can be viewed as a chain of related activities. The resources and capabilities required at each stage depend upon the nature of the activity being undertaken.

Value chain analysis, because of its focus on disaggregating the company and its main rivals into a set of distinct strategic activities, allows us to better understand their respective impact on product cost and differentiation—that is, to understand why spreads vary so widely across companies and how some add more value than others. By mapping the activities that the company performs and the linkages between activities, the value chain provides a representation of the company that can then be manipulated to suggest new ways of competing. New strategies can take the form of new configurations of the chain of activities. By reconstructing and rearranging the value chain, a company can erect entry barriers and create value. The end result of value chain analysis is often a reconfiguration or recombination of value chain activities that creates superior value for customers and earns a sustainable competitive advantage.

Several companies have competed successfully through redefining and reconfiguring the activities they perform. FedEx altered the nature of the delivery business by reconfiguring both the primary and the support activities to create the overnight delivery business. Another good example is provided by the airline industry. Southwest Airlines substantially lowered its operating costs by radically pruning the number of activities performed,

while American Airlines established a substantial differentiation advantage
by developing the Sabre ticketing system.

Porter proposed a fairly complex but useful version of the value chain
that distinguishes between "primary activities" and "support activities."

Primary Value Activities:

- *Inbound logistics*—Receiving inputs, material handling and ware-
  housing
- *Operations*—The direct activities that transform inputs into final
  product
- *Outbound logistics*—Order processing and output distribution
- *Marketing and sales*—Advertising, pricing, and channel manage-
  ment
- *Service*—Installation, training, repair, and parts

Secondary Value or Support (Staff) Activities:

- *Procurement*—Purchasing procedures and information systems
- *Technology development*—Improving the product and processes
- *Human resource management*—Hiring, training, and compensation
- *Company infrastructure*—General management, finance, account-
  ing, government relations, and quality management systems

As shown in Figure 9-4, a business' primary activities involve the
creation of physical product, the sale and distribution of the product to
customers, and creation of after-sale service. Support activities are
those necessary for the primary activities to take place, such as company
infrastructure, human resource management, technology development, and
procurement.

The value-creating potential of each primary and support activity
should be examined and ranked relative to competitors' abilities, with the
intent to determine areas where companies have the potential to create
value relative to their main rivals. To illustrate, each activity involved in
the inbound logistics category, such as materials handling, warehousing,
and inventory control used to receive, store, and disseminate inputs to a
product, is examined for its value-creating potential.

To guide the extent of decomposition, activities should be separated
only if they are strongly differentiated from an economic point view (or
have a high potential for differentiation) or represent an important proportion of costs. In either case, such focus helps isolate those activities

FIGURE 9-4 Porter's basic value chain.

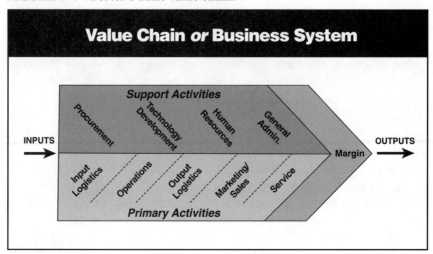

Source: Porter, op. cit.

that are most likely to create value. When using the value chain, a company's activities are progressively disaggregated into finer and finer details as more and more opportunities for competitive advantage are discovered.

It is also useful to distinguish between three different types of activities within each category of primary and support activities: direct, indirect, and monitoring. Direct activities are those that are directly involved in the value creation process, like the direct selling activities of the sales force. Indirect activities are those that enable the company to perform the direct activities and include such functions as maintenance, scheduling, and record keeping. Monitoring activities are those that ensure the reliability of the other activities and include items like inspection, testing, and rework.

Indirect activities, in particular, are becoming increasingly important in many industries. Because a company's indirect activities are difficult for other companies to observe, they represent a unique potential source for competitive advantage; it is much more difficult to imitate activities one cannot observe. In addition, because many companies lump indirect, monitoring, and other intangible costs together in overhead or burden accounts, they are passing up many opportunities for value creation that the value-based company can exploit. The quality management movement, for example, by bringing many manufacturing and business processes under control, eliminated the need for many of the monitoring activities and the costs associated with them, generating a distinct cost advantage for these companies.

Of course, a value chain is not just an array of independent activities; it is a *system* of interdependent tasks whose linkages themselves may be important sources of competitive advantage. If timely delivery is important to your customers, for example, careful coordination across operations, output logistics, and service is a must. The just-in-time management technique was developed with precisely this sort of linkage in mind. The linkages may go from support to main activities, or they may be between main activities. Identifying such linkages is a process that involves finding ways in which each value-creating activity influences the other activities of the chain. Since the management of these linkages requires timely and accurate information, effective information systems are a key requirement for transforming linkages into sustainable competitive advantage.

Not only are there linkages inside a company's own value chain, but also between the company and its suppliers and distributors. It is possible that both the company and its suppliers may benefit from a competitive advantage by optimizing the joint use of these activities or by improving the coordination between the chains. This is the idea, for example, behind many of the supplier initiatives undertaken within total quality management systems. The sharing will depend on the bargaining power of the suppliers. Coordinating, even vertically integrating, across the linkages with distribution channels—in the case of shipping suppliers, for example—can reduce costs and/or increase differentiation.

Customers also have a value chain, and the company's product is one of the inputs to their value chain. The particular degree of differentiation of a company arises from the way in which its own value chain is related to that of the customer. Each contact point between the value chain of the client and that of the company is a potential source of differentiation. A company can actually develop a competitive advantage for its customers by influencing their value chain. The Japanese recognized early on that U.S. customers valued quality as reflected by the finish of the automobile. This revelation happened to occur at about the same time Japanese automobile manufacturers developed processes that allowed them to perfect the finish of the car, transforming this link between the company's and its customers' value chain into a tremendously profitable competitive advantage that is still going strong today.

The value chain is also a fundamental tool that allows the determination of competitors' costs. Competitors' value chains are analyzed in the same way as the company's own, looking for ways to create and sustain a competitive advantage. In cases where an advantage is unlikely, seeking ways to minimize costs through long-term contracts, joint marketing agreements, technology licenses, joint ventures, and other coalitions can create measurable wealth.

A word of caution: Cost functions are difficult to estimate from traditional cost accounting methods. Rarely do the activities that make up the value chain coincide with their accounting classification. Accounting categories conceal linkages between activities particularly when the company is not structured along divisional lines or when the accounting system does not recognize the strategic business unit (SBU) as a data collection unit. Another challenge in using traditional accounting for value chain analysis is that there is little correspondence between the activities that create value and the responsibility centers collecting the data.

Once a value chain study of the business(es) is complete, we can identify the actual and desired competitive position(s) necessary in defining an optimal strategic path. Value chain analysis allows us to highlight our competitive advantages for those we should develop.

In summary, a business unit's competitive position in its product market determines its relative profitability. Business units with a competitive advantage based on either a differentiation, cost, or pricing strategy are capable of earning spreads above the average for their market (or, equivalently, of earning average spreads on increased market share) over time. Value chain analysis can aid the company in isolating those activities that hold the most promise for sustaining a competitive advantage. Lastly, it is not enough to earn a sustainable competitive advantage. For the competitive advantage to increase the value of the business, it must be large enough and sustainable enough to more than compensate for the investment required to gain and maintain that advantage.

THE LINK BETWEEN CURRENT STRATEGY AND VALUE: THE VALUE DRIVERS

Fundamentally, the value-creation approach means identifying, valuing, and adopting those strategies that produce a return that exceeds the cost of capital, therefore a competitive advantage, and maintaining that advantage for the longest time possible. The first step in this process is to identify and value the company's current strategy (e.g., the market attractiveness and relative competitive position of each of its businesses) and the sources of any competitive advantage (e.g., differentiation, cost, or pricing strategies, prevailing market conditions, and so on). The current strategy, once properly valued, will also provide a standard against which to

measure the added value of alternative strategies (or, more likely, portfolios of strategies).

The specific market and relative competitive economic features un-
covered by the strategic assessment of each business unit will clarify the
company's overall current strategy. The link between the current strategy
and the company's economic value depends on the impact of that strategy
on the level, risk, growth, and duration of the company's future cash flows.
The value of current and any competing alternative strategies, therefore,
depends on two things: (1) the appropriate formulation and specification
of the strategy, and (2) the quality and reliability of the forecasts of the
cash flows associated with that strategy. We discuss the latter issue here,
and we'll come back to the discussion of strategy formulation a bit later.

The most fundamental problem with the acceptance of value-based approaches by management may be forecast reliability. Managers are generally not taught how to make realistic forecasts. Most are suspect of forecasts in general and tend to favor projects with a quick recovery of funds
in a misguided attempt to mitigate uncertainty by shortening the forecast
horizon. Credibility is restored when forecasts are well grounded in a sensible, factual assessment of the internal and external economic environments of the company. The five forces examination of the average industry profitability, and the value chain assessment of those activities within
each SBU that are most likely to create and sustain above-average profitability, can lead to reliable forecasts of the level, risk, growth, and duration of economic cash flows associated with each strategy.

An example drawn from McTaggart[5] can help demonstrate what we
mean. The strategic characterization of a basic materials company began
with a market attractiveness assessment to determine whether the product
markets in which its businesses competed were currently profitable, how
fast they were growing, and the likely trends in both profits and growth
rates. This was accomplished with a five forces assessment of each of the
markets in which the company competes. In most cases, the profitability
and growth rates of competitors are not directly observable and must be
inferred through in-depth benchmarking, the analysis of publicly available
information such as analysts' reports or trade publications, and third-party
interviews with competitors' customers, suppliers, and employees.
Competitor analysis is made easier if management thoroughly understands

[5] McTaggart, Kontes, and Mankins, op. cit., pp. 114–124.

the links between its own economic environment and its profits and growth rates. Once the company was armed with a comprehensive market analysis, a detailed picture of the most likely sources of value creation in each market served emerged.

A profitability profile of the materials company and each of four competitors showed that only two of eight products supplied by this industry (Products A and B) earned a positive economic profit in 1992. An analysis of the structural factors responsible for the industry profit levels showed that there was tremendous excess capacity in 1992, coupled with surprisingly strong customer bargaining power and indirect competition. The excess capacity was due to the recession in 1991. A wave of consolidation among customers and the introduction of a new substitute product were responsible for pressure from customers and competitors. Five-year forecasts of each structural factor were made so that a profile of future industry profitability and growth could be constructed. This analysis showed that although increased capacity utilization would improve future market profitability, the improvement was but a fraction of what management had originally anticipated. Furthermore, pressures from customers and substitute products were forecast to persist, resulting in continued negative economic profits on fully half of the industries' eight products through 1997.

The next element of the strategic characterization is to analyze the relative competitive positions of each business unit. A relative competitive advantage—the ability to generate economic profits in excess of the industry average—is anchored in either a cost advantage or the ability to command a price premium by differentiating a product or service. As in the case of analyzing market attractiveness, the more comprehensive, fact-based, and objective the assessment, the more accurate and revealing the information. A differentiation advantage, for example, requires information on relative pricing (actual sales prices, not list prices), sales volume, market share, customer satisfaction, customer needs, and customer trends for each product of the company in question and its competitors. A relative cost advantage is more difficult to assess, given that internal cost data are generally proprietary. Relative economic costs can be surmised, however, by first developing a thorough understanding of the nature of your own cost structures through a detailed value chain analysis, followed by rigorous benchmarking of competitors' performance at each major stage in the value chain. An overview of how to link each activity in the value chain to specific drivers of cash flows, including costs, is provided in Figure 9-5.

FIGURE 9-5   Link between value chain and cash flows.

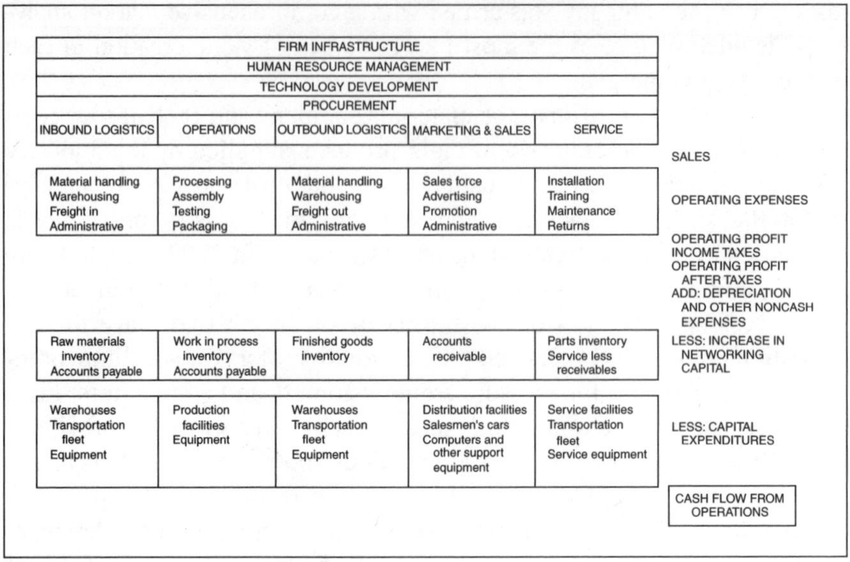

FIRM INFRASTRUCTURE					
HUMAN RESOURCE MANAGEMENT					
TECHNOLOGY DEVELOPMENT					
PROCUREMENT					
INBOUND LOGISTICS	OPERATIONS	OUTBOUND LOGISTICS	MARKETING & SALES	SERVICE	
					SALES
Material handling Warehousing Freight in Administrative	Processing Assembly Testing Packaging	Material handling Warehousing Freight out Administrative	Sales force Advertising Promotion Administrative	Installation Training Maintenance Returns	OPERATING EXPENSES
					OPERATING PROFIT INCOME TAXES OPERATING PROFIT AFTER TAXES ADD: DEPRECIATION AND OTHER NONCASH EXPENSES
Raw materials inventory Accounts payable	Work in process inventory Accounts payable	Finished goods inventory	Accounts receivable	Parts inventory Service less receivables	LESS: INCREASE IN NETWORKING CAPITAL
Warehouses Transportation fleet Equipment	Production facilities Equipment	Warehouses Transportation fleet Equipment	Distribution facilities Salesmen's cars Computers and other support equipment	Service facilities Transportation fleet Service equipment	LESS: CAPITAL EXPENDITURES
					CASH FLOW FROM OPERATIONS

Source: A. Rappaport, Creating Shareholder Value, *New York: The Free Press, 1999.*

The competitive analysis for the basic materials company revealed that two of its six products (Products A and B, again) were marginally advantaged relative to its competitors on differentiation and cost positions combined, and the remaining four were disadvantaged. Overall, then, the company was earning below-industry profits. As seen in Figure 9-6, the position was expected to improve somewhat by 1997, but not significantly. In fact, the management of this company did not expect to be able to earn above-industry profits over the next five years under the current strategy.

The preceding analysis can also be conducted by customer segments in addition to product groups, in many cases to great advantage. The five forces model helps isolate those customer groups with the lowest price sensitivity—those whose fraction of income spent on your product is small, for example—and the highest profit potential. Understanding how your product enters the value chain of each customer segment can help the company determine which strategy—differentiation, low cost, pricing, or some combination of the three—will generate and sustain the highest profits per segment.

This example demonstrates how a careful strategic value-added analysis of your company, products, segments, and markets can lead to dramatic changes in the strategic choices of management and the ultimate value of the organization.

FIGURE 9-6   Current and projected competitive advantage under current strategy.

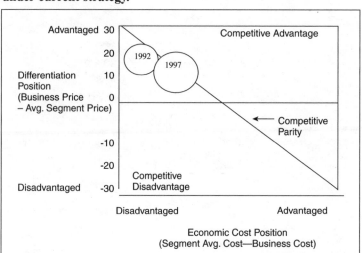

Source: McTaggart, Kontes, and Mankins, The Value Imperative, *New York: The Free Press, 1994, p. 117, Exhibit 7.3.*

Current Strategy and Value Drivers

As we saw in the materials company example and earlier in the Valuation module, corporate value is driven by free cash flows which, in turn, are determined by sales growth, operating margin, tax rate, capital investments, the cost of capital, and the interval of competitive advantage or "growth duration." The critical parameters that link the generic differentiation, cost advantage, and other strategies to value are summarized in Figure 9-7.

We need to translate the strategy into forecasts of cash flow, risk, growth, scale, and duration (the likelihood of sustainability), since these are the fundamental drivers of value.[6] There are often significant challenges in making this translation. For example, it is frequently difficult for line operators to see their impact on value drivers. Accounting systems sometimes fail to provide the balance sheet and cost information necessary to measure the impact on value. Because so much of the measure of value depends on the residual or terminal value generated after five years, it sometimes seems that the link between today's decision and eventual

---

[6] This discussion is drawn from "Putting Strategy into Shareholder Value Analysis" by George S. Day and Liam Fahey, *Harvard Business Review,* March–April 1990, pp. 156–162.

FIGURE 9-7   Value drivers and strategy.

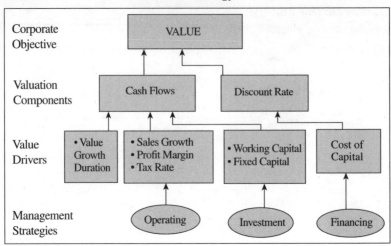

Source: Rappaport, op. cit.

economic value can be easily manipulated. Lastly, it is easy for managers to disagree about issues that influence the results—projected cash flows, the appropriate discount rate, and the duration or planning period.

Often these criticisms are more a matter of the way value-based management is implemented. For example, a preoccupation with calculating values and subjecting them to sensitivity analysis or computer-generated solutions can suppress strategic thinking or similar creativity. It is easy to become sidetracked with sophisticated quantitative analysis and forget that the qualitative judgment of management over the life of the investment is what is going to ultimately drive corporate value. The truth is that strategic thinking needs the rigor of the numbers that arise from a grounded economic analysis, and value-based management techniques need the creativity and judgment of strategic thinking.

Table 9-3 shows an overview of the fundamental differences between strategy analysis and value-based management. The critical difference between a focus on strategy and a focus on value is that while a focus on strategy may create delighted customers, the company can go bankrupt in the meanwhile! A value perspective is imperative for a company's survival.

For value-based management to work, managers must fully consider the economic context of the cash flows and ensure that cash flow forecasts and other value drivers are directly tied to the competitive analysis projections. We need to explicitly link the concepts of competitive advantage, strategy, and value creation. They must question whether cash outflows

TABLE 9-3   Strategy vs. VBM.

	Strategy Analysis	Value-Based Management
Objective	Superior quality in eyes of customer, lowest total cost	Maximize shareholder returns, free cash flows
Stakeholders	Customers, suppliers	Stockholders
Drivers	Inputs (resources, skills), intermediate outcomes (market share, relative cost, etc.)	Sales, costs, profit margins
Unit of Analysis	Product-market segments, business units, strategic groups	Company or divisions
Metric	Customer preferences, competitor comparisons, cost analysis, management judgment, and intuition	Stock returns for cash flows

contribute to competitive advantage and to what extent cash inflows are dependent on realizing these advantages. Specifically, they should broaden the range of strategy alternatives, challenge the inherent soundness of each alternative, and test the sensitivity of each alternative to changes in cash flows (inflows and outflows).

Checklist for a Critical Evaluation of Strategy's Link to Value Drivers

1. Uncover all the strengths and weaknesses associated with a strategy before attaching numbers to strategy alternatives.
2. Find solid evidence that a strategy will outperform the competition. Managers should ask penetrating questions about the requirements for success, and they should view all evidence critically. This is where strategy evaluation often flounders.
3. Scrutinize the validity of all underlying assumptions. All strategies are based on assumptions about competitors (present and future), customers, suppliers, government, industry, technology, and other economic conditions. Most of those assumptions are usually wrong. Assumptions about vulnerability to risk and ability to respond should conditions unexpectedly change are critical to the sound strategic foundation of cash flow forecasts. For example, a strategy to build

capacity makes the company more vulnerable in a downturn than a strategy to lease additional capacity.

4.   Questions to ask include: What will happen to key results if important assertions are proven wrong? If critical tasks are not accomplished? If program schedules slip badly? How likely are all these events to happen and when?

5.   No strategy, no matter how well conceived and carefully scrutinized, is worth much if it is implemented poorly, so the managers responsible for corporate strategy must also consider any problems that may arise with implementation, including manpower issues and distraction from other business units strategies. Many ideas that looked good on paper did not translate into value because of implementation issues. For example, one of the implementation issues faced by GM's Saturn included the time required to build a new system of supplier relationships with less than a third of the number of component suppliers. A company must ask itself, Does the organization have the necessary skills and resources to implement the strategy alternative successfully? If not, is there time and money to develop them?

6.   A critical review of strategy and its likely link to cash flows includes the question, How much would the cash flow forecasts have to change to make the strategy decision unattractive? By varying key parameters, managers can see which ones affect value the most and which can be most easily leveraged for value.

In sum, deriving cash flow and risk forecasts is much more an examination of the strategic fundamentals than a number-crunching exercise. It is the strategy analysis that gives us numbers that are worth crunching. Even the most sophisticated and defensible financial analysis of meaningless cash flow estimates is still meaningless. Without a basis in the hard organizational and competitive realities, value-based numbers have no meaning. When accompanied by sharp critical strategic thinking, the VBM approach gives reliable signals about a strategy's potential.

With the framework provided by the value drivers analysis, the qualitative aspects of strategy can be related to their quantitative financial results with a view toward enhancing corporate value. This requires using the material on strategy and the business economics framework set forth earlier, integrating them and identifying the key sources of competitive advantage, and linking the specific strategies to the key value drivers. Chapter 9 has focused on how one might do this at the level of the strategic business unit, starting with the unit's current strategy. An illustration of how this might be done is provided in Table 9-4. The table shows how the key valuation parameters, or value drivers, can be related to tactics supporting a competitive strategy such as a cost leadership or product differentiation.

TABLE 9-4   Relating strategy to key valuation drivers.

Value Driver		Strategies
Profit Margin	*Increase average price*	Product differentiation Market segmentation Pricing policy Market repositioning Tighten collections
	Decrease average cost	Value chain analysis New distribution channels Alter service terms Alter product guarantees Technological innovation Raw materials procurement Lengthen production runs Productivity gains
Working Capital	*Reduce working capital*	Improve inventory management Shipping terms Reduce accounts receivable Improve cash management
Fixed Assets	*Reduce fixed assets*	Outsourcing Productivity gains Licensing Franchising Technological innovation
Cost of Capital	*Increase leverage*	Stretch accounts payable Financial engineering Recapitalization
	Reduce equity	Share repurchase Special dividends

From Current to Alternative Strategies

The next component of the strategic characterization of the company is to summarize the most critical elements of the company's current strategy: What are the current and desired product markets served, and what are the actual and desired competitive positions in each of these markets over time? Condensing the comprehensive and detailed market attractiveness/competitive position analysis into its most basic elements is like panning for gold: Inconsistencies between what the company is planning to do and what it should be doing to increase value drift away like grains of sand, leaving only the gold nugget a clear strategy for striking it rich. For example, the current strategy may call for the company to grow aggressively in markets that will remain unprofitable or where customer pressures will prevent the company from ever achieving a sustainable competitive advantage.

This kind of fact-based strategic assessment of the company and its businesses and customer segments, with its focus on where value is being created and destroyed, is often quite sobering. Managers who undertake such assessments for the first time often come away with an entirely new perspective on their company. Where once new strategies were not even considered, now an urgent search for alternative strategies to grow value-creating segments of the business and divest value-destroying segments begins. There is nothing more motivating, for example, than discovering that your competitors have distinct cost advantages in a strategic input. The entire total quality movement of the early 1980s, for example, was nothing less than a wholesale reaction by some industries—the automotive industry, for example—to the discovery that Japanese competitors had created a competitive advantage in both quality differentiation and cost efficiencies.

From the industry and value chain analyses, the company identifies the competitive advantages it has, or should have, for each business unit. The company's products and those of its main rivals are compared in terms of their relative position on Figure 9-8, which shows the strategy and value creation matrix. Quite often the lesson learned from this analysis is that 80% of firm value is coming from 20% of the product groups or customer segments, ones that are currently being undersupplied or underserved.

Once each business unit is located on the value creation matrix, the strategic implications for the company's management are clear. Business units with sustainable competitive advantage in attractive markets (A) are almost certain to remain profitable for the foreseeable future and should receive ample funding for growth. Businesses with weak competitive positions in unattractive markets (F) are most likely to remain unprofitable;

FIGURE 9-8   Strategy and value creation.

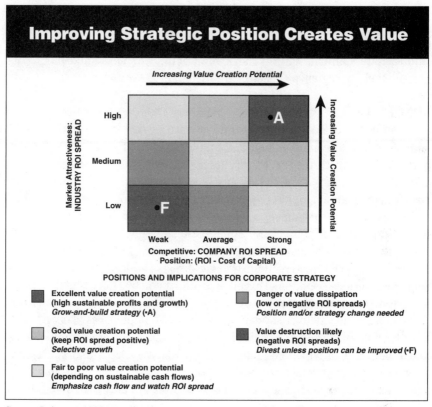

Source: Reimann, 1987, op. cit.

the value of the company will likely increase if these units are divested. The link between the economic factors driving market attractiveness and competitive position on the one hand and likely value creation on the other is clear and direct for these businesses.

The indicated strategy for those businesses somewhere in the middle is less clear. Businesses with strong competitive positions in weak markets are still typically profitable, although the duration of such profits is more dependent on the size and nature of the competitive advantage. Business units with weak competitive positions in strong industries are generally unlikely to recover over the long term and are highly dependent on the fortune of the industry, which is usually beyond the management's control. These units should probably be divested to improve the overall profitability of the company.

Corporate restructuring that divests value-destroying units and increases investment in more profitable units will result in dramatic creation of corporate value and improvements in stock price. Management can also create value through a regime of strategic alliances, joint ventures, acquisitions, retrenchment, and diversification activities. These and other corporate-level strategies are discussed in Chapter 10.

CONCLUSION

In general, there are numerous strategic thrusts that can underlie a sustainable competitive advantage and value creation. Two of the most important strategic thrusts were discussed earlier—namely, differentiation and low cost. However, strategies can have other thrusts. For example, focus strategies target a market segment or part of a product line. Preemptive strategies employ first-mover advantages to inhibit or prevent competitors from duplicating or countering. Synergistic strategies rely on the specific synergies between a business and other businesses in the same company.

Several other value-creating strategic thrusts can lead to market leadership. For example, operational excellence, illustrated by Dell Computer, leads to customer convenience and cost efficiencies. Dell created a radically different and efficient delivery system for personal computers based upon build-to-order manufacturing and mail-order marketing. Another example is customer intimacy in which companies such as Home Depot and Nordstrom excel at individual personalized service. Yet another example is product leadership where companies such as Johnson & Johnson and 3M strive to produce a continuous stream of state-of-the-art products and services.

After all is said and done, the bottom line is still this: Companies that create a sustainable competitive advantage in industries that are economically viable will create value and prevail. There is a bit more focus on *creating* a competitive advantage today rather than simply maintaining one. This is a good thing, but the advantage is still a function of the ownership of a set of unusual capabilities that are difficult for competitors to imitate. The most recent developments and ideas about strategy by Porter[7] and others hold that sustainable competitive advantage can be built around an unusual set of capabilities that are not necessarily housed within the company. A group of competitors that share an intense rivalry may also share a sophisticated competitive context that becomes part of each company's competitive skill set in dealing with a global marketplace.

---

[7] Michael Porter, *On Competition*. Cambridge, MA: Harvard Business School Press, 1998.

The preceding analysis has defined the firm's current strategy and the most significant opportunities for competitive advantage. The approach can give us significant insights into the current value-creating capabilities of a business or company. But sustainable competitive advantage is inherently dynamic, and before we can use this information to develop sustainable value-creating strategies, we must have a framework for properly assessing the impact of strategies on the dynamic economic value of the business or company. That is, before any organization can use any method for allocating resources in ways to maximize value, it must be able to properly assign value to the various "portfolios" of resource-allocation strategies at hand. Fundamentally, all of the market attractiveness-competitive position analyses are incomplete because they do not account for the value of flexible management over the life of the investment. Proper valuation techniques must recognize the value created by both (1) the interdependencies between SBUs and markets at a point in time, but also (2) the interdependencies through time between today's investment decisions and tomorrow's investment opportunities. We take up these critical corporate strategy issues in Chapter 10.

10

CORPORATE STRATEGY

VALUE MANAGERS CONDUCT A THOROUGH ANALYSIS of the current strategy and the internal and external economic environment of each of their business units and anticipate as much as they can about possible developments in product, capital, and labor markets, and the general competitive landscape. All of this is incorporated into their corporate strategic plan for maximizing the value of the company.

As soon as we embark on a given strategy, however, we begin learning anew about customer preferences, supplier costs, and competitor reactions. Value managers are active managers: They revise their strategies as new information becomes available in a continuing effort to make their strategies succeed.

A successful corporate strategy is one that adapts as markets evolve, businesses grow, and management learns. Corporate strategy is much more like a series of options than a series of static cash flows. Unfortunately, the most common financial method for evaluating strategy—discounted cash flow analysis—assumes that managers follow a predetermined path regardless of how events unfold. Discounted cash flow analysis describes a static world, but the business world is an inherently dynamic place.

For example, the sustainability of competitive advantage is a naturally dynamic issue. Once managers have identified areas of likely competitive advantage in the static environment presented in Chapter 9, their next challenge is to focus on those businesses where the competitive advantage can be sustained for the longest period of time, despite the internal and external economic forces pushing the business toward a zero-profit competitive equilibrium. Without sustainability, a competitive advantage is unlikely to be large enough to recover its costs and create value.

Since the goal of strategy is to create economic value, the method we use to choose among competing strategies should correctly incorporate the impact of strategy (both the current strategy and its possible future revisions) on value. Real options valuation, described in Chapter 8, does just that. In Chapter 8, we described how to get from the value of a static series of cash flows to the option value of a typical business strategy or investment, that is, how to get a number. In this chapter, we discuss how to use the real options valuation framework to formulate strategies that create sustainable competitive advantage—that is, that create economic value.

Luehrman[1] proposes a pragmatic approach to devising corporate strategy using real options that in practice is not that much more complicated than performing an NPV analysis. In this approach, corporate strategists map out potential projects on the basis of two option-value metrics, one calculated from NPV analysis and the other a risk measure. The results locate each existing or proposed project in one of six areas on a graph, allowing for the identification of strategically attractive projects. The idea is to structure future projects to maximize their overall value, including their option value. By actively seeking projects that have a high potential payoff, high degree of uncertainty, or high likelihood of successive growth opportunities, companies can make full use of real options thinking in strategic planning.

An options valuation framework can improve strategy in three ways. One, it improves value-based decision making by recognizing the value of managerial flexibility imbedded in various strategies. Two, the options framework can actually help the value manager in the creative process of formulating strategies that are more likely to add value to the company. Three, a real options framework can assist the management in maximizing shareholder value. How? Recall from Chapter 3 the empirical evidence documenting the favorable stock price reactions to strategic announcements. Now we know why: the market generally recognizes the real op-

---

[1] Much of the discussion in this chapter is based on Timothy A. Luehrman's "Strategy as a Portfolio of Real Options," *Harvard Business Review,* Sept.–Oct. 1998.

tion value of strategic decisions. We will have more to say about the importance of clearly communicating corporate strategies to the investment community in Chapter 14.

THE VALUE OF STRATEGIC MANAGEMENT: THE TOMATO GARDEN METAPHOR

Think of your company's projects like tomatoes in a garden. On any given day, the tomatoes in the garden and the projects in the business have varying growth prospects and potential for value creation. Some tomatoes if left on the vine will ripen, just like some projects if delayed will become more valuable. The option to delay—for projects and tomatoes alike—can be valuable.

Managing a portfolio of options is a lot like tending a garden of tomatoes. Most experienced gardeners are able to walk into the garden on any given day and distinguish between ripe tomatoes, rotten tomatoes, and the remainder that fall somewhere in between. These "in-between" tomatoes can be further classified into four groups: (1) those that are edible and could be picked now, but would ripen and grow beautifully with more time on the vine; the gardener should pick them now only if squirrels or competitors are likely to get them first; (2) those that are not yet edible (so it does not pay to pick them even if some will succumb to scavengers) but are sufficiently far enough along and there is enough time left in the season that many of them will ripen and eventually be picked; (3) those that look less promising, but with sun, water, and a little luck, some of these might make it; (4) those that are so small and green that no amount of time or nurturing will bring them to harvest. There is no value in picking them; they might as well be left on the vine.

Active gardeners understand that the fraction of tomatoes that fall into each of these six categories (the ripe, the rotten ones, and the four types of in-between tomatoes) can be influenced by how carefully and knowledgeably the gardener tends the garden, assuming that there is sufficient time left in the growing season. There are always the unknowns, like the weather, that are beyond the gardener's control, but the odds are that the well-tended garden creates a higher yield in most years.

In option pricing terminology, passive gardeners are simply making exercise decisions. They show up at the garden on the last day of the season, pick the ripe tomatoes (i.e., exercise their options, or NPV's "invest now"), and leave the rest (let the option expire, or NPV's "invest never").

In contrast, the active gardener monitors the options and looks for ways to influence the underlying variables that determine the option value.

There is another advantage to monitoring the individual tomato plants that compose the garden, (i.e., the individual businesses that make up the company). Monitoring allows the manager to update forecasts on the probabilities of success and the likely profits of each business, strategy, or investment. The sooner such forecasts are updated, the more value the manager can create by limiting unprofitable decisions and enhancing profitable ones. Clearly, the active manager is rewarded with a higher-valued company, just like the active gardener is rewarded with a better crop.

The garden plot can be usefully described by the option-value space in Figure 10-1. The space is defined by two option-value metrics. The value-to-cost ratio on the horizontal axis is the ratio of the underlying investment's value to the present value of its costs. When the value-to-cost ratio is greater than 1, the project is worth more than it costs. The metric

FIGURE 10-1   The real option-value space.

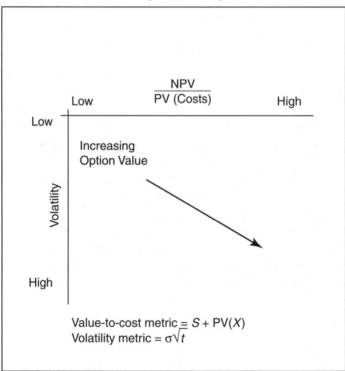

on the vertical axis reflects the investment's variability. Notice that the option space in Figure 10-1 is essentially the same as the options pricing table presented in Chapter 8. In both, (call) option value rises with volatility and the ratio of asset value to cost.

The option-value space can be divided into six distinct strategic regions, shown as numbers rising clockwise from 1 through 6 in Figure 10-2. Each of these regions corresponds to a different value-creating strategy.

Businesses in Regions 1 and 6 are those with the lowest volatility measures—that is, those for which all uncertainty has been resolved or, more likely, time has run out. Businesses in these two regions differ only in their value-to-cost metric, and it is easy to see what to do with them. For those with a value-to-cost ratio greater than 1—that is, with a positive NPV—the optimal strategy is to "invest now." These are the ripe tomatoes, in Region 1 of the figure. For those with a negative NPV and no time or remaining uncertainty, the decision is equally clear: "invest never." These are the rotten tomatoes, in Region 6 of the garden.

FIGURE 10-2   The real options tomato garden.

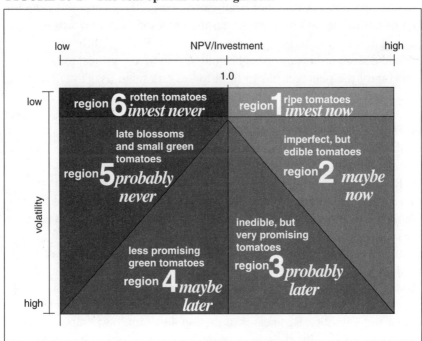

These "now or never" extremes are appropriately valued by standard net present value analysis. When time and uncertainty are no longer factors, net present value gives the same answer as option valuation. We saw this idea in Chapter 6, where we showed that the value of a company is the sum of its as-is value and the value of its future growth opportunities:

Value = Value of Assets in Place + Value of Future Growth Opportunities

$$V = \frac{\text{EBIT}_1}{k} + \sum_{t=1}^{\infty} \frac{I_t(r_t - k)}{k(1 + k)^t}$$

Recall that the value of assets in place is simply the present value of the perpetual EBIT stream generated by existing assets. The value of the latter term depends on the ability of the company to earn a return on new investment r in excess of the cost of the funds invested k and on the quantity of dollars of new investment I_t. Growth only contributes to value if the return earned by the company on its new investments exceeds the cost of capital—that is, if there is a positive spread. Otherwise, the second term in the above equation is negative. "Bad growth" destroys corporate value.

The real options valuation framework explicitly incorporates the impact of both time and uncertainty on the value of future growth opportunities. The more time there is remaining before a commitment must be made, the more information can be gathered about the project and the more opportunity the manager has to limit losses and magnify gains. The more uncertainty or variability there is associated with the cash flows of an opportunity, the greater the likelihood of large positive cash flows. It is true that uncertainty also increases the probability of large negative cash flows, but the real options framework recognizes that managers can take actions to minimize those negative cash flows.

Returning to the tomato garden in Figure 10-2, we can see that when time and uncertainty are factors, as they are in Regions 2, 3, 4 and 5, flexible management can make a significant difference in the value potential of a business. Strategy becomes at once more interesting, challenging, and certainly rewarding. To make the number of possibilities manageable, we divide the remaining areas of the tomato garden into four distinct "strategic" regions. Region 2 contains businesses and products with high value-to-cost and low volatility. Region 3 projects have both high value-to-cost and volatility. Businesses in Region 4 exhibit low value-to-cost and high volatility. Finally, those in Region 5 have both low value-to-cost and volatility.

Businesses in Regions 2 and 3 have high value-to-cost ratios. These are potentially very valuable, since the present value of their spreads is positive—they more than recover their costs over the projected life of the business. Depending on their volatility measures, however, some will create even more value if investment is delayed and more information about the business and the economic environment is gathered. Consider the businesses in Region 3: These are not the most valuable projects. However, because of the high levels of remaining uncertainty and/or time to expiration, many are likely to become more valuable, particularly with active management.

Investments in Region 2 are more interesting because, while there is sufficient time for these to benefit from active management, many create significant value now. Rather than suffer the losses from entrants and other competitors, value may be enhanced by investing now (i.e., exercising our option early or "picking the tomatoes"). What kinds of investments fall into this "optimal early exercise" category? Examples include impending patent expiration, preemption by a new entrant, and the loss of market share to aggressive rivals.[2]

This is an important point to repeat: For some business investments, *value may be lost by deferring.* Contrary to popular belief, real options valuation does not say that it always pays to wait. The proper decision depends on the *net* effect on value from waiting—the increase in value from information gained compared to the loss in value to faster-moving competitors. We come back to this point when we discuss the strategic implications of the real options framework.

Continuing to move clockwise around the option space, we move into Regions 4 and 5. Investments in these regions have value-to-cost ratios that are less than 1 (i.e., a negative NPV). If harvested now, these investments destroy value. NPV analysis would say simply "invest never." But real options valuation helps the manager to see that even these investments can be separated into those that are more or less likely to add value with time and active management. Those in Region 4—the less-promising green tomatoes—have enough time and uncertainty remaining for management to turn some of them around. Region 5 contains late blossoms and small green tomatoes, and there is so little time or opportunity left for them to

---

[2] The analogy to financial options pricing is straightforward. Recall that the underlying asset of a real option is some set of business cash flows. Any predictable loss of business cash flows is like a dividend payment on a financial call option. With pending dividends, it is sometimes better to exercise the option early and purchase the underlying stock in order to receive the dividend cash flow.

become valuable that value is actually enhanced if managers—gardeners—ignore these projects and spend their time and resources elsewhere.

Over time, businesses will naturally migrate within the option space toward the northwest region, where they are least likely to add value to the company. They migrate north along the volatility axis because option value declines as time to maturity approaches. They migrate west to a lower value-to-cost ratio because the denominator, the present value of the costs or $c/(1 + r)^t$, rises as time remaining, t, falls.

Only two forces can prevent the natural migration of businesses toward lower value regions: luck and active management. Neither should be ignored. Many times, good managers are those that consistently put the business in a position to benefit from "good luck." Nonetheless, it is easier for us to focus on the purposive actions managers can take to guide projects away from Regions 4 and 5 and toward Regions 2 and 3. As illustrated by the tomato garden option-value space, those actions take the form of improving the value-to-cost metric and increasing the volatility metric. We take each in turn.

Anything managers do to increase value or reduce cost will move projects to the right in the option-value space. Examples include the differentiation and cost advantage strategies of Chapter 9, including price or volume increases, tax savings, lower capital requirements, and cost savings.

Corporate managers rarely have the luxury of altering one value driver without affecting several others, however. Let's take the simple differentiation or market-entry strategy of adding a new product feature. The differentiation, if successful, will raise prices and increase the value-to-cost metric. However, the strategy will also entail additional investment costs that lower the ratio. There are also spillover effects from one metric to the other. If some of the additional investment costs are fixed, for example, leverage is increased, which, in turn, increases the variability of free cash flows and improves option value along the volatility axis.

The volatility measure, as the product of the variability of the future value of the underlying asset and the time remaining before "maturity," captures how much things can change before an investment decision must actually be made. The higher the volatility, the more opportunity for the project to become profitable. The longer the time frame, the more opportunity for management to turn the investment or business around. Managers can increase volatility by seeking high-risk or leveraged opportunities. They can expand the effective time frame by delaying the commitment to proposed projects through licensing or the use of staged financing, for example, or minimizing the competitive rivalry for existing projects.

By mapping a company's businesses within the option value space, managers can tell at a glance not only which businesses are creating value but also the likelihood of a business becoming even more valuable in the future. In this way, real options valuation enables managers to create more corporate value because it gives them a tool for deciding how to best spend limited time and resources. It enables them to focus on those businesses that have the greatest likelihood of responding to active management, to "cultivation," and creating a crop of wealth at season's end.

Both of the option value metrics—value-to-cost and volatility—are important value drivers. That is, management can influence both and each has a significant impact on competitive advantage. But *strategic* value drivers do more than increase profits or reduce costs: strategic value drivers create *sustainable* competitive advantage.

We argue that the true value of a strategy depends on the sustainability of the competitive advantage. Sustainable competitive advantage relies on preventing competitors from imitating your successful strategies. Conditions that are most likely to create barriers to imitation and sustain competitive advantage take two basic forms: exclusive or proprietary rights to the factors that generate the competitive advantage, and minimal competitive rivalry. These conditions are shown in Figure 10-3.

Proprietary options provide highly valuable, exclusive rights of exercise. These result from patents or the company's unique knowledge of a market or technology that competitors cannot duplicate. Proprietary options are an example of the classic barriers to entry discussed in Chapter 9 that protect a company's profits from competition.

Shared options are less valuable "collective" opportunities of the industry, like the chance to enter a market unprotected by high barriers or to build a new plant to service a particular geographic market. Projects to cut costs are often shared options, since competitors usually can and will respond with cost reductions of their own, thus minimizing the benefits to any one company.

As shown in Figure 10-3, the company in the upper right quadrant with an exclusive or propriety option and minimal competitive rivalry can fully capitalize on the value of flexible management. An example is Microsoft, who owns a proprietary option on the MS-DOS operating system and has a virtual monopoly in their market. The threat to their position from imminent imitation is remote.

Although proprietary options like patents prohibit imitation, some patented products fail to generate sustainable profits because of the availability of close substitutes produced by rival companies. The existence of a proprietary option, exclusive right, or unique managerial skill set is not necessarily enough

FIGURE 10-3   Strategy and option value.

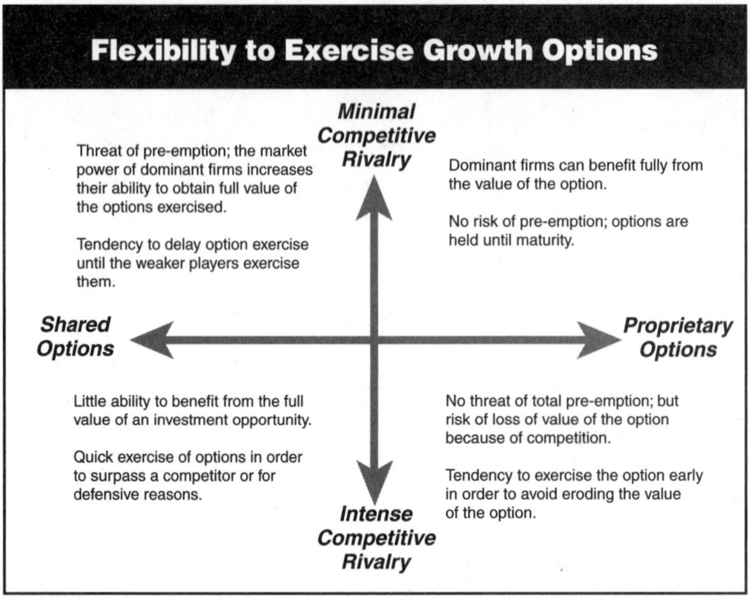

> Source: This and related ideas in this section are well discussed in Lenos Trigeorgis, *Real Options: Managerial Flexibility and Strategy in Resource Allocations,* Cambridge, MA: MIT Press, 1996.

to sustain a competitive advantage in the face of intense competitive rivalry. For example, drug companies own proprietary rights to brand-name drug products, but the competitive rivalry represented by generics undermines their ability to exploit the full value of the growth option. These are firms in the lower right quadrant of Figure 10-3. Some early exercise to prevent the erosion in value from lost market share is observed in businesses in this quadrant.

Firms in the lower left quadrant are those with shared options and intense competitive rivalry. These are the commodities industries. A typical option in this scenario is the option to expand production in a crowded market. Companies in these industries have little ability to benefit from the full value of an investment opportunity. Early exercise for defensive reasons is common.

Companies in the upper left quadrant enjoy some market power but own shared options. The automotive industry and other oligopolies occupy this space. The firms in these industries can obtain close to the full value of the options because of their market power, but because their options are nonexclusive, they sometimes cannot hold them to maturity. A typical option in this group is the right to expand production of a good—for example, four-door sedans—with a limited number of close substitutes.

The distinction between proprietary and shared options is one of the critical differences between financial options and real options. Unlike financial options, real options can be proprietary or shared. One of the most reliable strategic value drivers is the systematic quest to convert shared options into proprietary ones at both the business and corporate levels.

Even this strategic value driver, however, should be pursued judiciously in a value-based management framework. Consider, for example, the interaction between the proprietary nature of the option and the competitive intensity of the industry, as captured by the strategy-option value cross in Figure 10-3. If we take one common type of real option—the option to delay—and reexamine it from the framework of Figure 10-3, we see that if there were no barriers to entry and intense competitive rivalry ensued, the option to wait would have very little value. In this situation, investing in a proprietary option to wait would make little economic sense. Likewise, in situations with minimal competitive rivalry, like natural monopolies, proprietary options may not be necessary. Profits can be sustained because imitation cannot occur without rival firms.

One strategy for preventing imitation is to limit the intensity of the competitive rivalry (i.e., reduce the availability of close substitutes, increasing monopoly power). One way is to reduce the number of potential competitors by absorbing your rival through merger and acquisition activity. Another is through effective differentiation, which also reduces the number of direct competitors to your product.

Kester observed that companies frequently commit investment funds early rather than waiting despite their ability to defer, and interprets this as evidence that the cost of deferring exceeds the value sacrificed in early exercise.[3] He goes on to suggest that it pays a company to exercise its growth options earlier (i.e., commit the funds now) rather than later when

- The project's NPV is high.
- The level of risk and interest rates are low.
- Options are not proprietary; that is, they are shared.
- Industry rivalry is intense.

Interestingly, the first two conditions describe projects in Region 2 of the tomato garden, where early exercise was warranted. The last two describe conditions in the lower left quadrant of Figure 10-3, where commodities firms reside and early exercise is common.

---

[3] W. Carl Kester, "Today's Options for Tomorrow's Growth," *Harvard Business Review,* March–April 1984, pp. 153–160.

Real options valuation has the potential to make a significant differ-ence in the area of competition and strategy. Sustainable competitive ad-vantages resulting from patents, proprietary technologies, ownership of valuable natural resources and other scarce goods, managerial capital, rep-utation or brand name, scale, and market power all empower companies with valuable options to grow through more profitable investments and to more effectively respond to unexpected adversity or opportunities in a changing technological, competitive, or general business environment. In short, the real options framework provides a powerful method for visual-izing and valuing and alternative business and corporate strategies.

OTHER CORPORATE STRATEGY ISSUES

Corporate strategy should begin with an overall assessment of the company's current strategy and value creation, which is generally a consolidation of the strategic and financial analysis of each of the company's individual business units or strategic groups. As long as the financial forecasts for each busi-ness unit are strongly anchored in an objective assessment of internal and external economics, a bottom-up analysis of products, customers, and busi-ness segments should provide helpful information for management to com-bine with companywide analysis in their formulation of value-creating cor-porate strategies. The tomato garden options value assessment is the final screen for the identification of value-creating corporate-level strategies.

Care must still be taken to assess the impact of positive and negative interactions between business units and how they might affect the drivers of value. The identification of the strategic value drivers shared across mul-tiple business units is also a very important result of the consolidation.

Corporate strategy can focus on creating value for shareholders in three ways: (1) managing the corporate portfolio by adding businesses that will enhance value and divesting businesses that will destroy value, (2) proac-tively managing those strategic value drivers that span more than one busi-ness unit, and (3) exhibiting the leadership and designing the corporate governance attributes necessary to make value creation the single over-riding objective of all activities within the organization. This last issue is the subject of Chapters 12 and 13.

Managing the Corporate Portfolio: Profitable Acquisition and Divesting Strategies

As we saw in the BioTech example in Chapter 4, one of the most useful and practical results from consolidating business unit assessments into a corporatewide assessment is the discovery, in more cases than not, that a large fraction of corporate value is being created in a small subset of the company's businesses. An immediate implication of such a discovery is that simply by divesting value destroyers and by growing and expanding value creators, the company can increase its value significantly. This leads us to a discussion of how best to acquire and divest with an eye toward enhancing long-term corporate value.

Of the innumerable academic studies on the impact of mergers and acquisitions on corporate value, one clear fact emerges: Not all acquisitions create value.[4] It is useful to keep in mind that the acquisitions we observe are but a small subset of those considered and scrapped by management in its quest for value. In addition, it is quite difficult to accurately measure the impact of the completed merger on company value, since the only sensible benchmark for added value is how the target and bidder firms would have performed over the long term had they not merged. In effect, the researchers have to "rerun" history to determine the real impact mergers have had on value. As a result, there is considerable debate on the specific impact of mergers on value, but the fact remains that mergers and divestitures are one extremely useful method for implementing value-seeking strategies.

The most successful merger candidates have three characteristics in common: (1) the acquisition assists management in achieving a specific value-creating objective(s), (2) management can resist the "winner's curse" temptation to overpay, and (3) the acquisition can be successfully integrated into the existing company and its value-creating strategies. Together, these characteristics help to ensure that the acquisition will generate greater free cash flows than the total cost of the control premium and company integration combined.

Profitable acquisition strategies should focus on their strategic value drivers, or those value drivers that can be controlled by management and have the greatest potential impact of future value creation. Acquisition-related strategic value drivers tend to fall into three categories: unique demand synergies, unique cost synergies, and unique managerial economies.

Unique demand synergies are those that are difficult for others to imitate. Demand synergies can be created by combining complementary products or services, unbundling products or services to better match the preferences of a larger customer pool, or by otherwise extending differentiation into additional links of the company and user value chains.

Cost synergies typically result from the elimination of overlap in one or more links in the value chain, such as procurement, marketing, assem-

---

[4] In an ongoing study of the long-term impact of mergers on corporate value, S. Jarrell creates and tests a method for estimating what the value of the bidder and target companies would have been without the merger and finds that fully two-thirds of completed mergers do indeed create significant value over a five-year postmerger period.

bly, distribution, and research and development. In some select industries, such as banking and other financial services, cost synergies can be substantial and serve as the catalyst for significant sustainable improvements in value creation.

Unique managerial economies are difficult to predict; we tend to "know them when we see them," and then generally only in hindsight. Nonetheless, we know they are there and understand intuitively that these are the most significant sources of sustainable value creation available. Resources do not reallocate themselves, after all. Managerial economies are the extension of the ability to successfully manage resources to the activities of other companies, related or not. Such economies rely, in part, on the inherent skill set of the particular management and leadership in an organization, but they benefit significantly from the careful study and thorough, fact-based, and objective review of which management strategies have worked for this team and which have not.

An interesting variant of this source of corporate strategic value is the possibility of taking the company private. Management buyouts (MBOs) are the purchase, usually with high levels of debt, of the company by a small group of investors that include current or former management. Typically these are managers who are frustrated with the constraints imposed on them by the board or other senior executives with regard to which types of investments and strategies to pursue and what levels of risk the company can absorb. By taking the firm private, the MBO team can internalize both the risks and rewards of following their own strategic vision for the company. Managers in MBOs become owners and adopt the incentives of owners, thus reducing agency costs.

It is interesting to examine the value creation impacts of large management buyouts of publicly held companies. In those cases where the MBO goes public again, it is possible to gather market value data from both before and after the buyout transaction, and gain some insights into whether value was created or destroyed as a result of changes in strategy and incentives.

As shown in Table 10-1, companies taken private experienced significant improvements in performance and decreases in capital expenditures in the two years following the buyout. The management of these companies nearly doubled their companies' market values from the two months preceding the buyout announcement to the subsequent post-buyout sale, net of the stock markets' performance during that same period. It is clear that spectacular benefits can be realized by pursuing alternative business strategies and aligning the behavior of managers with the interests of the shareholders.

Strategies to identify value-creating divestments are actually just the flip side of value-creating acquisitions. When a company has discovered

TABLE 10-1   Effects of MBOs on corporate performance.

	Year −1 to +2	Average All Companies
Return on capital*	5.4%	11.3%
Capital spending/Capital	−1.3%	4.9%
Inventory/sales	−2.8%	13.8%

*EBIDT/Capital, where capital = Market value of equity + Book value of debt.
Sources: PC Plus Compustat, and S. Kaplan, "Effect of Management Buyouts on Operating Performance and Value," Journal of Financial Economics 24(1989), pp. 217–254.

that a business unit or product is destroying value and cannot be turned around in a cost-effective way using differentiation, cost, or other strategies, that unit becomes a candidate for divestment. These are businesses in Regions 3 and 4 of the tomato garden. Other candidates for divestment will arise as managers examine alternative strategies for future value. For example, units that no longer fit with the company's strategic direction and can be sold for a premium should be considered for divestment. Examining the unit from the potential acquirer's point of view will help the company to command the highest premium for the business.

MANAGING SHARED STRATEGIC VALUE DRIVERS

Shared strategic value drivers consist of organizational skills and expertise that must be centrally managed for the full impact on value creation to be realized. Examples include Kellogg's brand equity, which is shared across many product segments and geographic markets, and Wal-Mart's legendary restocking process, which is shared by each of its retail businesses. Other possibilities include activities exclusive to senior management, such as strategic resource planning and corporate development, and communication about corporate strategic intent with analysts and the rest of the investment community. Identifying these shared strategic value drivers is often a difficult task, but almost universally worthwhile. Generally, the most significant lesson learned from the hunt for shared strategic drivers is the realization that very few value drivers actually qualify as strategic—in other words, those that create unique organizational capabilities that are difficult to imitate and that create significant future value. Many organizations credit their success to having "the best people" or "the best recruiting and training," when in reality these value drivers are easily duplicated. Others go to great lengths to keep their total quality management or strategic planning processes secret, when essentially the same systems have been developed in each of their competitors' companies.

Managing shared value drivers involves three critical tasks. The first is making sure that sufficient resources are devoted to each capability. Shared value drivers are much like public goods, those from which we benefit but for which we do not pay. It is likely that no one business unit would want to foot the entire bill for a shared value driver that other units benefit from as well, so this is one of the primary responsibilities of a corporate strategy. The second task is ensuring that no one business unit exploits the shared value driver to the detriment of other business units and creates an overall value loss to the company. For example, if one unit exploits the brand name of the company in a less-than-appropriate application, the value of the brand name to the rest of the company may be irreversibly damaged. The premature application of new technologies developed in one unit may lessen the long-term value of the perfected second-generation technology to the other units. Lastly, the job of determining how units in a vertically integrated business should share strategic value drivers, including how to price transfer goods or spread overhead costs, is best left up to corporate level decision makers who are responsible for the current and future value of the overall organization.

The third task critical to effectively managing strategic value drivers is to leverage them to the fullest extent possible by seeking and exploiting opportunities to apply them outside the borders of the existing organization—for example, in new markets or through active new product development. This may be the most exciting opportunity for creation of value through focused management of shared value drivers.

Strategic Fit: The Ultimate Shared Strategic Value Driver

The common theme behind strategies that generate sustainable competitive advantage and the value creation that goes along with it is this: *Prevent (or significantly delay) imitation.* The "static" method for preventing imitation is to set up roadblocks to imitators, through patents, asset ownership, experience, minimum-efficient scale, and other barriers to entry. A more dynamic method is more complicated and may involve a fairly new corporate strategy referred to as "strategic fit" by Porter[5] and a web of "complexity and complementarity in strategic assets" by Oster.[6]

Porter points to the dominant firms in the New Economy as exemplars of successful strategic thinking. They do not regard strategy as a single ap-

---

[5] Michael Porter, *On Competition.* Cambridge, MA: Harvard Business School Press, 1998.

[6] Sharon M. Oster, *Modern Competitive Advantage.* New York: Oxford University Press, 1999.

proach or incremental improvement, rather as the "strategic fit" between every part of the company's value chain. In the absence of this kind of fit, strategies can quickly be reduced to short-lived tactics that are easily imitated and otherwise competed away. Companywide fit locks out imitators by creating a complex chain of complementary processes and assets that are difficult if not impossible for outsiders to duplicate. It is hard for outsiders or entrants to imitate these advantages when it is not even clear, by their complexity, what they are.

Fit is also related to Porter's latest work on "clusters," or regions where competitors congregate and businesses that are involved in each link of the value chain develop around them. Silicon Valley is a leading example of clusters. Ironically, geographic proximity turns out to be a key source of competitive advantage in the most highly developed, highly technological economies. Clusters create strategic value in many ways.[7] For example, it is easier to improve the interlocking value chains of customers, suppliers, and the company when viewed and managed from within the cluster. Management can more easily detect trends in demand and work more closely with suppliers, labor, distributors, after-sale service providers, and lenders. Finally, new technologies and best practices are diffused more easily when competitors and related companies and assets congregate.

CONCLUSION

The complete strategic module of the VBM framework is displayed in Figure 1-7 in Chapter 1. At center stage is the MA/CP value creation matrix. Industry analysis and competitive position analysis determine each business unit's actual and desired positions on the vertical and horizontal axes, respectively. Once each business unit is located on the value creation matrix, the strategic implications for the company's management are clear, and a set of growth strategies and investment opportunities available to the company are defined. The manager's decision should be guided by the pursuit of strategies and opportunities that are most likely to have the greatest impact on the value of the company and therefore the welfare of all its stakeholders.

Chapter 9 was concerned with business strategies, which involve such decisions as expansion into new markets, new product development, the choice of operating technology, the scale and scope of investment projects,

---

[7] Strategic fit may be one of the strongest examples of a barrier to imitation. In addition, the "cluster" has few true substitutes with which to compete.

and the completion of multiphase projects. We learned in Chapter 8 that each of these decisions contains embedded real options, such as the ability to make follow-on investments; to abandon, alter, or expand; or to wait and learn before investing.

This chapter focused on corporate-level strategy, which looks at the portfolio of businesses and includes decisions that reconfigure the businesses within the portfolio including:

- Expanding to a new market (e.g., through acquisition, joint venture, licensing, and so on)
- Exiting a market (divestiture, spinoff, and so on)
- Redeploying resources across business units, which takes a broader perspective and more authority than any one business unit manager has

Other related corporate level issues are the focus of Part IV of this book, including:

- Corporate governance issues—how to incent employees and managers to make value-enhancing decisions; how to link what they do to the corporatewide objective that they sometimes cannot see and usually cannot direct
- Communication to the outside community about the company and its mission, strategy, brand, soul, and value

Real options analysis applied to corporate strategies gives managers a method of identifying and valuing critical strategic decisions. Real options valuation, because it captures the value of strategic or flexible management, represents the final screen through which strategies should be viewed in a value-based management framework. Management must also address the exclusiveness of owning a strategic option and the effect of competition on the company's ability to fully appropriate for itself the value of the strategic option.

P A R T

FINANCE

11

C   H   A   P   T   E   R

ESTIMATING DISCOUNT RATES

T HE CENTRAL IDEA OF THIS CHAPTER is that all companies require capital, and capital isn't free. The cost of capital is the minimum return required by debt and equity holders. If the company is unable to generate that minimum return, investors will withdraw their funds in search of a competitive return elsewhere. A company that cannot attract capital cannot survive.

Up to this point in the book, discount rates have been assumed without explanation. How do we know which rates to use? How should they be estimated? Do they vary across assets, lines of business, and strategies? Can a company influence its cost of capital through its choice of capital structure? These are the issues addressed in this chapter.[1]

THE COST OF CAPITAL CONCEPT

While companies can experience varying degrees of market power in the sale of their products and services, they must compete with everyone else in the open and active market for financial capital. As in any other market, the price of capital is determined by supply and demand. When investors supply funds to a company by buying its stocks or bonds, they not only postpone consumption but also expose their funds to risk, and they

---

[1] This chapter draws heavily from R. A. Morin, *Regulatory Finance,* Public Utility Reports, Inc., Arlington VA, 1994.

FIGURE 11-1   Cost of capital determination.

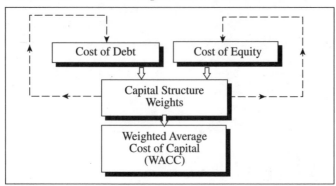

must be adequately compensated for both. The compensation they require is the "price" of capital," expressed as the percentage rate of return on the dollar amount of capital supplied.

The cost of capital is firmly anchored in the notion of *opportunity cost* from economics. A company will be unable to attract capital unless it can offer returns that recover the opportunity cost of the foregone return on alternative comparable investments—hence, the equivalence among the cost of capital, required return, and opportunity cost.

DETERMINING THE COST OF CAPITAL: AN OVERVIEW

The procedure for determining the company cost of capital is depicted in Figure 11-1. The costs of debt and equity capital are first determined separately, then weighted by the proportions of debt and equity in the capital structure, and summed to arrive at the weighted average cost of capital, or WACC.

Table 11-1 illustrates the computation of Georgia-Pacific's WACC in early 2000. To calculate the WACC, we need the costs of debt and equity, along with their respective proportions in the capital structure. The after-tax cost of debt is found by multiplying the current bond yield of 7.5% by

TABLE 11-1   Georgia-Pacific Corp. weighted average cost of capital.

Type of Capital	Market Value	Weight	After-Tax Cost	Weighted Cost
Long-term debt	$3,395	40%	4.5%	1.8%
Common equity	$5,006	60%	13.2%	7.9%
Total	$8,401		**WACC**	**9.7%**

(1 − Tax Rate), or 7.5% × (1 − 0.4) = 4.5%. The cost of equity is given as 13.2%; we show how to derive it later in the chapter. The weights are the proportions of debt and common equity employed by the company expressed in market values. In this example, the weights are 40% for debt and 60% for equity. The procedure for determining appropriate weights (i.e., the capital structure) is discussed in a later section as well.

COST OF EQUITY CAPITAL

There are three major approaches for estimating the cost of equity capital: risk premium, capital asset pricing model (CAPM), and discounted cash flow (DCF). No single methodology dominates all applications. Each requires judgment as to the validity of the assumptions made and applicability of the results to the valuation problem at hand.

Risk Premium

The risk premium method of determining the cost of equity recognizes that investors require higher returns on stocks than on bonds to compensate for the additional risk. The mechanics of the approach are straightforward: First, determine the spread between the return on equity and the return on debt, then add this spread of "risk premium" to the current debt yield to estimate the current cost of equity. The approach is useful partly because the required data—the yield on debt and the risk premium between classes of stocks and bonds—are readily available.

The risk premium approach is portrayed graphically in Figure 11-2. The horizontal axis measures risk, and the vertical axis measures required returns. The upward-sloping capital market line (CML) shows that the risk

FIGURE 11-2 Risk and return in capital markets.

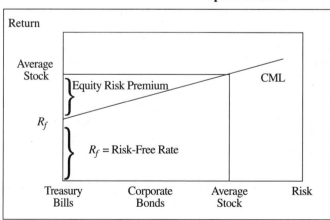

premium increases with risk. For example, stocks are riskier than corporate bonds, and their risk premiums are higher as well.

One approach for estimating the risk premium is to simply take the difference between the *historical* realized returns on stocks and bonds.[2] For example, if the current cost of debt is 6% and the historical spread between stocks and bonds is 7%, then the cost of common equity is 13%. At issue is how far back one should go in gathering historical data. We suggest using the longest period for which data are available. In this way, the influence of short-run deviations in the risk-return relationship will average out, and investor return expectations and realizations will converge.

Another approach is to measure the risk premium as the difference between the *expected* returns on common stocks and bonds as the risk premium. For example, if the current cost of debt is 6% and the expected risk premium between stocks and bonds is 7%, then the cost of equity for stock of average risk is 13%.

There are several methods for estimating the expected returns on the stock, all centered on calculating the expected risk premium on a market index, and adjusting it up or down depending on the relative risk of the stock. The expected risk premium on the market index can be computed by estimating the expected equity returns for a broad sample of companies using the DCF, as explained in the next section, for each of several future time periods and then subtracting the corresponding yields on debt from these estimates.

If the company's risk differs from the market's, the market risk premium needs to be adjusted to find the company's own risk premium. The adjustment factor can take many forms. One is based on the company's beta (discussed in the next section, Capital Asset Pricing Model) or the beta of a group of equivalent risk companies. For example, if the average market risk premium over the Treasury bond yield is 7%, and if the subject company has a beta of 0.60, the adjusted risk premium is $(0.60) \times (7\%) = 4.2\%$. This beta-adjusted risk premium is then added to the bond yield to arrive at the company's own cost of equity capital.

Another adjustment factor is the ratio of the company's standard deviation of returns to the average standard deviation of the equity market. In the case of a private company, the average deviation around the trend in its earnings per share or the variability in its book return on equity relative to that of a market index could serve as the basis for the risk adjustment. The adjustment can also be based on more qualitative risk meas-

---

[2] A useful data source is Ibbotson and Associates, which compiles historical returns and risk premiums from 1926 to the present for a variety of stock and bond portfolios.

ures, such as relative bond ratings, Standard & Poor's stock ratings, and Value Line safety ratings.

When examining historical returns, there is some debate about whether one should use the arithmetic or geometric mean of the return. Both measures are used in practice. The geometric mean measures historical holding period returns better, while the arithmetic mean summarizes expected returns better. Because the cost of capital is based on the return investors *expect* to achieve, we generally prefer the arithmetic mean.[3]

There is also some discussion about whether one should include a country risk premium in the calculation of the cost of equity for non-U.S. countries. If the risk is unsystematic, it should not be included in the cost of equity. If it is systematic but not captured in the calculated beta, some adjustment is warranted. Recent research suggests that the systematic country factor is significant in the case of many emerging equity markets.

Many valuation professionals add a country risk premium based on the spread between that country's government bonds and U.S. Treasury bonds of equivalent maturity. Another option is to incorporate risk adjustments in the cash flow forecasts, but this is difficult and highly judgmental, for it requires managers to forecast the likelihood and impact of such events as the repatriation of profits, expropriation, capital controls, and nonconvertibility. At a minimum, in cases where country risk may be important, one should probably examine the range in values that results from including and excluding country risk.

Capital Asset Pricing Model (CAPM)

The second approach in estimating the cost of equity capital is the CAPM. According to modern finance, a security's total risk can be partitioned into company-specific risk and "market risk," the nondiversifiable portion related to the general movement of the capital market:

$$\text{Total Risk} = \text{Market Risk} + \text{Company-Specific Risk}$$

The central idea behind the derivation of the CAPM is that the effects of company-specific risk on expected equity returns can be eliminated just by holding that stock in a diversified portfolio. This is shown in Figure 11-3. As the portfolio becomes progressively more diversified by the addition of securities, the specific risk component declines sharply until only market-related risk remains.

---

[3] In statistical parlance, the arithmetic average is the unbiased measure of the expected value of repeated observations of a random variable, not the geometric mean. See Morin, op. cit., for a formal demonstration.

FIGURE 11-3   Portfolio risk and diversification.

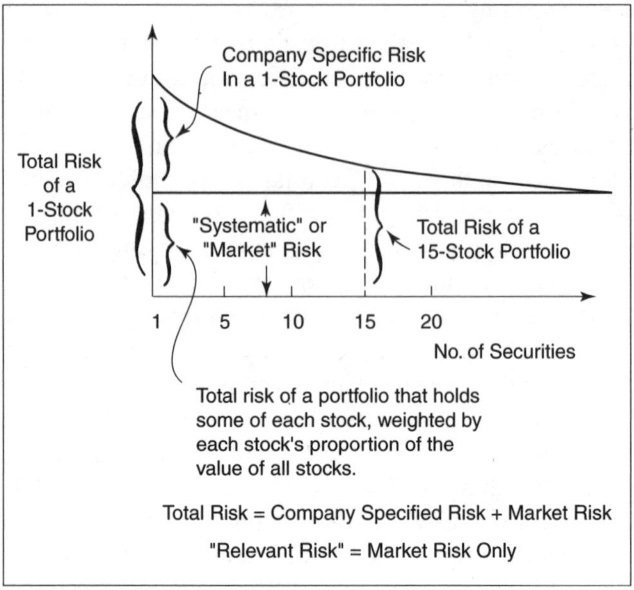

Source: Brigham, Gapenski, and Ehrhardt, op. cit.

Since investors can costlessly eliminate company-specific risk simply by holding a diversified portfolio, investors should expect to be compensated only for nondiversifiable risk, the variability in equity return driven by the market. Beta measures this market-driven volatility. For example, a beta of 0.75 indicates that a company equity return is 75% as volatile as the overall capital market. If the market rises 10%, the stock will rise by 7.5% on average. For diversified investors, beta is the only relevant risk measure. The CAPM formally quantifies this risk-return relationship:

$$K = R_F + \beta(R_M - R_F)$$

The seminal CAPM expression states that an investor expects to earn a return K that is equal to the return on a risk-free investment R_F plus a risk premium consisting of beta β and the market risk premium ($R_M - R_F$). This is portrayed graphically in Figure 11-4. Notice that the market portfolio has average risk, captured by a beta of 1.0. Stocks with less-than-average market risk, or with a beta of less than 1, are expected to earn less than the market. Those with a beta of greater than 1 are expected to earn a return greater than the market. Those with a beta of 0 are expected to earn the risk-free rate.

FIGURE 11-4   CAPM.

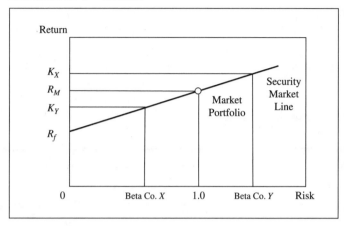

The graph in Figure 11-5 shows the relationship between the expected returns (measured as the sum of the dividend yield and expected growth rate) and betas of New York Stock Exchange (NYSE) common stocks as of early 2000. The securities are grouped into portfolios of ascending risk. It is clear that there is a strong positive correlation between expected returns and beta.

Despite the CAPM's conceptual appeal, using it to estimate the cost of equity does present some practical difficulties. For one, the model calls for expected values of the risk-free rate, beta, and the return on the market portfolio, but we must use historical data and proxies in estimating the

FIGURE 11-5   Return vs. beta risk, NYSE stocks, 1/2000.

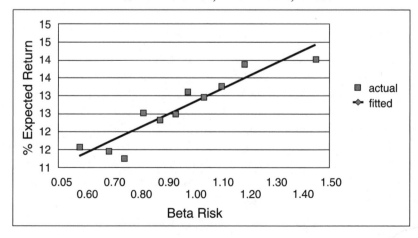

CAPM. As different practitioners choose different historical data periods or proxies, the CAPM results will vary as well. Nonetheless, some guidelines on choosing the best proxies have evolved.

The yield on long-term government bonds is a good proxy for the risk-free rate because investments in common stocks are typically long term and we eliminate a potential source of measurement error by trying to match maturities of the terms in the CAPM—likewise, when the CAPM is used to price equity capital raised to finance the purchase of long-lived company assets.

The second CAPM variable we need to estimate is beta. A useful starting point for measuring beta is the company's historical beta, particularly if the company's market risk is expected to remain fairly stable. Historical betas are available from several commercial sources including Value Line, Bloomberg, Merrill Lynch, Standard & Poor's, BARRA, and others. Industry betas or the beta from a portfolio of comparable risk securities are also useful proxies for a company's beta.

The last required input for the CAPM is the expected market risk premium. There are two methods of estimating the market risk premium: prospective and historical. The prospective method is implemented by applying the DCF methodology to a representative market index, such as the Standard & Poor's 500, Value Line Composite, or the NYSE Index. For reasons of consistency, the market portfolio used here should be the same as the market index used in deriving beta estimates. Subtracting the current risk-free rate from that estimate produces one valid estimate of the market risk premium.

A second valid approach is to assume that investors anticipate about the same risk premium in the future as in the past and estimate the expected market risk premium directly from historical market risk premiums. For example, from 1926 to 1999 the risk premium on the overall stock market averaged close to 7.5%.

With these proxies, it is straightforward to use the CAPM to estimate the cost of equity capital for a company. Let's illustrate with BellSouth. We use the current yield on long-term Treasury bonds of 6.5% to proxy for the risk-free rate. Historically, the Bell Regional Holding Companies' stock price has changed 0.9% for each 1% change in the market index, indicating a beta of 0.90 for telecommunications companies like BellSouth. For the market risk premium, an estimate of 7.5% is used, based on the Ibbotson Associates compilation of historical returns, which shows that a broad market sample of common stocks outperformed long-term U.S. government bonds by 7.5% from 1926 to 1999. Putting these estimates together, BellSouth's cost of equity capital according to the CAPM is 13.25%:

$$K = 6.5\% + 0.90\,(7.5\%) = 13.25\%$$

Size effect.   Although the CAPM is often used to estimate the cost of capital, the evidence indicates that the model is incomplete. Factors beyond beta seem to play some role in explaining variation in long-run average returns. The most important missing factor is a *size effect.* Smaller firms (as measured by market capitalization) tend to generate higher returns than indicated by the CAPM, possibly because of a missing risk factor, or because small firms are underpriced, or some combination of the two. Financial theory cannot yet explain the small-firm effect.

It is well established that the CAPM underestimates the cost of equity for companies with betas of less than 1.0. "Expanded CAPMs" have been developed which relax some of the assumptions thought responsible for the bias. These expanded CAPMs typically produce a risk-return relationship that is "flatter" than the traditional CAPM, producing higher estimates at lower betas, and lower return estimates at higher betas. An example, known as the Empirical Capital Asset Pricing Model (ECAPM),[4] is shown in Equation 1:

$$K = R_F + a\ (R_M - R_F) + (1 - a)\ \beta\ (R_M - R_F) \qquad (1)$$

The constant term a is empirically determined. Returning to the BellSouth example (risk-free rate of 6.5%, beta of 0.90, market risk premium of 7.5%), and letting $a = 0.25$, the ECAPM produces a cost of equity of 13.4%:

$$K = 6.5\% + 0.25 \times 7.5\% + 0.75 \times 0.90 \times 7.5\% = 13.4\%.$$

DCF Approach

The traditional DCF formula states that under certain assumptions[5] the equity investor's expected return K_e can be viewed as the sum of an expected dividend yield, D_1/P_0, plus the expected growth rate of future dividends and stock price g:

$$K_e = D_1/P_0 + g$$

[4] See Morin, op. cit., for a full discussion of ECAPM and related literature.

[5] The traditional DCF model requires the following main assumptions: a constant average growth trend for both dividends and earnings, a stable dividend payout policy, a discount rate in excess of the expected growth rate, and a constant price-earnings multiple, which implies that growth in price is synonymous with growth in earnings and dividends. The traditional DCF model also assumes that dividends are paid annually, when in fact dividend payments are normally made on a quarterly basis. The assumptions underlying this valuation formulation are discussed in detail in Morin, op. cit., Chapter 4.

where K_e = Investors' expected return on equity
D_1 = Expected dividend during the coming year
P_0 = Current stock price
g = Expected growth rate of future dividends

Through trade, investors set the equity price in order to obtain a fair rate of return. The expected returns implied by a given market price are not directly observable, however, and must be estimated. The DCF approach estimates K_e from the expected dividend yield and an estimate of expected future growth.

The expected dividend yield in the DCF model can be obtained by multiplying the current dividend yield by the growth factor $(1 + g)$. Dividend yields are readily available in the popular press and financial databases. The principal difficulty is in estimating the unobservable expected growth rate. For this, two proxies are typically employed. The first is historical growth. Under conditions of stability, this is a reasonable proxy. The second is analysts' long-term growth forecasts. Both IBES and Zacks Investment Research provide consensus analysts' earnings growth forecasts for publicly traded companies. To illustrate, using the rewritten DCF model, $K_e = D_0(1 + g)/P_0 + g$, and market data for The Southern Company (current dividend of \$1.34, current stock price of \$24.00, expected dividend growth of 7%), we find a cost of equity capital of 13%.

If investors expect some growth pattern other than constant infinite growth to prevail in the future, the general DCF valuation framework can handle such situations. Also note that the standard DCF model does not apply to high-growth stocks. In the development of the standard DCF equation, it was necessary to assume that the company's growth (g) was less than the required return (K). This assumption is realistic for most established companies. Although it is possible for a firm to generate very high growth rates for a few years, no firm could double or triple its earnings and dividends indefinitely.

DIVISIONAL COST OF CAPITAL

The companywide WACC is frequently not appropriate for individual divisions or projects with varying risks. It is only applicable to scale expansions of the company or divisions with the same risk profile as the company. Capacity expansion projects for example, are riskier than routine maintenance projects and should be assigned higher costs of equity capital.

Investment and valuation strategies that employ a single companywide cost of capital may systematically destroy economic value. Managers who use the WACC to analyze all projects accept too many high-risk projects and too few low-risk ones.

The message is crucial: The cost of capital for a division, investment project, or specific asset depends on the riskiness of the cash flows of that investment, not on the variability of the cash flows of the company that undertakes the project. The cost of capital depends on the use of funds and not on the source of funds. This is because the cost of capital is fundamentally the opportunity cost of the investor, that is, the foregone return on comparable risk investments.

Management Comparisons Approach

So how does one estimate the risk of a division, a nontraded asset? One possibility is the management comparisons approach. Under this approach, the beta of an industry or other group of firms identified by management as having the most similar risk, structural, and/or economic characteristics as the division is used in the CAPM or ECAPM to estimate the divisions' cost of equity capital. One difficulty with this approach is that although the reference companies may have the same business risk, they may have different capital structures. Observed betas reflect both business risk and financial risk. Hence, when a group of companies is considered comparable in every way except for financial structure, their betas are not directly comparable.

Specifically, an increase in financial leverage (debt capital) will increase the equity beta of a company, all else remaining constant. Intuitively, the fixed interest payments on debt increase the variability of the residual income available to shareholders, with higher debt ratios increasing income during boom periods and decreasing income during bust periods. The following equation decomposes a company's (levered) beta into a business risk (unlevered) component, and a financial risk component related to the use of debt financing:

$$\beta_L = \beta_U \left[1 + (1 - T)\, D/E \right]$$

where β_L = Observed levered beta of a company
β_U = Unlevered beta of the company with no debt in its capital structure
D/E = Ratio of debt to equity expressed in market value terms
T = Corporate income tax rate

Intuitively, this expression states that the total risk of a company β_L is the sum of business risk β_U and a financial risk premium that depends on the magnitude of the company's debt ratio D/E. The unlevered beta of a company β_U is influenced by the type of business the company operates in and its cost structure, the level of fixed versus variable costs.

Example.   The following example demonstrates a two-step procedure for determining the beta of a division whose business risk is comparable to a sample of reference companies in the same industry, but with a different capital structure. Georgia-Pacific Group is a "letter stock" reflecting the nontimber operations of Georgia-Pacific Corporation, one of the largest manufacturers of paper and building products. The company wishes to estimate its cost of capital, but its brief operating history eliminates the standard estimation models. For example, the company has no data on its beta yet. The company looks to a reference group of companies in the paper products industry. Their average levered beta is 0.80, and average market value debt ratio is 28%. Georgia-Pacific Group's own debt-equity ratio is 40%, and its corporate tax rate is 40%.

The first step in estimating Georgia-Pacific Group's equity beta is to purge the pure-play companies' average beta of the effects of financial leverage and obtain the unlevered beta using the beta equation:

$$\beta_L = \beta_U [1 + (1 - T) \, D/E] \qquad\qquad (2)$$
$$0.80 = \beta_U [1 + (1 - 0.40)28/72]$$

Solving the above equation, $\beta_U = 0.65$. The second step is to estimate the levered beta of Georgia-Pacific Group using the same above equation in reverse, this time using Georgia-Pacific Group's own debt-equity ratio:

$$\beta_L = \beta_U[1 + (1 - T)D/E] = 0.65[1 + (1 - 0.40)40/60] = 0.91$$

The estimated equity beta for the division of 0.91 is then used in the CAPM to estimate the cost of equity capital for the Georgia-Pacific Group division.

The pure-play methodology assumes that the pure-play companies have the same business risk as the division, and that, indeed, such pure-play companies can be identified to begin with. One difficulty with the approach is to identify undiversified "single line of business" proxy companies. The pool of pure-play companies is shrinking as companies become more diversified over time. In fact, most companies are not perfectly homogeneous in risk and have multiple lines of business. Moreover, to the extent that the universe of pure-play companies is dwindling, the influence of outliers on the proxy cost of capital estimate increases. In addition, the choice of screening parameters and cutoff points in defining a sample of pure-plays is arbitrary and subjective. Finally, the technique does not consider corporate synergies; it assumes that the risk of total company is simply the sum of the risk of its parts.

The CAPM Approach

The CAPM framework provides an alternative method for determining a division's cost of capital. A parent company can be viewed as a portfolio of assets or divisions. In the absence of significant synergy, the risk of the parent's common stock, as measured by beta, is a weighted average of the betas of its divisions, say, Divisions 1, 2, and 3:

$$\beta_p = w_1\beta_1 + w_2\beta_2 + w_3\beta_3 \tag{3}$$

where w_1, w_2 and w_3 represent the weights and β_1, β_2, and β_3 are the betas of the three divisions. To estimate the weights, the average percentage contribution of each division to consolidated operating income over a reasonable historical period can be used. Assuming that the weighted betas sum to the aggregate beta and given the weighted betas of two of the three divisions, the beta for the remaining division can be estimated. The CAPM formula can be used to measure the cost of equity of the "residual" division. The problem is that this approach is only useful in the limited case of one unknown division. The following two-division example illustrates the method.

Example. The electric utility industry is being restructured and disaggregated into two distinct components: the generation business and the wires business. The former is to be deregulated and subjected to the forces of competition, while the latter will continue to be regulated. In 1998, the Southern California Edison Company (SCE) was interested in quantifying the cost of equity for its regulated wires business.

Given that the weighted betas of the two unbundled businesses of an integrated utility like SCE must add up to the parent's aggregate beta, and given the weighted beta of one of the two business segments, the residual beta applicable to the remaining business segment can be calculated. The CAPM formula can be used to measure the cost of equity of the "residual" business segment.

The aggregate beta (β_{parent}) of SCE's vertically integrated operations is known from market data, and it must be equal to the weighted average beta of its wires and its generation businesses:

$$\beta_{parent} = w_w\,\beta_w + w_g\,\beta_g$$

Solving the preceding equation for the beta of SCE's wires business, we obtain the following:

$$\beta_w = \beta_{parent}/w_w - w_g \, \beta_g/w_w$$

We know SCE's aggregate beta, which at the time was 0.75. The beta of the generation business was estimated at 0.80, based on the betas of comparable risk companies in similar businesses, namely oil and gas producers. The weights of the wires and generations businesses were 55% and 45%, respectively. Inserting these quantities in the preceding equation, we obtain a wires business beta of 0.71:

$$\beta_w = 0.75/0.55 - 0.45 \times 0.80/.55 = 0.71$$

Earnings Beta Approach

Another approach is needed in the case of a business entity that is not publicly traded. Since beta is a measure of the relationship between the returns of a company and the overall market, and since the relationship is, to a large extent, determined by the relationship between the company's earnings and corporate earnings in the overall economy, an *earnings beta* can be computed and used instead. The slope coefficient from a time series of quarterly earnings regressed on the corresponding index of aggregate quarterly corporate earnings published by the Commerce Department is the earnings beta. The earnings beta is basically a measure of earnings cyclicality—that is, the extent to which fluctuations in a company's earnings mirror the fluctuations in aggregate earnings—and is well correlated with market beta. A similar measure of risk can be constructed using accounting returns (ROEs) instead of earnings.

Example.   Two steps are required to implement the earnings beta approach. First, a general relationship between equity beta and earnings beta must be established for a large sample of publicly traded stocks. Second, the estimated relationship is used to infer the division's beta. Take, for example, the following regression between the published betas of a large sample of publicly traded stocks and their earnings beta:

$$\text{Stock Market } \beta = 0.564 + 0.251 \text{ Earnings } \beta$$

If a division's beta, obtained by regressing a time series of the division's quarterly earnings on an index of aggregate quarterly corporate earnings over the last 10 years, is 0.90, then the stock market beta of that division, obtained by inserting the division's earnings beta into the above equation, is as follows:

$$\text{Stock Market } \beta = 0.564 + 0.251 \times 0.90 = 0.73$$

ESTIMATING THE COST OF DEBT

The cost of debt (k_d) should be based on current market rates of interest and expressed on a net-of-tax basis because it is after-tax cash flows that are being discounted. In most settings, the market rate of interest can be converted to a net-of-tax basis by multiplying it by 1 minus the marginal corporate tax rate.

For privately held debt, yields are not quoted, but stated interest rates on bank term loans or leases may provide a suitable substitute if interest rates have been fairly stable. In the case of convertible debt, its true cost is far higher than the coupon yield quoted on the bond because convertibles offer investors a valuable option on the firm's common equity, one that can be costly to the company's stockholders.

The cost of preferred stock, since its dividends are perpetual, is simply the stated dividend divided by the current price. If, for example, Southern Company's preferred stock pays a dividend of $1.20 in perpetuity and the stock is trading at $120, then the current required return, or cost of preferred equity, is $1.20 divided by $120, or 10%.

CAPITAL STRUCTURE AND THE COST OF CAPITAL

The weights assigned to debt and equity in the WACC represent their respective fractions of total capital provided, measured in terms of market values. Computing the market value for debt should not be difficult. It is reasonable to use book values if interest rates have not changed significantly since the time the debt was issued. Otherwise, the value of the debt can be estimated by discounting the future coupon and principal payouts at the company's current interest rate, with the help of a standard financial calculator.

What is included in debt? Short-term as well as long-term debt? Payables and accruals? The answer depends on how free cash flows are calculated. Since the cash flows are those available before servicing short-term and long-term debt, both short-term and long-term debt should be considered a part of capital when computing the WACC. Since the servicing of other liabilities, such as accounts payable or accruals, has already been considered when computing free cash flows, internal consistency requires these not be considered a part of capital when computing the WACC.

There is an inherent logical circularity in assigning a market value to equity, because value is what we are trying to estimate in the first place. How can the manager assign a market value to equity at this intermediate stage, when value will not be known until all the steps in the valuation process have been completed?

One satisfactory approach is to use "target" ratios of debt and equity to capital for this intermediate calculation. Another is to use a reasonable initial guess for the value of equity, perhaps based on some multiple of next year's earnings forecast, as a weight in the calculation of an initial WACC. The initial WACC is, in turn, used in the discounting process to generate an initial estimate of the value of equity. That initial estimate can then be used in place of the guess to arrive at a new WACC, and a second estimate of the value of equity can be produced. This iterative process can be repeated until the value used to calculate the WACC and the final estimated equity value converge.

Example

We now return to Table 11-1 to complete the estimation of Georgia-Pacific's WACC as of early 2000. The book value of debt was used to proxy for market value. The market value of equity was obtained by multiplying the book value of equity by the company's M/B ratio. The resulting market value weights of debt and equity were 40% and 60%, respectively.

The cost of debt is simply the current yield on Georgia-Pacific's outstanding debt, 7.5%. The after-tax cost of debt $7.5\% \times (1 - 0.40) = 4.5\%$. The cost of equity is estimated with the CAPM. The current yield on long-term Treasury bonds of 6.5% is used as the risk-free rate. GP's beta was assumed to be 0.91, based on the average beta of the companies in the paper industry, as reported in Value Line. A market risk premium of 7.5% is used based on the historical spread between stocks and bonds reported by Ibbotson Associates. Putting these estimates together, GP's cost of equity capital is 13.3%, and the weighted average cost of capital is 9.7%.

Optimal Capital Structure

The broader question of whether there exists an optimal set of weights in computing the WACC is now addressed. We know that the value of a company is estimated by discounting the free cash flows to the providers of capital at the WACC. This is shown in simplified form in the following equation. Clearly, if the cost of capital is reduced, the value of the company will increase.

$$\text{Value} \uparrow = \frac{\text{Cash Flow}}{\text{Cost of Capital}} = \frac{C}{k \downarrow}$$

Because the objective of a company is to maximize value, this can be accomplished by minimizing the cost of capital.

The relationship between capital structure and the cost of capital is shown graphically in Figure 11-6. The horizontal axis is the debt-to-total capital ratio, D/C, assuming that no other form of senior capital exists. The graph depicts the return requirements of bondholders and shareholders in response to a change in capital structure as the firm progressively substitutes debt for equity capital. Taxes are ignored for the moment.

The required return on debt is relatively flat for a debt ratio from zero up to some critical debt ratio value, say, 50%. Beyond that point, an increase in debt increases the required return on bonds as debtholders perceive a significant increase in financial risk. The actual value of the critical threshold can be determined by examining the reaction of interest rates to increases in the debt ratio of companies with the highest-quality bonds (Aaa). As debt is increased but remains below the critical debt ratio, the risk to bondholders and return to debt is essentially unchanged, but as the debt is increased beyond the critical value, bond risk and required returns increase significantly in a manner consistent with the quality gradient observed for company bond yields and debt ratios. The points on the bond graph in Figure 11-6 can be estimated by observing the actual bond yields and debt ratios for companies in a given industry rated Aaa, Aa, A, and Baa, respectively, at a moment in time. Access to debt financing is likely to be severely curbed beyond the Baa rating level.

The curve depicting the behavior of shareholders as the debt ratio is increased is developed as follows. At a zero debt ratio, the return on equity coincides with the return on total capital, since the firm is all-equity

FIGURE 11-6 Relationship between capital structure and cost of capital.

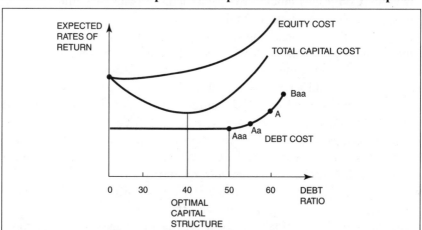

Source: Morin, op. cit.

financed at that point. Shareholders only have to contend with business risk and do not have to deal with financial risk at that juncture. Beyond that point, with each successive increase in the debt ratio, equity returns rise moderately at first in response to increasing financial risk to the point where the bond ratings begin to deteriorate. We encountered this fundamental concept in finance earlier when we discussed financial risk. As the debt ratio reaches very high levels where the solvency of the firm is endangered, shareholders' required returns rise sharply.

The relationship between the WACC and capital structure emerges directly from the assumed behavior of bond returns and equity returns. This is also seen in Figure 11-6. At a zero debt ratio, the cost of capital is the cost of equity. With each successive substitution of low-cost debt for high-cost equity, the average cost of capital declines as the weight of low-cost debt in the average increases. A low point is reached where the increased risk and required return of equity exactly offset the cost advantage of debt. This is the optimal capital structure point. Beyond that point, the cost disadvantage of equity outweighs the cost advantage of debt, and the weighted average cost of capital rises accordingly.

The most salient characteristic of the graph is the U-shaped nature of the total cost of capital curve, pointing to the existence of a value-maximizing (i.e., cost-minimizing) capital structure. Despite the rise in both debt and equity costs with increases in the debt ratio, the WACC reaches a minimum. Beyond this point, the low-cost and tax advantages of debt are outweighed by the increased equity costs. This occurs just before the point where bond ratings start deteriorating, and the cost of capital increases rapidly at higher debt ratios. Companies should strive for a capital structure that minimizes the composite capital cost, thus maximizing value.

Despite the conceptual appeal of this "trade-off" view of the optimal capital structure, it is difficult in practice to quantify the optimal level of debt. There are intangible costs and distress costs associated with a higher debt ratio. The yield advantage of a higher bond rating increases dramatically in adverse capital market conditions. Bond flotation costs increase as bond ratings decline, particularly in years of difficult financial markets. Low-rated bonds also carry shorter maturities, especially in poor years. The result is a maturity mismatch between the firm's long-term capital assets and its liabilities. Moreover, lower bond quality is associated with more years of call protection, particularly during difficult financial markets; since bonds are frequently called after a decrease in interest rates, bonds that carry call protection for a greater number of years are more costly to companies. As bond ratings decline, the probability that a company will reduce the dollar amount or shorten the maturity of their bond issues increases dramatically. This in turn reduces the marketability of a bond issue and hence increases its yield. Finally, the optimal capital structure shifts over time with changes in capital market conditions and changes in business risk. Perhaps more importantly, companies should maintain a borrowing reserve, using less debt in normal times so as to build reserve debt capacity when needed.

Several have studied the empirical relationship among the cost of capital, capital-structure changes, and the value of the firm's securities. They find evidence consistent with the existence of a tax benefit from leverage, and a positive relationship between leverage and the cost of equity. The studies report that cost of equity increases between 34 and 237 basis points when the debt ratio increases from 40% to 50%, with an average of 138 basis points in the theoretical studies and 76 basis points in the empirical studies. This translates into a 7.6 to 13.8 basis point increase per percentage increase in the debt ratio, with the more recent studies leaning toward the upper end of that range.

One immediate implication is that important changes in the leverage should be taken into consideration when estimating the cost of equity. For example, when capital structure is expected to vary in a predictable way, such as in an LBO, recapitalization, joint venture, or project financing, the cost of equity should be explicitly adjusted to reflect the changing leverage (unless the APV method from Chapter 6 is used instead).

Example
Eastern Power Company's cost of equity is estimated at 12% based on the company's existing capital structure, which consists of 35% debt and 65% equity in market value terms. The current borrowing rate is 8%, and the corporate income tax rate is 40%. The management of Eastern Power Company has decided to alter its capital structure to 40% debt and 60% equity. The revised cost of equity can be obtained by solving the Modigliani-Miller relationship between the cost of equity and financial risk (leverage) using the revised debt ratio:

$$K_e = \rho + (\rho - i)\,(1 - T)\,D/E$$

where K_e = Cost of equity
      ρ = Cost of equity for an unlevered company
      i = Interest rate on debt
   D/E = Debt to common equity proportion
      T = Income tax rate

The cost of equity bears a positive and linear relationship to financial risk. The first term of the expression p represents the shareholder's compensation for business risk, the company's cost of equity in the absence of debt financing. The second term, $(\rho - i)(1 - T) D/E$, represents the additional compensation for bearing financial risk.[6]

To solve for K_e, the cost of capital for an all-equity financed firm ρ is required. This can be done by solving the above equation for ρ under the old capital structure, $12\% = \rho + (\rho - 0.08)(1 - 0.40) 0.35/65$, from which we find $\rho = 11.02\%$, then inserting this ρ into the same equation under the new capital structure:

$$K_e = 0.1102 + (0.1102 - 0.08)(1 - 0.40) 0.40/0.60$$
$$= 0.1223 = 12.23\%$$

The market value of equity is easily obtained by multiplying the current stock price by the number of shares outstanding. The market value of debt is obtained by applying orthodox bond valuation formulas. Book values can be used as an approximation if market values are unobservable.

Another way to tackle the problem is to compute an unlevered beta, then relever the beta with the new capital structure, as in an earlier example in the chapter. The CAPM formula is then employed to measure the cost of equity under the new capital structure.

The major thrust of the example is that a changing capital structure will affect the estimates of the cost of equity capital. The revised cost of equity can be estimated with either the Modigliani-Miller or the levered beta-CAPM equations.

Example: Finding the Optimal Capital Structure

The management of National Electric Company is of the opinion that the cost of debt is a function of the debt ratio and that this function is reflected in the schedule shown in the first and second columns of Table 11-2.

The first column shows the increasing debt-to-total-capital ratio (D/C). The second column shows the after-tax cost of debt K_d, assuming a tax rate of 40%. (In an actual situation, such a schedule could be derived from the actual bond yields and debt ratios for company bonds in different quality rating groups averaged over a number of years.) The company's man-

---

[6] The "ρ" term is often referred to as the unlevered cost of capital. It is, in fact, the appropriate discount rate to use in computing the present value of the base case component of the APV approach to valuation discussed in Chapter 6.

TABLE 11-2   Capital structure and cost of capital.

D/C	K_d	K_e	WACC
0%	5.0%	11.00%	11.00%
10%	5.0%	11.15%	10.54%
20%	5.0%	11.60%	10.28%
30%	5.0%	12.35%	10.15%
40%	5.5%	13.40%	10.24%
50%	6.0%	14.75%	10.38%
60%	7.0%	16.40%	10.76%
70%	8.5%	18.35%	11.46%

agement also believes that the company's cost of equity K_e can be expressed as the sum of the risk-free rate R_F, a premium for business risk b, and a premium for financial risk f, as follows:

$$K_e = R_F + b + f$$

The risk-free rate is measured by the yield on long-term Treasury bonds at 7%. The premium for business risk demanded by company investors is estimated at 4%. The premium for financial risk is an increasing function of the debt ratio; the premium rises slowly at first and then accelerates rapidly as the debt ratio reaches prohibitive levels. The behavior of the premium for financial risk is assumed to be proportional to the square of the debt ratio, and the proportionality constant is 0.15. Substituting into the preceding equation, the cost of equity function can be expressed as $K_e = 7\% + 4\% + 0.15\ (D/C)^2$ and is shown as a schedule of equity cost for various debt ratios in the third column of Table 11-2.

WACC for each level of debt ratio is calculated by adding the cost of debt and the cost of equity corresponding to each debt ratio, weighted by their relative proportions. This calculation appears in the fourth column of Table 11-2. The cost of capital plotted in Figure 11-7 reaches a minimum at a debt ratio of 30%. National Electric Company's optimal capital structure thus consists of 30% debt and 70% equity.

The functional relationship between the cost of equity and leverage is specified by employing the Modigliani-Miller expression discussed in the previous example and repeated in the following:

$$K_e = \rho + (\rho - i)(1 - T)D/E$$

FIGURE 11-7   National Electric Company's cost of capital vs. leverage.

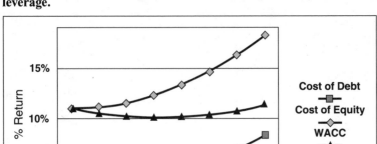

For example, with an unlevered cost of equity of 11%, a cost of debt of 8%, and a tax rate of 40%, the preceding equation yields the following functional relationship between the cost of equity and financial leverage:

$$K_e = 0.11 + (0.11 - 0.08)(1 - 0.4)D/E = 0.11 + 0.012\ D/E$$

Another way to specify the functional relationship between the cost of equity and leverage is to compute the beta of the company at various degrees of leverage using the levered beta equation discussed in the previous section and substituting the resulting beta into the CAPM to obtain the cost of equity.

CONCLUSIONS

The implementation of VBM can have dramatic financing implications in a company. In setting a target capital structure, a company should aim for a debt ratio that retains financial flexibility while taking full advantage of the tax benefits of debt. LBOs, for example, substitute debt for equity, typically reduce the cost of capital, and clearly alter the company's focus from earnings per share to the cash flows that are required to service the debt. They also create value through the tax shield on interest and because they ease investors' fears that management may make unproductive investments.

Much confusion remains in corporate circles about the role of debt in the capital structure. The value of borrowing is not so much from the tax benefits it creates but the operational efficiencies it inspires. The need to service heavy interest and principal payments intensifies managers' commitment to hard work, efficiency, productivity, and rigorous screening of investments.

Stock repurchases are another financial strategy aimed at creating value for shareholders. In most cases, share repurchase results in an appreciation of market value. While the reason offered is typically that "the stock is undervalued relative to assets," the truth is also that repurchases create value by lowering the cost of capital, thus making more efficient use of the corporation's equity base.

The inherent conservatism of corporate America, with its focus on maintaining a superior bond rating or a debt/equity ratio of under 50%, stands in the way of value optimization. Balance sheet ratios lose their meaning when intangibles are expensed, or inventories are valued on a LIFO (last in, first out) basis, or the book values of property, plant, and equipment are a small fraction of their replacement cost, or the current value of equity is understated. More importantly, however, cash flows, not balance sheet ratios, service debt.

Maintaining the highest-possible bond rating does not necessarily result in the lowest cost of capital. Even when a company's bonds are downgraded, the cost of capital can be reduced through the greater use of debt. Some corporate acquisitions that involve high takeover premiums become viable from the shareholders' standpoint for this reason alone. Debt is used to buy equity; thus, the corporation's equity base is used more efficiently.

Long-term achievement of at least an A rating or preferably a Aa rating is in a company's best interests.[7] Debt leverage targets should be set in the lower part of the range required to attain this optimal rating. The required range is obtained from the observed capital structure of industry peers and/or from the debt ratio guidelines specified by bond rating agencies for a given bond rating. If the company maintains its debt ratio close to the bottom end of the optimal range required for a AA bond rating, its overall cost of capital should be minimized.

If the company reduces its debt ratio below that point, it would be giving up the tax benefits associated with debt but would not reap the benefits from a lower cost of debt and equity. If the company operates at a debt ratio beyond that point, the cost of debt and equity will rise. The latter rise will occur at an increasing rate if the operating environment deteriorates. Moreover, the company will reduce its financing flexibility. In normal times a company should conserve enough unused borrowing capacity so that during periods of adversity it can use this capacity to avoid foregoing investment opportunities.

---

[7] See the optimal capital structure simulation model developed by Morin, op. cit.

PART IV

CORPORATE GOVERNANCE

12

PERFORMANCE METRICS

AS MENTIONED IN AN EARLIER CHAPTER, value-based management consists of three components: finance, strategy, and corporate governance. The previous chapters dealt with the strategic and financial components of VBM. The next two chapters focus on corporate governance, which consists of performance evaluation, compensation, and investor relations.

In a recent CFO magazine survey, 65% of the responding companies indicated that they were reexamining their performance metrics. Companies are realizing that accounting-based measures are often poor indicators of value creation, and they are searching for appropriate value-based measures of corporate performance.

Value managers today are faced with a daunting array of value-based metrics: economic value added (EVA), total shareholder return (TSR), cash flow return on investment (CFROI), and shareholder value added (SVA), to name the most prominent. Several of these value metrics are linked to consulting firms: Stern & Stewart with EVA, Boston Consulting Group with CFROI, and L.E.K. Consulting, LLC with SVA. Each claims that their measure is best. This metric war complicates the managers' task of deciding which performance metric or set of metrics is best for their company.

In this chapter, some of the more popular performance metrics are introduced and illustrated. A summary table comparing the strengths and weaknesses of each measure and our guidelines for matching the metric to the situation is provided in Table 12-10 at the end of the chapter. We find that no single measure is best for all organizational levels within the company. As displayed in Figure 4-11 in Chapter 4, we recommend market-based measures such as relative TSR to measure value at the corporate level, and economic value creation metrics such as SVA for the business unit or segment level. At the operational level, the focus should be on the value drivers that simulate market value creation. A well-planned and implemented performance-metric system ensures that the measures at all three levels are aligned and consistent with the overall goal of maximum shareholder value.

There is a popular saying in management that "what gets measured gets done." This is especially true in the case of value-based management. Value creation is not a naturally occurring phenomenon. It requires a complex and well-functioning financial information system that appropriately measures value and focuses the attention of management and employees on value creation.

The first step in choosing an appropriate performance measure is to develop suitable criteria for comparing the various measures. We suggest the following:

1. *Accuracy*
    - Does the measure account for the amount of future cash flows?
    - Does the measure account for the timing of future cash flows?
    - Does it account for the risk of the cash flows?

2. *Strategic decision making*
    - Can the measure value strategies?
    - Can it be used as a basis for strategic decision making?

3. *Performance measurement and compensation*
    - Does it provide an accurate measurement of employee performance?
    - Can it be used as a basis for compensation?
    - Is the measure subject to manipulation by employees?
    - Will the adoption of the measure lead to employee behavior and actions that maximize value?

4. *Complexity*
    - Is the measure easy to calculate?
    - Can it be communicated easily to analysts, shareholders, and employees?

5. *Organizational levels*
    - Can the measure be applied to the corporate, business unit, and operational levels of the company?

- If not, can it be decomposed into a series of value drivers that can be applied at the business unit and the operational level?

6. *Robustness*
- Is the measure appropriate at all stages of a company's life cycle: start-up, growth, maturity, and decline?
- Is it equally applicable during various market conditions: bull markets and bear markets, expansion and recession?

Of course, no single measure of value satisfies all six criteria. But this provides a useful framework for understanding the trade-offs between various value metrics. Based on this framework, managers might decide to use multiple value measures, for example, one metric for decision making and another for performance evaluation.

ACCOUNTING METRICS

Traditional performance metrics such as earnings per share (EPS), book value (BV), return on equity (ROE), return on assets (ROA), and return on invested capital (ROIC) are based on accounting numbers. These standardized measures are easy to calculate and widely popular. The fundamental difficulty with accounting metrics is that they do a poor job of capturing the three fundamental determinants of value creation: the amount, timing, and risk of the future cash flows of a company.

Accounting earnings are a single-period measure whereas economic value is driven by the cash flows generated over the life of the asset, typically several periods hence. Even over a single period, however, earnings correspond poorly to cash flows, since they omit working capital and fixed asset investments. By ignoring capital investments, earnings give no indication of the cost required to produce the earnings and therefore say nothing about value creation. Ratios such as return on assets and return on invested capital, because they take into account the capital employed, are a modest improvement over earnings alone, but these ratios are still single period and fail to account for risk, which is the cost of capital. Because investors confront a myriad of investment opportunities, they have an opportunity cost when investing in a company. Ultimately, they will invest in a company only if it offers returns greater than or equal to the opportunity cost of capital, which is the cost of capital of similar investments. By ignoring the cost of capital, accounting measures fail to give an indication of the company's ability to create market value.

Some use ROA or ROIC in excess of the cost of capital as indicators of value creation. The difficulty with this comparison is that accounting

TABLE 12-1 Accounting metrics and value.

Projected Income Statement						
Fluff Co.	2001	2002	2003	2004	2005	2006
Sales	$100	$105	$110	$116	$122	$128
Cash Expenses	−$70	−$74	−$78	−$82	−$86	−$90
Depreciation	−$20	−$20	−$20	−$20	−$20	−$20
EBIT = NI	$10	$11	$12	$14	$16	$18
True Value Co.	2001	2002	2003	2004	2005	2006
Sales	$100	$105	$110	$116	$122	$128
Cash Expenses	−$70	−$74	−$78	−$82	−$86	−$90
Depreciation	−$20	−$20	−$20	−$20	−$20	−$20
EBIT = NI	$10	$11	$12	$14	$16	$18

returns are single-period earnings on historical book value, while the cost of capital is market-based and forward-looking. Comparing the two often produces misleading results. A better measure of economic returns in this case, if used with caution, is the Internal Rate of Return (IRR), which is based on the expected future cash flows of the company. IRR can readily be compared to the company's cost of capital, as both are based on the investors' perceptions of the long-term prospects of the company.

The following numerical example demonstrates the difficulty of evaluating performance using accounting-based measures.[1] Consider two companies, Fluff and True Value. Both companies are assumed to have no interest or taxes, so that EBIT (earnings before interest and taxes) is equal to NI (net income). The two companies are private with no P/E data available. The projected income statements of Fluff and True Value are shown in Table 12-1.

Which company has more value? Both companies have the same earnings, but without balance sheet information on costs, we cannot evaluate the companies on the basis of value created. Table 12-2 displays the projected cash flow statements from the two companies. Cash flow statements combine information from both the income statement and the balance sheet, and allow a better view of value creation.

[1] Source: Weston & Copeland, *Managerial Finance,* 9th ed., Dryden 1992, Ch. 17.

TABLE 12-2 Accounting metrics and value.

Projected Cash Flow Statement

Fluff Co.	2001	2002	2003	2004	2005	2006	Cumulative
EBIT = NI	$10	$11	$12	$14	$16	$18	$81
Depreciation	$20	$20	$20	$20	$20	$20	$120
Capital Expenditure	-$60	$0	$0	-$60	$0	$0	-$120
Increase in Inventory	-$25	-$1	-$1	$4	$5	-$2	-$20
Cash Flow	**-$55**	**$30**	**$31**	**-$22**	**$41**	**$36**	**$61**
Cost of Capital	10%						
NPV at 10%	**$29**						

True Value Co.	2001	2002	2003	2004	2005	2006	Cumulative
EBIT = NI	$10	$11	$12	$14	$16	$18	$81
Depreciation	$20	$20	$20	$20	$20	$20	$120
Capital Expenditure	-$20	-$20	-$20	-$20	-$20	-$20	-$120
Increase in Inventory	-$15	-$1	-$1	-$2	-$2	-$2	-$23
Cash Flow	**-$5**	**$10**	**$11**	**$12**	**$14**	**$16**	**$58**
Cost of Capital	10%						
NPV at 10%	**$38**						

311

Clearly, True Value creates superior value. A careful look at the cash flow statements tells us why. Fluff replaces expensive manufacturing equipment every three years; True Value replaces less expensive manufacturing equipment every year. Also, True Value does a better job of managing its working capital. Its focus on earnings created and capital used distinguishes this company as a true value creator. Value-based metrics focus on the long-term projected cash flow statements, thereby providing an accurate picture of a company's value creation potential.

Because accounting measures are single period, they are especially ill-suited to strategic decision making, which involves projects whose impact is felt over several years. Moreover, accounting measures look backward, while strategic decisions project the firm into the future. In fact, a focus on short-term accounting earnings can lead to decisions that systematically destroy long-term value. Consider the following situation: Company A has two business segments, one a cash cow and the other high growth. Its strategy is to reallocate cash from the cash cow to the high-growth business. In this situation, because of its increased earnings and decreasing capital base, the cash cow's ROI is likely to be higher than that of the high-growth segment. Based solely on accounting numbers, one might conclude that a harvest strategy is superior to a growth strategy. This is not necessarily the case. In fact, the value created by the high-growth segment may be far superior based on the projected cash flows from each segment. A value-based metric based on long-term cash flows would accurately indicate the superiority of the high-growth segment.

The accounting model enables managers to influence reported earnings through their choice of accounting methods. This practice, known as *earnings management,* decreases the accuracy of accounting information and renders it questionable for performance evaluation and compensation criteria. For example, if used to compute compensation, managers might have the incentives to maximize single-period earnings at the expense of long-term value creation. For this reason, companies such as AOL, Microsoft, and HBOC have been publicly criticized for managing their earnings. Managed earnings practices include managing revenues by the choice of the recognition period, earnings by timing of asset sales and recognition of gains or losses, and cost of goods sold by the choice of inventory valuation method.

The biggest benefits of accounting measures are their simplicity and familiarity. Accounting measures are easy to calculate and to communicate to the investment community and to employees at all levels of the organization. The wide spectrum of accounting measures is another factor contributing to their popularity. There is a measure suited to each organizational level within the company. ROE can be used at the corporate level, ROIC at the divisional level, and decomposed ROA at the operational level, as discussed further at the end of this chapter.

The most theoretically accurate valuation model is useless if it fails to capture how the market values companies. Recall from Chapter 3 that the empirical evidence clearly indicates that the market is neither naive nor myopic, but values companies based on their expected long-term cash flows. The market's message to managers is clear: Adopt value-based measures, not accounting ones.

In summary, accounting-based measures, while simple to calculate, familiar, and eclectic, fail to accurately measure value, have limited use for strategic decision making, can be manipulated, and serve as a poor criteria for performance evaluation and compensation.

ECONOMIC VALUE METRICS

In earlier chapters we learned that DCF is the most accurate approach to valuation because it takes into account the amount, timing, and risk of the future expected cash flows of an investment project. The difficulty with DCF lies in forecast accuracy. Cash flow forecasts are sensitive to many factors, including (1) economywide forces such as inflation, interest rates, and money supply; (2) industry forces such as competitive rivalry, supplier and buyer power, and the availability of substitutes; and (3) company forces such as strategy, management, and capacity. If forecasting cash flows were an easy task, there would be no need for any other measures of value. DCF would be used for everything: corporate decisions, performance evaluations, and compensation.

A good performance measure should not only be accurate but also easy for all its users to understand. DCF can be fairly complex, especially if managers are accustomed to working with financial ratios and other accounting metrics. Moreover, since DCF relies on cash flow forecasts, it is inherently subject to manipulation. Managers who are evaluated on the basis of DCF have incentives to be overly optimistic in their estimates of cash flows. Corporate managers often do not have enough information regarding individual projects to recognize and make the appropriate allowances for their optimism.

The adjusted present value (APV) approach, a variant of the DCF approach discussed earlier in Chapter 6, suffers from the same drawbacks as NPV and has been around for a relatively short time. Some managers consider it more complex than NPV. It may be difficult to explain the idea of

APV to investors and employees at the operational level. On the other hand, APV clarifies the fundamental value drivers of a business better than NPV and hence could be invaluable for setting compensation targets at the operational level.

In recent years we have witnessed the proliferation of several alternative value measures, including economic profit, economic value added, market value added, shareholder value added, cash flow return on investment (a variant of the internal rate of return), total shareholder return, and the balanced scorecard. These metrics and their characteristics are described in Table 12-10 at the end of this chapter.

ECONOMIC PROFIT

In the economic profit (EP) model, the value of a company is equal to the amount of capital invested plus the present value of the economic profit created each year going forward. The EP in any given time period takes into account not only the accounting expenses but also the opportunity cost of the equity capital invested in the business.

$$EP = \text{Net Income} - (\text{Invested Capital} \times \text{Cost of Capital})$$

Dividing and multiplying by invested capital and noting that the return on invested capital (ROIC) is net income divided by invested capital yields a useful variation of the EP formula:

$$EP = \text{Invested Capital} \times (\text{ROIC} - \text{Cost of Capital})$$
$$= \text{Invested Capital} \times \text{Spread}$$

When a company has a positive spread, its economic profit is improved by investing more capital. In the case of a negative spread, more capital actually decreases economic profit. This distinction between good growth and bad growth is an important concept in value creation.

GOOD GROWTH	BAD GROWTH
Spread > 0	Spread < 0
r > k	r < k
Creates Value	Destroys Value

Suppose Company C has $2000 in invested capital, a 20% return on capital, and a 10% cost of capital. The economic profit created is $200:

$$\text{Economic Profit} = \$2000 \times (20\% - 10\%)$$
$$= \$200$$

Now suppose that next year, Company C invests $100 in capital, resulting in $2100 in total capital. The spread remains the same. Company C's economic profit increases to $210. Conversely, suppose the company makes no incremental investments in capital but improves its return to 25%. Company C's economic profit increases to $300.

The preceding example illustrates two different strategies for creating value: (1) investing more capital at high spreads and (2) improving the spread while maintaining the capital base. The spread could be improved either by decreasing the cost of capital or increasing the return on capital.

EVA: CALCULATION

Three inputs needed to calculate EVA, a popular variant of EP: (1) net operating profit after taxes (NOPAT), (2) invested capital, and (3) cost of capital. The example shown in Table 12-3 provides a simplified EVA calculation.

The main advantage of EVA is that it focuses attention on spread and capital growth, the fundamental concepts of value creation. EVA encourages management to invest more capital when the spread is positive and reduce capital and harvest the business when the spread is negative. Quaker Oats reduced inventories from $15 million to $9 million and eliminated 5 of its 15 warehouses after adopting EVA. Coca-Cola divested business units with negative spreads.

EVA possesses several objectionable features, however. As a single-period metric, it often fails to encourage long-term value creation, as illustrated in Table 12-4. In this example, a company is evaluating a project that costs $500 in initial capital and produces cash flows in years 1 through 4.

Despite healthy EVAs in all four years, this project has a negative NPV. This is the danger in using single-period metrics for multiperiod decisions. Notice if we take the present value of these EVAs and compare it to the initial investment, we get the same reject decision as with NPV. This is an important point: Value is not a function of the EVA in a single period, or even the incremental EVA between two periods, but rather the discounted value of all future cash flows associated with an investment project.

EVA looks back instead of forward. It is based on historic (sunk) capital base and ignores the stock market's expectations for the future performance of the company. As a solution, some suggest forecasting EVA into the future, which requires forecasts of NOPAT and capital, but then we have come back full circle to DCF. Why not just forecast the free cash flows directly and use DCF instead?

EVA also sometimes creates a disincentive for capital growth, as illustrated in Table 12-5. Notice that the reinvestment in year 5 dramatically re-

TABLE 12-3   Calculating EVA: example.

Selected income statement information:

Net sales	$20,000.00
Cost of goods sold	$12,000.00
Selling, general, and administrative	$6,000.00
Net operating profit	$2,000.00
Other income	$120.00
Earnings before interest and taxes	$2,120.00
Cash operating taxes	$927.00
NOPAT	**$1,193.00**

Cash taxes are computed as follows:

Provision for taxes	$975.00
Increase in deferred taxes	($35.00)
Cash taxes actually paid	$940.00
Tax shield of interest expense	$42.00
Tax on interest income	($55.00)
Cash operating taxes	$927.00

Selected balance sheet information:

Capital employed		
Net working capital	$2,500.00	
Net property, plant, and equipment	$3,500.00	
Other assets	$337.00	
Total Capital Invested (TCI)	**$6,337.00**	
Cost of capital		15.00%
ROIC	NOPAT/TCI	18.83%
Spread	ROIC - COC	3.83%
EVA	**Spread * TCI**	**$242.45**

duces year 5 EVA. If performance reviews and compensation were based on EVA, managers would have the incentive to underinvest for long-term growth.

Calculating EVA frequently requires some fairly complex accounting adjustments to reexpress the accounting book value of capital as a cash flow. These adjustments are the main difference between EVA and another

TABLE 12-4   EVA and value creation: an example.

	0	1	2	3	4
NOPAT		$100	$150	$200	$250
Capital	$500	$500	$375	$250	$125
Depreciation		$125	$125	$125	$125
Net capital	$500	$375	$250	$125	$0
Cash flow	($500)	$100	$150	$200	$250
Cost of capital		17.00%	17.00%	17.00%	17.00%
Capital charge		$63.75	$42.50	$21.25	$0.00
EVA		$36.25	$107.50	$178.75	$250.00
Incremental EVA			$71.25	$71.25	$71.25
Discounted EVA at COC		$30.98	$78.53	$111.61	$133.41
NPV		($39.89)			
Present value of EVA		$354.53			
Initial investment		($500.00)			
Value created		($145.47)			

metric known as residual income. Stern & Stewart lists approximately 164 useful adjustments to book values to arrive at useful EVAs, although in practice the following seven seem to be the most significant:

1. Capitalize R&D expenses.
2. Capitalize operating lease expenses.
3. Add back LIFO reserves and deferred tax reserves.
4. Add back bad debt reserves and warranty reserves.
5. Add back one-time restructuring charges.
6. Add back amortization of goodwill.
7. Replace accounting depreciation with economic depreciation or sinking-fund depreciation. Sinking-fund depreciation depreciates the asset so that the return on the asset is constant over its economic life.[2]

---

[2] The following article provides a complete discussion including numerical examples of accounting adjustments to calculate EVA: David Young, "Some Reflections on Accounting Adjustments and Economic Value Added." *The Journal of Financial Statement Analysis.* Winter 1999.

TABLE 12-5 EVA and growth incentive.

Case 1: EVA with no capital reinvestment

			Periods			
	Year 0	Year 1	Year 2	Year 3	Year 4	Year 5
NOPAT		100	200	300	200	100
Capital	1000	1000	800	600	400	200
Depreciation		200	200	200	200	200
Net capital	1000	800	600	400	200	0
Cost of capital		0.125	0.125	0.125	0.125	0.125
Capital charge		$100.00	$75.00	$50.00	$25.00	$0.00
EVA		$0.00	$125.00	$250.00	$175.00	$100.00

Case 2: EVA with capital reinvestment

			Periods			
	Year 0	Year 1	Year 2	Year 3	Year 4	Year 5
NOPAT		100	200	300	200	100
Capital	1000	1000	800	600	400	200
Depreciation		200	200	200	200	200
New investment		0	0	0	0	1000
Net capital	1000	800	600	400	200	1000
Cost of capital		0.125	0.125	0.125	0.125	0.125
Capital charge		$100.00	$75.00	$50.00	$25.00	$125.00
EVA		$0.00	$125.00	$250.00	$175.00	($25.00)

The problem with these adjustments is that many of them require inside information, and hence external evaluators such as raiders or investors are likely to come up with different measures of performance than managers of the company.

EVA is highly dependent on company size. Consider a company with two divisions, A and B. Both divisions have the same cost of capital, 10%. Division A is larger than Division B. The EVAs of the two divisions are calculated as follows:

	Division A	Division B
NOPAT	$150.00	$50.00
Net capital	$1,000.00	$250.00
ROIC	15%	20%
Spread	5%	10%
EVA	**$50.00**	**$25.00**
Standardized EVA	**5%**	**10%**

Which division creates more value? EVA points toward A, but ROIC and spread point toward B. The answer is Division B: It utilizes its assets better and generates a higher return per dollar of capital invested.

This size bias poses considerable problems for using EVA to determine compensation or compare performance across companies or divisions. By construction, EVA favors established, capital-intensive divisions over smaller, newer divisions with less capital invested. By using EVA to allocate capital, more capital is allocated to the bigger divisions, resulting in even higher EVA for these divisions. This is often a mistake, since the smaller divisions are usually growing faster and are of more strategic importance to the company.

Standardized EVA, or EVA divided by the total capital employed, measures the wealth created per unit of capital employed and is a more appropriate measure for comparing the performance of different-sized companies and divisions. In the above example, standardized EVA identifies Division B as the better performer.

Although EVA has done a poor job empirically of explaining market returns,[3] managers who use EVA to evaluate performance also use assets more intensively and increase share repurchases, both of which tend to increase company value.

In conclusion, although EVA has several advantages, its short-term orientation limits its relevance as a value measure.

MARKET VALUE ADDED

The market value added of a company is defined as the difference between the market value and book value of the company:

MVA = Market Value of the Company − Book Value of the Company

---

[3] Biddle, Bowen, and Wallace. "Evidence on EVA." *Journal of Applied Corporate Finance,* Summer 1999.

Company value consists of debt value plus equity value. If we make the reasonable assumption that the market and book values of debt are the same, the MVA of the company simplifies to

$$MVA = Market\ Value\ of\ Equity - Book\ Value\ of\ Equity$$

The market value of equity is simply the stock price multiplied by the number of shares outstanding. Calculating book value is more controversial. Stern & Stewart Co. propose using economic book value (EBV), which is the accounting book value adjusted to reflect the true economic value of the underlying assets. The adjustments are similar to those made when calculating EVA. MVA is not easily manipulated by management.

A primary drawback of MVA is that it leaves out dividends, another important component of shareholder wealth [a weakness not shared by Total Shareholder Return (TSR), covered later]. In addition, it is difficult to measure to MVA of an individual business unit. MVA is also heavily influenced by company size. Some use MVA standardized by the amount of capital employed to try to control for the size bias. To illustrate, let us compare the MVA of two well-known electric utility companies, Northern States Power and Northeast Utilities.[4] As of the end of 1998, both companies had roughly the same total market value, $7.6 billion for NSP and $7.9 for Northeast. The performance of the two companies varied widely, however. Northeast invested $7.9 billion of capital to produce $7.9 billion in value, whereas NSP needed only $5.8 billion of capital to produce $7.6 billion in value:

$$MVA = Total\ Market\ Value - Total\ Capital\ Invested$$

$$Northern\ States\ Power\ MVA = \$7.6B - \$5.8B = \$1.7\ B$$

$$Northeast\ Utilities\ MVA = \$7.9B - \$7.9B = \$0.0\ B$$

NSP shareholders, who own a company worth $1.7 billion more than the capital they invested, are much better off than Northeast shareholders, who just break even.

Table 12-6 shows, however, that the top MVA companies are not the leaders when it comes to capital efficiency as measured by standardized MVA.

---

[4] See S. R. Rajan, "Turning Capital to Wealth: A Ranking of U.S. Utilities." *Public Utilities Fortnightly.* December 1999.

TABLE 12-6 Top MVA companies.

Top Five Utilities Ranked by 1998 MVA

Company	1998 MVA Ranking	1998 Standardized MVA Ranking
Duke Energy	1	4
Southern Company	2	38
Con Edison	3	13
Florida Power and Light	4	10
Edison International	5	49

Top Five Utilities Ranked by 1998 Standardized MVA

Company	1998 Standardized MVA Ranking	1998 MVA Ranking
IPALCO Enterprise	1	29
Black Hills Corporation	2	61
Montana Power Co.	3	26
Duke Energy	4	1
Louisiana Gas & Light	5	18

Source: S.R. Rajan, "Turning Capital to Wealth: A Ranking of U.S. Utilities," *Public Utilities Fortnightly*, December 1999.

SHAREHOLDER VALUE ADDED

The shareholder value added (SVA) approach was introduced by Alfred Rappaport. Shareholder value is defined as corporate value less the value of debt. Corporate value is equal to the DCF value of the company plus the value of the nonoperating assets and marketable securities, shown in Figure 12-1.

SVA focuses on the change in value. It is simple to calculate SVA in each period once we have the market values of debt and equity in each period. However, in order to be useful in decision making, we need a measure that can be forecast over a longer planning horizon. The internal SVA of a company can be estimated over the forecast period using a process similar to that of NPV calculation. As in the case of NPV, the SVA analysis begins by forecasting the cash flows over the planning period. The steps involved in calculating SVA are as follows:

1. Forecast cash flow from the value drivers.
2. Calculate the residual value at the end of each year by capitalizing the cash flow before new investment.

FIGURE 12-1   SVA approach to corporate value.

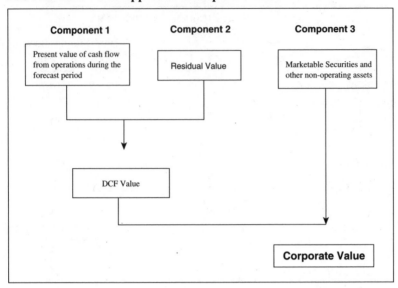

3.   Discount the cash flows and the residual value back to the present using the cost of capital.

The cumulative present value of the cash flow and the residual value of each period together represent the value created for that period. The change in value from the previous period is the SVA of that period.

The following example illustrates the calculation of SVA.[5] First, a few definitions are in order. Cash flows are calculated using a value driver approach:

Cash Flows = Cash Inflows − Cash Outflows

= [(Sales) (Operating Profit Margin)
(1 − Cash Income Tax Rate)] − [(Incremental Sales)
(Fixed and Working Capital Investment Rate)]

= [NOPAT] − [Incremental Investment]

The residual value in each year is the capitalized (discounted) value

---

[5] Rappaport, op. cit.

of the NOPAT in that year. It represents the value of perpetual no-growth cash flows from that point forward:

$$\text{Residual Value} = \text{NOPAT/Cost of Capital}$$

Table 12-7 shows a sample SVA calculation. The value drivers are held constant for the entire forecasting period for the purpose of simplification.

Rappaport also proposes an alternative, somewhat simpler approach to calculating SVA. Because the cash flow of a company in each period is the difference between NOPAT and incremental investment, SVA can be calculated using these two factors. Specifically:

1. Calculate the incremental NOPAT in each year.
2. Capitalize the incremental NOPAT by dividing by the cost of capital.
3. Discount the capitalized incremental NOPAT back to the present.
4. Calculate incremental investment.
5. Discount incremental investment back to the present.

The SVA of each period is the difference between the discounted values of the capitalized NOPAT and incremental investment.

The alternate approach is illustrated in Table 12-8 using the same data and finding the same result.

SVA is an attractive measure of value in many respects. It accounts for the amount, timing, and risk of cash flows. It allows for a period-by-period evaluation of value creation by providing a complete snapshot of the value created in each year of the planning period. Finally, by breaking value down into its two components—NOPAT and incremental investment—SVA allows managers to see more clearly the impact of operational and capital allocation decisions on value.

SVA has its drawbacks, however. Like DCF and NPV, it relies on forecasts, which are complex and subject to manipulation. SVA is a more difficult concept for managers not already familiar with DCF. SVA still does not enjoy the same acceptance in the investment community as accounting measures or even EVA, and there is limited empirical evidence on SVA. Despite these limitations, SVA is the best metric for the divisional and business unit level because it links business unit performance to shareholder value creation at the corporate level. SVA can also be easily made operational by following the value driver approach, discussed at the end of the chapter.

TABLE 12-7   SVA calculation: An example.

ESTIMATING SVA

The five-year forecast for the firm is given below:

(In millions except for percent)

Sales (last historical period)	$100.00
Sales growth rate	11%
Operating profit margin	8%
Incremental fixed capital investment	24%
Incremental working capital investment	19%
Cash income tax	35%
Cost of capital	10%
Marketable Securities & Investments	$3.00
Market value of debt	$10.00

Step 1: Calculate cash flows from the drivers.

Year	Sales	Cash Inflow	Cash Outflow	Total Cash Flow
0	$100.00			
1	$110.50	$5.75	$4.50	$1.24
2	$122.10	$6.35	$4.98	$1.37
3	$134.92	$7.02	$5.50	$1.52
4	$149.09	$7.75	$6.08	$1.68
5	$164.74	$8.57	$6.72	$1.85

Step 2: Calculate residual value by capitalizing cash inflow.

Year	Residual Value
1	$57.46
2	$63.49
3	$70.16
4	$77.53
5	$85.67

TABLE 12-7   SVA calculation: An example (*Continued*).

Step 3: Discount cash flows and residual values using the cost of capital.

Year	Cash Flow	Present Value	Cumulative PV of Cash Flows	Residual Value	Present Value of Residual Value
1	$1.24	$1.13	$1.13	$57.46	$52.24
2	$1.37	$1.13	$2.26	$63.49	$52.47
3	$1.52	$1.14	$3.40	$70.16	$52.71
4	$1.68	$1.14	$4.55	$77.53	$52.95
5	$1.85	$1.15	$5.69	$85.67	$53.19

Step 4: The SVA in each year is the incremental cumulative PV of cash flows and residual value.

Year	Cumulative PV + Residual Value	SVA
1	$53.37	$1.37
2	$54.74	$1.37
3	$56.11	$1.38
4	$57.50	$1.38
5	$58.89	$1.39
+ Marketable Securities and Investments	$3.00	
Corporate Value	$61.89	
− Market value of debt	$10.00	
Shareholder value	$51.89	

Source: Adapted from Rappaport, op. cit., pp. 48–49.

INTERNAL RATE OF RETURN

The IRR of a series of cash flows is the discount rate which makes their NPV equal 0. It is calculated by trial and error, facilitated by today's financial calculators and spreadsheet functions. The IRR is compared to the cost of capital to decide whether or not to invest: Projects with an IRR greater than their cost of capital are accepted, while those with an IRR below the cost of capital are rejected.

Even though IRR remains a popular valuation tool, its use is difficult to defend. The value of IRR lies in the fact that it yields a return that can readily be compared to the cost of capital. But if the cost of capital is

TABLE 12-8   SVA: an alternate calculation.

	Historical	Forecast 1	Forecast 2	Forecast 3	Forecast 4	Forecast 5
1 NOPAT	$5.20	$5.75	$6.35	$7.02	$7.75	$8.57
2 Change in NOPAT		$0.55	$0.60	$0.67	$0.74	$0.81
3 Change in NOPAT/K		$5.46	$6.03	$6.67	$7.37	$8.14
4 Change in NOPAT/ [K (1 + K)^t − 1]		$5.46	$5.48	$5.51	$5.53	$5.56
5 Incremental Investment		$4.50	$4.98	$5.50	$6.08	$6.72
6 PV of incremental investment		$4.10	$4.11	$4.13	$4.15	$4.17
7 SVA (4-6)		$1.37	$1.37	$1.38	$1.38	$1.39

Source: Adapted from Rappaport, op. cit., pp. 48–49.

known, why not use NPV, which is a far more accurate valuation method and avoids the many disadvantages of IRR?

IRR suffers from many disadvantages and has to be used with caution, as outlined in the following section.

The Borrowing/Lending Problem

Consider the following projects for a company with a cost of capital of 10 percent.

Project	Cash Flows C0	Cash Flows C1	IRR	NPV at 10%
A	−2000	2500	25%	$247.93
B	2000	−2500	25%	($247.93)

IRR ranks the projects the same. But clearly Project B is undesirable because you receive $2000 today but have to pay back $2500 next year. IRR is not able to distinguish between Projects A and B. Project A involves lending money, while Project B involves borrowing money. When borrowing money, higher value for the borrower is associated with a lower, not a higher, return. NPV leads to the correct decision in this case.

Multiple Rates of Return

The following is a series of cash flows from a mining project. The negative cash flow at year 6 represents the expenses involved in environmental cleanup of the mine.

Cash Flows ($ thousands)

0	1	2	3	4	5	6
-1000	800	150	150	150	150	-150

There are two IRRs for this project—50% and 15.2%—one for each sign change in the cash flows. Which is correct? We have no way of knowing. Clearly, IRR is not suitable for valuing projects with both cash inflows and outflows.

Mutually Exclusive Projects

IRR results are misleading when comparing projects of different scales. Consider Projects A and B. Both are good projects. IRR chooses A, yet B is clearly superior to A in terms of cash flows. In this case, IRR does not yield the correct decision, since the projects are different in scale.

Cash Flows

Project	C0	C1	IRR	NPV at 10%
A	-10,000	20,000	100%	$7,438.02
B	-20,000	35,000	75%	$10,743.80

Changing Cost of Capital

IRR is difficult to use as a decision-making criterion when a company's cost of capital changes over time, as in the case of an LBO. The question arises as to which discount rate is compared to the IRR.

IRR and NPV both require the same inputs, but NPV has all the advantages of IRR and none of the disadvantages. As such, it is difficult to understand the enduring popularity of IRR. The proponents of IRR claim that it is easier to explain to non-financial managers than NPV. While this might be true, managers should recognize that IRR has severe limitations when it comes to accurately valuing projects. IRR is particularly misleading in situations of capital rationing, which require managers to choose among mutually exclusive projects.

Basing compensation on IRR is equally problematic. IRR-based compensation gives managers incentives to search for high-IRR projects. These are usually short-lived projects with relatively little up-front investments, which may not add much to the long-term value of a company. This is not a robust measure, as it is not applicable to high-growth companies. IRR fails in all but one of the six performance measure criteria introduced earlier; simplicity is not enough to save this measure.

CASH FLOW RETURN ON INVESTMENT (CFROI)

Cash flow return on investment (CFROI) is the company-level equivalent of IRR. It reflects the average underlying IRR on all of the company's existing assets. The measure was originally developed by Holt Consulting, which was later acquired by the Boston Consulting Group. CFROI is especially useful for measuring the true economic profitability of assets of capital-intensive companies. There are four inputs into CFROI:

1. *Gross investment (GI)* is computed by adding back depreciation to the net asset value to estimate the original investment in the asset. Intangible assets such as goodwill are netted out. The gross investment is converted into a current dollar value by adjusting for inflation:

    Gross Investment = Net Asset Value +
        Cumulated Depreciation on Asset + Current Dollar Adjustment

2. *Gross cash flow* (GCF) is the cash flow earned in the current year by that asset calculated by adding noncash charges such as depreciation and amortization to the after-tax operating income of the company. The operating income is adjusted for accounting effects such as operating leases.

    Gross Cash Flow = EBIT $(1 - t)$ + Current Year's Depreciation

3. *The expected life of the assets in place (n)* is the third input. CFROI is concerned about the economic life of the assets at the time of the original investment.

4. *The salvage value (SV),* or the expected value of the assets at the end of its useful life, is the final input. The salvage value is adjusted to current dollar terms. The salvage value is usually computed from the percentage of the asset that is not depreciated.

CFROI is the IRR of these four cash flows. It is the discount rate that equates the present value of the gross cash flows and salvage value to the gross investment and hence is the composite internal rate of return, in current dollar terms.

The following example illustrates the CFROI calculation.[6] Consider a company whose book assets are two years old and have a net value of $100 million. Accumulated depreciation is $25 million. The assets have a remaining life of five years and 25% of the assets are not depreciable. Inflation has been 5% over the last two years. Current EBIT is $30 million, depreciation is $2 million, and the company has a marginal tax rate of 35%. CFROI is estimated as follows:

Step 1: Calculate gross investment.

$$GI = (100 + 25)(1.05)^2 = \$137.8 \text{ million}$$

Step 2: Calculate gross cash flow.

$$GCF = 30(1 - .35) + 2 = \$21.5 \text{ million}$$

Step 3: Calculate expected salvage value.

$$SV = GI(0.25) = 137.8(0.25) = \$34.5 \text{ million}$$

Step 4: Calculate the IRR of the cash flows.

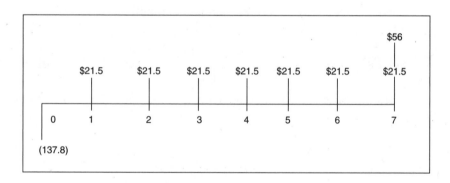

The IRR of the cash flows = CFROI = 11.2%

The CFROI can then be compared to the real (inflation-adjusted) cost of capital to evaluate whether the companies' assets are creating value. For projects that do not have the same risk as the company, the CFROI is compared to the appropriate hurdle rate that reflects the risk of the project.

The preceding example assumes that the inflation-adjusted cash flows are constant over the life of the project. The cash flows can easily be modified to account for real growth.

[6] The example is drawn from A. Damodaran, "Value Creation and Enhancement: Back to the Future," FMA International/CICB World Markets.

CFROI can be adjusted easily for economic depreciation. The latter is defined as the reduction in present value of the asset. For the purposes of calculating CFROI, economic depreciation is the annual amount that needs to be set aside in a sinking fund earning the cost of capital over the life of the gross depreciating assets to provide for their replacement. In practice, economic depreciation is calculated as the gross depreciating assets multiplied by a sinking-fund factor, determined by the cost of capital and the life of the assets. The assumption of economic depreciation will result in constant cash flows over the life of the asset. CFROI each year is computed as:

$$\text{CFROI} = \frac{\text{Gross Cash Flow} - \text{Economic Depreciation}}{\text{Gross Investment}}$$

Assuming a cost of capital of 10% and economic depreciation of $10.9 million in the preceding example, CFROI evaluates to 7.69%:

$$\text{CFROI} = \frac{21.5 - 10.9}{137.8} = 7.7\%$$

Economic depreciation has resulted in a dramatic decrease in CFROI from 11.2% to 7.7%. The reason is that a portion of the cash flows from the assets has to be set aside to replace depreciating assets. These sinking-fund cash flows get reinvested at the cost of capital instead of the IRR.

Return on gross investment (ROGI) is a simple alternative to CFROI. ROGI is the ratio of cash flow to cash investment and is calculated using

$$\text{ROGI} = \frac{\text{Gross Cash Flow}}{\text{Gross Cash Invested}}$$

ROGI moves in the same direction as CFROI, but usually exceeds it.

CFROI has its drawbacks. Essentially, it is a backward-looking measure. CFROI is concerned with the original investment in the project, a sunk cost. In cases where the market values have risen, CFROI is probably higher than the cost of capital, yet management is likely better off selling the assets. To illustrate, consider the case of a company that needs to assess the profitability of a piece of equipment. The equipment was purchased five years ago at a price of $10,000 in current dollars. It has a life of nine years with annual cash flows of $1700 and a salvage value of $3000 (in current dollars). The cost of capital is 10%.

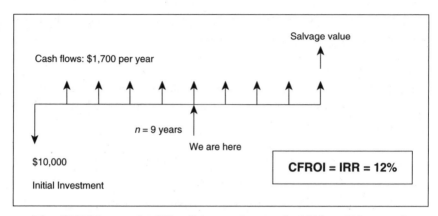

The CFROI over the life of the equipment is 12%, a 2% spread over the cost of capital. Management could congratulate themselves on taking on a profitable project. But recall that we are five years into the life of the equipment. The equipment has retained its value well, and the current market value is $9000. Based on the CFROI of 12% should management continue the project? To answer this question, we have to look at the NPV of the remaining cash flows:

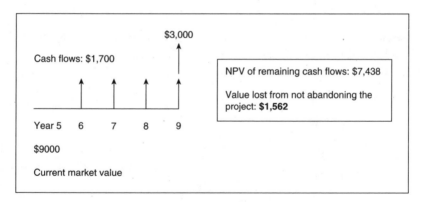

The NPV of the remaining cash flows is $7438. When compared to the current market value of the equipment, $9000, we see clearly that this investment is a losing proposition. Management should abandon the project and sell the equipment. Blind adherence to CFROI in this case would have led to value destruction.

In contrast to single-period traditional accounting measures that are based on book value, CFROI is not biased by asset depreciation and does reflect the complete life of the asset. However, it focuses on assets in place and ignores future growth opportunities. As such, it is a questionable valuation technique for high-growth companies.

TOTAL SHAREHOLDER RETURNS

The total shareholder (TSR) returns of a company over a given period are the actual dividend yields and capital gains to the company's stockholders over that period:

$$TSR = \frac{P_1 - P_{0-}}{P_0} + \frac{D}{P_0}$$

$$\downarrow \qquad \qquad \downarrow$$

Capital Gains Dividend Yield

For example, Company A had a stock price of $60 in the beginning of January 2001. During 2001, the company pays two dividends of $2 each, one in January and one in June. At the end of 2000, Company A's stock is $70. The risk-free rate during this period is 6%:

$60		**$70**
$2	**$2**	
1/2001	6/2001	12/2001

Reinvesting the first dividend at 6% for 12 months yields a cash flow of $2.12 at the end of 2001. Reinvesting the second dividend at 6% for the remaining six months yields $2.06 at the end of 2001:

Cash Flow from D_1 = $2.12

Cash Flow from D_2 = $2.06

Total Cash Flow from Dividends = $4.18

Capital Gains in 2001 = $70 − $60 = $10

$$TSR = \frac{\$10}{\$60} + \frac{\$4.18}{\$60} = 23.6\%$$

$$\downarrow \qquad \qquad \downarrow$$

Capital Gains Dividend yield

Relative TSR is simply TSR that has been indexed to the market or a peer group. It is designed to filter out the external noise and industrywide factors that affect the market returns of a particular company.

TSR is a comprehensive measure reflecting all activities or decisions by a management team (e.g., dividend changes, share repurchases, acquisitions, capital structure changes, improvement in operations, new-product introductions, market share or volume increases, and growth by expansion). TSR is virtually impossible to game. It provides a very effective early warning signal of when past company strategies have reached the limit of effectiveness. Most of the publicly traded companies that have been targeted by shareholder activists were singled out because of their poor TSRs, even though their accounting performance was fine. TSR is conveniently reported in corporate 10K forms[7] and is widely reported in the financial press.

The choice of TSR as a measure of value creation is motivated by the fact that it overlaps one-for-one with individual investor's and professional fund manager's performance scorecard. TSR is the combined capital gain and dividend yield of the stocks held in the portfolio and is usually judged in relation to the return of similar portfolios (e.g., growth funds or dividend funds) or the overall market. For fund managers, relative TSR determines both the manager's compensation and the capital the fund is able to attract over the long term.[8]

Both TSR and MVA are based on market returns. The main difference between the two is that TSR includes dividends, while MVA does not. TSR offers a number of additional improvements over MVA, summarized in Table 12-9.

TSR is a superior measure of shareholder wealth creation. Recognizing this, the *Wall Street Journal* publishes a yearly report called "Shareholder Scoreboard" that ranks the 1000 major U.S. companies on TSR.

On the negative side, absolute TSR is not very robust. It is affected by swings in the market place, and as such, it is an imperfect performance metric for compensation. (Relative TSR was developed to address this problem.) Because it is based on marketwide stock returns, it is not applicable to private companies and individual business units.

INTERNAL TSR/TOTAL BUSINESS RETURNS (TBR)

The Boston Consulting Group has introduced an internal TSR measure known as total business return (TBR) that extends TSR to private companies and divisions within public companies. TBR compares the sum of the estimated future value of a business unit (the capital gains) and the free

---

[7] As a matter of fact, it is concerned about high levels of executive compensation that have resulted in SEC-mandated TSR reporting in corporate proxy statements. TSR must now be reported in the annual 10K filing so shareholders can assess the validity of executive compensation.

[8] More information on TSR as a measure of value creation performance is in Chapter 13.

TABLE 12-9   TSR versus MVA.

TSR Capital Gains + Dividends	MVA Market value − Book value
Comparable across companies	Biased by company size
Clear indicator of current value creation	Unclear indicator of current value creation
Independent of accounting	Subject to book accounting conventions
Established key measure for investors	Not widely used by investors
Market impact could be removed by indexing to the market or peers	Difficult to index and hence impacted by market conditions
Required by SEC for financial reporting	Not required by SEC

Source: Implementing value-based measures workshop, November 18, 1997, The Boston Consulting Group.

cash flows to the parent (dividend yield), to the current investment in the business unit or project. This is a direct internal analog to TSR.

$$\text{TSR} = \frac{\text{Actual Capital Gains} + \text{Dividends}}{\text{Initial Value}}$$

$$\text{TBR} = \frac{\text{Modeled Capital Gains} + \text{Free Cash Flow}}{\text{Initial Value}}$$

TBR can be calculated either looking backward (comparing the current value to the initial value) for compensation purposes or looking forward (comparing the current value to the estimated future value) for planning and capital budgeting purposes. To serve as a basis for performance measurement, TBR is compared to the cost of capital.

There are many ways in which the beginning and terminal business values can be calculated, including:

EBITDA multiple: Value = EBITDA × Multiple

Capitalized Value Added:

$$\text{Value} = \frac{\text{Book Capital} + \text{Value Added (EVA or SVA)}}{\text{WACC}}$$

BCG spot model: Value = Simulated Future Cash Flows (DCF)

BALANCED SCORECARD

Introduced by Robert Kaplan and David Norton, the balanced scorecard supplements traditional investor-oriented financial measures with criteria that measure performance from three additional perspectives: customers, internal business processes, and learning and growth (also called innovation).

The balanced scorecard is unlike any other accounting or value-based measure in that it does not provide an aggregate number for company value. The purpose of the scorecard is not so much to measure company value but to focus the management on achieving the objectives that will result in value creation.

Our own feeling is that while the process of developing the balanced scorecard may be a useful in identifying the value drivers of the company, the approach is difficult and cumbersome to measure and maintain, and its complexity and subjectivity make it unsuitable as a compensation criterion.

CONCLUSION

Table 12-10 compares the various performance measures based on the six criteria identified at the beginning of the chapter: accuracy, complexity, strategic decision making, compensation, applicability to all organizational levels and robustness.

It is clear that each measure has its own strengths and weaknesses. Trade-offs must be made, particularly between complexity, linkage to shareholder value, and manipulability. Figure 12-2 displays the complexity-linkage-manipulability trade-off among the various metrics. A careful examination of the strengths and weaknesses and the trade-offs involved in each performance measure will guide management in adopting the best measure for each objective of the company.

NPV is the most accurate measure of value, since it is a true reflection of the DCF valuation. However, as a performance evaluation and compensation measure, NPV has considerable limitations. The measure is based on forecasts and hence is heavily influenced by subjective judgments by management. Besides, expected future cash flows are not the best criteria for evaluating employee performance and deciding compensation. Regardless of the final choice, it is comforting to note that the ability of a performance measure to focus management's attention on value creation is more important than the accuracy of the dollar value it produces.

A common limitation of all performance measures not based on stock prices is their failure to consider option value. As we saw in Chapter 8, real options are of critical strategic importance for all companies.

TABLE 12-10 Performance measure comparison.

Measure	Accuracy	Complexity	Decision making	Compensation	Robustness	Organizational Levels
ROI	Low. Not based on cash flows. Single-period measure.	Low. Easy to calculate and communicate to investors and non-financial managers.	Low. Decisions based on accounting measures do not maximize value.	Low. Easily manipulated by employees.	High. Could be applied at different life-cycle stages of the company and under different market conditions.	High. Applicable at both the corporate and business unit levels. Easily decomposed into operational drivers.
NPV	Highly accurate. Accounts for amount, risk, and timing of future cash flows.	High. Difficult to calculate and communicate to non-financial managers.	Medium. NPV is an aggregate measure and it does not capture the managerial flexibility (option value).	Low. NPV relies highly on forecasts. Not an accurate measure of employee performance.	High. Could be applied at all stages of a company. Internal measure, not impacted by market conditions.	High. NPV is equally applicable at the company, business unit, and project levels.
APV	Highly accurate. Accounts for amount, risk and timing of future cash flows.	Medium. Easier to calculate than NPV. Difficult to communicate to non-	Higher than NPV since APV unbundles the DCF value into components. The measure	Low. Relies highly on forecasts. Not an accurate measure of employee	High. Could be applied at all stages of a company. Internal measure, not	High. APV is equally applicable at the company, business unit, and project levels.

	Accuracy	Simplicity		Performance	Applicability	
	financial managers.	does not capture flexibility.	performance.	impacted by market conditions.	High. Equally applicable at the company, business unit, and project levels. Easily decomposed to value drivers.	
EVA	Low. Single period measure. Not based on cash flows.	Low. Relatively easy to calculate and communicate. Widely accepted in the investment community.	Low. Decisions based on EVA do not maximize value. Does not capture flexibility.	Low. Easily manipulated. Short-term measure.	Low. Not applicable at the high-growth stages of a company since it stunts growth.	High. Equally applicable at the company, business unit, and project levels. Easily decomposed to value drivers.
SVA	Highly accurate. Accounts for amount, risk, and timing of future cash flows.	High. Complex measure to calculate and communicate.	High. Allows management to isolate the effects of growth and profitability on company value. Does not capture flexibility.	High. Compensation could be based on the SVA of each period.	High. Could be applied at all stages of a company. Internal measure, not impacted by market conditions.	High. Equally applicable at the company, business unit, and project levels. Easily decomposed to value drivers.

(continued)

TABLE 12-10 Performance measure comparison. (*Continued*)

Measure	Accuracy	Complexity	Decision making	Compensation	Robustness	Organizational Levels
MVA	Medium. Leaves out dividends and hence does not capture free cash flow to shareholders.	Low. Easy to calculate and communicate to investors and non-financial managers.	High. Managerial flexibility reflected in the measure.	Low. Market based measure only suitable at the corporate level.	Low. Only applicable to public companies and biased by size. Impacted by market conditions.	Low. MVA is an aggregate measure applicable at the corporate level, not the business unit and operational levels.
IRR	Low. High IRR does not necessarily translate to high DCF value.	Medium. Easier to communicate to non-financial managers.	Medium. Useful decision-making tool when compared to cost of capital. Decisions made based on IRR may not maximize value.	Low. Relies highly on forecasts. Not an accurate measure of employee performance.	High. Could be applied at all stages of a company. Internal measure, not impacted by market conditions.	High. IRR is equally applicable at the company, business unit, and project levels.
CFROI	Low. Focuses on the value of assets in place. Poorly accommodates growth.	High. Difficult to calculate and communicate.	Low. Maximizing CFROI does not necessarily maximize value.	Medium. Employees could manipulate the measure by decreasing gross investment.	High. Could be applied at all stages of a company. Internal measure, not impacted by market conditions.	High. Equally applicable at the company, business unit and project levels. Easily decomposed to value drivers.

TSR	High. The future cash flows are reflected in the capital gains. Dividends reflect free cash flows.	Low. Readily observable market based measure. Easy to communicate to investors and employees.	High. Managerial flexibility reflected in the measure.	Low. Market based measure only suitable at the corporate level. The internal proxy TBR suffers from the same drawbacks as NPV.	Low. Only applicable to public firms. Impacted by market conditions. Could be improved by using relative TSR indexed to the market or a peer group.	Low. TSR is an aggregate measure applicable at the corporate level, not the business unit and operational levels.
TBR	High. The future cash flows are reflected in the modeled capital gains. Dividends reflect free cash flows.	Medium. The beginning and terminal business values have to be estimated using value models.	Medium. Does not capture managerial flexibility.	Low. TBR relies highly on forecasts. Not an accurate measure of employee performance.	High. Applicable to both private and public firms. Not impacted by market conditions.	High. Equally applicable at the corporate, divisional, and project level. Easily decomposed into value drivers at the operational level.
Balanced Scorecard	Low. Does not quantify value.	Complex to calculate, but conceptually not difficult.	High. Consists of a series of objectives and targets that could be set as criteria for decision making.	Low. The measure is too complex and contains subjective measures.	High. Could be applied at all stages of a firm. Internal measure, not impacted by market conditions.	Medium. More applicable at the operational than the corporate and business unit levels.

FIGURE 12-2   Performance measures: Accuracy vs. complexity.

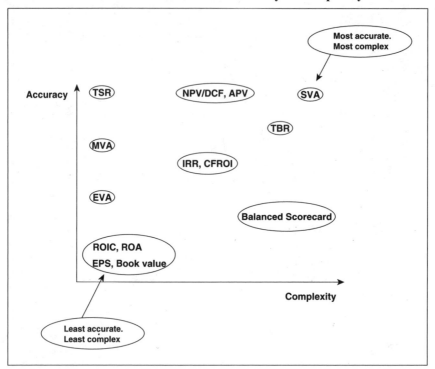

Although there is no perfect performance measure that answers a company's every need, it is clear that some measures are superior to others. Figure 12-3 displays a hierarchy of metrics suitable at various organizational levels. At the corporate level, relative TSR is the appropriate measure. The measure is directly correlated with shareholder wealth maximization, is not biased by company size, and can easily be indexed to the market or peer group. More importantly, the measure is easy to calculate and widely accepted by the investment community.

But TSR is not the perfect measure for the business unit and operational levels. At the business unit level, SVA is a more appropriate measure of performance. Focusing on the incremental shareholder value in each year will allow management to maximize value without relying on subjective performance forecasts. At the operational level, NPV, or its variant APV, in combination with real options value, is the best measure for capital budgeting purposes. But for compensation and performance evaluation purposes, value drivers targets are preferred. SVA can easily be de-

FIGURE 12-3 **Hierarchy of performance metrics.**

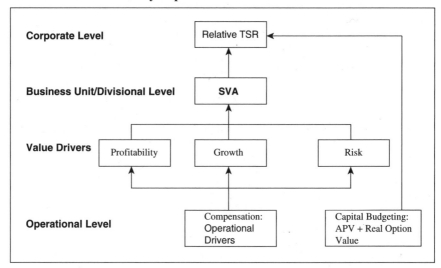

composed into value drivers such as sales growth, operating profit margin, working capital investment, and fixed capital investment. Focusing on these drivers at the operational level will maximize SVA, which in turn will lead to higher TSR. This decomposition is shown in Figure 12-4.

The DCF value of a company can be decomposed into is critical value drivers, risk, return, and capital, as shown in Figure 1-2 and elsewhere throughout the book. Return, capital, and risk drive value at the aggregate level. These factors can in turn be decomposed further into operational drivers, or "micro drivers," as shown in Table 9-4. The spread between return and cost of capital that is so important to value creation can be improved by improving the profit margin, reducing SG&A costs, or by decreasing the cost of capital. Cost of capital could be reduced by increasing leverage or by reducing equity.

Growth is determined by both internal and external factors. Internal factors include the nature of the company's tangible and intangible assets and incremental working capital and fixed capital investments. External factors include competitive forces and the economic growth. In addition to the rate of growth, the duration of growth is also important for value creation. Sustainable growth is created through strategies that result in competitive advantage.

Even though each aggregate value-based measure can be decomposed into its own unique set of value drivers, there are seven generic value driv-

FIGURE 12-4   SVA: Decomposed into value drivers.

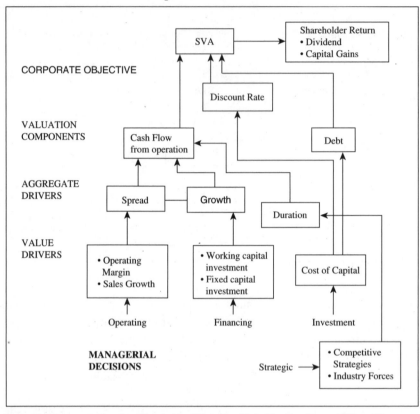

Source: A. Rappaport, *Creating Shareholder Value,* New York: The Free Press, 1999, p. 56.

ers that are common to most value-based measures, as first identified by Alfred Rappaport:[9]

1.   Sales growth
2.   Cash profit margin
3.   Cash tax rate
4.   Working capital
5.   Capital expenditure
6.   Cost of capital
7.   Competitive advantage period

[9] A. Black, P. Wright, and J. Bachman, *In Search of Shareholder Value: Managing the Drivers of Performance.* London: Pitman Publishing, 1998, p. 49.

All companies can improve value by focusing on the seven generic value drivers. But each company is different in terms of the competitive environment they face and the strategies they follow. The value driver method can be further refined by combining the generic drivers and strategy. Companies can choose to focus on all seven generic value drivers or a selected few. Once the drivers to focus on have been identified, the next step is to formulate strategies to maximize these drivers, as illustrated in Table 9-2.

This is where companies diverge. For example, one company could choose to maximize profit margin by following a low-cost strategy, while another company might choose to do the same by following a differentiation strategy. Companies choose the strategy that is best suited for their internal and external environment. Once the company develops strategies, a number of operational drivers that are key to implementing the strategy have to be identified. By focusing on these operational drivers, the company's strategy is successfully implemented, which in turn improves the value drivers, creating aggregate value.

13

CORPORATE GOVERNANCE AND EXECUTIVE COMPENSATION

AS WE SAW IN **FIGURE 1-1** FROM **CHAPTER 1,** value-based management consists of integrating the three components of corporate value creation—strategy, finance, and corporate governance—into a common value-based framework.

Corporate governance is an often overlooked but critical component of value creation. It is defined as the policies and guidelines that govern the relations between boards of directors, senior management, operating units, and investors. The three main areas of corporate governance are performance measurement, the compensation system, and investor communications.

An effective performance measurement and compensation system is critical to the successful implementation of VBM. It governs how executives behave, what kinds of executives the organization attracts, and how effectively the corporate vision gets translated into tangible value for the shareholders. The recent shift in the U.S. economy from bricks and mortar to intellectual capital reinforces the importance of compensation plans in effectively focusing and harnessing the brainpower of employees to add shareholder value.

The executive compensation practices of corporate America are of great interest to investors, business media, consultants, and academic researchers. Much of the focus has been on the role played by stock options. Stock options now constitute more than half of the CEO compensation in the top U.S. companies. With the record-breaking bull market of the 1990s, mere average performers garnered huge windfall bonuses in compensation.

There is an urgent need for today's managers to understand the importance of the compensation system to the successful implementation of value-based management. A well-conceived and well-executed compensation system can represent a formidable sustainable competitive advantage for the company. To do so, it must do three things: (1) align managerial and shareholder interests at minimal cost; (2) attract, motivate, and retain managerial talent; and (3) focus efforts on long-term value creation. We take each in turn.

ALIGN MANAGERIAL AND SHAREHOLDER INTERESTS AT MINIMAL COST

In most companies, ownership and control are separated. The owners (shareholders) entrust management with the responsibility to maximize the value of their investment. The ownership structure of most publicly held companies is quite disperse; no single shareholder has a large enough stake in a firm to make it worth their while to actively monitor the management. When managers are self-interested and unmonitored, at times they maximize their own wealth at the expense of the shareholders. This leads to an "agency problem" where the agent (the manager) fails to act in the best interests of the principal (the shareholders).

Agency costs are the costs incurred by shareholders to mitigate the agency problem—that is, to align the manager's actions with the shareholders' interests. Three examples of the agency problem are noteworthy: (1) excessive perquisite consumption, where the managers engage in activities that improve their own status and prestige at the expense of shareholder interests, such as buying corporate jets and building opulent headquarters; (2) underinvestment—given the truncated time horizon of managers relative to shareholders, managers may neglect to invest in strategic activities that increase the long-term value of the company; and (3) taking excessive risks—managers' truncated time horizon may induce them to engage in high-risk activities that have high short-term payoffs but destroy long-term value.

Shareholders appoint boards of directors who are responsible for aligning the interests of management with shareholders. The board can either

(1) directly monitor management's actions or (2) devise a compensation plan (a kind of "indirect" monitoring) that incents managers to choose to act in the interest of shareholders.

Empirical evidence shows the two alternatives are viewed by most companies as a trade-off. Companies with high degrees of monitoring, either through proactive boards committees or by virtue of belonging to a highly regulated industry, have lower levels of compensation and fewer performance-based features in their compensation plans.

Optimal monitoring is difficult. Initially, increased monitoring probably adds value as managers are held accountable to shareholders for their choices. At higher, excessive levels, monitoring can demoralize management, interfering with their desire and ability to maximize corporate wealth.[1]

Another factor that affects the effectiveness of monitoring is the information asymmetry between managers and shareholders. Boards typically have limited prior information on the actions that maximize company value, and even if they do, it is difficult to verify whether management has undertaken these actions. Thus, even the best monitoring system is unlikely to ever completely resolve the agency problem.

A good compensation plan can encourage the manager to self-monitor by rewarding the manager for taking actions that benefit shareholders. Compensation systems do not constrain managers' actions, and hence the value of flexible management should not be not compromised.

Barings Bank: The Case of a Fatally Flawed Compensation System

Barings Bank, a renowned British bank established in 1762, declared bankruptcy in 1994, largely due to the actions of a rogue trader, Nick Leeson. Leeson was supposed to be engaged in arbitrage arising from the price differentials of the Nikkei 225 futures between the Osaka and Singapore exchanges. Instead of maintaining counterbalancing long and short positions on the two exchanges, Leeson had purchased securities in both markets, making an enormously risky bet that the Nikkei 225 would rise. Instead, it fell, and by March 1999, Barings had suffered over $1.4 billion in damages. Barings was sold to ING, and the company's owners lost their entire investment. The collapse

---

[1] R.E. Hoskisson, and M.A. Hitt. 1988. "Strategic Control Systems and Relative R&D Intensity in Large Multiproduct Companies." *Strategic Management Journal,* 9, pp. 605–622.

was ultimately due to the bank's poorly designed compensation system, which gave incentives for excessive risk taking to the traders but failed to encourage managers to monitor or otherwise control the traders. Barings traditionally paid out 50% of gross earnings as annual bonuses. Managers participated in the profits, but not in the losses, thus encouraging excessive risk taking. (*Source:* Adapted from Brickley, Smith, and Zimmerman, "The Economics of Organizational Architecture," *Journal of Applied Corporate Finance,* Vol. 8, No. 2, Summer 1995.)

ATTRACT, MOTIVATE, AND RETAIN MANAGERIAL TALENT

A compensation strategy that offers potentially unlimited pay for performance can attract the top managerial talent, motivate them to create value, and retain them in a competitive market for managerial talent. The changing trends in business, including the arrival of the information age and global competition, have resulted in an increasing demand for experienced senior executives who have the ability to adapt in environments marked by high uncertainty, speed, and change.

The Importance of Compensation in Retaining Talent: The Case of GE

General Electric has been extremely successful in retaining its top executives. Behind this longevity is a compensation plan that pays the top performers considerably more than their average counterparts. Jack Welch is the sixth highest paid CEO in the Fortune 500, according to the 1999 Business Week Executive Pay Scorecard. The $83 million Welch received in 1999 is composed mainly of long-term compensation. GE is one of the rare conglomerates that has managed to consistently add shareholder value. One of the reasons some conglomerates fail is the increase in agency costs from increased decentralization and the information asymmetry between the corporate office and the disparate divisions. It could be argued that an effective compensation system is even more important in a conglomerate than in a specialized company. GE's success in implementing effective compensation plans is certainly a critical factor in their enduring success in shareholder value creation.

FOCUS EFFORTS ON LONG-TERM VALUE CREATION

A properly designed compensation system creates value by (1) aligning the time horizon of shareholders and managers/employees, and (2) defining and focusing managers/employees on the key value drivers of long-term shareholder value.

Shareholders have a much longer time horizon than managers and employees. By tying management and employee incentives to measures of the long-term value of the company, like the stock price, a compensation system can focus management's attention on sustainable value creation.

Home Depot: Compensation That Synchronizes Value Creation at All Levels

Home Depot is one of the top 10 retailers in the United States. The company has provided its shareholders with an annual total return of 44.8% over the past 10 years, well above the industry average of 21.6%. Over 70% of Home Depot's stock price is based on the market's expectation of its future growth (PVGO). Home Depot's compensation system focuses attention on value by linking compensation to the value drivers—that is, the growth in new stores and sales per store. A sensitivity analysis reveals that a one-year delay in currently scheduled store openings would destroy 16% of the company's market value. (*Source:* Adapted from Rappaport, op. cit., pp. 129–130.)

EXECUTIVE COMPENSATION PLANS

Compensation strategy is an essential link between strategy formulation and implementation: It focuses attention on the critical activities necessary to implement a value-maximizing strategy at all levels of the organization. A successful compensation strategy decomposes the business strategy into a series of value drivers and appropriate time horizons, and creates performance incentives to link employee actions with changes in the value drivers. The steps required in formulating a compensation strategy are as follows:

1. Identify the corporate and business level strategies.
2. Decompose the strategies into a series of value drivers at each organizational level.
3. Design performance measures by incorporating value drivers and the appropriate time horizon.
4. Translate performance measures to compensation criteria by incorporating additional factors such as competitive information.
5. Periodically review and adapt strategy as business conditions change.

Executive compensation plans (ECP) occupy a critical role in an over-all compensation strategy. Executives' major role in the organization is to formulate and implement value-creating strategies. The role of the CEO is especially important—imagine Intel without Andy Grove and Disney without Michael Eisner.

The stock market recognizes the critical role played by CEOs. When Kodak hired George Fisher as its CEO, the stock moved up nearly 5 points in a day, creating $1 billion in shareholder value. Conversely, when Maurice Saatchi, the CEO of the advertising giant Saatchi & Saatchi, was replaced, the share price of the company fell from $8 to $4 in one day.

ECPs have two primary objectives: (1) to attract, retain, and motivate managers and (2) to align the objectives of the management with share-holders. Constructing an optimal ECP is difficult because of the conflict-ing objectives of managers and shareholders. Besides the agency problem, shareholders hold stocks for the long-term and have diversified sources of wealth. Managers have relatively short time horizons and undiversified sources of wealth (in the sense that most of their wealth is likely to come from the company) and, as a result, may take actions that maximize value over a shorter time frame and with less risk exposure than shareholders would prefer. ECP has to effectively balance the long-term and short-term nature of the conflict between management and shareholders, as well as optimize their differing risk profiles.

The elements of a typical compensation plan consist of salary, annual bonuses, benefits, and long-term compensation. Each of these elements can have a long- and short-term component. A 1999 *Business Week* sur-vey on executive compensation at 365 of the largest companies in the United States[2] found

- The average pay of the CEO of a large public company was $10.6 million in 1998, up 36% from 1997 and an astounding 442% over 1990. In comparison, the S&P 500 index rose 27% from 1997 to 1998, while the earnings for the companies in the index fell 1.4%.
- Long-term compensation consisted of 80% of the average CEO's pay, up from 72% in 1997. Exercised options were the major com-ponent of the long-term compensation package.
- The average salary and bonuses fell for the second year in a row to $2.1 million.

---

[2] J. Reingold, 1999. "Executive Pay: Special Report." *Business Week.* April 19, 1999, pp. 72–90.

The important finding from the survey is the shift from fixed to variable pay, which coincided with the sustained bull market over the period. The major indices have seen a nearly 100% increase from 1995 to 1997, and the Dow was up 263% from 1990 to 1999. What is not clear is whether the rise in variable pay caused the bull market or the bull market caused the rise in variable pay. A 1993 compensation survey of the Fortune 100 companies from The Conference Board sheds further light on the issue.[3] The key finding are as follows:

- From 1991 to 1993 the compensation packages for top executives in the surveyed companies shifted from base salary to bonuses and stock option grants.
- Compensation is based on both financial and nonfinancial criteria.
- CEO short-term compensation (base salary and bonuses) is tied closely to improvements in pretax profit margins and return on equity, while long-term CEO compensation in the form of option grants correlates closely to total cumulative shareholder returns.
- Executive stock ownership bears no significant relationship to company performance.

Much attention has been focused on the differences between the corporate governance systems in the United States, Japan, and Germany and how they impact executive compensation plans. The U.S. corporate governance system is market-based. U.S. capital markets are relatively liquid, and stock ownership is dispersed. Managers are monitored by both an external market for corporate control and by outside board members. In contrast, governance systems in Germany and Japan are based on intercorporate relationships. Managers are monitored by banks and large corporate shareholders. Ownership is concentrated and capital markets are relatively illiquid. The external markets for corporate control are very small and sometimes absent altogether.

Research has found that in all three countries, executive turnover and cash pay rises with increases in stock price and earnings of the company. U.S. executives, however, do own signficantly more stock and options than their German and Japanese counterparts.

These findings could be interpreted as indicating that the relationship-oriented governance system in Germany and Japan leads to more efficient

---

[3] M.A. Klein, "Top Executive Pay for Performance." The Conference Board Research Report. Number 1113-95-RR, 1995.

monitoring of managerial actions and consequently reduces the agency costs associated with the separation of ownership and control, and the need for self-monitoring devices such as stock options.

Employee stock ownership and other methods for linking executive compensation to corporate performance are being increasingly used in the global marketplace. Expansion by foreign companies into the United States (Daimler-Chrysler and BP Amoco are examples) and the global competition for talent will lead to an increase in the role of equity-based compensation in foreign companies.

Empirical studies have shown that the announcement of stock option plans results in average market-adjusted excess returns of between 2% and 3%. The market recognizes that stock option plans create value by aligning the interests of the managers and shareholders, and provide managers with incentives to maximize shareholder value. Management is also more likely to initiate stock option plans when they think the company will do well—hence, the positive market reaction to the announcement.

DESIGNING AND IMPLEMENTING AN EFFECTIVE COMPENSATION PLAN

The design phase consists of identifying the parameters of the plan, and the implementation phase consists of deciding on the specific instruments for executing the parameters. The design phase consists of the following factors:

1. Choose the appropriate mix of fixed and variable compensation at each level of the organization.
2. Select the appropriate value-based performance measures at all organization levels.
3. Decide on the appropriate time horizons for the salary, bonus, and long-term components of the compensation plan.
4. Decide on the appropriate level of leverage.

Let's look at each of these individually.

1. Fixed and Variable Compensation Mix

In pure pay-for-performance, the entire pay will vary from year to year as performance outcome varies. This is impractical for several reasons, the most important being that employees are too risk-averse to have their entire pay fluctuate. Another difficulty is identifying the outcome measures that correspond most closely to performance, an especially heavy requirement when pay is entirely based on outcomes. This is a difficult task considering the information asymmetry that exists between different levels of the organization.

The pay packages of most top executives contain a significant variable portion, often in the form of stocks or stock options. More than one-half of the 200 largest U.S. companies require executives to buy and hold sizable blocks of stocks, ranging from a market value of 5 to 15 times their base salary.[4] Companies such as Caterpillar and Coca-Cola impose substantial penalties on executives that do not comply with the stock ownership guidelines, including withholding stock options until the guidelines are met.

At progressively lower levels of the organization, the task of linking pay to performance becomes increasingly complex. Using stocks and stock options as incentives may not be as relevant at lower organizational levels, since the employees at these levels are not likely to have much control over the stock price movements of the company. It becomes necessary at these levels to decompose value creation into a series of operational factors, which can then be used as a basis for variable pay. Since risk aversion tends to decrease with total wealth, operational-level employees are likely to be more risk-averse than top management, and it is unlikely that variable pay will constitute a major portion of total pay for employees at these levels. As a result of all these factors, operational employee pay is largely fixed. Many companies do grant stocks and stock options to employees at these levels as incentives, but they are usually a negligible portion of the employees' total pay package.

2. Performance Measures

Before we can identify performance reward measures that are aligned with shareholder value, we need to understand what drives shareholder value in a company. The appropriate driver at each level corresponds to the operating factors that have the greatest impact on shareholder value and over which employees have the greatest control. Observed performance metrics include both accounting-based and market-based measures, many of which were defined in Chapter 12. Here, we focus on their role in compensation plans.

---

[4] P. Gogoi, 1999. "The Boss's Pay; False Impressions: More Companies Require Top Executives to Own Stock; The Result Isn't What Everybody Expected." *Wall Street Journal*, April 8, 1999.

Accounting-based measures. Popular accounting-based measures of performance include operating profit, net income, earnings per share, return on investment, and return on assets. The main advantages of accounting-based measures are their relative simplicity and ease of calculation. Employees at all levels of the organization are familiar with these mea-sures and understand them easily. These measures are routinely calculated for financial reporting purposes and do not require any special adjustments.

The disadvantages of accounting measures, however, outweigh their advantages. Accounting-based measures are appropriate measures of performance only when they correspond closely to shareholder value maximization, and this is usually not the case. Value depends on long-term economic cash flows. Accounting measures are one-period and focus on accounting earnings or similar statistics. As a result, when compensation is based on accounting measures, managers tend to shorten their time horizon and concentrate on projects with short-term value, ignoring investments with long-term payoffs.

Another disadvantage of accounting-based measures is that they do not reflect the cost of invested capital. A project can show accounting profit without creating any true economic value. Company value is increased by investing in projects with good growth, where the return exceeds the cost of capital. Finally, accounting-based measures are easily manipulated, limiting their effectiveness as objective measures of management performance.

Despite their limitations, the simplicity and ease of calculation of accounting-based measures have resulted in their sustained popularity as performance measures. In certain industries, net income corresponds closely to cash flows, which may explain its endurance.

Market-based measures. There is no doubt that stock prices are closely correlated with shareholder wealth. The question is whether the stock price is an appropriate measure of executive performance. Top management's job is to design strategies that maximize long-term company value. The market is the best judge of the effects of strategy and other business decisions on shareholder value, and the empirical evidence shows that the market rewards decisions that maximize long-term value. Hence, stock price is indeed an appropriate macro-level measure of the top management's performance.[5]

---

[5] The discussion in this section applies to market value added (MVA), which is closely related to stock price.

One major concern about using stock price as a compensation benchmark is the issue of control. Stock price is affected by many external developments in addition to managerial actions, including changes in interest rates, inflation, and international competition. One solution might be to use relative or indexed stock prices to focus compensation on the performance of the company relative to the market. One idea is to peg the exercise price of executive stock options to an industry or market index. The value of the option then moves with changes in the relative performance of the company, but not with economywide or industrywide shocks.

One disadvantage of using relative stock performance in compensation is that it gives managers the incentive to take actions that reduce the exposure of the company to industry- or economywide shocks. Many companies cite this as the reason for avoiding the practice. John Shiley, the president and CEO of Briggs & Stratton, a $1.3 billion manufacturer of air-cooled gasoline engines, said "We believe an executive's response to uncontrollable events is fundamental to value creation. The market's digestion of negative and positive uncontrollable events will ebb and flow. Therefore, an executive who effectively plays the cards he or she is dealt will show a superior MVA over time."[6]

The choice between a market and peer group index involves trade-offs. Stock options indexed to the market are easily measured and tracked, but a market index ignores the special circumstances affecting an industry. Options tied to a peer group index are a better judge of management's contributions; however, it is sometimes difficult to identify and track an appropriate peer group, especially for diversified companies.

The use of stock price as a measure of performance is harder to justify at the business unit level. The effects of any single business unit performance on the aggregate performance of a multiunit company would be negligible. In the absence of clear linkage between performance and stock price, it is unlikely that the company's stock price can act as an effective incentive at the business unit level. Often, companies have turned to corporate restructuring solutions such as divestitures, letter stock issuance, and equity carve-outs for this problem. Another solution that does not involve restructuring is the creation of a phantom stock to track the performance of the business unit. This is a less than ideal solution, since the absence of an efficient external market for the stock reduces the validity of the phantom stock price and compromises the compensation plan.

[6] J.S. Shiley, 1996. "Is Value Management the Answer?" *Chief Executive.* December 1996. 119. pp. 54–57.

Many private companies rely on a phantom stock to measure shareholder value creation. An alternative is to use internal proxies for stock returns. Two such proxies, SVA and TBR, were discussed in Chapter 12. These internal proxies are correlated to shareholder value creation and hence are appropriate compensation criteria at the business unit level. An additional benefit of the internal measures is that they can easily be decomposed into a series of value drivers. By combining these value drivers with the company's strategies, company-specific strategic value drivers can be identified at the operational level and used as a basis for compensation for frontline employees and managers.

Total shareholder return. Total shareholder return (TSR) measures the combined capital gains and dividends to the shareholder over a certain period. TSR is a good measure for companies that have high dividend payout rates and low P/E ratios. TSR has an important advantage in that the future growth prospects of the company are reflected in this measure through the capital gains term, which in turn depends on the stock price. Using TSR relative to the market or a peer group insulates the measure from fluctuations in the stock market.

Economic profit. Economic profit measures such as residual income and economic value added adjusts accounting profits for the opportunity cost of invested capital. Either absolute or incremental economic profit measures could be used as the basis for compensation.

Economic profits, although superior to accounting profits, are still one-period measures. Rewarding managers on the basis of such short-term measures might cause them to concentrate on short-term returns, forgoing long-term value in the process. One solution to this problem is called "banking." In banked compensation plans only a portion of the compensation earned in one year is paid out in that year. The rest accrues in a bank and is paid out depending on the performance in later years. Banking creates powerful incentives for executives to aim for sustainable levels of performance. Long-term value is not sacrificed for unsustainable short-term performance.

Another disadvantage of economic profit methods is that companies with a relatively small tangible capital base, such as technology and service companies, have higher economic profit figures, all else the same. In other words, EP measures have a size bias. This problem is especially acute when comparing the performance of different business units of a company.

Measuring incremental economic profits instead of absolute economic profits mitigates but does not solve the problem. A better solution is to express the economic profit as a percentage of the capital invested.

Shareholder value added (SVA), discussed in Chapter 12, addresses the short-term orientation of EP measures. Recall that SVA is calculated by discounting forecast cash flows for a specified period and subtracting the incremental future investments anticipated for that period. Rappaport argues for compensating managers based on Superior Shareholder Value Added (SSVA), shareholder value above and beyond the expectations of the shareholders. As shown in Figure 13-1, SSVA is calculated by first identifying shareholder expectations for value in the specified period. Once the baseline value is established, managers are rewarded for superior value creation. This is similar to the standard business practice of rewarding managers for beating budget targets, but the budget in this case is based on investor not manager expectations.

Cash flow. Since the market values a company based on its discounted cash flows, cash flows provide a better estimate of the company's performance than accounting measures. Cash flow is also less subject to manipulation. Incremental cash flow and cash flow return on investment (CFROI) are two of the performance measures based on cash flow. The main disadvantage of CFROI is that it is a backward-looking measure that focuses on the return from the assets in place. This measure is not an accurate measure of long-term value creation.

Ideally, companies should customize their executive compensation plans by using different combinations of value drivers and compensation

FIGURE 13-1   Superior shareholder value added.

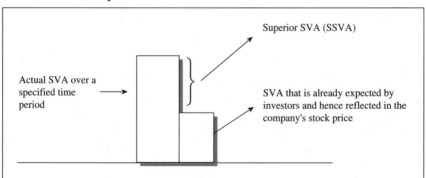

plan components (salary, bonus, and long-term incentives). A case in point is that of Briggs & Stratton (see box).[7]

Briggs & Stratton: A Complex Approach to Value Creation

The company has in place a leveraged stock option (LSO) plan for its executives. The LSO plan is linked to the company's EVA compensation plan by relating the number of LSOs awarded to the EVA bonus payout for the year. The EVA plan sets annual performance goals and target incentives that together determine bonus payouts for the year. The potential bonus is equally weighted between corporate and divisional performance targets. Briggs & Stratton also has a novel approach for the time horizon problem. The bonus amount that is 125% over the target incentive is banked. One-third of the bank balance is paid out in each year with a positive bank balance. However, in any year, the banked bonuses are subject to forfeiture if a negative bonus is accrued because of unsatisfactory performance in achieving targeted EVA goals. Once the bonus amount is determined, each executive receives an out-of-the money option, with a current market value equal to 10 times the amount of the EVA payout. The options are exercisable at the end of three years. The exercise price for the LSO is linked to the company's cost of capital for a five-year period. The LSOs go in the money only when the stock price exceeds a deemed cost of capital return for the five-year period. Long-term value is added by consistent delivery of strong EVA annual performance. By linking the annual EVA bonuses and long-term LSOs, Briggs & Stratton has structured their compensation plan to maximize both short- and long-term performance.

Compensation at the business unit level.   Should compensation at the business unit level be based only on the performance of the business unit? If, in fact, managers' compensation is based only on the factors over which they have control, clearly the answer is yes. But what about the interrelationships among the business units? For most companies with diverse busi-

---

[7] Shiley, op. cit.

ness units, significant synergies exist between the units. Cooperation between the different business units is essential to realize these synergies. As such, it makes sense that a portion of the compensation of the business unit manager should be based on the performance of other business units or on the aggregate corporate performance. The best measure of performance evaluation and compensation at the business unit level is a weighted measure of corporate and business unit performance. SVA is an accurate judge of business unit performance and hence is an appropriate criterion for business unit compensation. A sample plan at the compensation level will be a weighted average of the business unit SVA and the corporate-level TSR.

Recent years have seen a substantial number of restructuring such as equity carve-outs, letter stock issues, and divestitures. In many cases the rationale behind these restructuring efforts is to create a readily observable measure of the business unit performance, which can then be used to base the managers' compensation on. The presence of an accurate and readily observable measure of business performance is a critical component of company value creation. Diversified companies lack such a measure, and this may be one of the reasons for their poor market performance.

Compensation at the operational level.   Contribution to value and controllability should be the two main criteria used to identify compensation criteria at the operational level. In value-based management, the operational processes that underlie each activity should be closely linked to the value drivers. Basing compensation at each activity level on the appropriate value driver will greatly facilitate creating this linkage.

Because value is a function of three variables—future cash flows, risk, and time horizon—the operational value drivers are those factors that influence those variables. Recall the seven generic operational value drivers from the previous chapter: sales growth, profit margin, the tax rate, working capital, capital expenditure, cost of capital, and competitive advantage period.

Superior shareholder value is created by companies that are able to sustain their cash flows at a level above the rest of the industry. This is achieved by the strategic decisions made by top management. Once strategies that maximize the generic value drivers are identified, they could be decomposed into a series of strategic drivers. For example, the drivers important to a strategy of low-cost leadership are different from those for a strategy of differentiation. The process of identifying strategic drivers and basing compensation on them will focus the attention of frontline employees and management on these drivers, thereby resulting in the strategy being implemented.

Operational drivers can also be identified by the decomposition process discussed in the previous chapter, using the DuPont formula for example.

Once operational drivers have been identified, the next task is to assign the appropriate drivers to each division and organizational level and to base incentives on these operational drivers. The process is as follows:

1. Formulate strategy.
2. Decompose into operational drivers.
3. Assign appropriate drivers to each division and organizational level.
4. Base compensation on the value drivers.
5. As employees focus on maximizing the value drivers, the strategy is implemented.

If this process is implemented properly, strategy formulation and implementation should be a smooth, fluid process that flows from upper management to the operational level. As value-maximizing strategies are implemented, shareholder value is maximized.

3. Time Horizon

An effective compensation plan should strike the optimal balance between short-term and long-term goals of the company. Short-term financial results are certainly important, but they should not come at the expense of long-term growth. Choosing the appropriate time horizon for incentives is a critical element of compensation plans. Once the time horizon is chosen, there are a number of tactics to implement this. Examples include vested stock options, where the options can be exercised only after a certain period, and banking, where a portion of the incentives in a given period is held back and put at risk for the subsequent periods' performance. These delivery instruments ensure that the incentive-earning performance is sustainable before actually paying the incentive.

4. Leverage

Leverage can be defined as the change in value of the incentives for a given change in the underlying performance measures. The higher the leverage, the higher the incentives paid per incremental improvement in the performance measure. Designing the proper leverage is difficult and depends on (1) the particular underlying incentive measure, (2) the scope and time frame of the company's strategy (strategy that needs to be executed sooner may require more leverage on the measures that correspond to the critical strategy drivers), and (3) the company's external competitive environment.

The process of setting leverage consists of the following steps:

1. Identify the performance factor or the minimum performance measure threshold that deserves an incentive.
2. If appropriate, select a target performance range.
3. If appropriate, select a maximum cap on the incentives.
4. Define the leverages corresponding to the appropriate performance ranges among the threshold, targets, and maximum.
5. Quantify the effects of different compensation scenarios on the company value.
6. Modify leverage based on the employees' risk profile.

In the plan design illustrated in Figure 13-2, leverage differs with different target ranges. The first target range is levered more highly than the second. The floor represents a base level of incentives, regardless of performance, while the cap is the highest level of incentives to be paid out.

Alternately, as Figure 13-3 illustrates, the pay could vary directly with performance with no caps or floors, once a minimum performance threshold is reached.

In practice, a critical but often overlooked part of leverage design is whether the incentive compensation is affordable to the company. Quantifying the effects of compensation on company value is critical to

FIGURE 13-2   Compensation leverage design.

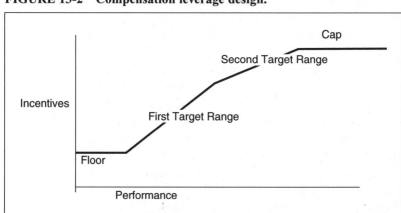

FIGURE 13-3   Alternative leverage design.

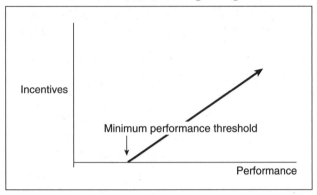

ensure that the compensation scheme is affordable. This is difficult to do *a priori,* but the case of Computer Associates (see box) illustrates the perils of blindly setting compensation schemes without understanding the effects of compensation payout on the company value.

Another relevant factor in setting leverage is the risk profile of the employee. Obviously, this is a difficult factor to identify. Even if the risk profile and utility functions of employees can be accurately identified, the question remains whether the compensation packages should be modified to accom-

---

Value Destroying Compensation: The Case of Computer Associates

In May 1995, the Long Island-based software company Computer Associates granted its three top officers, including its CEO, Charles Wang, the right to millions of company stock under a variety of future performance scenarios. One of these scenarios came to pass on May 21, 1998, when the company's stock closed above $53.33 per share for the 60th day in a 12-month period. Mr. Wang was given 12.15 million free shares worth $670 million. The total payout to the three top executives was $1.1 billion. The company booked the entire charge of $1.1 billion in its 1998 fiscal year, resulting in an after-tax charge of about $675 million. In the same announcement, the company also warned that its revenues and profits for future quarters would be affected by the Asian economic crisis. The price of Computer Associates immediately plunged from $57 to $39.5, a decline of 30.7%. A shareholder lawsuit has been filed against the

company, complaining that the company was issuing bullish statements on its future until the date of the announcement. The suit further claimed that the news of the Asian crisis was withheld from the
stockholders long enough for the top management to collect their
$1.1 billion reward. The $1.1 billion award represents 43% of the
entire profits for the company for the three-year period. Considering
that Computer Associates total shareholder return was in the 67th
percentile of a peer group during the same period, this is clearly a
case of excessive compensation.[8] The compensation committee set
the targets back in 1995 without an understanding of the performance necessary to achieve these targets and without controlling for
the effects of a sustained bull market.

modate these factors. The goal of executive compensation is not to optimize
the risk of the executive, but rather to align the executives' incentives with
those of the shareholders. To the extent that executives' risk aversion affects
the incentive effect, risk aversion has to be taken into account in designing
compensation plans. When a risk-averse executive is given a highly leveraged
compensation package, he or she might try to mitigate the risk in two ways.
The first way is by hedging the risk through actions such as early exercise of
options and selling stocks. Empirical studies have shown that CEOs do hedge
some of their risk by selling their stock or exercising their options for cash.[9]
The second way is by taking managerial actions that reduce the risk of the
company, such as investing in projects with low returns variability.

Most shareholders are well diversified. Their holdings of a single company's stock are likely to be a part of an overall portfolio. As such, when
it comes to risk, stockholders are primarily concerned with the beta or the
systematic risk of the company. On returns, stockholders are similarly concerned with relative performance or how the company performed relative
to their diversified portfolio. On the other hand, the wealth of executives
correlate closely to the absolute performance of the company. Executives
are concerned with absolute performance and absolute risk. Absolute risk
coincides with the volatility of the company's value. A compensation pack-

[8] "Mr. Wang, Give Back Those Shares." Crystal Report. July 28, 1998, www.crystalre-
port.com/page_artcle.asp?id=56.

[9] E. Ofek, and D. Yermack. "Taking Stock: Does Equity-Based Compensation Increase
Manager's Ownership?" Unpublished draft, 1997.

age leveraged to company value might cause risk-averse executives to focus on reducing volatility (measured by sigma) instead of the more relevant beta. This is likely to result in managerial actions that reduce stockholder value, such as the avoidance of high-risk, high-return projects that are optimal from the perspective of well-diversified shareholders. Since this is clearly an unwelcome effect, executive risk aversion remains a matter of concern to the board. Boards might choose to address this problem by uncoupling executive salary and bonuses from company value.

COMPENSATION INSTRUMENTS

The important factors to be considered in selecting the optimal compensation instrument are as follows:

1. The type and appropriate mix of payment
2. Use of stock (real, phantom, restricted)
3. Use of options (at-the-money, in-the-money, out-of-the-money)
4. Tax effects (corporate and individual)
5. Timing of payment
6. Restrictions on incentive delivery

The objective of delivery strategy is two-fold:

1. To ensure proper implementation of the design strategy
2. To minimize the cost of incentive delivery to the company

STOCK OPTIONS

Stock options have become the delivery instrument of choice for many companies, and value-based managerial incentives can no longer be understood without a solid understanding of stock options. The average CEO stock option grant increased from $155 thousand to $1.2 million between 1980 and 1994, representing a 700% increase. In the largest publicly traded companies option grants are larger than the combined average salary and bonuses, and more than 90% of CEOs now hold stock options.[10] The direct correlation to shareholder value, along with the fact that stock options are essentially free to the granting company, make them an attractive alternative to cash bonuses.

Another reason for the popularity of options is the comparative reporting costs of salary versus bonuses. On the upside, very large bonuses have

[10] B.J. Hall, and J.B. Liebman. "Are CEOs Really Paid Like Bureaucrats?" *Quarterly Journal of Economics.* 1998, 113, pp. 653–691.

high reporting costs and tend to attract negative attention from the media and the public. Stock option gains, although subject to some criticism, is much less controversial. On the downside, large decreases in salary and bonuses are resisted by the executives. Boards are often quite friendly with the executives and may find it politically difficult to impose meaningful penalties on their colleagues. On the other hand, the decrease in executive wealth due to large holdings of stock and options following substantial decline in the company's stock price is surprisingly well tolerated by the executives. Thus, the political costs of executive pay have resulted in options being the high-powered incentive of choice for many companies.

Of course, stock options do not come without costs. Their main disadvantage is that they dilute existing shareholders' interests in the company. Another criticism is that their cost is not reflected in the company's financial statements. Currently, companies are required to disclose the cost of fixed-price option grants in footnotes to their financial statements, but they are not required to charge the cost against earnings. The absence of earnings impact has led many companies to view options as "free money to be spread around widely and deeply."[11] In a dramatic example, *The Economist* reports that if Microsoft had accounted for the cost of all outstanding options (including those granted during the year) in 1998, the company had a loss of $18 billion compared to the declared profit of $4.5 billion during the year.[12]

Warren Buffet offers this explanation for the explosion of option grants: "Accounting principles offer management a choice: pay employees in one form and count the cost, or pay them in another form and ignore the cost. Small wonder then that the use of options has mushroomed." Mr. Buffet is outspoken in his criticism of options: "Although options can be an appropriate and even ideal way to compensate and motivate top managers, they are more often wildly capricious in their distribution of rewards, inefficient as motivators, and inordinately expensive for shareholders." He argues for accounting for options as a real expense. "If options are not a form of compensation, what are they? If compensation is not an expense, what is it? And, if expenses should not go into the calculation of earnings, where in the world should they go?" When Warren Buffet bought General Re Corporation in 1998, he replaced the option plan with a cash-based incentive program, taking a $36 million charge to income.

---

[11] S. Hays, 1999. "Overdoing Stock Options May Decrease Returns for Shareholders." *Workforce*. June 1999. p. 148.

[12] "Special: Share Options." *Economist*. August 7, 1999, pp. 18–20.

One way to address the issue of dilution is by granting stock appreciation rights (SARs). SARs carry the benefits of an option, but no shares change hands. Holders get a cash payout equal to the difference between the strike price and the stock price at exercise. Another advantage of SARs is that unlike options, they represent a real expense for the company, resulting in a more cautious approach to executive pay. The newly formed Daimler-Chrysler has put in place a stock appreciation right plan, replacing the bonus plan of Daimler-Benz and option plan of Chrysler. For stock options to create value, the benefits from the incentive effect have to outweigh the costs from the dilution effect. By actively managing the factors that contribute positively to the incentive effects of stock options, boards can maximize the value impact of options.

Another issue is complexity. For options to align the interests of managers and shareholders, the incentives provided by them have to be well understood both by executives and by the boards that grant them. A case in point is the common misconception regarding the downside risk of options. The familiar hockey stick payoff of traded options, where the option need not be exercised if it is out-of-the-money, has increased this misconception. Stock option grants are an important component of the executives' pay package, and any downswings in the option value represent real decreases in the executives' wealth. Some have argued that stock options have more downside risk than stock.[13] Let's say, for example, the sensitivity of an option's value to the value of the underlying stock is 0.55—that is, for every dollar change in the value of the stock, the value of the option changes by 55 cents. A company can give a greater number of stock options than stock shares to its executives, to arrive at the same *ex ante* value transfer, since each option is worth less than each share. If, in a typical case, a company can transfer three times as many options as shares for the same *ex ante* value transfer to the executive, the total sensitivity of the option grant is 1.7 (3 times 0.55).

The sensitivity is even greater for out-of-the-money options than in-the-money options, since the company can give the executives a higher number of out-of-the money options than at-the-money options for the same *ex ante* value transfer. In that case, for the same value transfer to the executive, options have greater sensitivity to stock price movements than stocks, and out of-the money options have greater sensitivity than at-the-money options.

---

[13] B.J. Hall, "The Pay to Performance Incentives of Executive Stock Options." NBER working paper 6674, 1998.

To produce the desired shareholder value-enhancing behavior in executives, it is important that executives be constantly aware of the upside and downside movements of their option package. Pay-to-performance incentives are undermined if the executives do not properly understand them. If boards adopt the policy of valuing option packages on a regular basis, the executives would be much more aware of the sensitivity of their option packages to changes in shareholder wealth, and incentive effects of options would improve significantly.

Indexed Stock Options

The value of stock options is directly correlated to the stock price of the company. The question remains of how much the stock price is affected by managerial actions and how much by overall market conditions such as inflation and interest rates. During a bull market, option packages are likely to result in windfalls to the executives regardless of their performance. An indexed option, where the exercise price rises over time according to some market index, is a solution to this problem. The index could either be an aggregate stock market index such as the S&P 500 or an index made of peer companies. Either way, the executive is rewarded only when the company's stock price rises above a hurdle rate. Shareholders of a company are interested in relative value, or how the company performs relative to the market. By using indexed options, executives are rewarded on the value created in excess of the overall market or industry group.

The question remains as to why out-of-the money and indexed options remain unpopular as incentive contracts, when in fact they serve the shareholder interests better than their popular alternative, at-the-money, unindexed options. Part of the answer is the risk aversion of executives. Many risk-averse executives will either resist or demand a premium for accepting an option package consisting of the riskier out-of-the money and indexed options. Risk aversion significantly impacts option exercise behavior, and consequently the long-term incentive effects of options. If stock options are exercised early and in times of stock market volatility,[14] their long-term incentive effect is significantly undermined. Longer vesting periods might be the answer to this problem.

Another drawback of indexed options is that they do not enjoy the same favorable accounting treatment as fixed-price options. Currently, companies are not required to charge the cost of fixed-price stock options

[14] S. Huddart, "Patterns of Stock Option Exercise in the United States." In *Executive Compensation and Shareholder Value: Theory and Evidence.* London: Kluwer Academic Publishers, 1999.

against their earnings. In the case of indexed options, the difference between the stock price and the exercise price must be reported each year as an expense. The requirement to expense indexed options discourages companies from adopting indexed option plans.

The advantages and disadvantages of options are summarized in Table 13-1.

TABLE 13-1   Stock options: pros and cons.

Advantages of Options		
	Intervening Factors	Suggested Board Actions
Incentive effects	Complexity of options	Make sure executives are constantly aware of the upside and downside movements of their option package
	Windfalls from bull markets	Indexed options.
Leverage		Increase leverage through out-of-the money options.
Long time horizon	Early exercise	Longer vesting periods.
Tax benefits		

Disadvantages of Options		
	Intervening Factors	Suggested Board Actions
Dilution effects		Grant stock appreciation rights instead of actual shares.
Executive risk aversion		Design compensation package to fit the executives' risk profile or hire executives with the desired risk profile.
Gaming effects (Executives might engage in arbitrage with the market using their superior information)	Information asymmetry	Investor relations; timely communication of company value to the market.

TRENDS IN EXECUTIVE COMPENSATION

Between 1980 and 1994, the mean value of stock options granted exploded, rising by 683% from $155,000 to $1.2 million. The median value of stock option grant increased from 40 to $325,000.[15] The percentage of CEOs receiving stock option awards during the year increased from 30% in 1980 to nearly 70% in 1994. The percentage of CEOs holding stock options increased from 57% to 87% in the same period. Long-term compensation, mostly from option exercises, made up 80% of the average CEO's pay package, up from 72% in 1997. The 100 largest American companies granted stock and stock options amounting to 2% of their outstanding shares in 1998, up from 1% in 1989. Added to the grants made in previous years, the total outstanding stock and options in incentive schemes amount to 13.2% of corporate equity, around $1.1 trillion dollars. In 1989, equity awards formed 6.9% of corporate equity. Stock option grants to chief executives accounted for a record 53.3% of the compensation given by America's top 100 companies in 1998, compared to 26% in 1994 and 2% in the mid-1980s.[16]

The combination of increasing option grants and the sustained bull market of the 1990s and early 2000 has brought a great deal of wealth to American executives, focusing increasing attention on the relation between option grants and performance. The debate continues as to whether the compensation is justified by performance or whether it is merely a windfall from the bull equity market.

Many critics argue that in a rising equity market, unindexed option packages actually sever the link between pay and any objective standard of performance. The option windfalls reward both passable as well as truly great performance. The 100 largest companies in the S&P 500 account for 9% of the rise in the market. The stocks of several companies have underperformed, yet pay raises are not limited to the overperformers. Cyprus Amax Minerals CEO Milton Ward had a pay package of $2.1 million in 1998, consisting of salary and bonuses, along with 450,000 options, while the stock plummeted 36% during the year. Michael Eisner has helped Disney's stock rise 450% in the past 10 years. Disney's stock has trailed the market in the past two years, and earnings have fallen 13% in 1998. Yet Eisner was granted 24 million shares in 1997, ranking him number one in the *Business Week's* list of the CEOs who gave their shareholders

[15] Hall and Lieberman, op. cit.
[16] "Special: Share Options." *Economist.* August 7, 1999, pp. 18–20.

the least for their pay. Federal Reserve Chairman Alan Greenspan has publicly criticized the level of CEO pay and favors options that are indexed, either to the peer group or to a market.

Advocates of options have asserted that they are responsible for the outstanding performance of the equity market. Critics worry that companies are outsourcing compensation to the shareholders and setting untenable levels of pay expectations for the future while creating hefty dilution. In fact, the mushrooming stock option grants have focused attention on the dilution effects of options. According to Watson Wyatt Worldwide, the average overhang of American companies (options already granted plus the options available for grant, divided by the number of outstanding shares) increased from 5% in 1998 to 13% in 1997. Institutional investors have reacted by voting against any plans where the potential dilution is over 10%.

An important question is what would happen to compensation plans in a bear market. Will options still continue to be the primary component of compensation, exposing executives to significant losses? A look back at history suggests otherwise. In the 1970s, a prolonged bear market made options worthless. Instead of maintaining them, companies switched over to bonus plans based on the achievement of cash-based goals.

Another way options are breaking the link between pay and performance is through repricing, whereby the exercise price of out-of-the money options is reset to make them in-the-money. A case in point is Henry Silverman, the CEO of Cendant. When Cendant's stock fell in the late 1990s, the compensation committee repriced Silverman's options at $9.1, well below their original range of $17 to $31. Repricing is often justified as a strategy to retain executives when the company is stumbling. Even though repricing may not be the optimal strategy, it is true that pay linked to company performance makes it extremely difficult for underperforming companies to attract and retain managerial talent. In light of the current shortage of managerial talent practices such as repricing and retention, bonuses will continue to flourish.

Another consequence of the shortage of managerial talent is the cost of attracting new executives, especially from companies who are performance leaders. Often the executives leave behind attractive compensation packages and expect their new employers to make them whole for the foregone package, while showering them with a whole new set of incentives. The pay package offered by Hewlett-Packard to Carleton Fiorina in 1999 is a case in point. Apart from salary and bonuses, the package includes $28 million in stock options and $66 million in time-lapsed restricted stock. The restricted stock grant is the largest amount of restricted stock ever conferred on a CEO in a given year. The size of the award is surprising, especially in light of the fact that HP is well known for performance-lapsed restricted share awards. In fact, in 1998, Fiorina's predecessor Lew Platt was required to give back to HP a substantial number of shares he had been awarded years earlier for failing to deliver the requisite amount of performance. Platt's share return amounted to a negative compensation of $2.4 million in 1998. HP justified Fiorina's compensation package by citing the need to remunerate her for the substantial compensation package she was leaving behind at Lucent Technologies. These types of giveaway compensation packages do nothing to align the new executives' incentives to the interests of the company shareholders. One answer is to link the make-whole pay to the achievement of specific goals.

Although few companies have adopted indexed options, companies such as Monsanto and Procter & Gamble have introduced several alternative performance-based equity incentives over the last few years. Although these are better than plain-vanilla stock options and achieve some of the benefits of indexed options, the targets specified are not tied to superior shareholder returns. These alternative equity incentives include (1) premium priced options, (2) performance vesting options, and (3) performance-based restricted stock.

In a *premium priced option,* the exercise price is set at a premium to the market price. The premium can either be fixed over the life of the option, or it could be a series of increasing exercise prices over the option term. Although premium priced options measures are better suited to measuring superior performance in an up market, the difficulty of achieving premium prices makes them impractical in a down market.

Performance vesting options carry an extended vesting period, usually 10 years. The vesting period is accelerated if prespecified performance targets, usually specified in terms of the stock price, are met. An important advantage of performance vesting options is that they do not incur any accounting charges, unlike indexed options. However, a major disadvantage is that these options vest at the end of their term, regardless of performance. As such, they are less performance-sensitive than indexed options.

In the case of *performance-based restricted stock,* executives are granted a large up-front block of shares based on achieving specified goals such as a target level of relative TSR. At the end of the performance period, the participant receives a portion of the initial grant (0% to 100%) based on his or her performance. Companies adopting this plan do incur an annual accounting charge. The other disadvantage is meeting the specified target in a down market.

Indexed stock options are the best equity-based performance incentive. The compensation earned through indexed options is always correlated with superior shareholder value, regardless of whether a bull or bear market is prevailing over the time period in question. Indexed option plans are administratively simpler than performance-based vesting and restricted stocks, since there is no need to establish targets and update them periodically. Because the indexing eliminates the effect of market and industry-specific price movements, indexed options are less influenced by events outside the management's control. However, for indexed options to be effective, it is imperative that the peer group or index used should be a fair basis of comparison. Management must accept the fairness of this comparison for the incentive to produce the intended motivation and actions.

CONCLUSION

Figure 13-4 summarizes the framework of how compensation plans can create value. The starting point of any compensation plan is the business strategy. It is important to keep in mind that an effective compensation plan based on bad strategy is likely to destroy not create value. At best, strategy is the link between the company's internal capabilities and resources and the external competitive environment, and if executed successfully, it provides the company with sustained, above-average cash flows. The compensation plan design follows from the strategy. The critical component is identifying a series of value drivers at the aggregate and operation level that correspond closely to value creation. Once the plan is designed, appropriate instruments are selected to deliver the plan. When the plan is executed and compensation is based on a hierarchy of value-based performance measures, managers and employees are expected to make decisions that maximize shareholder value. A number of factors such as risk aversion and performance sensitivity to compensation may interfere with the effectiveness of compensation plans in producing value-creating managerial actions.

An effective compensation system clearly defines the appropriate value drivers at each organizational level. Incentives based on share price appreciation might be an appropriate performance measure at the corporate executive level, but less so at the business unit and divisional level. The individual business unit or division performance is likely to be a key component of performance measurement at this level. If the objective of a pay-for-performance system is increased performance, it seems logical that pay be based on the factors that the employees have control over. As a result, appropriate performance measures must be identified for each organizational level. Whereas a business unit manager might be rewarded based on

FIGURE 13-4 How compensation plans add value.

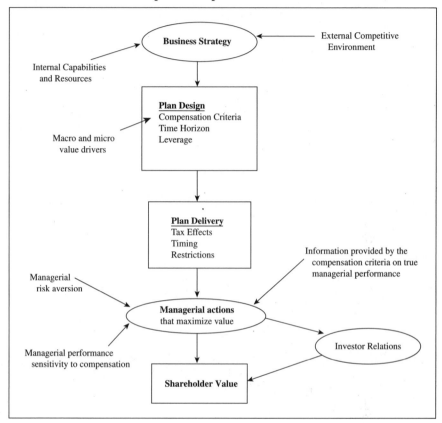

the performance of the entire business unit, a plant manager might be rewarded based on the performance of the individual plant.

Of course, there is an important drawback to limiting pay-for-performance to the factors managers have control over. In some instances, this may actually discourage cooperation between divisions. The important point is that appropriate value drivers at each level have to be those that are tied most to long-term value creation. In public companies, corporate management sets the strategy that is implemented in increasing detail at each organizational level. It is important that the compensation system synchronizes value creation at all levels.

14

BECOMING A VBM COMPANY

THIS CHAPTER FOCUSES ON MAKING **VBM** A CORE COMPETENCE. The broad process and critical success factors for a successful introduction of VBM in your company are outlined.

To successfully institutionalize the VBM approach, there are six critical success factors:

1.   Top management support
2.   Education and training
3.   Strategy review process
4.   Value-based incentive compensation
5.   Keep it simple
6.   Investor communications

Let's look at each factor individually.

TOP MANAGEMENT SUPPORT

To implement VBM successfully, it is absolutely critical to get the strong support and commitment from the top; otherwise, the implementation of VBM risks becoming just another finance exercise. With the CEO leading the way, top management must be actively involved in promoting the use of VBM throughout the company and in the key business processes that influence behavior: strategic planning, resource allocation, performance measurement, incentive compensation, internal reporting, and investor communications.

The decision to adopt VBM is often precipitated by a company's poor total shareholder return (TSR) performance relative to the market or its peers, and the inevitable subsequent change in leadership. A change in strategy is needed, and a new CEO arrives on the scene with a mandate to transform the company from top to bottom. VBM is championed as part of a major transformation package and is adopted to change behavior and alter the mind-set and culture of the organization and to encourage managers and employees to think and act like owners.

Prior to embarking on the road to VBM, companies are often income statement driven. The focus is on sales and budgets, with incentive compensation tied to the budget. Budgets are gamed, driven by bartering, with little or no incentive to use budgets efficiently. Capital expenditures are allocated on the basis of track record, accounting impact, and size of business unit instead of long-term value creation. Management gradually realizes what investors knew all along: that profitability is less than the cost of capital, and a change in strategy and direction is needed.

EDUCATION AND TRAINING

Effective and ongoing training and education are critical success factors for VBM implementation. Successful VBM companies often start training before the implementation itself, and training is a never-ending process that continues well after the VBM program is deployed across the entire company and that must be driven down through all levels of the organization.

If key management decisions in such areas as new products, new business development, financing, operational management, and corporate restructuring are to be made from a value creation perspective, managers must first understand the basic concepts of valuation, its interaction with competitive strategy, and how their decisions impact value.

To be effective, the education program must include active involvement by senior management to show support and also to help communicate the corporate-level value creation perspective. The initial sessions should be held with the CEO and the top executive group and then with selected groups of key executives throughout the organization. These executives meet in small groups to discuss valuation and strategy concepts applied to a variety of internal case studies. Training programs can be conducted internally and/or with the periodic assistance of outside subject matter experts.

Business unit managers must become actively involved in analyzing, presenting, and discussing case studies drawn from their own businesses that illustrate competitive strategy concepts and methods. These studies are then critically analyzed and discussed by their peers. One or more representatives from top management should always be present at these sessions. In the process, business unit managers will not only learn all the new strategic concepts and techniques, they will learn more about their own businesses and those of some of their peers in the corporation.

Operating managers at the lower levels must understand that they can impact the value of the company and how to make value concepts part of their behavior. This is particularly important insofar as performance is going to be judged on how well the employees did versus the value driver targets assigned to them. Hands-on active participation in easy-to-understand exercises, case studies, and role-playing will help business unit managers identify specific value drivers, giving them a broader, more strategic perspective and language. This will in turn greatly facilitate communication between various business units and other parts of the organization.

Of course, cultural change is not immediate. Adopting a VBM system is a lot like implementing any change. People are naturally resistant to change. In the case of VBM, people's basic beliefs about what drives their businesses are challenged, and frequently these beliefs must change significantly. Value-creating strategies frequently contradict conventional wisdom. For example, size is not a guarantor of business success. VBM shows that the opposite frequently creates more value. Better focus and/or downsizing (shrinking) may be required to gain or sustain competitive advantage.

This is unpopular with managers whose compensation is tied to conventional measures such as sales or earnings. Operating managers are reluctant or unwilling at first to think and act strategically in value creation terms. They often have little or no knowledge of the tools and concepts of valuation and competitive strategy because of their backgrounds in such technical areas as engineering or accounting. Furthermore, they are accustomed to being rewarded for measurable short-term results such as cost reduction, sales increases, or accounting profitability. This means that participation, buy-in, and ultimate ownership are crucial to successful implementation.

The cultural change takes place gradually. Business unit managers become more and more comfortable with the concepts of valuation and their interaction with competitive strategy analysis, and with how to translate these concepts into action plans. They gradually begin to think in a more external and future-oriented manner about their business. A common language evolves in the business plans submitted to top management, including terms such as "economic profit," "market attractiveness," "sustainable competitive advantage," "value chain," "substitute products," "value drivers," "product differentiation," and "focus."

STRATEGY REVIEW PROCESS

At the heart of every successful VBM effort is a business-level focus on strategy. Shareholder value creation is a high-stake process that requires a stubborn assessment of the value creation potential of marketing, technological, and operating strategies of each business unit and prospective new business opportunities,

As discussed in Chapters 9 and 10, the two primary strategic determinants of value creation are market attractiveness and competitive position. Market attractiveness and competitive position drive future prices, profit margins, volume, required investment, and the cost of capital (business risk). These factors in turn determine free cash flows and economic value. Consequently, business unit strategies must be validated by a process that explores market attractiveness and competitive position to discover where value is created today and in the future. This entails the development of an externally validated cash flow forecast supported by a realistic assessment of market attractiveness and competitive position, as well as the current strategy for calculating the value of each business unit. Evaluating the alternative strategies ensures the ones selected are those which create the most value.

One successful way to introduce a VBM program in your company is through a thorough, interactive, cross-functional strategy review process. The idea is for management to link shareholder performance (relative TSR) and free cash flow analysis with the company's strategic intent. In addition to the CEO, COO, and the corporate planning staff, the strategy review sessions should include the top executives from functions perceived as critical to the key strategic issues of each business—marketing, finance, production, information technology, legal, human resources, and R&D. This enhances the chance of each business manager to get top management attention, as well as feedback, when presenting their strategic plans. The review process reinforces the education program as well.

Based on the business plan, each business unit determines the capital and resources needed to meet its targets. This information is then funneled back to corporate, where it is tested against market expectations and evaluated to ensure that shareholder value is enhanced.

The lessons learned in the training sessions must be constantly rein-forced by giving managers the opportunity to practice and demonstrate their newly acquired skills. The review process should allow sufficient time to cover key strategies and issues with an open discussion period, as well as a formal presentation by each business unit. Senior management must take an active role in the review process and provide plenty of encour-agement and constructive criticism.

Business-level managers of most non-VBM companies are generally not inclined or prepared for value-based competitive strategy analysis. Some simply extrapolate historical information on a spreadsheet, assum-ing that the future will reflect the past. Others resort to pie-in-the-sky "hockey stick" approaches and project unrealistic sudden increase in prof-itability during the forecast period, making the economic value of the busi-ness look good despite poor current and past performance.

VALUE-BASED INCENTIVE COMPENSATION

The success of VBM is closely linked to manager and employee value-based compensation. Without this crucial connection, VBM is just another flavor of the week from the finance group. The best education, training, and strategic review process in the world won't make any lasting impres-sion unless managers are given more tangible incentives for their efforts. Just because business managers know which strategies have the greatest chance of creating economic value doesn't mean they will be eager to pur-sue any of them. They need to know that their efforts will be rewarded. Top management must develop an effective system for assessing and re-warding a value-based orientation among executives at all organizational levels.

Building an effective compensation system to reward executives for long-term shareholder value appreciation is the most difficult part of the VBM process, and it is frequently the weakest link in implementation. Two major hurdles must be overcome. First, reliable and valid measures of long-term value-creating performance are needed. Second, equitable incentives must be clearly linked to these performance measures.

Excessive reliance on accounting-based measures of success is inap-propriate because of their short-term focus and because it encourages ex-ecutives to choose strategies that will make their units look good now but may hurt their chances for sustained value creation later. For example, a harvesting strategy with very low investment can improve current ac-counting returns, but only at the expense of competitive position and prof-itable growth in the future.

Although more and more companies are introducing value-oriented performance measures, most companies still do not link performance measures and goals with total shareholder returns. Common shortcomings include budget-based goals rather than goals linked to value-maximizing strategies, annual goals rather than multiyear goals, insufficient use of value drivers, and the improper use of economic profit and other residual income measures.

A number of value-based performance measures—among them EVA, SVA, TSR, TBR, and CFROI—were discussed in Chapter 12 and evaluated on the basis of their accuracy, simplicity, and relevance. These criteria are important, since a considerable portion of the employee's compensation is to be tied to the measure of choice. After evaluating each metric on the basis of these three criteria, most companies will conclude that no one metric satisfies all the needs of the company. Tailoring value metrics to the particular circumstances and needs of the company becomes a critical success factor for VBM implementation. A combination of metrics is usually desirable, taking into consideration accuracy, simplicity, and relevancy, with different metrics applicable to different levels of the organization. An hierarchical scheme of metrics is depicted in Figure 4-11 in Chapter 4.

As discussed in Chapter 12, TSR relative to a peer group is a reasonable metric to use at the senior management level. Top management is rewarded when the company's performance exceeds that of the peer group. Targeting rewards to superior total shareholder returns sends a clear and powerful signal to the rest of the organization and to the investment community that management is totally committed to exceeding peer total shareholder return performance.

Indexed stock options also provide excellent vehicles for linking senior management rewards to superior total shareholder returns. Rewards for superior performers and penalties for inferior performers can be provided by designing a stock option with an exercise price indexed to a stock market index or to the stock performance of a peer group. Peer indexing data are readily available from the *Wall Street Journal's* annual Shareholder Scoreboard and are also used in the SEC's disclosure requirements.

In addition to receiving incentive compensation pay, top managers should have a financial stake in VBM by being required to buy stock to align their interests more closely to those of their shareholders. Company directors should also be encouraged to behave like owners as well by having a substantial portion of their retainer—say, 40% to 50%—in common stock, creating a personal interest in shareholder value.

To involve all managers and employees at the operating level in the quest for value and to make operating managers into owners/shareholders, key value driver goals should be established for each business. Key value drivers are defined as measurable and easily communicated current accomplishments that have a significant positive impact on the long-term value of the business. The operational value drivers for each division have to be identified and a portion of the front-line employees' compensation tied to the achievement of value driver targets.

A company should offer incentives to its managers through an incentive plan with both short- and long-term compensation components. In the short term, the value gains by operations are calculated, and managers are rewarded based on the continuous improvement in this measure of value—SVA, for example. To encourage a longer-term perspective, a combination of indexed stock options are offered deep within the company. A portion of the divisional managers' compensation is tied to both SVA and corporate relative TSR. The company could also implement phantom stock to simulate a sense of ownership among the managers in their various business segments.

Incentive compensation must be driven all the way down to the operational level. Almost every employee should be tied to shareholder value in one way or another. The result of linking employee compensation to the value creation process is that employees think and act like owners, and thus employees' and shareholders' interests become aligned. Incentive-based compensation tied to some measure of value fosters an atmosphere in which employees are committed to the company's success; dedicated to value creation, personal excellence, quality, and productivity; and willing to assume reasonable risks.

KEEPING IT SIMPLE
Because the principal reason for adopting VBM is to change the behavior of managers and employees and encourage them to think like owners, the VBM tools must be kept simple, streamlined, easy to understand, and easy to translate into terms that all levels of the company can comprehend and trust. Simplification is essential for showing employees that VBM is not viewed as simply another finance exercise disconnected from operating performance. It is important to simplify what can often be a complex calculation by minimizing the number of value measures employed. The performance evaluation and compensation system should be consistent with the same performance metrics calculated uniformly for everybody.

During the training and education phase, there is no need to make operational managers experts on valuation models and performance metrics, as long as they understand the portion of the calculation for which they are responsible. The focus should be placed on a few key concepts and their application to the functional operations. Understanding the concepts that can change management behavior is far more important than understanding the technicalities of the actual calculations.

INVESTOR COMMUNICATION
The final step is to communicate with your investors. The investor relations function is a key element of a program aimed at enhancing long-term shareholder values. Investor communication entails orienting the investor-relations function toward providing more relevant information to investors. It is important to identify your influential shareholders and explain to them your actions and strategies and how they will contribute to economic value. The CEO and the senior management of the various subsidiaries should communicate the vision of the company and its long-range business plan to the investment community. An investor communication program requiring full disclosure of relevant data will enhance credibility with your investors and enable them to do a better job of forecasting future cash flows. Such communications include annual and quarterly reports, meetings with analysts, and the many day-to-day contacts that take place between corporate executives and investors.

Investors should be informed effectively and early about the conversion to VBM. Most companies who have implemented VBM not only experience an almost immediate behavioral and cultural change as a result of linking compensation to value, but the stock price often rises following the announcement of adopting a VBM culture. The company is viewed favorably by the investment community, and VBM companies typically exceed market and peer group stockholder performance.

The business and the environment in which the business operates should be explained clearly to investors so that the market does not discount the stock for something it does not understand. The focusing should be placed on strategies and opportunities for long-term value enhancement rather than the outlook for the near term. Future prospects rather than historical performance should be emphasized. The past is relevant only to the extent that it helps an investor assess future prospects. This means explaining how much capital is to be allocated to the various businesses, how the company is to be financed, and perhaps most important, what performance objectives are motivating management to perform. Investors need to know how management evaluates its own operating profitability and on what basis it rewards its people.

The creation of hype and overexpectations must be avoided, because when actual results fall short of expectations, the reaction usually more than offsets any benefit that may have been gained by a temporary run-up of market values.

Market Signals Analysis

Companies and the stock market are engaged in an ongoing two-way signaling and monitoring process. Companies provide information via published reports, news releases, and other communications. Investors incorporate this information into their expectations and collectively express their view of a company's prospects in the stock price. Stock price, in turn, signals what performance is required if shareholders are to earn their required return. Stock prices convey important, low-cost, continuous information to management.

If a shortfall in the value of the current business plans relative to market expectations exists, identifying opportunities to close the gap should become management's top priority. If, on the other hand, a realistic valuation of the plans exceed the current stock price, management may need to do a better job of communicating future prospects. In any case, understanding any value gap is essential for decisions ranging from issuing new shares, repurchasing shares, and financing acquisitions.

Understanding and beating market expectations is essential to creating superior shareholder value. A process called *market signals analysis,* developed by L.E.K. Consulting, helps managers understand what their companies' stock price is signaling about market expectations. The stock price of a company reflects the long-term cash flow prospects of a company. However, the market's expectations of these prospects do not necessarily coincide with management's expectations.

L.E.K. Consulting proposes a three-step process for market signals analysis: (1) performing investor market research, (2) estimating value creation implications, and (3) determining implications for management.

Performing Investor Market Research

The most important source of information about market expectations is stock analysts. Many publications and websites contain consensus analysts' consensus forecasts on a company's fundamentals. In addition, during meetings with their analysts, managers should make a concerted effort to understand the analysts' opinions about their firm. The minimum information that should be gathered is as follows:

- Consensus forecasts for revenue, profits, and free cash flows for the company and individual business units
- Analysts' perception of management and management's ability to meet their commitments
- The performance indicators that analysts find important
- The extent to which analysts find the company fairly valued

- The analysts' opinion of the company's corporate and business strategies

Estimating Value Creation Implications

After exploring analysts' expectations, the next step is to translate this information into the value analysts expect the company to create over time. This is obtained by subtracting from a baseline value the discounted cash flow business value reflected in the analysts' views:

$$\text{Value Creation} = \text{Discounted Cash Flow Value} - \text{Baseline Value}$$

$$\text{Baseline Value} = \frac{\text{Net Operating Profit after Tax}}{\text{Cost of Capital}}$$

By comparing the value expectations of analysts and management, managers can determine which of these forecasts generates the most value to shareholders.

Determining Implications for Management

The comparison between management and analysts' expectations can result in three possible outcomes, each requiring very different management actions. As displayed in Figure 14-1, either management's value expectations exceed, equal, or are inferior to those of the market.

Figure 14-2 displays the managerial implications. If management's expectations exceed those of analysts, the company is undervalued. There are two potential reasons why a company may be undervalued. First, the management's plan may be considered unrealistic and difficult to achieve by the analysts. Second, the market may not have given the plan its fair credit. Several options exist for management action: (1) investor communications could be improved to communicate more information to the market, (2) share repurchases could communicate the management's belief that the company's shares are undervalued, and (3) corporate restructuring should be considered if a particular business unit is the source of undervaluation. In this case, management should consider a spin-off, liquidation, or sale.

If market expectations closely mirror those of management, the company is fairly valued. The management's focus should be to exceed their own expectations. Performance targets and incentives could be designed to ensure that the plan represents a minimum threshold of performance.

If management's expectations are less than those of analysts, the company is overvalued. Management has two courses of action. First, business strategy could be reexamined to find ways to close the strategy gap and deliver the type of performance reflected in the stock price. Strategies to

FIGURE 14-1   Management vs. market expectations.

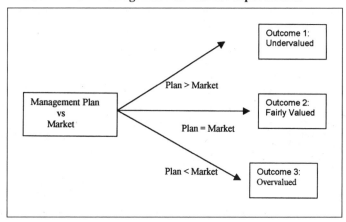

create value more in line with expectations include entering new markets, performing synergistic acquisitions, pruning value-destroying divisions, improving marketing and distributions practices, and selling the firm to a strategic buyer at a hefty premium. Second, management can communicate to the market that it is being too aggressive in pricing the company. This will strengthen management credibility, a key ingredient in managing investor expectations over the long term.

The example shown in Figure 14-3 illustrates the market signal analysis process. Technology Corporation had a strong record of delivering su-

FIGURE 14-2   Implications for management actions.

Outcome	Management Actions
Under Valued	Share repurchases/Increase in dividends
	Investor Communications
	Corporate Restructuring
Fairly Valued	Continued focus on investor relations
	Strategic priority to exceed plan performance
	Ease expectations downward
	Do nothing
Over Valued	Strategic priority to fill the gap
	Review investor relations practices

Source: "Market Signals Analysis: A Vital Tool for Managing Market Expectations," L.E.K. Consulting Shareholder Value Added Newsletter.

FIGURE 14-3   Market signals analysis: Illustration.

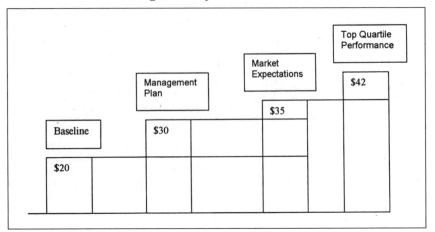

perior shareholder returns. After comparing internal and external value forecasts, management concluded that the market was overvaluing its shares.

The baseline value for the company was $20 per share plus an addi-
tional $10 per share from the value creation opportunities identified by
management, or $30 per share. Market expectations justified $35 per share,
$5 above management's expectations.

The first step was to determine why market expectations exceeded those
of management. In talking to analysts, management found that the analysts re-
garded the company's forecasts as too conservative. Moreover, the market had
underestimated the capital expenditures necessary to grow the business. Since
management compensation was tied to achieving superior TSR over those of
Technology Corporation's peer group, top quartile share price performance
was a top priority. This necessitated a share price of $42. Management iden-
tified three strategies designed to fill the $12 per share value gap:

- Entering new geographic markets through an acquisition
- Productivity improvements for cost reductions and superior margins
- Redesigning new products to reduce capital requirements

Since implementing these strategies, Technology Corporation has remained in the top quartile of share price performance in its peer group.
The market signal analysis process provided management with impetus to
explore new avenues of value creation.

For management to be consistently creating shareholder value, they
must examine market expectations and find out ways to exceed them. This

process is made more difficult by the fact that the market adjusts its expectations upward for consistently strong performers. Companies like Microsoft, Dell Computers, and Intel have to deliver increasing levels of performance year after year to maintain their share price momentum. The three-step market signal analysis process provides a systematic approach for management to understand and possibly exceed market expectations and thereby ensure shareholder value maximization.

RECIPE FOR VBM SUCCESS

This chapter and the BioTech experience in Chapter 4 identified the critical success factors of a VBM program:

1. Support
2. Education
3. Strategy process
4. Compensation
5. Simplicity
6. Investor communications

The guidelines to follow in adapting VBM to your company are as follows:

- VBM should have complete top management support and a strong advocate at the chief executive level.
- The managers and employees at all levels should be trained extensively on VBM both before and after implementation.
- VBM requires a strategy review process whereby business unit strategies are anchored on the development of an externally validated cash flow forecast supported by a realistic assessment of market attractiveness and competitive position. Evaluating the alternative strategies ensures the ones selected are those which create the most value.
- Compensation should be linked to shareholder value creation. An effective value-based performance metric or set of metrics is important for this.
- The VBM calculations and measures should be kept simple and consistent. This is essential for the program to be understood, endorsed, and trusted by all managers and employees.
- VBM requires an effective investor communication program. This enhances credibility with your investors, enabling them to do a better job of understanding your actions and strategies, how they will contribute to economic value, and forecasting future cash flows.

Index

WACC, 114, 282. *See also* Cost of
    capital
Wal-Mart, 153, 275
Wall Street Journal, 334
Walt Disney, 30, 56, 79
Wang, Charles, 362
Ward, Milton, 369
Weaver, S. C., 77

Weighted average cost of capital (WACC),
    114, 282. *See also* Cost of capital
Welch, Jack, 348
Wells Fargo, 30
Working capital, 255

Xerox, 228

ABOUT THE AUTHORS

Roger A. Morin, Ph.D., is a professor in Georgia State University's Robinson College of Business Administration. Dr. Morin has lectured at Wharton, Dartmouth, and the University of Montreal School of Business, and has over a quarter century of experience in executive training and corporate consulting for dozens of clients, including AT&T, Bell South, and Price Waterhouse. His work has appeared in numerous journals, including *Journal of Finance, Journal of Business Administration, International Management Review*, and *Financial Review*.

Sherry L. Jarrell, Ph.D., is assistant professor of finance and economics at Wake Forest University's Babcock Graduate School of Management. In Dr. Jarrell's ten years of MBA education experience, she has been a professor or lecturer at Columbia University, Emory University, Georgia State University, Indiana University, Southern Methodist University, and the University of Chicago. A popular lecturer for organizations across the country, she also has written and reviewed for numerous publications including *Journal of Business, Financial Management, Quality Managers Journal, Financial Practice and Education*, and *Harvard Business School Press*.